BROWN UNIVERSITY STUDIES

VOLUME XXI

SAMUEL JOHNSON
IN
GRUB STREET

BY
EDWARD A. BLOOM

BROWN UNIVERSITY PRESS
PROVIDENCE, RHODE ISLAND
1957

Library of Congress Catalog Card Number 57-11203
COMPOSED, PRINTED AND BOUND BY
GEORGE BANTA COMPANY, INC., MENASHA, WISCONSIN

FOR MY MOTHER
in memory of
ROBERT AND IRVIN BLOOM

PREFACE

THE PURPOSE of this study is to examine and evaluate the journalistic career of Samuel Johnson. Others have treated specialized aspects of this subject, but they have not developed it comprehensively as a related part of his literary output. Johnson was often contemptuous of the periodical press and of most of those who wrote for it; yet he served long and honorably as journalist and editor. For almost four decades he contributed to the growth of British journalism. He drew much from those who preceded him and in turn added to the periodical development. Except for a brief interlude in Birmingham after he left Oxford, Johnson spent most of his time in London, the capital of British journalism. There he grubbed in uncongenial conditions; unlike most journalists of the time, he managed to survive with distinction.

He had a hand in virtually every kind of journalistic publication and writing. Thus, his career coincided with the expansion of eighteenth-century journalism, and he participated in the four major types of periodicals which came to maturity during this century: newspapers, essay serials, magazines or miscellanies, and review serials. Not everything he published in periodicals has been identified, but what is known is impressive both for quantity and literary quality. He made many friendships in the literary underworld of Grub Street, and some of his earliest journalistic practices he later exhibited in his most substantial works. He learned early to form and express judgments on a variety of topics connected with journalism and hence with literature, such as authorship, patronage, copyright, freedom of the press.

Certain of my choices of organization and presentation may appear less satisfactory than other possibilities. A few comments here will perhaps anticipate the most serious objections. Many of Johnson's journalistic pieces have never been collected in any edition of his works and, consequently, are relatively unknown except as bibliographical items. These are not easily accessible. Since my aim has been to provide as inclusive a study as possible, I have frequently examined and analyzed writings individually and in their appropriate relationships. This is best illustrated in Chapters I, III, and V. As an alternative, I could have confined myself to samplings from essays when subject matter or technique seemed to overlap; but any gain in compactness would have meant the sacrifice of little-known pieces which deserve prominence. Within reasonable limits, I have also provided frequent quotations. Johnson's words, if apology for them is necessary, often convey pungency and immediacy which the modern writer cannot recreate through paraphrase. As he retorted to Wilkes' complaint that quotation is pedantic, "No, Sir, it is a good thing: there is a community of mind in it."

Some items in the journalistic canon (Appendix B) may appear at first sight arbitrary; yet their inclusion is appropriate. I have deliberately viewed as journalistic the largest possible area of Johnson's relationship to the periodical press. For that reason I have included even literary and political advertisements. My principle has been to include any piece which first appeared in a periodical publication (thus accounting for the omission of pamphlets), though in a few instances I have added items which were reprinted rather than initially printed in a journal. Generally, however, I have considered reprintings only incidentally, in the text and notes.

It was difficult to treat the essay serials—the *Rambler, Adventurer,* and *Idler*—without duplicating previous commentators. Details of inception and publication are germane to the limits of this study. As for analysis of contents, I have confined myself to those matters pertinent to Johnson's journalistic activities. Hence, the reader will find a full discussion of his concepts on a host of problems, including the miseries of authorship, the writer's responsibilities, and the transience of fame. In these serials are recorded some of his most astute reflections on journalism, and on literature in general. Reluctantly, I have avoided extensive or formal discussions of his literary criticism, and also questions of morality not directly relevant to his journalistic writing. These are massive esthetic-moral concerns better treated in another context.

Johnson stands out as a journalist against the backdrop of Grub Street, during his own times and earlier. Throughout, aside from the customary authorities, I have drawn upon contemporary periodicals and pamphlets to present the most authentic possible view of journalistic conditions. I have invoked writers as famous as Defoe, Fielding, Goldsmith, and Smollett, and as obscure as the legion of anonymous hack writers. Johnson compares favorably with the best London journalists of the century, while conforming to the traditions of writing invectives, editing poor things, scribbling poetry, composing moralistic biographies, sound reviews, and the like.

Acknowledgment of the encouragement and assistance I received while this work was in progress is pleasant. The late Professor Walter Graham first stimulated my interest in Johnson and in eighteenth-century journalism. After his death, I was fortunate to have the guidance of Professor Arthur W. Secord. At various stages, my typescript was read by Professors Secord, James L. Clifford, Fredrick S. Siebert, Frederick W. Hilles, Harris F. Fletcher, Arthur Sherbo, and Robert G. Noyes. They gave freely of their time, experience, and knowledge. Professor Clifford made available manuscript materials which have strengthened sections of this book. Others to whom I am indebted for suggestions are Dr. Benjamin B. Hoover, Mr. Herman W. Liebert, and Dr. George Luck. Parts of Chapters VI and VII first appeared in journals: "Samuel Johnson on Copyright," *JEGP,* XLVII (1948), 165-172; "Johnson on a Free Press: A Study in Liberty and Subordination," *ELH,* XVI (1949), 251-271. In employing what seems to me an almost inevitable title, I trust there will be no suspicion that I have encroached upon the charming essay of S. C. Roberts, "Johnson in Grub Street," *Cornhill Magazine,* n.s. LXV (1928), 440-451. Our aims have taken us in different directions. Mention should be made of courtesies extended by staffs of various libraries, chief among them the University of Illinois, Brown University, Harvard University, Yale University, the New York Public Library, Tulane University, and the British Museum. But my deepest sense of obligation is to my wife, Lillian D. Bloom, who patiently saw this through from beginning to end, as editorial counselor, indexer, typist, and mainstay of my spirits.

E.A.B.

Providence, Rhode Island
September, 1956

CONTENTS

NUMB. XXVIII.

THE
BIRMINGHAM JOURNAL.

MONDAY, *May* 21. 1733.   [*To be continued Weekly.*]

To the PUBLICK.

Gentlemen,

AS *some of our particular Friends, who have been Encouragers of this our Weekly Paper, have represented to us the Pleasure we should do the Publick, and the Advantage we might make to ourselves by altering the Day of our Publication; and as we have discover'd a ready Inclination to gratify our Readers, upon their first Request, we hope it will not be taken amiss that we postponed our last Thursday's Paper, and assure them, that all our future Papers, shall be publish'd on the Monday; containing in them, all the material News of that Morning's-Post.*

As we are determin'd to spare no Cost nor Pains, we hope, to furnish our Readers with as good a Collection of News as can be met with, or desir'd in any Country Paper.

We acknowledge with Gratitude the Acceptance our Paper has already met with in most Places where it has been distributed, and Hope those whose Candour and Ingenuity had a regard to it in its Infancy, will not forsake it in its riper Years.

THURSDAY'S POST.

FOREIGN AFFAIRS.

From the Daily Courants.

ITALY.

Leghorn, April 25.

THE Master of a French Vessel arrived here the 21st inst. from Metelline, reports, that on the 16th of the same Month, being in the Height of Cape Bona, he heard the firing of Guns at Sea for some Hours, with great Fury; which makes it believed, the combined Fleet of the Spanish and Maltese Men of War have attacked that of Algiers, coming in Company with the Turkish Sultana's from the Ports of Turky, with some Ottoman Troops on board. We expect every Moment to hear the Success of the Combat, if any.

SPAIN.

Brussels, May 10. The day before yesterday was sent to Luxemburg, a Brigade of Gunners, with several Pieces of Cannon, some Mortars, and a proportionable Quantity of other warlike Stores, under and Escorte of a Detachment of War [...], in order to fill the Magazines of that Place, which makes some People believe, that the Tranquillity of that Part of Europe [...] to be shaken. The Regiment of Vehlen, Dragoons, is [...]

here from Aix-la-Chapelle, from whence it is, with two Battalions of War [...] to proceed to Luxemburg, to reinforce [...] Garrison. They talk also of sending thither the [...] Squadrons of the Regiment of Don Emanuel of Portugal.

GERMANY.

Ratisbon, May 10. Not long since, several of the Suabian and Franconian Subjects arrived here by Water, on their way to settle in Hungary; the Reason whereof is not conceived, because we see daily so many return from thence, begging to their own Country. The Minister of Brandenburg has disposed every thing necessary for the Reception of the Emigrants of Berchtolsgaden, who are every Moment expected here, Those called Bishopwizers, consisting of 80 Souls, are to rest here for some [...]. The R[...] Catholicks were not a little surprized, when they perceived that the Magistrates who met the said Emigrants, had a Flag carried before them, with the British and Hanoverian Arms. More Money and Books have been brought hither from Augsburg to be distributed amongst the most Needy of the Emigrants of Berchtolsg[...] The first Au[...]ian Commissary [...] of the Empire de Count de Stremberg [...] his Departure for Vienna, being nominated Ld. Steward of the Houshold to the Eldest Caroline Archdutchess, who (we hear) will very shortly be betrothed to the Duke of Lorrain.

HOLLAND.

Hague, May 13. The States of Holland and West-Friesland assembled this day. M. Cornelius Hop, Ancient Echevin and Counsellor of the City of Amsterdam, formerly Ambassador of France, and afterwards Minister-Plenipotentiary at the Congress of Soissons, took the day before yesterday his Seat in the Council of State, on the part of the Republick of Holland; and M. William-Henry Bentink de Wittenstein in the Chamber of Accompts of the Generality; on the part of the Province of Over-Yssel. The Count de Sinzendorff, Minister Plenipotentiary of the Emperor, was yesterday in Conference with some Lords of the Regency. We have received advice, that M. de Bilderbeek, Resident of this State at Cologn, died the 16th Instant at Manheim, whither he went to execute [...] Commission on the part of their High Mightinesses the States-General, with his Electoral Highness Palatine.

FRANCE.

Paris, May 16. We have received Advice from Warsaw, that on the 27th past, the Opening of the General Dyet of Convocation was made very quietly, and that all the Deputies to that Assembly seemed inclinable to prevent, by their good Agreement, what might retard the holding of the Dyet of Election.

The 11th Instant, about seven in the Evening, the Queen felt some Labour-Pains, and in a very short time after, her Majesty was delivered of a Princess, which is in as good a State of Health, as can be expected; as is also her Majesty in her present Condition. Her Delivery was so precipitate, that there was not Time sufficient to call M. Peyrac, her Majesty's Man-Midwife, who went but just before into the Garden, which occasioned the Woman that nurses her Majesty to receive and deliver the Infant to M. Helvetius, first Physician to the Queen who was in the Chamber, with the Ladies of the Palace; after which that Princess received Private Baptism, with the usual Ceremonies.

IRELAND.

Dublin, May 1. We hear from Carlow, that a Man being to be hang'd for Cow stealing, the Sheriff was at a great Loss for a b[...]d experienced Jack-catch, when a Fellow who was in Goal for his Fees very readily offered his Service, who disguised himself in Woman's Cloaths, blackened his Face, and dexterously did the Business, and so was discharged. The Sunday following [...] went to T[...]ls [...]hr[...] and [...] his C[...]science; but seeing [...] of the Folks [...] in the Ceremony who was reputed worth Money, he slunk away, and went to the Priest's House, robbed him of 30 Guineas, two Suits of Cloaths and two Cheeses: The Priest offered a Mod[...] Reward for the taking him, and we hear after a diligent Search he was taken last Sunday, and is in a fair Way of following a late Patience.

On Saturday last a Child of five Years old, of one Jones a Plaisterer, at the Carteret's Head in Stephen's-street, followed his Father to a Gentleman's House where he was at work, and unheeded fell into a Well of a very great Depth, he lay till Monday before it was suggested what could become of him: It is said an old Aunt of the Child's dreamed he was in the Well, and by that Means was found out.

Sunday last one Doyle was murdered at Carlow by one Courran, being drinking together they fell out about the Payment of the Reckoning, Courran stabbed the other in the Belly with a Case-Knife, of which Wound he instantly died, Courran was secured and sent to Goal.

This week one Terryl, a Shoemaker, in Hammond-lane, poisoned himself, being jealous of his Wife.

On Sunday morning one Nehemiah Richardson was taken in a House in Mals-lane near the Inns, on Suspicion of Robbing on the Highway, and now lies in Irons in the Black-Dog, when he was taken he had a case of Pistols and a Blunderbus, lying loaded on the Table before him, he appeared to be a Gentleman, being very well drest, having on a good ruffled Shirt, and a Seal Ring on his Finger.

The same Day one Mr. Barker, who keeps the black Bull in Sycamore-Alley, and one or three more Persons were walking in the Right Hon. the [...]

CHAPTER I

JOURNALISM AT ST. JOHN'S GATE

I

POVERTY and melancholia were principally responsible for driving Samuel Johnson into journalism. Because of lack of funds, which probably intensified his pathological gloom, he left Pembroke College, Oxford, in December, 1729, after a thirteen-month residence, and thus brought to a close the hope of a career in the law, ministry, or one of the other learned professions.[1] Despondent and aimless, he returned to the uncongenial home of his parents in Lichfield, where the death of his father Michael, early in December, 1731,[2] necessitated his employment. Lichfield offered him few opportunities for gaining a livelihood, and his assistance was not needed in the family book business, which was now easily managed by his mother and his younger brother Nathaniel.

After a short and unhappy teaching experience in the school at Market Bosworth, Leicestershire, and a period of enforced idleness, Johnson perhaps late in 1732 accepted the invitation of a former schoolmate, Edmund Hector, a surgeon, to visit him in Birmingham. Johnson was familiar with this industrial city close to Lichfield, where he had frequently visited friends and relatives.[3] Hector seems to have asked Johnson to join him because he knew he was unemployed. Furthermore, Thomas Warren, Birmingham's first bookseller, had begun the *Birmingham Journal,* a weekly newspaper, in November, 1732; and Hector, who lodged and boarded with Warren, perhaps hoped Johnson's talented pen would add merit to the new paper. Boswell has given credence to this possibility by asserting that Johnson contributed essays to the *Journal.*[4] But to seek specimens of Johnson's writings in the *Journal* would be idle, since only one issue (No. 28, for May 21, 1733) of this short-lived paper is known to exist. What remains of the *Journal* is now significant only as a sample of British provincial journalism. Revealing no signs of individual authorship, the surviving number is comprised mainly of domestic and foreign news items copied from other newspapers and the customary sprinkling of advertisements. Warren's ambition, as he advised his public, was "to spare no cost nor pains, . . . to furnish our readers with as good a collection of news as can be met with, or desired in any country paper." But he was frustrated in his hope that "those whose candour and ingenuity had a regard to [the *Journal*] in its infancy, will not forsake it in its riper years." If Johnson was assigned the usual hack work of conning, clipping, and rewriting, it is likely that he also wrote original essays, now lost. But Johnson had given up working for the *Journal* before May, 1733, and positive evidence of original contributions must await discovery of the earlier numbers. His tantalizing silence about these earliest journalistic activities is as expressive as the contemptuous remarks he frequently uttered about the news craft. Newspapers he regarded as the products of "narrow and mercenary minds" (*Idler*, No. 7), undiscriminating and trivial repositories of "cheap and easy knowledge."[5]

During this Birmingham interlude Johnson had more on his mind than newspaper editing and hack writing: after six months as Hector's guest, he took his own lodgings, a fair indication that he intended protracted residence in Birmingham. Emotional complications affected the melancholy young man, for in 1733 he probably met his future wife, Elizabeth Porter, twenty years his senior.[6] Whatever attraction might have existed between them at the time was futile because her merchant husband, Harry Porter, did not leave her a widow until August or September, 1734. More pertinent to Johnson's intellectual development and his residence in Birmingham was his undertaking a translation and abridgment of Father Jerome Lobo's *Voyage to Abyssinia* from a French version which he had read at Oxford (the original had been written in Portuguese). Commissioned for the task by Warren, Johnson was prodded and coaxed by the faithful Hector, who took dictation while the reluctant translator lay in his bed; and Hector then virtually saw it through the press. In 1735 Warren published the *Voyage* in Birmingham, although on the title page he pretentiously assigned it to London. Unwelcome as the chore apparently was, Johnson earned five guineas, which he considered equitable; and he long retained a kindly feeling for Warren,[7] who saw him through a difficult financial and emotional period. Meanwhile Johnson must have been casting about for additional sources of income. An ingenious, if unconfirmed, theory is that he interested himself in the spinning machine which Lewis Paul and John Wyatt of Lichfield had set up in Birmingham, and in which Warren and Cave were later unsuccessful investors.[8]

Lucy Porter, Johnson's stepdaughter, once told Boswell that Johnson was disliked in Birmingham, but by whom or for what reason the record does not reveal.[9] Whether this alleged unpopularity had anything to do with his departure is problematical; a more likely assumption is that he could not earn an adequate living. To procure employment he returned to Lichfield in 1734 and published proposals for printing by subscription the Latin poems of Politian, a Renaissance author.[10] When nothing came of this, he returned to Birmingham and made his first bid to awaken in London the attention of Cave, publisher of the flourishing *Gentleman's Magazine.* In an unsigned letter dated November 25, 1734, Johnson volunteered the services of a fictitious "anonymous friend" for the improvement of the periodical, and he asked that a reply be sent to "S. Smith" at Birmingham. As proof of his familiarity with the magazine's contents, he alluded flatteringly to Cave's generous £50 prize contest for the best poem in Latin or English on "Life, Death, Judgment, Heaven and Hell." With his customary forthrightness, however, Johnson suggested that Cave appeared "no less sensible than [his] readers of the defects of [his] poetical article," a regular feature of the *Gentleman's Magazine* named "Poetical Essays," which consisted of five or six pages of both original and reprinted poetry. Johnson's "friend" offered "on reasonable terms, sometimes to fill a column" to improve this department, and to provide "short literary dissertations in Latin or English, critical remarks on authours ancient or modern," and other contributions in both the arts and sciences. "By this method," Johnson predicted, "your literary article, for so it might be called, will . . . be better recommended to the publick, than by low jests, aukward buffoonery, or the dull scurrilities of either party."[11] Such a blunt statement from an unknown correspondent could hardly have pleased Cave; yet Hawkins believed the bookseller answered the letter on December 2 in order to accept

Johnson's services.[12] There is no evidence, however, that Johnson was commissioned to write for the *Gentleman's Magazine* as early as 1734.

Even if some kind of understanding with Cave had resulted from this exploratory letter, it would not have given Johnson the kind of income he now needed to fulfill his family obligations. On July 9, 1735, he married Mrs. Porter.[13] Again he attempted teaching, advertising for students to be enrolled in a school which he founded at Edial, near Lichfield.[14] Unsuited for the discipline of a schoolroom, Johnson found this experiment as disastrous financially and emotionally as the earlier one at Market Bosworth. He then decided to take up residence in London and work on *Irene,* of which he had written three acts in Edial. But he hoped to earn his immediate living as a translator while aiming toward his theatrical ambitions. His wife remained in Lichfield while he and a former Edial student, David Garrick, rode horseback to London in the spring of 1737, armed with letters of recommendation from their friend, Gilbert Walmesley.[15] They arrived impoverished—as they had set out—but at Garrick's suggestion they were able to borrow five pounds from Thomas Wilcox, a bookseller who, according to legend, was more impressed by Johnson's brawn than his literary potentialities.[16] If, as has been suggested, Walmesley gave Johnson a letter to Henry Lintot the bookseller, it did not bring employment; nor is there any indication, contrary to one contention, that Johnson received aid from any other booksellers prior to joining Cave's staff in 1738.[17]

While writing *Irene* in Greenwich, Johnson again communicated with Cave (July 12, 1737), this time over his own signature, and possibly met the bookseller about this time.[18] Now he proposed a translation of the *History of the Council of Trent* from the Italian of Father Paul Sarpi with Le Courayer's notes from the French. During the summer, while awaiting the commission which he subsequently received, he returned to Lichfield to complete his drama; but in the autumn he came back to London, accompanied by Mrs. Johnson. His hopes for staging *Irene* were long frustrated, its production being delayed until 1749.

Facing the dreary prospect of a return to Lichfield or the grimmer one of starvation for himself and his wife, Johnson at the age of twenty-eight was being driven almost inexorably toward entrance into London journalism, which in 1737 was tantamount to becoming a literary adventurer. Since his Birmingham experience he had seen in journalism nothing more than an unfortunate alternative to literature. When his prospects failed to improve after the encouraging reception of his poem *London* (May, 1738), he seemed to have no choice but the drudgeries of Grub Street. But still unreconciled after a year or more of these labors, he applied in the summer of 1739 for a teaching position in a Leicestershire school. He was disappointed once again, now for lack of a master's degree. Pope, who knew Johnson only indirectly as the talented author of *London* and of the political pamphlets *Marmor Norfolciense* and *A Complete Vindication of the Licensers of the Stage* (1739), recommended him to Lord Gower (probably upon an intermediary's request); and Gower in his turn wrote on August 1, 1739, to a friend of Dean Swift in Dublin to grant Johnson the degree from Trinity College. "They say [wrote Gower] he is not afraid of the strictest examination, though he is of so long a journey; and will venture, if the Dean thinks it necessary; choosing rather to die upon the road, *than be starved to death in translating for the booksellers;* which has been his only subsistence for some time past."[19] Perhaps Johnson had overstated his plight, but even his limited experience in translating for booksellers gave him a basis for his discontent. By this time he had done the substantial rendering of Father Jerome's *Voyage* (1735) and Crousaz's *Commentary* (late in 1738 or early in 1739), as well as a part of Father Paul's *History* (in 1738 and 1739). It is understandable that the tediousness, even futility, of this kind of task and irritating editorial pressures embittered him, causing him to regard translation as hack work justified only by necessity. Despite all efforts and good intentions, Johnson failed to get the degree and was obliged to resort to journalism.

II

An understanding of Johnson's association with the *Gentleman's Magazine* contributes heavily to an assessment of his literary position in the latter half of the eighteenth century, for from his beginnings in journalism, as he struggled to meet the assignments and deadlines of

a gelid publisher, emerged the significant body of his works. Despite
the poverty which kept him in the squalor of Grub Street, he was
not a Grubean. He maintained his integrity, assurance, and ability
throughout this difficult period. Associates like Richard Savage and
Samuel Boyse, lacking his talent and spiritual strength, sank into
a journalistic humus, but Johnson matured, mellowed, and ultimately
achieved greatness. Almost from the very outset it became apparent
to an efficient, perceptive judge like Cave that Johnson, for all his
antipathy and seeming indolence, was superior in talent to his fellow
journalists. The long relationship between these two men, which
can be reconstructed only from superficial details, became more than
merely one between employer and employee. At first, to be sure,
Cave attempted to keep Johnson in his proper place and to impress
upon him the importance of St. John's Gate. Although the struggling
young Johnson seemed diffident, Cave probably recognized a kindred
spirit, for both had been frustrated in their early literary ambitions.
In addition, Johnson shared Cave's capacity for friendship and for
common sense, traits which soon made him a trusted, valuable assistant, despite disagreements. "On all difficult occasions, Johnson
was Cave's oracle" and "advocate."[20]

Edward Cave founded the *Gentleman's Magazine* in 1731 and
managed it under the pseudonym of "Sylvanus Urban of Alderman-
bury, Gent." He first called it the *Gentleman's Magazine: or, Trader's
Monthly Intelligencer,* but soon renamed it with the more comprehensive title of the *Gentleman's Magazine: and Historical Chronicle.*
It was "printed, and sold at St. John's Gate, by F. Jefferies in
Ludgate-street." From 1735, however, it was "printed by Edward
Cave, at St. John's Gate." Thus, in four years Cave had achieved considerable solidity as a bookseller and printer, although it was several
years before he did any extensive book printing.

He instituted the magazine as a timesaver for the busy British
people. Its intention, he stated in the first number, was to compile

monthly a view of all the pieces of wit, humour, or intelligence, daily
offered to the publick in the newspapers (which of late are so multiplied,
as to render it impossible, unless a man makes it a business, to consult them
all), and in the next place we shall join therewith some other matters of
use or amusement that will be communicated to us.[21]

Cave did not intend the *Gentleman's Magazine* to be primarily a repository of original articles and poems, but rather a reprint of the best articles and poems from other journals, which he carefully credited both on the monthly title page and at the heads of individual pieces. He divided his periodical into customary departments: essays, poetry, personal notices, foreign affairs, some original feature articles, financial notes, and book notices. Until 1738 he supplied a yearly supplement devoted to factual reports of parliamentary proceedings, but then substituted the disguised monthly *Debates in the Senate of Magna Lilliputia.* The *Gentleman's Magazine,* though not the first miscellany in England, soon became the most important,[22] and it continued to be significant for the next two centuries. Numerous periodicals, many with decided partisan policies, existed in 1731, and Cave though he himself sought to remain politically neutral drew upon them freely. Among them were the *Craftsman, London Journal, Universal Spectator, Applebee's Journal, Reade's Journal, Free Briton, Hyp-Doctor, Grubstreet Journal.*

Although Johnson's testimony implies that Cave gave him a fair stipend, and probably, therefore, was equally fair with his other writers, it is questionable whether Cave's generosity was as great as has been maintained.[23] Nevertheless, Cave encouraged literary efforts by the payment of prizes. Two constant prize winners were Moses Browne and John Duick, both of whom supplemented their incomes as pen cutters by contributing poetry and judging contests. In addition, Cave was able to secure the services of eminent men, like Dr. Thomas Birch and Dr. Cromwell Mortimer, secretary of the Royal Society. Richard Savage wrote for the magazine as early as 1733. Both Pope and Johnson served as constant judges.[24] As the periodical acquired more prestige, fewer gleanings and more original essays appeared in its pages.

Johnson, who always maintained a warm feeling for his employer, was strongly impressed with his establishment, beholding St. John's Gate the first time "with reverence." Well might he entertain this feeling, for in 1738 the *Gentleman's Magazine* was already firmly established as one of the leading periodicals of the day.[25] To Johnson fresh from the provinces, the magazine was truly a seat of learning and literaure. In his own words, written sixteen years later, it was "a periodical pamphlet, of which the scheme is known wherever the English language is spoken," and "one of the most successful and lucrative pamphlets which literary history has upon record."[26]

Various publications in 1738, in the spirit of the age, were attacking Cave as he was attacking them. His most bitter rivals were a group of booksellers who had begun the *London Magazine* in 1732 in direct competition. Unscrupulous, powerful, and able, they closely imitated Cave's departments and makeup.[27] They did not stop at imitation, however, and a verbal war developed. For instance, *Common Sense* complained that the *Gentleman's Magazine* had "murdered common sense" and mangled truth and spirit in writing. The *London Magazine* quoted the complaint, and in a pseudo-news item of February 20, 1738, described Cave as breaking from his house in a frenzy, running distracted through the streets, and raving against the *London Magazine,* before being confined. Cave retorted, sending out a call for letters and poems in his defense.[28] Among these pieces, which Cave published, was Johnson's first contribution, the formal, highly laudatory verses *Ad Urbanum.*[29]

This poem marks Johnson's debut in London journalism, for it "appears that [he] was now enlisted by Mr. Cave as a regular co-adjutor in his magazine."[30] But Johnson early became more than Cave's coadjutor; he assumed the functions of an editor almost immediately, and exercised them at least until 1745. His consequent influence on the magazine was strong. He succeeded Browne and Duick as poetry judge, made abstractions, answered correspondents, and from June, 1738, helped edit the *Parliamentary Debates* written by William Guthrie, and the contributions of other correspondents.[31] Johnson, therefore, became responsible for a large, diversified share of Cave's editorial burdens. Cave was not easily satisfied, as a letter addressed to him by Johnson in September, 1738, reveals.[32] Working at first in his own lodgings (although he was eventually assigned a room at St. John's Gate) rather than under the keen surveillance of Cave, and with his usual indolence, Johnson was probably greater in promises than in production. Cave was especially perturbed by Johnson's failure to complete the translation of Sarpi's *History of the Council of Trent,* which he had undertaken to produce in two volumes, and in advance of which he had paid Johnson a considerable sum of money. Between August 2, 1738, and April 21, 1739, Johnson acknowledged in a receipt, Cave had given him £49.7*s.* and a seemingly additional 2*s.*6*d.*; but whether this money was for the Sarpi alone, or for other assignments as well, the receipt fails to make clear. Under prodding Johnson admitted "impediments, which I hope, are now at an end; and if you find the progress hereafter not such as you have a right to expect, you can easily stimulate a negligent translator." Despite the drudgery which Johnson considered his tasks for Cave to be, his principal occupation for the next seven years was editor and contributor to the *Gentleman's Magazine.*[33]

About Johnson's formative period certain facts emerge which obviously contradict some previous opinions. For instance, in his limited journalistic sphere Johnson was a man of ability whom Cave could invest with responsibility; certainly he was not just another hack writer as has been insisted.[34] No matter how distasteful his assignments may have been and how perfunctory he sometimes was in their execution, he brought to them a remarkable talent which was probably more than many of them deserved. Without knowing it at the time, he was preparing for more serious accomplishments and he had no need to feel shame about his labors for Cave. Furthermore, too much stress has been placed upon Johnson's early naïveté, mainly as a consequence of the anecdote concerning Cave's desire to "dazzle him with the splendor of some of those luminaries in literature," like Moses Browne.[35] Even though the young Johnson, despite his vast learning, might have been a callow countryman, he was not dazzled long by his colleagues, for in the main he was confident of his powers. Nor is there any reasonable support for an ingenious contention that Johnson in those days had attributes of self-restraint and diplomacy for which he is seldom given credit.[36] As a matter of expedience, he usually did what was wanted of him; but when he became aroused, he did not often hesitate to show his displeasure. Johnson had a job which he performed to the best of his ability until he could relieve himself of the compulsion to continue it.

Identification of Johnson's contributions to the *Gentleman's Magazine* is still and always must be incomplete, owing to the amorphous nature of his early writings. He was casual about his small works; and Boswell, Hawkins, and other early biographers have left gaps in the canon. What has been established, however, is extensive and important enough to allow for a satisfactory evaluation.

ESSAY CONTRIBUTIONS TO THE *Gentleman's Magazine*

Johnson wrote voluminously under Cave, his known contributions to the *Gentleman's Magazine* filling nearly three of the eleven volumes of the *Works* (Oxford, 1825). His compositions were scant until November, 1740, when he began to write the *Parliamentary Debates*. After that date he sometimes turned out copy for as much as one-half of the usual fifty pages of the magazine. The reports of the debates averaged fifteen to twenty pages, and in addition he wrote biographies and essays which ran from two to ten pages each. The quantity of his writing is less impressive when we consider that he had a month in which to prepare the materials for an issue, and that frequently during his affiliation with the *Gentleman's Magazine* he had no other employment. He nevertheless possessed two abilities useful for Cave's purposes—the all-important knack of good impromptu writing and the versatility to cope with the editorial prob lems invariably encountered by a large publication.

1. *Prefatory Essays*

One of the most irksome, and yet in many ways one of the most important, practical demands laid on the editor of the *Gentleman's Magazine* was to find an effective means of competing with other journals, especially the *London Magazine*. A common procedure (apart from attempting to produce a superior magazine) was to vilify one's opponents with charges of venality, moral turpitude, plagiarism, or any other vice which came to mind. An eighteenth-century periodical writer, relatively secure from the infrequently enforced libel laws, had to be proficient in meeting the charges of editors with counter-charges. This undignified editorial warfare was not only accepted but demanded.

Among Johnson's major editorial duties was that of composing prefaces or addresses to the readers for each of the seven bound volumes of the magazine between 1738 and 1744. These seven essays and two additional articles, upholding the good name of Cave and attacking rival booksellers, are interesting examples of contemporary invective. Though infrequently the papers were written with unexpected moderation and depth of thought, their total effect is militant and shallow. The fact that most were compressed into one or two pages intensifies this impression; and it is obvious that several were calculated to insult and enrage opposing journals as well as to prove to the *Gentleman's* readers that it could conduct itself vigorously in a literary war. This practice, further, provided an effective circulation-building device by securing free advertising for the warring parties. Johnson, who during his Grub Street career helped improve the status of journalism, also thus continued one of its worst customs. If excuse is necessary, his obligations to his employer were such that he had no alternative but starvation; and, for that matter, he perhaps even enjoyed the combat.

Divorced from urbanity, some of Johnson's early writings contain a degree of zestful malice which shows he was well versed in the invective of the day. In his first preface (1738) he alluded to the "clamours, rage, and calumnies" of many competitors, among them the *Craftsman, Common Sense,* and *Universal Spectator,* which he accused of various sins. His chief target, the *London Magazine,* he said willfully stole Cave's plan after Cave had refused to share his profits with a group of booksellers interested in joining with him. In spite of its tactics, the *London Magazine* was left with 70,000 copies "mouldering in their warehouse . . . unsold, unread, and disregarded," a statement which certainly exaggerated the truth.[37] Johnson implied that, owing to its sponsorship by a union of booksellers, the *London Magazine* could influence larger numbers of people than could the *Gentleman's Magazine.* Despite this prestige, he said, it resorted to scurrilous advertisements and hired news writers to attack Cave's periodical. Johnson deplored the continuation of an argument [about the respective merits of their parliamentary reporting] with such an unworthy foe, but trusted that the lessons derived would be of value against a better adversary, should one ever come along. To show how inept the *London Magazine* was, he proposed to reprint verbatim—except for "marking a few pretty words in italicks"—an article in which it attempted to refute one of Cave's strictures against it.[38] The words italicized—mainly *read* and *publish* —have no other effect than to make the *London's* writer appear vapidly repetitious, as indeed he is. Johnson was merely resorting to an old journalistic trick of seemingly innocent quotation, while by emphasizing the words of his opponents he distorted the context in which they appeared. At the same time he was drawing attention away from his open charges of "deplorable stupidity" and "weakness and folly."

Johnson's 1739 preface was more restrained and philosophical than the previous one, and he proudly stated that the *Gentleman's Magazine* was becoming more original in its contents. This led him to set down one of his earliest opinions on the qualities of an author and the subject of authorship, in anticipation of numerous periodical essays in which he expounded his high regard for serious literary craftsmanship. "The character of an author," he stated, "must be allowed to imply in itself something amiable and great; it conveys at once the idea of ability and good-nature, of knowledge, and a disposition to communicate it. To instruct ignorance, reclaim error, and reform vice, are designs highly worthy of applause and imitation."[39] But the untruthful writer, he observed in the same preface, invites abhorrence. Political truth is especially important, and writers must do what they can to clear the good names of rulers involved in factions. Yet it is not the function of the writer either to extol or defame any one man as a regular policy, and to do so is shameful. Writers, Johnson continued, must also ward against encroachments upon individual liberty. Here is an early key to the writer's credo which he always respected, and to the moderate libertarian aims which he cherished throughout his life. Tacitly rejecting censorship, he felt that any question of it would be precluded if journalists assumed an honorable attitude toward their responsibilities. In delineating authors, Johnson even revealed a compassion for "the laborious drudgeries which they are forced to undergo in the recess of Parliament, or a time of inaction, to give expression to wornout thoughts, to say something when they have nothing to say, and to find, in the most barren months, some field of praise or satire as yet untouched." Attitudes such as these were motivated by personal experience. The distinguishing characteristic of this essay is its tone of reasonableness and its plea for moderation. Conceding that men are never wholly good nor bad, Johnson observed that "A fool sometimes stumbles on the right, and the wisest man may deviate into error and misconduct." For this reason, then, periodical writers should take seriously their obligation to censure what is blameworthy and to credit what is praiseworthy; to be, in short, judicious at all times.

Mellowness and assurance underlie much of Johnson's introduction to the tenth volume (1740) of the magazine, but characteristic strains of reproach against other periodicals and journalism are also present. None "of the common topicks of prefaces are now left us," he asserted, and he saw no reason to belabor the obvious—the high quality of the *Gentleman's Magazine* and the inferiority of its rivals. As a substitute, therefore, he printed an "ingenious dissertation" on the Roman *Acta Diurna* which he attributed to an unidentified writer. But the style and attitudes are unmistakably Johnson's; and, as on later occasions, he demonstrated a critical and historical understanding of periodicals.[40] The essay has two functions, one of which is to describe the *Acta* and to quote examples; the other of which is to show the analogy between ancient and modern news-gatherers. Initially published during the first consulship of Julius Caesar, the *Acta* were the daily newspapers of Rome and were officially authorized. They contained news of a public nature which was drawn up by officials (*actuarii* or *actarii*) assisted by clerks and reporters (*notarii*). And they also contained news of a private nature—births, marriages, scandals, and the like. Wealthy citizens of Rome and the provinces frequently employed scribes (*operarii*) to copy the *Acta* for them. But the reports were disseminated more widely by being posted daily on a whitened board. After a reasonable interval, they would be taken down for deposit in the public archives. Though no genuine fragments are extant, the *Acta* are preserved in numerous passages by ancient authors. Johnson included many of these historical details, citing allusions to the *Acta* by such writers as Suetonius, Tacitus, Cicero, and Juvenal. He also reproduced translated portions of the *Acta* as they appeared in Pighius' *Annals* and Dodwell's *Camdenian Lectures,* to suggest their flavor. He realized, however, as did others that their authenticity is dubious.[41]

But Johnson's brief historical discussion was motivated by a desire to comment upon contemporary journalism. The essay, he said, "will serve to illustrate the thought at the beginning, by shewing the analogy of customs, and besides furnish a good authority for the readers of news-papers (who may for the future appeal to the practice of the old Romans). . . ." Seeing a small degree of utility and a larger one of triviality in the reading of newspapers, he concluded, "that the use and amusement resulting from these diurnal histories, render it a custom, not likely to be confined to one part of the globe, or one period of time." Blandly ironical, Johnson's comparison was hardly flattering to English writers, whom he considered even more attracted to the trivial than were the ancients.

The Roman gazetteers are defective in several material ornaments of style. They never end an article with the mystical hint, *this occasions great speculation.* They seem to have been ignorant of such engaging introductions, as *we hear it strongly reported;* and of the ingenious, but thread-bare, excuse for a downright lie, *it wants confirmation.* It is also observable, that the praetor's daughter is married without our being told, that *she was a lady of great beauty, merit, and fortune.*

Almost extraneously, further, he derived from accounts in the *Acta* of the Romans' "great regard" for "a false and ridiculous religion" a grave contemporary lesson:

I shall only add, that if the Romans thought a strict practice of religious rites transmitted to them . . . absolutely necessary to the preservation of discipline and morality, how much more ought those, who live under a true and divine religion, which enjoins no precepts but what are rational, no ceremonies but what are significant, to shew a proper regard for it upon all occasions, at least, never to discover by their lives and discourse, that they have lost all sense, not only of solid piety and virtue, but of common decency.

The preface of 1740 is in many respects the most significant which Johnson wrote for the *Gentleman's Magazine.* In the manner of his later periodical essays, especially the *Idler,* it is a pointed commentary on one of the social customs of his day. While Johnson's premises are erudite as well as reflective of his durable prejudices, he presents them for the most part with an interesting urbanity that lightens but in no way lessens the gravity of his opinions. Now committed to journalism, Johnson—probably voluntarily—had begun to examine its origins as part of the social and historical fabric of his own civilization. Unlike the other prefaces, because Johnson felt no need to engage in personal abuse and self-justification, the present article is unusually elaborate, combining as it does elements which are journalistic, academic, and moralistic. Here one finds definite anticipations of the periodical essayist.

After 1740 the prefaces in the *Gentleman's Magazine* lose the sparkle of many of the earlier introductions. The journal's rapid expansion is reflected in a tone which is both self-satisfied and independent. The paper war with other periodicals continued, of course, but the prefaces focused less on controversy than on positive accomplishments. Adding nothing essential to what he had already said in his prefaces, Johnson obviously was bowing to the convention which decreed such essays. He could boast (1741) that the *Gentleman's Magazine* was widely circulated and that portions of it were being reprinted in both foreign and British journals. Enterprisingly he promised greater variety and bulk than were offered by competitors. He stressed the trend of the *Gentleman's Magazine* toward original pieces, and denied all charges of political partisanship. As a matter of form he censured the *London Magazine* and its followers.[42] The preface for 1742 contained still another puff for the *Gentleman's Magazine* and its purposes, including praise for the verity of the *Debates,* the "impartiality and perspicuity" of its extracts, and its general literary excellence.[43] The fulfillment of its readers' demands, Johnson professed a year later in the preface for 1743, would continue to be the magazine's principal aim.[44] He admitted that political news generally had been too engrossing; and although the magazine did not intend to neglect politics, it was striving for variety with the introduction of articles on morality, commerce, and philosophy. By the end of 1744 peace in the editorial war was hinted.[45] At least, in his preface for that year Johnson said the controversy with other magazines had ended. This was a portent of greater dignity, though a footnote to his article charged that the *London Magazine* still lied about its circulation. The growth of the *Gentleman's Magazine* continued. On the whole, therefore, he had some justification for the statement he had made in the 1742 preface, that "applause has rather increased than relaxed our application, and . . . victory has not lulled us in security, but excited us to vigilance."

Several years after he had ceased active participation in the *Gentleman's Magazine,* Johnson probably wrote one more preface for Cave, that to the first index of 1753.[46] Under any circumstances this brief piece would be of interest as a product of Johnson's pen and as an indication of his continuing interest in the magazine. It is for the most part utilitarian and explanatory; its formal duty is to retail the events reported in the periodical for the preceding twenty years. But the tranquil tone is markedly different from that of many of the earlier prefaces. Compressed though it is, it contains a paragraph of political and philosophical attitudes which exhibits the growth of Johnson's thinking as a nationalist, despiser of rebellion, and exponent of public liberty. One statement in particular merits inclusion with his notions of liberty and subordination, for he defended the right of political opposition to Walpole, "a statesman as able perhaps as any that ever existed." This opposition, he maintained, produced a series of debates indicative of the "right of the Crown and the privileges of the people, so as for ever to prevent their being confounded in the cause either of tyranny or of faction." By 1753 Johnson, even as a journalist, was politically independent. The essay is notable also in revealing that Cave's substantial position permitted the new, satisfying dignity of completely ignoring the rivals of the *Gentleman's Magazine.*

Johnson's prefatory essays must be regarded as assignments from Cave; and, therefore, except for incidental reflections, they were not necessarily expressive of his own attitudes. Despite such an obvious restriction, these essays chart the improvement of eighteenth-century journalism and foreshadow Johnson's later literary achievements. In the prefaces spread over seven years may be detected the gradual change in the attitudes of the *Gentleman's Magazine,* a change largely attributable to its favorable reception. With this came a greater emphasis upon self-improvement and a concurrent lessening of abusiveness. The *Gentleman's* broad interests anticipated the cultural and intellectual position that such miscellanies would eventually assume in England. While Cave's motives for combatting the monopolistic aims of the *London Magazine* were obviously materialistic, his triumphant survival was an omen for the possibilities of independent journalism. And Johnson, especially in his remarks on the character of an author, was able to inject an idealistic note for the promulgation of truth, liberty, and dignity.

2. *Biographies*

Following the ancients and the writers of the Renaissance, Johnson observed in *Rambler,* No. 60, that no form of writing is more valuable than biography. From other men's lives we derive delight and instruction, for to some degree we participate in common motives, fallacies, hopes, dangers, desires, and pleasures. These universal experiences he tried to make evident in the biographies he wrote while he was contributing to the *Gentleman's Magazine*. Without being a technical innovator during the St. John's Gate period, he developed a remarkable proficiency in biography, the form in which he was ultimately to display some of his maturest criticism. Further critical principles enunciated in the *Rambler* essay are worth noting as a guide to his practice. He admitted, for instance, the value of catching attention with famous names, but held that public greatness is less significant than the minutiae of private daily life in which prudence and virtue are exposed. More can be learned of a man's true character from those who knew him personally than from a formal chronological account from birth to death. Honesty, above all else, is important. The biographer, writing from personal knowledge as Johnson wrote about Savage, must not permit friendship to cause him to conceal or invent. It is no "act of piety to hide the faults or failings of . . . friends, even when they can no longer suffer by their detection." The lessons to be drawn from a man's life rather than panegyric should be the primary intention of biography.

Johnson's respect for historical accuracy adds to the value of his biographies. He was contemptuous of histories which became inflated through the use of "flying reports" and unsubstantiated facts, as he said in the life of Boerhaave. And though as a journalist he was not concerned with original research, he made every effort to avoid or rectify errors.[47] He regretted that the paucity of biographical information, as in the life of Sydenham, sometimes necessitated skepticism about unusual achievements. Usually he was careful to name his authorities, especially when there was an obvious danger of prejudice, as in the letter of Barretier's father or the anecdotes of Burman's friend, Dr. Osterdyke. Whenever possible Johnson relied upon generally available sources, such as Wood, Clarendon, Burnet, and Wotton. He derived data about Roscommon from Fenton's notes on Waller and Aubrey's *Miscellany*. Less frequently he used other kinds of documents, such as Albert Schulten's *Oratio Academica in Memoriam Hermanni Boerhaavii,* extracts from letters, Fontenelle's *Éloge de Morin,* and Le Courayer's commentary on Father Paul. For the life of Savage he could augment the meager printed accounts with his personal knowledge. The range of his materials, as might be expected, contributed to a diversity of treatments, from the general and objective to the particular and subjective.

Writing for a periodical, Johnson necessarily limited his biographies to from three to five pages in each issue; however, because of the popularity of some of his subjects, he frequently serialized them over three or four issues. Despite the handicaps of space, Johnson always strove to write well-rounded biographies. Little of his factual material was new; but this did not hinder his free interjection of personal opinions, especially about the morality of his subjects. In addition he evaluated their contributions to society, pointing out the lessons to be drawn from their lives, and in general elaborating as he saw fit on even the most obvious qualities of the men he was memorializing. Subtlety, as Johnson himself would have admitted, was a refinement that eighteeenth-century writers reserved for a more discerning and sensitive audience than the readers of periodicals. In this early stage of Johnson's career most of his biographies were of non-literary people; yet from his lessons in biography writing for the *Gentleman's Magazine* he acquired the technique later demonstrated to advantage in the *Lives of the English Poets,* in which he wrote from a more experienced and mature point of view and for a more literate audience. He was, furthermore, no longer cramped by space nor harassed by monthly editorial deadlines. By the time he undertook the *Lives,* Johnson could employ his earlier lessons in compression of material, and in stating his own opinions whenever he felt the need to amplify an issue or drive home a moral.

His interest in men of science, history, and travel was characteristic of the latter half of the eighteenth century, when science and historical inquiry were regarded as the keys to truth.[48] Many literary men of the time were absorbed in science or natural and experimental philosophy. Adam Smith and Edward Gibbon studied anatomy; Thomas Gray investigated Linnaeus' *Systema;* Gibbon and Johnson experimented in chemistry. Eighteenth-century thinkers were concerned with synthesizing or classifying knowledge; and history to them was a broad, general term embracing the sciences as well as the political past of a nation. Johnson kept abreast of world developments, whether in science, in exploration, or in naval affairs. His was an era of international expansion in which the world had been shrunk by the travels of William Dampier, Jean Baptiste Labat, R.A.C. Renneville, and others. In 1735, furthermore, Jean Baptiste du Halde had published his second-hand yet important account of China. That Johnson was well aware of these developments is amply reflected in his articles about Blake, Drake, Du Halde, the Amazons, and in his *Foreign Histories*.[49]

There are both complaint and apology in his preface of 1742 that much of the biographical emphasis in the *Gentleman's Magazine* appears to be upon foreigners. The reason he ascribes to British apathy toward the lives of its own distinguished men, in consequence of which adequate information about them is wanting. That he was unremitting in his belief is evident in the opening sentence of the life of Cowley, where he complains of "the penury of English biography." His own selections of biographical subjects, both British and Continental, were dictated mainly by the likelihood of their appeal to a popular audience. Precocious scholars and philosophers like John Philip Barretier,[50] as Johnson intimated in his life of the German prodigy, and Peter Burman[51] were sure to excite curiosity. Scientists and physicians like Herman Boerhaave,[52] Louis Morin,[53] and Thomas Sydenham[54] were renowned figures, contemporary or nearly so, whose lives commanded a similar interest. Cave, in addition, had material interest in the biographies which were related to his publishing ventures. As one of the booksellers projecting a translation by Johnson of the *History of the Council of Trent*, he deemed it profitable to print a short life of the sixteenth-century Venetian author, Father Paul Sarpi.[55] He also published Sydenham's works in 1742, and he intended Johnson's essay—which he appended to the edition after its appearance in the magazine—to promote their sale. The heroic exploits of Blake and Drake, which made a stirring appeal to British nationalism, may well have been intended as a reminder of former naval victories and present defeats, and also to stimulate interest in the war against Spain.[56] The introduction to the life of Blake is sufficiently inflammatory to warrant this conclusion.

Johnson probably influenced Cave in the selection of several subjects who were not only well known, but whose lives had a personal appeal for the biographer. The three scientists—Boerhaave, Morin, and Sydenham—are remarkably similar to Johnson in moral elevation and, the first two, in physical suffering. The projected life of Savage, also, is marked by Johnson's sympathy (as well as acquaintance with the poet), an interest stronger than Cave's regard for a late employee. "They only who live with a man can write his life with any genuine exactness and discrimination."[57] The life of Drake, aside from its expressed distaste for Spaniards, revealed Johnson's characteristic antipathy to the wilds of America or, for that matter, any aspect of untamed nature.

As in his other literary productions, so also in his journalistic biographies is forceful opinion a characteristic. Self-identification, he states explicitly in the *Rambler* essay, is an inevitable part of biographical reconstruction. Johnson's attitudes, however, are integrated with the factual details which motivate them and are almost never permitted to stand isolated as though they are more important than the life being described. The essay on Blake offers a significant exception, for in Johnson's introductory paragraph he alludes harshly to the "insults, ravages, and barbarities" of the Spaniards in his own day, and calls for vengeance. For the most part, however, he opens in a milder tone, beginning immediately with the customary details of birth, family, ancestry, schooling or apprenticeship, and subsequent career. His lives would be drab if he had confined himself to this kind of strict chronology, for the moralistic, philosophical interpretations give his writings vitality. Of Boerhaave's pain-ridden life, thus, he comments that illness "taught him to compassionate others." In discussing Sydenham he pauses to refute Sir Richard Blackmore's imputation that Sydenham was "a physician by accident and necessity" and that his training was rudimentary and informal.[58] "That it should be imagined that the greatest physician of the age arrived at so high a degree of skill, without any assistance from his predecessors; and that a man, eminent for integrity, practiced medicine by chance, and grew wise only by murder is not to be considered without astonishment." At times skepticism of his subjects' accomplishments forces another kind of interpolation. For instance, he was hard-pressed to believe that Barretier mastered five languages at the age of nine. That faith in precocity should be so tempered is understandable in one who was to regard Pope's boyish *Ode on Solitude* as "nothing more than other forward boys have attained."[59] Yet Johnson conceded that he was perhaps influenced by prejudice, and he admitted that "an account is not to be immediately censured as false, merely because it is wonderful." Throughout the biographies, thus, Johnson's biasses are evident; but then so is his broadmindedness.

Johnson's somber reflections on death and his evaluations of moral traits indicate that the center of his biographical interests was in ethical excellence. It is no objective historian who writes of Boerhaave, "The history of his illness can hardly be read without horrour"; or, "May his example extend its influence to his admirers and followers! and those who endeavour after his knowledge, aspire likewise to his piety!" Similarly he concluded of Barretier: "His constant application to learning suppressed those passions which betray others of his age to irregularities, and excluded all those temptations to which men are exposed by idleness or common amusements." Related traits earn Johnson's praise in his discussions of Burman and Sydenham. And though he had profound respect for bravery in military men, he set even more store by their piety and firmness of moral character. This is seen in his aphoristic remark about Drake, that "virtue is the surest foundation both of reputation and fortune, and . . . the first step to greatness is to be honest." The conclusion of the Blake essay is a vindication of the admiral's religious sincerity and humaneness.

Characteristically a champion of lost causes and a rebel against tyranny in any form, Johnson in his biographies often expressed his sympathy for the oppressed. Much of his admiration for Father Paul, for instance, can be traced to the cleric's anti-papal attitude and his harassment by the Inquisition. Many of Johnson's early subjects, indeed, were controversial figures. Boerhaave was virtually driven from the ministry by accusations of atheism when he attempted a reasonable explanation of Spinoza's seemingly heretical notions. He wished above all, said Johnson, to live "at liberty, without any restraint upon his books, his thoughts or his tongue, and at the utmost distance from all contentions of state parties."[60] The vindication of Sydenham against people like Blackmore, who accused him of professional incompetence, and of Savage against those who found him immoral, is typical of Johnson's belligerently protective attitude. That the body of Blake, a Puritan admiral, was desecrated during the Restoration, Johnson held abhorrent. "Had he been guilty of the murder of Charles the first, to insult his body had been a mean revenge; but, as he was innocent, it was, at least, inhumanity, and perhaps ingratitude." It was sufficient for Johnson that Blake had served his country well, even if his principles were mistaken, and that he was religious, if only "according to the pretended purity of these times." A man may be righteous in his convictions and behavior, according to Johnson, without conforming to the moral and religious standards of the majority; and certainly he should not be persecuted for deviations.

Attention to moral qualities is important in Johnson's biographies, but not to the exclusion of specific details which his readers expected. He achieved a skillful balance between the exposition of abstract virtues and the description of concrete realities which makes his subjects credible. His most obvious means of establishing realism was through the use of historical facts, such as dates, names of people, and particular incidents. Johnson also realized the importance of narrative continuity implemented by small, revealing domestic details, perhaps unimportant in themselves but valuable for creating an intimate atmosphere. Descriptions of home life and illnesses served this purpose. His lives of the admirals, whose adventures he colorfully delineated, also exhibit this realism. When Blake in pursuit of pirates sailed into Tunis (March, 1666) the governor sent him an insulting note. "Fired with this inhuman and insolent treatment," Johnson wrote, "he curled his whiskers, as was his custom when he was angry," and proceeded to decimate his rash enemy. "This was so bravely executed, that with the loss of only 25 men killed, and 48 wounded, all the ships were fired in the fight of Tunis." Of Drake's adventures, Johnson provided dates of four voyages, names of ships, and even the fact that the sailor carried with him "a complete service of silver for his own table." Descriptions of strange fish and animals and of savage customs contribute to this rounded, picturesque biography. Such concreteness, intended for the entertainment of magazine readers, also anticipated the biographical thoroughness of the *Lives of the English Poets.*

Johnson turned to biographical translation in 1741, to extol the

French scientist Morin. His rendering of Fontenelle's *Éloge de Morin* demonstrates his thesis that translations must be exact or literal.[61] Fontenelle was a fortunate choice of biographer since both authors were compatible in moral attitudes. Johnson, thus, was able in his account of Morin to present a sequel to the Boerhaave with few changes or interpolations. Fontenelle's French style, furthermore, accommodates itself very well to Johnsonian phraseology. In an evaluation of Johnson's early biographical writings, the Morin translation may be considered as much a part of the canon as the original pieces, both for choice and treatment of subject.

A member of the French Academy, Morin was a student of botany, a physician, and a philosopher well received in royal circles. With his usual moral gravity, Johnson followed Fontenelle's discourse on Morin's exemplary personal traits and professional integrity. Morin was extremely charitable, frugal, and pious. "Thus abstinence and generosity discovered themselves with his passion for botany, and the gratification of a desire indifferent in itself, was procured by the exercise of two virtues." (*Déjà avec le goût de la botanique, la libéralité et la sobriété commençaient à éclore en lui et une inclination indifférente ne se développait qu'accompagnée de ces deux vertue naissantes.*) In his later years, Morin was made pensionnaire of the Academy and a plant, *Morina Orientalis,* was named after him. Fontenelle, like Johnson, recognized the ephemeral nature of fame. Johnson, in a spirit that foreshadows his disillusioned views, translated: "[A] plant is a monument of a more durable nature than a medal or an obelisk; and yet, as a proof that even these vehicles are not always sufficient to transmit to futurity the name conjoined with them, the *Nicotiana* is now scarcely known by any other term than that of tobacco." (*Une plante est un monument plus durable qu'une médaille ou qu'un obélisque. Il est vrai cependant qu'il arrive des malheurs même aux noms attachés aux plantes; témoin la nictiane, qui ne s'appelle plus que tabac.*) Johnson quoted a maxim attributed to Morin, but one which could be applied as well to himself in his own gruffer moments: "Those that come to see me do me honour, and those that stay away do me a favour." (*. . . ceux qui me viennent voir me font honneur, ceux qui n'y viennent pas me font plaisir.*) Throughout his sketch, Johnson demonstrates a competence in translation. And here, as from many of his other biographies, he draws support and inspiration for his own life.

Except for the life of Roscommon and the notice of a forthcoming life of Savage, Johnson did not write biographies of literary men for the *Gentleman's Magazine*.[62] Not until he began the *Rambler* and contributed to the *Literary Magazine* was he to emerge fully, in his journalism, as a literary critic and reviewer; his criticism in the *Gentleman's Magazine* was mainly exploratory. The journalistic study of Roscommon was neither forceful nor adequate, although Johnson later enlarged this cursory account and included Roscommon in his gallery of English poets. The first version is a mere patchwork of references and notes, the latter of which are more representative of Johnson than the body of the essay. Aubrey's report of the manner in which Roscommon predicted the death of his father is examined gravely; Johnson's resulting skepticism of miracles is anticipatory of his role in the Cock Lane hoax. As for provocative critical evaluations, Johnson merely recommended Roscommon as "perhaps the only correct writer in verses before Addison," and he praised him for having few faults. In final evaluation, Johnson stated only that his "character as a writer is eminent." Despite its inadequacy, the Roscommon essay provides a comparison with the mature biographical and critical qualities of the later *Life,* which was an outgrowth of these outline materials. Greater enthusiasm is observable in the biography of Richard Savage, Johnson's dissolute colleague on the *Gentleman's Magazine* and companion in the London streets. Actually the *Life of Savage* bears only an oblique relationship to the *Gentleman's Magazine*. Johnson proposed the biography in a letter appearing in the magazine; but it was published in a pamphlet by James Roberts in 1744 and later included in the *English Poets*. The *Proposal* is interesting largely because of Johnson's friendship with Savage during these Grub Street days and his deep sense of responsibility for a fellow hack whom he vowed to protect from calumny. His intimacy with Savage is implicit in the *Proposal,* though details of biography and criticism were withheld until the appearance of the pamphlet. The *Life of Savage* is an exception to Johnson's own remark, in 1773, that no English literary biography had been well written.[63]

Scattered through his contributions to the magazine, especially in the book reviews and study of epitaphs, is literary criticism. Although the biographies seldom required such judgments, Johnson made random statements which exhibit his early critical interests. Thus, despite his skepticism of Barretier's precocity, he commented on notes which the prodigy, at the age of eleven, drew up in connection with a French translation from the Hebrew of Rabbi Benjamin. These notes, "out of the common road of learning," Johnson found afforded "many instances of penetration, judgment, and accuracy." Of Peter Burman, a celebrated Dutch scholar and attorney, as of Barretier, Johnson wrote mainly to describe unusual erudition and piety. But he also had something to say about his ability as a writer, even though with a definite reservation. His style he judged to be "lively and masculine, but not without harshness and constraint, nor, perhaps, always polished to that purity, which some writers have attained." These faults were offset by high moral quality, "and if reputation be estimated by usefulness, he may claim a higher degree in the ranks of learning than some others of happier elocution, or more vigorous imagination." Literary criticism was not Johnson's major concern at this time, but he introduced as much evaluation as possible, because every aspect of a subject's career was material for him.

Although Johnson never popularized his biographical essays by a lowering or sensationalizing of style, he was nevertheless able to communicate to the diversified readers of periodicals. His use of concrete, often personal, details established a reassuring tone of authority; and the fluency of his writing was as appropriate in the pages of the *Gentleman's Magazine* as in those of more serious works. He impressed his audience with his gravity without overwhelming it. For his most substantial pieces, furthermore, he selected subjects who would be popular despite their eminence. Playing on such themes as patriotism, unusual attainments—especially of triumphs over adversity—and moral or ethical probity, Johnson virtually assured public sanction. Considered in their journalistic contexts, thus, the biographies have much to commend them. But they did not suffer the usual quick extinction of periodical pieces. They were quoted and reprinted and moral axioms were taken from them, sometimes long after their initial publication. Their lasting influence may be attributed to the accomplishments and lofty characters of their subjects, but also to the skillful portrayals and reflective philosophy which distinguished these biographies from the journalistic productions of the day. The knowledge that Johnson was their author of course helped in later years to enhance their value.[64]

3. *Travel Essays*

Once Boswell said he might publish an account of his European travels, and Johnson advised against it. "What can you tell of countries so well known as those upon the continent of Europe, which you have visited?" Nor would he write of his own foreign travels, for intelligent readers had seen more of France than he had. In his conversations and in his writings, Johnson maintained that the narrator of travels must have the useful purpose "of contrasting one mode of life with another." But these were philosophical and even supercilious considerations which he had not yet formulated while he was writing for Cave. Perhaps, further, he had not yet achieved the sophistication which was to make him reject this kind of literature. As a matter of necessity as well as of curiosity he was more responsive to books about distant places, such as Lobo's treatment of Abyssinia. And in the first few years of his association with the *Gentleman's Magazine,* South American and Chinese themes provoked Johnson's wonderment, giving him materials for articles. Contemporary interest in the Amazons was colored by incredulity, as would appear from the translation of Abbé de Guyon's *Dissertation on the Amazons* which Boswell attributed to Johnson.[65] Thus Johnson characteristically advised his readers that scarcity of information about this female society was no reason for disbelieving its existence. Considering the exoticism rather than the moral implications of the subject, Johnson—as in his life of Drake—developed primitivistic details most likely to attract English periodical readers: the customs of the Amazons, their dress, warlike traits, and abnormal lives. From these materials, apparently, Johnson later developed *Idler,* No. 87, a satire in which he compared English women with the Amazons. Echoing the earlier piece, he declared "it may reasonably be imagined, that many ancient historians are unjustly suspected of falsehood, because our own times afford nothing that resembles what they tell."

China was another penumbral region for most eighteenth-century

Englishmen, but the regular traffic of East India Company ships between China and England piqued curiosity for information about the East. In 1735 British interest was intensified by the publication of Jean Baptiste du Halde's *Description de la Chine*. Consequently Cave, between 1735 and 1742, had been promising a complete translation of Du Halde's work, and intermittently he had been publishing selections which had been rendered by William Guthrie and one Green. In 1736 he printed a few sections submitted by an impatient reader in anticipation of the entire *Description*. Cave's publicity was enhanced by his feud with another bookseller, John Watts, who in 1736 brought out Richard Brookes' translation of Du Halde. Despite all this, insufficient subscribers were attracted and Cave's edition remained incomplete.[66]

Johnson's part in the publication of Du Halde's *Description* began sometime in 1738, probably before July. In that month Cave ran a letter signed "Eubulus," on *Du Halde's History of China*. Ascribed to Johnson by John Nichols, the letter has been generally overlooked by most commentators, including Boswell.[67] Although there is no positive evidence of authorship, "Eubulus" bears enough resemblance to Johnson in style, tone, and subject matter to suggest that he wrote at least the introduction to the letter at a time when he was attempting a connection with Cave. The author thanks Cave for making the *Description* available to English readers, and he justifies the translation because it contains valuable, novel information about China and possesses a morality analogous with that of Britain. The main purpose of the letter, contained in the second half, is to praise the honorable spirit of an English nobleman; the opening paragraphs show the parallels between two cultures, as well as advertise Du Halde. The first five paragraphs—sonorous, balanced, and gravely moral—if not Johnson's are a remarkably good imitation, exemplified in this passage:

Any custom or law unheard and unthought of before, strikes us with that surprize which is the effect of novelty; but a practice conformable to our own pleases us, because it flatters our self-love, by showing us that our opinions are approved by the general concurrence of mankind.[68] Of these two pleasures, the first is more violent, the other more lasting; the first seems to partake more of instinct than reason, and is not easily to be explained, or defined; the latter has its foundation in good sense and reflection, and evidently depends on the same principles with most human passions.

The second half of the letter lacks distinction, and it may well be that Johnson had been called upon merely to write an introduction. The account of the nobleman, unquestionably commonplace, could have been written by any of Cave's hacks. The opening sentiments, on the other hand, and their similarity to Johnson's later comments on Du Halde make plausible Nichols' identification of Johnson with at least this share of "Eubulus." Ironically, thus, the first two prose pieces in the *Gentleman's Magazine* attributable to Johnson were only partially his. The introduction to the first of the *Debates in the Senate of Magna Lilliputia,* which had appeared in June, was apparently written by him, as was the opening of the "Eubulus" letter in July. These collaborative essays (and his subsequent work on the *Debates* in 1738), indeed, show that Cave at first found Johnson more useful to the miscellany as an editor than as an author.

In a letter to Cave, September, 1738, Johnson alluded to his part in the *Description:* "The Chinese Stories may be had folded down when you please to send, in which I do not recollect that you desired any alteration to be made." Johnson's function was to select portions of the translation for printing in the magazine; but Cave was not pleased with Johnson's dilatoriness. Johnson, for his part, was not satisfied with the quality of the translation; even forty years later he recollected its inaccuracy. Despite his ostensible familiarity with China, Du Halde, a Jesuit, had never made a trip of more than ten leagues from Paris, and he compiled his account from *Mémoires* of Jesuit missionaries. Voltaire, who knew this fact, nevertheless praised the usefulness of the *Description.* Johnson added to his own selections a eulogistic critique in which—like "Eubulus"—he announced that this, differing from most other travel books, was truthful and authoritative. And in conversation he recommended the *Description* as a book of reference.[69]

Opinions about travel writing which as an employee of Cave he had been unable to express Johnson made clear enough in later years. "Those whose lot it is to ramble can seldom write, and those who know how to write very seldom ramble," he told Mrs. Thrale. The deficiency of many travel writers, he felt, lay in their inability to interpret what they had seen, for to set down mere physical observations would be inexcusable. Only if a traveler were to communicate significant cultural and ethical matters, to compare the mores of a foreign land with his own, could he justify his authorship.[70] For Johnson, travel like any other activity must be socially useful and, as he wrote in *Idler,* No. 97, "He that would travel for the entertainment of others, should remember that the great object of remark is human life."

> Every writer of travels should consider, that, like all other authors, he undertakes either to instruct or please, or to mingle pleasure with instruction. He that instructs must offer to the mind something to be imitated, or something to be avoided; he that pleases must offer new images to his reader, and enable him to form a tacit comparison of his own state with that of others.

When ultimately Johnson produced a travel book, *A Journey to the Western Islands of Scotland* (1775), he demonstrated his practical belief in his own dicta.

4. *History of the Council of Trent*

Encouraged by Walmesley, William Caslon the type-founder, and Dr. Birch, Johnson began in 1738 a translation of Father Paul Sarpi's *History of the Council of Trent* from the Italian, with the notes and biography from the French of Dr. Pierre François le Courayer. Father Paul was a precocious sixteenth-century Venetian whose encyclopedic knowledge—like that of Barretier and Burman—delighted Johnson, and whose *History* he felt merited a translation better than one already published (1736). In anticipation of this project he composed a brief life of Father Paul for the *Gentleman's Magazine,* which he signed "S. J.," drawing his materials wholly from Le Courayer and condensing freely.[71] He emphasized Father Paul's scholarship and his mastery of languages, impressed that "his application was unintermitted, his head clear, his apprehension quick, and his memory retentive." But even more, Johnson respected him for his courageous independence in Church matters which brought him into frequent collison with the Inquisition and led to attempts upon his life. Father Paul had written *The History of the Council of Trent* in order to deny the Pope's claims to omnipotence and to attack corruption in the Church. When he died at the age of seventy-one, he was "Hated by the Romans as their most formidable enemy, and honoured by all the learned for his abilities, and by the good for his integrity." To this eulogy Johnson added with obvious relish a quotation from one of Father Paul's letters: "There is nothing more essential than to ruin the reputation of the Jesuits: By the ruin of the Jesuits, Rome will be ruined; and if Rome is ruined, religion will reform of itself." Johnson, further, was able to discover evidences in the *History* of Father Paul's admiration for the Church of England. The life of Sarpi takes on importance as an early expression of Johnson's liberal principles. Of the *History* he said, "the reader finds liberty without licentiousness, piety without hypocrisy, freedom of speech without neglect of decency, severity without rigour, and extensive learning without ostentation." To these qualities Johnson added the opinions of Bishop Burnet and Wotton that Father Paul was a model for historical writing equal to any in antiquity as well as his own conclusion that the *History* was "a work unequalled for the judicious disposition of the matter, and artful texture of the narration." For Johnson, thus, Father Paul was an ideal biographical subject, permitting him to expound on such favorite themes as intellectual genius, liberalism, anti-Catholicism, and victory gained despite seemingly insuperable odds. He treated Father Paul admiringly, as a figure whose career should serve as a symbol for aspiration.

Unfortunately, Johnson's plans to translate the *History* proved abortive, for another person engaged simultaneously in the same project read one of Cave's newspaper advertisements and publicly protested that his own work was being infringed. By an oddity of circumstance this person was also named Johnson—the Reverend John Johnson—keeper of Archbishop Tennison's library near St. Martin's in the Fields.[72] The Reverend Mr. Johnson, who claimed the patronage of eminent clergymen and the personal encouragement of Le Courayer, implied that S. Johnson's surname was a fiction intended to capitalize upon his own prior and superior project. At St. John's Gate the Sarpi translation had already reached the stage of advance publicity and Johnson had been receiving payments since August 2, at least two months prior to John Johnson's protest. Cave could not afford to stand by idly. Six thousand copies of a proposal, no longer extant, had been distributed. Further, advertisements of the proposal had been run in the *Daily Advertiser* (October 11, 1738; also on October 12, 19, 20, and 25), and in the *Weekly Miscellany* on October 21. The *History's* size was set and the price stipulated. Subscriptions were being taken by the booksellers Dodsley, Rivington, and Cave. Johnson also took subscriptions and apparently even kept a list of subscribers.

Thus, when John Johnson's letter of protest appeared in the *Advertiser* on October 20, Cave inserted a crisp response the following day, asserting the independence and value of his own project and maintaining that "Mr. Johnson's sirname is no new acquisition." For evidence of the originality of Johnson's scheme, the bookseller offered to make available the proposals which had been dated and submitted more than a year earlier. Although the letter of October 21 in the *Advertiser* is signed "Ed. Cave," there may be some basis to a recent contention that, from internal evidence—essentially of style and syntax—it should be ascribed to Samuel Johnson.[73] The confusion caused in the daily press by reports of the competition between the two Johnsons resulted in the nullification of both translations, and despite the life of Sarpi which appeared in the *Gentleman's Magazine,* November, 1738, Cave's expenses were in vain. From Johnson's manuscript he printed perhaps six sheets of the *History,* most of which were subsequently converted to wastepaper in spite of plans to save a few copies.[74] As for John Johnson, a report at the time of his death (February 27, 1747) held that he had continued to work—futilely— on his own translation of the *History.*

5. *Crousaz and Pope*

There was generally rapport between Cave and Johnson through their association, which lasted until Cave's death in 1754. But frictions were inevitable, as in the first year of Johnson's full-time employment. The now famous letter [November, 1738?] signed *impransus* tacitly refers to a rebuke administered by Cave because Johnson failed to keep his printers supplied with assigned copy; and it plainly expresses Johnson's willingness, out of keeping with the later independence, to conciliate his new employer.[75] The letter sheds light on this early relationship and Johnson's frequently eccentric working habits, but it has an even greater importance. In it we first

learn of Johnson's part in the translation from the French of Jean
Pierre de Crousaz's *Commentaire* on Pope's *Essay on Man,* a work
distinct and separate from Crousaz's *Examen* of the *Essay,* which was
translated by the future bluestocking Elizabeth Carter, a fellow contributor to the *Gentleman's Magazine.* Johnson urged that her work
be advertised at once, probably to forestall any rival translations, and
Cave printed the *Examination* in 1738. While Miss Carter had been
engaged in her translation, Johnson had been translating—or at least
had been assigned to translate—the *Commentary on Mr. Pope's Principles of Morality.* But both he and Cave were dubious of the success
of the project; "for as the names of the authors concerned are of
more weight in the performance than in its own intrinsick merit, the
publick will soon be satisfied with it."

Johnson's obvious unwillingness to settle down to the *Commentary*
was one cause for its delayed publication until sometime in 1739.
Another, perhaps, was the appearance in 1738 of Charles Forman's
incomplete edition of a *Commentary upon Mr. Pope's Four Ethic
Epistles* issued by Edmund Curll. When it became apparent to Cave
that Curll's version would not be completed, he may have urged
Johnson to proceed. Once Johnson overcame his inertia, he wrote
with his usual rapidity, admitting composition of forty-eight quarto
pages of the annotated translation of the *Commentary* in one day.[76]

Crousaz's criticism of Pope has been evaluated elsewhere, but a
brief summary of the controversy will help to clarify Johnson's connection with it. Pope's *Essay on Man* was first translated into French
prose by Silhouette (1736) and into verse by the Abbé du Resnel
(1737). Crousaz, professor of mathematics and philosophy in the
University of Lausanne, read both versions. A pious man who distrusted metaphysics and Pope's optimism (and, according to one
critic, incompetent to understand Pope's meaning and purpose),
Crousaz identified Pope's views with those of Leibnitz and Spinoza,
concluding in the *Examen* that the *Essay* was irreligious. Bishop Warburton, who earlier had been a friend of many of Pope's dunces and
had himself criticized Pope, nevertheless vindicated him in a series
of letters, in 1738 and 1739. To Pope's relief and gratitude, Warburton in opposition to Crousaz strongly denied that Pope favored
fatality, or that he rejected revelation. Unwilling to let the matter

drop, Crousaz wrote the *Commentaire* in rebuttal, prefacing it with one of Warburton's letters "Written to Mr. Crousaz on his Examen of Mr. Pope's Essay on Man."[77]

Johnson's translation of the *Commentaire* is relevant to this discussion because it is the basis of an essay which he wrote for the *Gentleman's Magazine* in 1743, several years after the rendering of the Crousaz work.[78] But special mention deserves to be made of the notes on the *Commentaire,* which are significantly representative of his earliest literary criticism.[79] The additional point should be made that the largest part of Johnson's comments have to do with the quality of Du Resnel's verse translation of the *Essay on Man* (which Johnson interlineated with the English version whenever Crousaz made a direct allusion). Because of the inadequacy of the Abbé's work, Crousaz, who admitted his ignorance of English, arrived at interpretations which had no foundation in Pope's original. For the most part, then, Johnson's literary criticism was aimed at Du Resnel rather than Crousaz. He accused the French translator of missing Pope's meaning and his "fire and precipitation" (p. 8n.). Of one passage which Du Resnel had inflated from the original sixteen lines to thirty-three Johnson noted, "it is not necessary to make any other remark than may be made in general on the whole work, that it is extremely below the original in spirit, propriety, and notwithstanding the diffuseness of his expression, perspicuity" (p. 67n.). Despite Du Resnel's being his major target, Johnson was not indifferent to occasional literary faults for which Crousaz was accountable. Here, the chief complaint was one of carelessness, for had Crousaz made a closer comparison between the texts of Du Resnel and Silhouette he would not have let some of Pope's "nonsense pass without censure." Furthermore, at times he even was guilty of misinterpreting Du Resnel's lines. Mistaken at one point about Pope's meaning of death, according to Johnson, Crousaz "seems to have forgotten either the candour of a moralist, or the sagacity of a commentator" (p. 30n.). And Johnson, early in his translation, urged his readers to "observe with indignation the dull introduction, and common remarks which are interwoven with Mr. Pope's animated sentiments" (p. 6n.).

To encourage the sale of the translated *Commentary,* Johnson in a

two-part article for the *Gentleman's Magazine* acted as referee in the
indecisive quarrel between Crousaz and Warburton. Since the latter's
name had not been mentioned directly in the *Commentary,* Johnson
had not taken issue with his arguments. Now, however, without specifically analyzing Warburton's critique, he was less sympathetic to
him than to Crousaz. By extension, further, it may be inferred that
Johnson's displeasure touched upon Pope, who was enjoying Warburton's protection. Assuming a public manner somewhat different
from that which he had revealed in his letter to Cave, Johnson expressed a belief "in the importance of the subject." But he also
acknowledged the reputations of Crousaz and Warburton as well as
the enthusiasm with which each had argued his position. Deploring
an unseemly dispute which had led to irrelevancies and name-calling,
he felt that the main issues had been obscured. He considered the
affair particularly unfortunate, "because it has not been proved that
either the poet, or his commentator wrote with any other design than
that of promoting happiness, by cultivating reason and piety." Annoyed by Warburton's injudicious attacks upon Crousaz's character,
Johnson selected specimens from the translation of the *Commentary*
—which make up more than half the essay—to show that Crousaz
was "far from deserving either indignation or contempt," even
though his comments were not always pertinent. Johnson's presentation of these quotations and his return to them in the later life of
Pope are ample testimony of his partiality for Crousaz's views as
opposed to Pope's and Warburton's.

The most significant quotation in the *Gentleman's Magazine* essay
is from Crousaz's lengthy refutation of the "ruling passion," to
which Pope subscribed. Among other things, Crousaz had asserted
that far from being felicitous the doctrine of the ruling passion[80]—
devotion to instinct at the expense of reason—could result in "calamities and follies." And in a parallel statement, which Johnson did
not quote in the *Gentleman's Magazine,* Crousaz hypothesized instances of gamblers, debauchees, robbers, and murderers justifying
their misconduct as the operation of ruling passions. At least in general agreement with Crousaz, Johnson had devoted his most elaborate
note in the *Commentary* (p. 109*n.*) to a modification of this idea.
Recognizing "many reasonable objections against this system, of a

Ruling Passion," Johnson professed to be "conscious of none but the general desire of happiness, which is not here intended, so that there appears equal evidence on both sides." Neither Crousaz's attitude nor Pope's seemed thoroughly tenable to him. While he admitted that some individuals did indeed seek to appease a single passion, he moderately added that "there are others who do not seem to act in pursuance of any fixed or unvaried principle, but place their highest felicity sometimes in one object sometimes in another, and these make undoubtedly the gross of mankind." Reflecting upon this concept in his biography of Pope, Johnson took a more decisive stand, declaring the doctrine of the ruling passion "pernicious as well as false; its tendency is to produce the belief of a kind of moral predestination or overruling principle which cannot be resisted."[81] Toward the end of his life, thus, he adopted Crousaz's intransigent attitude.

Except for occasional notes, such as the one on the ruling passion and those on critical interpretation, Johnson gave no indication that the *Commentary* held any more interest for him than he had admitted to Cave. The article in the *Gentleman's Magazine* four years later is even less enthusiastic, for aside from his introductory paragraphs he made no attempt to discuss the Crousaz matter. The quotations, unannotated and isolated, are mere gestures anticipating the expectations of a periodical audience. That he participated in the quarrel because of his obligation to Cave is plain enough; and that he was laboring despondently as a hack while hoping for more serious literary achievements is equally manifest, from our knowledge of his career. Yet the *Commentary* and his article about it now have abundant interest, for they echo many of his later moral and critical atitudes. In the article, especially, one detects between the lines quoted from Crousaz his own deep concern not only for such principles as the ruling passion, but for those on the attainment of happiness and universal truth. There is also a cryptic reference in the article to a statement in page thirty-five of the translation, which he does not trouble to quote (hoping, perhaps, that readers will consult the original), but which he urges "every author . . . to impress upon his mind." The observation by Crousaz which Johnson apparently had in mind was this:

The more reputation an author is arrived at, the more cautious ought he to be, that nothing drops from his pen, from which men of corrupt inclinations may take advantages in opposing religion.

As axiomatic as many remarks which he himself wrote on the subject, it is as meaningful as though it were of his own composing. The opening paragraph, likewise, is reflective of the consistent judiciousness and sensible reasoning which he brought to his onerous task:

It would not be found useless in the learned world, if in written controversies as in oral disputations, a moderator could be selected who might in some degree superintend the debate, restrain all needless excursions, repress all personal reflections, and at last recapitulate the arguments on each side, and who though he should not assume the province of deciding the question, might at least exhibit it in its true state.

Perhaps Johnson intended in this statement something more than an unrealizable ideal, for he concluded his essay with an offer to carry on the discussion in a subsequent number of the miscellany, if correspondence warranted it. He would "show how Mr. Pope gave sometimes occasion to mistakes, and how Mr. Crousaz was misled by his suspicions of the system of fatality." The correspondence, however, could not have been very lively, since an interval of nine months elapsed between the two sections of the article. For want of public enthusiasm the series expired, thus justifying Johnson's earlier foreboding about his translation of the *Commentary*. Many years later he praised Crousaz as a pious philosopher whose "intentions were always right," and he again found Warburton guilty of imprudence, inaccuracy, and arrogance, for all the breadth of his learning. Johnson also recommended to advanced students of logic the writings of Crousaz, along with those of Watts, Le Clerc, Wolfius, and Locke.[82]

6. *The Cock Lane Fraud*

Johnson limited his activities on the *Gentleman's Magazine* after 1747; yet he continued as an occasional editor and contributor of poetry, and possibly wrote miscellaneous articles which have not yet been identified.[83] Johnson's interest in the supernatural involved him in an examination of the notorious Cock Lane case, the results of which in 1762 comprise the last essay that may be placed definitely with his other writings in the *Gentleman's Magazine*.[84] London was fascinated by the printed accounts of a twelve-year-old girl, in Cock

Lane near West Smithfield, thought bewitched by a woman who had died by foul means.[85] The child insisted that she heard mysterious knockings and that her bed moved without human agency. She discussed the method of the woman's death, heard a whirring of unseen wings, and predicted the hanging of the villain. So sensational was the case that numerous dignitaries—Horace Walpole, the Duke of York, Lady Northumberland, Lady Mary Coke, Lord Hertford, and perhaps the Earl of Dartmouth—made grave examinations of the girl and the premises in which these supernatural goings-on occurred.[86] The *Gentleman's Magazine* considered the girl's claims to be fraudulent, and Johnson was skeptical; but he would not judge the affair an imposture until he had examined the evidence personally. It is not apparent that Johnson actually went to Cock Lane and interviewed the principals. But he consulted with individuals who had done so— the Reverend Dr. John Douglas ("the great detecter of impostures," later Bishop of Salisbury) and others—to conclude a fraud had been perpetrated. Then in the presence of his fellow investigators, he wrote the article which appeared in the *Gentleman's Magazine*. Presenting his data with judicious objectivity, Johnson never intimated his acceptance of the details. Rather, he was convinced "that there is nothing preternatural in the responses that are given to the querists on this occasion," and "that the child has some art of making or counterfeiting particular noise, and that there is no agency of any higher cause." Clearly enough, Johnson far from being taken in contributed materially to exposing the imposture. William and Elizabeth Parsons (the parents of the girl), one Mary Frazier, a clergyman, and a merchant were subsequently prosecuted and punished for gulling the public.[87] Newspaper readers had been following the case avidly, and they required a victim to heighten the merriment and ridicule. Charles Churchill intended to provide the fun, even at the cost of distorting the facts. Although he admired Johnson for the literary excellence of *London* and *The Vanity of Human Wishes,* and was aware of his fame as author of the *Rambler* and *Dictionary,* and as projector of the forthcoming edition of Shakespeare, he saw him also as exceedingly dignified and dictatorial. Hence, Johnson made an excellent "Pomposo, insolent and loud" for the *Ghost,* a satirical attack upon ignorant superstition, and upon the writers of the day who helped propagate it.[88] London laughed heartily, but Johnson's literary position remained unaffected.

The Cock Lane hoax might be regarded as merely an amusing interlude in Johnson's career, except that it gives rise to speculation about several important parallels in his philosophical and religious position. Quite impervious to the ridicule which he had excited, Johnson in the following years continued to ponder the supernal implications of the deception. Discussing in 1778 a comparable case in which John Wesley had been involved, Johnson regretted "that John did not take more pains to inquire into the evidence for it." The question of ghosts, "after five thousand years [since the creation of the world], is yet undecided; a question, whether in theology or philosophy, one of the most important that can come before the human understanding." As a superbly rational individual, Johnson recognized the tenuousness of belief in the supernatural; but as a pious Christian, fearful that annihilation might follow death, he took partial comfort from an ability to suspend judgment. To him, therefore, the appearance of Parson Ford's ghost at the Hummums was not an impossibility. Torn as he was between the claims of reason and superstition, he maintained his judicious attitude on this as on other related matters. "All argument," he said, "is against it; but all belief is for it." In his late years, he became less inclined to doubt the relation between ghosts and the existence of the soul. "A total disbelief of" apparitions

is adverse to the opinion of the existence of the soul between death and the last day; the question simply is, whether departed spirits ever have the power of making themselves perceptible to us; a man who thinks he has seen an apparition, can only be convinced himself; his authority will not convince another, and his conviction, if rational, must be founded on being told something which cannot be known but by supernatural means.

Similarly, the vision of Parson Ford's ghost was "true as related, there was something supernatural." The man who had experienced the phenomenon was the sole authority; "and there it remains." Boswell, who was indignant over the misrepresentations of Johnson as "weakly credulous," wisely adduced

that Johnson had a very philosophical mind, and such a rational respect for testimony, as to make him submit his understanding to what was authentically proved, though he could not comprehend why it was so. Being thus disposed, he was willing to inquire into the truth of any relation of supernatural agency, a general belief of which has prevailed in all nations and ages [as Imlac had also said].

Thus, Johnson, "who insisted upon all his friends the importance of perpetual vigilance against the slightest degree of falsehood," as in the Cock Lane matter, was able to find a spiritual belief in ghosts which contributed to his inner life and seemed to him perfectly consistent with truth.[89]

VERSE CONTRIBUTIONS TO THE *Gentleman's Magazine*

One of the popular features of the *Gentleman's Magazine*—as of other eighteenth-century miscellanies and newspapers—was its poetry department, which appeared regularly in the monthly numbers, and of which Johnson's verses were an occasional part. While his poetic contributions, as compared with his prose, were relatively few and unimportant, they are an indispensable segment of his journalistic writings. In a strict sense, of course, they are tangential rather than directly journalistic, since—with the possible exception of poems like *Ad Urbanum* and *To Lady Firebrace* (1738, pp. 156, 486)—they have no material connection with his employment by Cave. Nevertheless, they have a significance today because of what they reveal about Johnson and the poetic tastes of neoclassical readers of periodicals. Although Johnson was not always writing consciously for this particular audience, he had a facility for pleasing popular tastes. Broadly representative, then, his poetry in the *Gentleman's Magazine* may be regarded as the essence of what was being read in the journals of his day. Some of these pieces he had written long before he came to London, while he was a student in Lichfield, Stourbridge, and Oxford. Gleaned from among his many other youthful poems, these early efforts include translations of a Horatian ode and Pope's *Messiah,* and original lines on the themes of authorship and friendship. All except the *Messiah* and *To Posterity,* written as part of a pamphlet after he came to London, were published for the first time in the *Gentleman's Magazine.* Once Johnson took up residence in London, much of his poetry was printed initially in the magazine, though never in large quantity, and it appeared irregularly until the year after his death.[90]

Some of this poetry is little more than formal or conventional versification. Its appearance in the *Gentleman's Magazine* was not a matter of strong literary concern to him. Despite his habitual revisions, he made no intensive efforts to polish as he did for publication in more enduring form. A seemingly random attitude toward these pieces is implied in the note preceding the Latin translation of Pope's verses *On His Grotto at Twickenham* (1743, p. 550): "it was the casual amusement of half an hour." This indication of unconcern is further supported by the publication of impromptu verses on Claudy Phillips (1740, p. 464) and the unknown Laura (1743, p. 378). The appearance of laudatory verses on his acquaintances—Savage, Miss Carter, Miss Aston, Dr. Birch (1738, pp. 210, 211, 429, 654) —suggests that even in his first year with Cave, Johnson submitted poems at will rather than as assignments. At least once, however, Cave asked him to write a poem, the commemoration of Lady Firebrace which Johnson reluctantly produced. His frank opinion is recorded in a letter to the publisher (1738): "The verses to Lady Firebrace may be had when you please, for you know that such a subject matter neither deserves much thought, nor requires it."[91] The resulting poem is as superficial and trivial as Johnson considered the subject to be:

> At length must Suffolk's beauties shine in vain,
> So long renowned in B———n's deathless strain?
> Thy charms at least, fair F———e, might inspire
> Some zealous bard to wake the sleeping lyre.
> For such thy beauteous mind, and lovely face,
> Thou seem'st at once, bright nymph, a Muse and Grace.

None of the other poems were written under this kind of compulsion. One may conjecture from Johnson's often expressed contempt for gratuitous authorship, and from his need in the early years, that he received at least nominal payments for the poems he himself contributed. The added conjecture may be made that he did not submit poetry under any fixed arrangement with Cave. He or his friends offered it casually, as it became available. Several poems were reprinted in other periodicals, and Cave also duplicated a few of the pieces. In the month following his publication of *An Essay on Epitaphs* (November, 1740), Cave drew from it the Latin verse and

English prose translation of epigrams in the *Greek Anthology* (p. 595). From the political pamphlet *Marmor Norfolciense,* which John Brett had published in the spring of 1739, Cave shortly thereafter reprinted the radical lines *To Posterity* (p. 269, the Latin lines; p. 324, the English translation).[92]

Part of Johnson's training in the grammar schools at Lichfield and Stourbridge consisted of the translation and imitation of the classic poets. Attracted by the current enthusiasm for Horace, he developed while he was at Lichfield a fondness for the odes. Not until much later was he attracted to the epistles and satire. The earliest of his verse translations which he preserved was the *Integer Vitae* (*Ode* I. 22). Probably written in Lichfield in 1725, it was subsequently revised and published in the *Gentleman's Magazine* (1743, p. 380).[93] His youthful interest in lyricism persisted when he went to Stourbridge, so that he continued to translate from Horace, not always with exactness, both odes and epodes.

The translation of Horace's *Ode* I. 22, though only a schoolboy exercise, he apparently regarded as a sufficiently adequate piece of versification for inclusion in the *Gentleman's Magazine*. While Johnson's incentive for offering it to Cave was probably financial, he nevertheless revised it before publication. The revisions are much slighter than they were to be when the poem appeared in Duncombe's edition of Horatian translations in 1757.[94] The major change for the *Gentleman's Magazine* consists of the correction of an actual error in translation. The Horatian lines *nec Iubae tellus generat, leonum / arida nutrix* Johnson originally translated:

> None fiercer Juba's thirsty land
> Dire nurse of raging lions, bore.

Going over the poem before its appearance in the journal, Johnson realized that he had made a schoolboy's typical error in misplacing a modifier, for *arida* did not modify *tellus* but *nutrix*. Thus, for the *Gentleman's Magazine* the revised line reads:

> None e'er more fierce Numidia's land
> The lyon's thirsty parent, bore.

The translation, with its conventional diction, its Christianized generalizations, and formal imagery (Johnson even substituted the vapid name of Chloe for the significantly connotative name of Lalagé, which he later replaced) is primarily important because of the light it throws on Johnson's journalistic ethic. Knowing that the poem would be regarded as little more than journalistic filler, he still made some effort at revision. If the effort was not a great one, it was probably equal to the quality of the poem, the position it would fill in the magazine, and the limited cultural attainments of his audience.

Johnson's Latin translation of Pope's *Messiah* is another youthful composition, probably written Christmas, 1728, for his tutor William Jorden, at Pembroke College, Oxford. There he had also turned out a few other original Latin poems and a Latin translation of Dryden's epigram on Milton. The translation of *Messiah,* it has been said, was "first printed for old Mr. Johnson, without the knowledge of his son, who was very angry when he heard of it."[95] The translation appeared next in John Husband's *Miscellany* in 1731. In 1752, after making a few unimportant revisions (e.g., *jam . . . jam* for *nunc . . . nunc, terget* for *tergit, garrula . . . murmura* for *murmura . . . garrula, palmisque rubeta* for *Spinetaque Palmis*), Johnson allowed the poem to be reprinted in the *Gentleman's Magazine* for April (p. 184), with the original in parallel columns. The critics of this poem have been many, their applause and censure being equally vehement. Actually it is the skillful versification of a university undergraduate. An analysis reveals that Johnson regarded its composition as a challenge, intellectual rather than poetic. It was an exercise in which he strove to outsmart by ingenuity both Pope and Virgil. Even then, as in the later *Lives,* Johnson saw little merit in Pope's *Messiah* and his Virgilian model. On the whole, he keeps close to the Popean original, even at the risk of a few twisted and tortured expressions, such as l. 44 *ille cutim spissam visus hebetare vitabit,* in order to render l. 39 *He from thick films shall purge the visual ray.* This line, incidentally, Warton found "reprehensible." The number of Virgilian reminiscences in Johnson's translation is surprisingly small, even though Pope had adapted several passages from Virgil's fourth eclogue. He probably deliberately forbore looking up the original of Pope's adaptation. Thus, while Johnson captures successfully the bucolic flavor of Virgil's eclogue, only rarely does he borrow an expression or a group of words from Virgil. An example is l. 9 *qualis rerum mihi nascitur ordo.* This is weak compared with Virgil's *magnus ab integro saeclorum nascitur ordo* (1. 5), but it shows that Johnson consciously avoided any too facile association. Because he was intimately familiar with the Messianic eclogue, he could not, despite himself, avoid all Virgilian echoes. At one point he contracted three lines of Virgil into one of his own (Virg. Ecl. IV, 13-14, 31, condensed into Johnson's l. 20). But in the main Johnson's efforts to avoid the Virgilian diction and style were successful. And the baroque imagery and rhetorical fireworks which Warton found so "reprehensible," but which Johnson admired,[96] suggest the taint of late Latin poetry through the works of Statius and Claudianus, for example. The translation, helping to clarify Johnson's youthful poetic attitudes and methods of composition, is one of the most ambitious and serious poems which he contributed to the *Gentleman's Magazine*.

Consonant with neoclassical poetic practice, Johnson gave an outward impression of neutralizing or at least disguising private emotion. Like his contemporaries he aimed at restraint, urbanity, and generalization. Most of his poems in the *Gentleman's Magazine* were written in the tradition of gentility, with the conscious awareness that versification was a polite, formal pastime. Both subject and manner were to be notable primarily for elegant cleverness rather than for the evocation of emotional responses. But this should not be inferred as evidence that Johnson did not feel deeply or that he could not write subjectively. Even within the limitations of the quatrain and heroic couplet and the conventions of frequently austere diction, he was capable of powerful statement. His best poems, indeed, are those written with an almost passionate conviction. These are the long satires, *London* and *The Vanity of Human Wishes,* intended for a more appreciative audience than periodical readers. In the *Gentleman's Magazine* also, however, there are occasional rumblings of controlled anger and the tender voice of subjective emotion, the symptoms of a poet who wrote out of his own need. *To Posterity,* which synthesizes the political theme of *Marmor Norfolciense,* is a bold and obvious poem; yet the attack on Walpole's government, loaded though it is with commonplace imagery, cannot be mistaken for innocuous, formalized reproach. In its direct, guileless clarity,

and in its intensive piling up of metaphorical charges, it supports
the author's intention of forceful accusation. Individual couplets provide generalized epigrams. But read in context they contribute to an
infectious tension. It is a poem which successfully grows out of the
cumulative listing, from disastrous cause to disastrous consequence,
reaching a climax in the rebellious line *Kings change their laws, and
kingdoms change their kings:*

> Whene'er this stone, now hid beneath the lake,
> The horse shall trample, or the plough shall break,
> Then, O my country! shalt thou groan distrest,
> Grief swell thine eyes, and terror chill thy breast.
> Thy streets with violence of woe shall sound,
> Loud as the billows bursting on the ground.
> Then thro' thy fields shall scarlet reptiles stray,
> And rapine and pollution mark their way.
> Their hungry swarms the peaceful vale shall fright
> Still fierce to threaten, still afraid to fight;
> The teeming year's whole product shall devour,
> Insatiate pluck the fruit, and crop the flow'r:
> Shall glutton on the industrious peasant's spoil,
> Rob without fear and fatten without toil.
> Then o'er the world shall discord stretch her wings,
> Kings change their laws, and kingdoms change their kings.
> The bear enrag'd th' affrighted moon shall dread;
> The lilies o'er the vales triumphant spread;
> Nor shall the lion, wont of old to reign
> Despotic o'er the desolated plain,
> Henceforth th' inviolable bloom invade,
> Or dare to murmur in the flow'ry glade;
> His tortured sons shall die before his face,
> While he lies melting in lewd embrace;
> And, yet more strange! his veins a horse shall drain,
> Nor shall the passive coward once complain.

Consistent with Johnson's political attitudes in *London* and later
writings, *To Posterity* is earnest and recriminating in tone, reflective
of his lifelong contempt for oppressors, and an early actualization of
a rebellious spirit that is at odds with the patina of conservatism. It
is not surprising that Cave, who professed impartiality and seldom
printed political verses, included *To Posterity* in the *Gentleman's
Magazine.* Apart from competitive reasons, he saw that it was too
good a poem to be omitted.

To Posterity affords the only poetic instance in the *Gentleman's*

Magazine of Johnson's declamatory private reaction to a public situation. And even here it might be argued that since his attitude was only that of a large number of his countrymen, he was protesting for them as well as for himself. Occasionally, however, he would introduce a purely personal mood, as in *An Ode* (1747, p. 240), a footnote to which informed the readers that the author suffered from gout at the time of composition:

> Unhappy! whom to beds of pain
> Arthritic tyranny consigns,
> Whom smiling nature courts in vain,
> Tho' rapture sings, and beauty shines.
>
> Yet, tho' my limbs disease invades,
> Her wings imagination tries,
> And bears me to the peaceful shades,
> Where ———'s humble turrets rise.

Such slight lines should not be burdened by analysis, and should be read merely as they reflect Johnson's love of versifying. Elsewhere in the poem there is an embarrassing lack of conviction in the pursuit of nature as *A guide, a father, and a friend* and *The silent grandeur of retreat*. Perhaps we know Johnson's attitudes too well to believe his romantic invocation. He never rises in this poem above prose statements, even in his expressions of melancholy, social concern, and disillusionment. *An Ode* is an occasional piece, interesting at this point for its contrast of range to the preceding poem. Johnson was not always successful with the graceful touch, and here he was handicapped by the commonplace subject of *arthritic tyranny* and the restorative of nature. Boswell gravely considered the piece "characteristick" and "a learned description of the gout," but he was perplexed because he knew that Johnson did not suffer from this ailment until late in life. Wisely, however, he resolved the perplexity for himself and for us, concluding the poem to be a fiction. "Why may not a poet suppose himself to have the gout, as well as suppose himself to be in love?"[97] The poem should be permitted to stand as an unimportant fabrication.

Anything but fabrication, however, is Johnson's tribute to his old household companion, Dr. Levet, "the obscure practiser in physick among the lower people" whom he met in 1746 and who died January 17, 1782, aged seventy-seven. An occasional tippler, crude in manner, but a kind and charitable man, Levet won Johnson's deep respect, as is evident from the comment on the day of his death: "He was an old and faithful friend . . . *Commendavi*. May God have mercy on him. May he have mercy on me."[98] The poem which Johnson wrote was entered in *Thraliana* (April 18), though it was first published in the *Gentleman's Magazine* (August, 1783, p. 695). It was also transcribed by Miss Carter and Frances Reynolds. The close personal identification which Johnson achieved in the much revised *On the Death of Dr. Robert Levet*[99] makes it one of his most moving poems. And because it has been much anthologized and discussed, it is one of his best known poems. Despite all this attention, the Levet memorial is by no means a work of unusual creative power. The rather too obvious occasional manner of the poem lessens the possible impression of spontaneity, though there can be no question of Johnson's sincerity in composing it. More than any other poem which he wrote, this has a subjective quality and an air of intimacy. But Johnson as a poet was too typically neoclassic, stifling feeling under generalized diction and contrived if effective figuration.

In both philosophy and structure, *On the Death of Dr. Robert Levet* is reminiscent of Gray's *Elegy*, though Johnson's piece has a considerably more limited focus and inward purpose, and though mortuary themes and the use of quatrains were conventional. Yet Johnson's admiration for the *Elegy* inevitably calls attention to that earlier work as a possible source of influence. His praise for Gray's universalized images and sentimentality, and for his dignity may also be applied to him. Less can be said for Johnson's "happy selection of images," his own being perfunctory, or for his variety and originality.[100] The feeling, implicit and repressed, is formal; and while he individualizes Levet's traits, the response which he evokes for him is only indirectly sympathetic. The portrait could be that of any good man. The difficulty appears to lie in a strained juxtaposition of individualized and generalized elements belonging to both personal remembrance and philosophical speculation. Although Johnson describes his friend as *Obscurely wise, and coarsely kind,* and gives sufficient evidence of his admiration, he never projects the description through concrete image or illustration. Personification and moralized exposition become substitutes for imagination.

Moralization in fact most concerns Johnson and gives him his most effective expression. The reader is glad to know that Levet was *Of ev'ry friendless name the friend* and is touched by his appearance *In misery's darkest caverns known.* But he is more acutely struck by the philosophical passages. The importance of the poem resides in the reflections which tell us about Johnson's attitudes and are thus biographical. The opening line, *Condemn'd to hope's delusive mine,* temporarily expresses Johnson's pessimistic melancholy and carries it through the first quatrain. The final stanza is likewise informative, intimating his fear of death and the perhaps hopeful relief that death may bring tranquillity. In the stanza beginning *His virtues walk'd their narrow round,* we find a reiteration of Johnson's intensive piety. And throughout the poem is a sense of philosophical affirmation in the face of death for which he long struggled, but which he did not always attain so positively as here. The poem, then, more about Johnson than Levet, is justly one of his valuable writings.

Except for general observations, little need be said of the remaining poems in the *Gentleman's Magazine. Friendship: an Ode,* originally done at Stourbridge, about 1726, seems to be the work of a poet more mature than the sixteen-year-old schoolboy. The indications are that it was revised, for the precocious work circulated in manuscript form before its publication. Sometime between 1735 and 1740 Lady Mary Wortley Montagu acquired a copy from an unknown source and transcribed it into an album of contemporary verses. Her version, different from that in the *Gentleman's Magazine* (1743, p. 376), suggests that changes had been made.[101] The ode has a vague affinity with the elegy on Levet, since both deal with the theme of friendship. But *Friendship,* considerably more abstract, is characteristic of a student's exercise in classical subject matter. If the poem was inspired by a particular person, his identity is unknown; the likelihood is that it was the outgrowth of reading in some such work as the popular *De Amicitia* of Cicero. Johnson's poem contains unmistakable resemblances to the Ciceronian concept (which in its turn had a Hellenistic origin), chief of which is the constant interplay of friendship and virtue. Amity, both maintain, can exist only among good men, and they who lack virtue are incapable of friendship.

> Thy [friendship's] gentle flow of guiltless joys
> On fools and villains ne'er descend.

Also directly Ciceronian is the notion that

> In vain for thee [friendship] the monarch sighs,
> And hugs a flatterer for a friend.

Coincidentally, Cicero was only sixteen-years-old—like Johnson who was probably aware of the parallel at the time he composed the poem —when he heard the old Roman lawyer Scaevola repeat the discourse of Laelius on friendship. *De Amicitia,* of course, was written many years later. Johnson likewise early formulated his ideas on a subject which he was to touch upon frequently in subsequent years.

Another youthful piece is *The Young Author,* which he probably wrote in 1729 during his brief residence at Oxford,[102] and which he later altered and published in the *Gentleman's Magazine* (1743, p. 378). At the age of twenty Johnson, thinking about a career in litera-ture, was already anticipating the disappointments as well as the as-pirations of authorship:

> So the young author panting for a name,
> And fir'd with pleasing hope of endless fame,
> Intrusts his happiness to human kind,
> More false, more cruel than the seas and wind.

At this time his experiences were limited to his own academic and psychological difficulties. But these, coupled with evidences of liter-ary frustrations among others in the Oxford environment, precipi-tated his pessimistic outlook. He saw the writer fleeing

> Where no sour criticks damn, nor sneers molest,
> Safe from the keen lampoon and stinging jest;
> There begs of heav'n a less distinguish'd lot;
> Glad to be hid, and proud to be forgot.

Unconsciously, he was writing a prelude to the more fully developed observations on authorship in *The Vanity of Human Wishes,* the *Rambler,* and elsewhere. In the light of his Grub Street experiences, projected against the circumvented aspirations of himself and many of his companions, *The Young Author* is a remarkably prophetic poem.

Rarer than the personal mood in Johnson's miscellaneous poetry is his wry humor, as in *To Lyce, an Elderly Lady* (1747, p. 240). Here he uses a playful, familiar conceit:

> Her teeth the night with darkness dyes,
>   She's starr'd with pimples o'er,
> Her tongue like nimble lightning plies,
>   And can with thunder roar.

However, on the grounds that it is uncharacteristic, there has been frequent hesitancy about attributing this piece to Johnson. A free imitation of Horace's *Ode* IV. 13, *To Lyce* may be an early poem which Johnson had at hand and contributed to Cave at a time when he was called upon for material.[103] He was capable of writing impromptu whimsy and on occasion, as in *An Ode,* he could improvise subject matter. Certainly one would like to believe that *To Lyce* is from his pen.

Having already come to Henry Hervey's rescue with the composition of a sermon in 1745,[104] Johnson perhaps did his friend further service by writing for him two poems intended for a young lady. These, *To Miss* [Alicia Maria Carpenter] *on her Giving the Author a Gold and Silk Net-Work Purse of her own Weaving* and *To Miss* [Carpenter] *on her Playing upon the Harpsicord,* are in a collection of transcripts made by or for Hervey. Also in the Hervey collection and attributed to Johnson are *Stella in Mourning* and *The Winter's Walk.* Three were printed in the *Gentleman's Magazine* and the fourth, *To Miss* [Carpenter] *on her playing upon the Harpsicord,* was printed in the *Museum* (November, 1746).[105] Conceived with a pleasing delicacy, the first two poems are trivial and stylized in their themes of love and flattery. Yet as examples of the kind of occasional verse Johnson could write they are interesting. The poem acknowledging the purse (1747, p. 239) illustrates well an ability to transmit a cheerfully ethereal quality that would have been acceptable to many a seventeenth-century lyricist:

> Though gold and silk their charms unite,
> To make thy curious web delight,
> In vain the vary'd work would shine,
> If wrought by any hand but thine,
> Thy hand that knows the subtler art,
> To weave those nets that catch the heart.
> Spread out by me, the roving coin,
> The nets may catch, but not confine,
> Nor can I hope thy silken chain
> The glitt'ring vagrants shall restrain;

> Why, Sylvia, was it then decreed,
>   The heart, once caught, should ne'er be freed?

The Winter's Walk (1747, p. 240) is again marked by poetic convention and, except for the despondent mood, little consequence. Here Johnson makes empathic use of standardized nature imagery to complement the emotion of a despairing lover:

> Behold my fair, where-e'er we rove,
>   What dreary prospects round us rise,
> The naked hills, the leafless grove,
>   The hoary ground, the frowning skies.
>
> Nor only through the wasted plain,
>   Stern winter, is thy force confest,
> Still wider spreads thy horrid reign,
>   I feel thy pow'r usurp my breast.
>
> *   *   *   *
>
> Tir'd with vain joys, and false alarms,
>   With mental and corporeal strife,
> Snatch me, my Stella, to thy arms,
>   And hide me from the sight of life.

Later he revised the final line to read *And screen me from the ills of life,*[106] suggesting greater restraint and resignation. The note of melancholy is characteristic, but for the most part the poem is stiff and unimaginative, the generalized diction and concepts effectively choking off an emotional response even to his inner fears. In *An Ode,* which appeared in the same number of the *Gentleman's Magazine,* Johnson employs similar terminology, though perhaps with a broader, more philosophical intention:

> Stern winter now, by spring repress'd
>   Forbears the long-continu'd strife,
> And nature, on her naked breast,
>   Delights to catch the gales of life.

Johnson's verse illustrates one of his many editorial connections with Cave. For not only was he poetry editor and judge, but a facile poet *ex officio* as well, though he contributed irregularly and sparsely; he was probably glad of the opportunity to add to his earnings. But Cave also thought well enough of Johnson's poetry to regard it as a literary asset to his periodical. If pieces like the translations have commendable qualities, the occasional poems—except for the elegy on Dr.

Levet and *To Posterity*—are second-rate at best. Yet on the whole Johnson's poetry exemplifies his creative interest and competence in conventional devices and subjects; he experimented with odes, couplets, quatrains, classical imitations and translations, formalized imagery and praise. By comparison with *London* and *The Vanity of Human Wishes,* they also make clear that his poetic forte was the barb of satire rather than the subtlety of lyricism, compliment, and subjectivity.

THE PARLIAMENTARY DEBATES

Laws prohibiting the dissemination of English parliamentary news except by state-authorized organs had long been on record and had long been violated, especially during periods when Parliament recessed. There were hazards, of course, for those of the Trade who exposed themselves; but they tended generally to disregard the risks as long as they could rely on public appetite for legislative news and on the laxity of prosecution. Reporters who sat in the galleries of Parliament depended on their memories when they wrote their reports, though frequently they chanced note-taking, as Cave testified in 1747 when he and Thomas Astley of the *London Magazine* were brought before the House of Lords for publishing accounts of the trial of Simon Lord Lovat.[107] When questioned about the *Parliamentary Debates* in the *Gentleman's Magazine,* Cave admitted personal responsibility. He said that he had concealed himself in the House, "and made use of a black lead pencil, and only took notes of some remarkable passages; and, from his memory, he put them together himself." He insisted that this was true even of the long passages. Some "very eminent persons" had sent him speeches, Cave testified, and some members of Parliament had taken notes for him. Curiously, the Lords neglected to ask the names of the guilty informants. By payment of bribes to easily accessible door-keepers and even to members of Parliament who had made speeches, owners of periodicals thus assured themselves of a constant supply of procedural information, which they received directly and by post. The existence of prohibitive laws necessitated various subterfuges. Cave, for instance, originally identified speakers participating in debates only by initials. While strictly accurate reporting was not his primary concern, he was prudent enough customarily to print his debates in the second half of each year, during the recess of Parliament.

On April 13, 1738, shortly after Johnson became a contributor to the *Gentleman's Magazine,* the House of Commons firmly resolved against any publication of its proceedings at any time. But when Parliament recessed on May 20, Cave immediately circumvented the restriction, publishing in the June number his first report of the *Debates in the Senate of Magna Lilliputia,* which were in reality an account of the Parliament's proceedings thinly disguised as the travels to Lilliput of Gulliver's grandson. As prompt as Cave was to meet the challenge imposed by the parliamentary prohibition, Cave's rivals had been even more alert. This fact probably hastened the appearance of Cave's debates, a number of which in revised form he drew from the *London Magazine.* In May, 1738, an unnamed correspondent of the *London Magazine* had anticipated the *Senate of Lilliputia* by transparently reporting legislative matters as the *Proceedings and Debates* of a fictitious political club whose members dined together thrice weekly.[108] Although the members were designated by Greek and Roman names, it was understood that they were loyal Englishmen, the only persons invited to the meetings of the club. The editors of the *London Magazine* in their preface for 1738 claimed total impartiality, maintaining that they published the debates for the information and benefit of all people. So little pretense of concealment did either magazine make that both offered keys to identify the speakers. Cave published his *Anagrammata Rediviva* in 1739. The *London Magazine* was more leisurely, bringing out its identifications in 1742.[109] These debates in the two magazines became so popular that Parliament made no attempt to prosecute the offenders.

An early, if only occasional, contributor to the debates in the *Gentleman's Magazine* was Cave's close friend, Dr. Thomas Birch. Until 1740, however, the chief writer was the Scot, William Guthrie, who was perhaps the first historian to have access to parliamentary journals, and who had been employed by Cave for this purpose. His knowledge of political maneuvering became so extensive that the government eventually pensioned him to guarantee his silence. Johnson had a grudging respect for Guthrie. "Sir," he said, "he is a man of parts. He has no great regular fund of knowledge; but by reading so long, and writing so long, he no doubt has picked up a good deal."[110]

Although Guthrie bore the initial responsibility for writing the debates, Johnson quickly became their editorial supervisor. His duties are implicit in a portion of a letter which he wrote to Cave in the autumn of 1738. "If I made fewer alterations than usual in the debates, it was only because there appeared, and still appears to be, less need of alteration."[111] Was he satisfied with the quality of Guthrie's work, or was he simply indifferent to a chore which he regarded as routine? There is no way of knowing, but in all likelihood Johnson's statement was affected by both attitudes. He could not have had a higher regard for his editing of the debates than for any of his other hack duties. Yet he was too conscientious to let pass unacceptable writing, and apparently he had made changes before. Now, in spite of Cave's complaint, or at least inquiry, Johnson felt he had fulfilled his obligation.

As editor, furthermore, Johnson seems to have been close to the debates from the beginning. The suggestion has been made that the allegorical format was the invention of his "fertile mind," and that he wrote the introduction to the first debate, the *Appendix to Capt. Lemuel Gulliver's Account of the Famous Empire of Lilliput.* The Lilliputian fiction was a necessary expedient for matching the ingenuity of the *London Magazine.* The stylistic basis on which the attribution of the *Appendix* was first made has since been examined with some attention to syntactical devices, such as parallelisms and antitheses.[112] While general inferences and statistical checks are no more conclusive than other kinds of speculation, they have not been without bearing. Likewise, it may now be fruitful to argue additionally in favor of Johnson's authorship by reference to certain characteristic attitudes as well as phraseology.

Any comic bent which Johnson had was essentially conversational rather than authorial. The wit and humor which his friends (to his own surprise) thought "were his shining talents,"[113] are not evident in the *Appendix,* a rather heavy-handed imitation of Swift's satire lacking narrative sparkle and subtlety. As an example of the author's bearish humor, Gulliver's grandson

resolved, as the most effectual method of vindicating his memory, to undertake a Voyage to Lilliput, that he might be able at his return to confirm his grandfather's reports by ocular testimony, and for ever silence those aspersions, which were, in his opinion, founded on nothing but extreme ignorance of both geography and human nature.

Except for the use of fabricated names—Lilliput, Man Mountain, Degulia, etc.—and a sketchy recapitulation of the Lilliputian empire, the *Appendix* can be read as a straightforward essay on a political situation. This very fact, indeed, brings the early Johnsonian technique into relief; barring unusual coincidence, there can be no doubt of the ideology and the forcefulness of its enunciation. For instance, one is reminded of Johnson by allusions, cynical though they are, to truthfulness. Gulliver "has, with the success almost always attendant on probity and truth, triumphed over all opposition, gained belief from the most obstinate incredulity, and established a reputation in the world, which can fear no diminution, nor admit of any increase." Despite the satiric intention of the passage, the concept of truth as a virtuous force bears comparison with *Rambler,* No. 96. In this Johnson allegorizes the militant triumph of truth over falsehood and her minions, one of whom is suspicion (easily equatable with incredulity).

Other instances of Johnson's beliefs are also exemplified in the *Appendix.* As a case in point, regret is voiced "that the ingenious traveller" was unable to report on the history, laws, customs, art, and nature elements of this strange land. In a political vein, the author of the *Appendix* condemned censorship by the government, which forbade, "under the pain and penalty of death, any person or persons to give the Man Mountain the least information relating to the state of any other country." And he denounced tyranny by King and Pope. These were all frequently expressed aversions of Johnson which do not require the belaboring of documentation. To be sure, the evidence is inferential, for many others had written on the same subjects. But it would be a curious accident or extremely clever imitation—at a time when there was no incentive for imitating Johnson—if another author had brought together in a single essay so many attitudes which were to become identifiable with Johnson's intellectual and political development. Beyond the mere conjunction of ideas on morality, libertarianism, and travel, the *Appendix* is written in such celebrated

Johnsonian form—the seriation of clauses and nouns, the polysyl-labics, and the like—as to arrest attention. The union of form and content, the reminders of the periodical essays, of articles and reviews on travel literature, and of moralizing judgments on political situa-tions, all these draw consideration to the *Appendix* as one of John-son's earliest prose essays in the *Gentleman's Magazine*.

Cave probably had more enthusiasm for the Lilliputian scheme in reporting the debates than did Johnson. The bookseller would have been more alert to the practicality of using the format of a book whose names had become familiar through wide reading. If Johnson fell in with the scheme it was because he had to rather than because he admired the author or the book. It was not often that Johnson reversed his opinions, and as far as the record goes he was consist-ently disparaging about Swift and *Gulliver's Travels*. In 1738 he had no personal reason for disliking the Dean (and Boswell asserted there was insufficient evidence that Johnson's failure to get the Irish de-gree ever colored his opinion), but he had surely read the book by then. Of it he would admit only that the inventory of the Man Mountain's pockets was good; he thought "no rules of judgment were applied to a book written in open defiance of truth and regu-larity," and that Book IV contained filthy images. On the other hand, perhaps sardonically, he regarded *Gulliver's Travels* as "a production so new and strange that it filled the reader with a mingled emotion of merriment and amazement."[114] Prompted by Cave and despite his own adverse reaction, therefore, Johnson could have agreed to employ the Lilliputian materials in the *Appendix,* in the editing of the de-bates, and in his own composition of them. The satiric possibilities perhaps even attracted him.

Responding to public interest during the first year of the debates, Cave exploited them with ancillary materials. In October he pub-lished a eulogistic poem, *To Mr. Gulliver,* which had been submitted by an unknown contributor. And he terminated the supplement of the *Gentleman's Magazine* with advertisements of the debates and the proposals for *Anagrammata Rediviva*. Recently it has been con-jectured that the latter notice was written by Johnson, but the evi-dence appears too limited for conclusiveness. Another attribution, more tenable, holds that the advertisement of the debates was written by either Guthrie or Johnson.[115] Of the two, Johnson is the more likely choice as author of the piece, which is brief enough to be quoted whole:

It is scarce necessary to add any thing further concerning Mr. Gulliver's Memoirs of the Debates in the Senate of Lilliput, which we began in June last, and have continued as far as the usual room would permit. They have been so well received by our readers in general, and so highly approved by all good judges, that we receive gratulations in prose and verse from all quarters: We have, indeed, given place only to the ingenious epistle, p. 543 [*To Mr. Gulliver*], signed J.A. whose name, as we have not the honour to know, we are the more obliged to him. To our future account therefore, of Senatorial affairs, we may, perhaps, subjoin some sketches of the Lilliputian history, and particularly the lives of their senators, and great men and women of distinction; for however remote from us, and how little soever this people may seem in the eyes of Europeans, yet their religious, their moral and political character, are not of less account. The most celebrated moralists of antiquity have given us lessons from the animal creation, and our famous Gay has sent a prince to learn of brutes;[116] but as successful as this method has been accounted, it must appear forced and unnatural to a royal pupil, in comparison of a real history of princes and governors of mankind; and especially if the moral does not naturally strike, and if the deduction, as is often the case, is not the result of right reasoning, but only brought in to serve a purpose or flatter a party. Mr. Gulliver being a stranger in the country, can have no bias to partiality; if such a suspicion should be entertained with regard to any passage on account of its being abridged, we shall be ready to turn to, and clear it up by his larger account; that we may in every instance deserve the applause already given us for our honesty, impartiality, and exactness.

Extensive proofs would overburden such a slight performance, and there are undoubtedly arguments which could be mustered against Johnson's authorship. These, having mainly to do with his distrust of Swift and *Gulliver's Travels,* and already developed in connection with the *Appendix,* are equally pertinent here. Positively, however, attention should be directed to the passage, *and especially if the moral does not naturally strike . . . but only brought in to serve a purpose or flatter a party,* as a Johnson-like turn of phrase and thought. Candidly a puff for the debates and the magazine, the advertisement— claiming to *deserve the applause already given us for our honesty, impartiality and exactness*—has the flavor of the prefaces which Johnson composed for the yearly volumes of the *Gentleman's Magazine.* It also has the mark of a man who edited and helped write the debates.

As usual Cave was a difficult man to please. Boswell is authority for the supposition that Johnson edited the debates between June, 1738, and November 19, 1740, and that thereafter he was the sole author. Reade, however, contends that Johnson was not continuously employed during this period, for he and Cave had quarreled in 1739 because of Johnson's long delay in awarding a prize for the best poem on the "Divine Attributes." In 1739 Johnson was travelling around England in search of employment, and he made no contributions to the *Gentleman's Magazine* between May, 1739 (the address *To the Reader*), and June, 1740 (the *Life of Blake*).[117] Reade's hypothesis is a reasonable analysis of Johnson's relationship to the *Gentleman's Magazine* and Cave during these thirteen months. In June Johnson resumed his duties as editor and contributor. The only information that Johnson gave Boswell about the actual time of his participation was that he was sole composer of the debates for only three years; Boswell set the period between November 19, 1740, and February 23, 1743.[118] Although the terminal date is acceptable, recent indications are that Johnson's first printed essay (other than the *Appendix*) concerns the debate of November 25, 1740.[119] Nor was this performance his exclusively, for the debates between November 25 and February 13, 1741, were perhaps rewritten from Guthrie's original or from notes taken by others. Nor are the dates on which the proceedings took place a close indication of the time of composition, since frequently long periods elapsed between the debates and their publication in the *Gentleman's Magazine*.[120] Johnson's steady authorship probably began with the debate of February 13 (published July, 1741) and continued through that of February 22-25, 1743 (the last part of which was published March, 1744).

The debates Johnson wrote were better than Guthrie's, but they were certainly less accurate. He did not attend parliamentary sessions or, at most, he attended only once.[121] Sometimes he was obliged to prepare articles about the proceedings with information no more precise than the names of the speakers and a general notion of their views. With these scanty materials he wrote the debates hastily. He was further impeded by such physical and mental suffering that he became accustomed to sleeplessness. When he wrote he isolated himself in the room assigned him at St. John's Gate and admitted no one but the compositor or one of Cave's employees.[122] He composed these legislative proceedings very rapidly, turning out three columns in an hour, and one day the equivalent of ten or twelve double-column printed pages.[123]

Johnson's debates, written with deft and imaginative skill, seem to have been responsible for a substantial increase in the circulation of the *Gentleman's Magazine*. That Cave's material fortunes were expanding at this time is reflected in his purchase of a decrepit coach and a pair of poor horses. So proud was he of his status, indeed, that on the coach and on his silver he emblazoned the sign of St. John's Gate.[124]

For a long time, perhaps until the celebrated dinner given by Samuel Foote, Johnson concealed as best he could his authorship, a fact not generally known until after his death. Yet, Johnson is said to have once warned Smollett against using the debates as source material for his *History of England,* a piece of advice which (if given) Smollett apparently declined to accept.[125] The degree to which the English public was denied reports of parliamentary proceedings and kept in ignorance of major details of original debates is accentuated by the credence usually given Johnson's accounts at the time they appeared. Possibly because he was troubled to learn that his debates were being translated into French, Spanish, and German by the end of 1742, he brought them to a conclusion.[126] It is inconceivable, however, that he was innocently unaware of his readers' acceptance of them as genuine reports. The *Gentleman's Magazine* itself was hardly modest in its claims for the veracity of the debates, and even Johnson made an issue of their importance and accuracy. He denounced the fraudulent aims of party writing and implied that his published debates were authentic. Later, however, he suffered qualms about his political inventions, admitting "that the only part of his writings which then gave him any compunction, was his account of the *Debates* in the *Gentleman's Magazine;* but that, at the time he wrote them, he did not think he was imposing on the world." To the well-known accounts of his alleged confession of authorship[127] may be added a revealing sentence from his own preface to the *Literary Magazine* (1756): "The speeches inserted in other papers have been long known to be fictitious, and produced sometimes by men who never heard the debate, nor had any authentic information." Despite

Johnson's protestations, as late as 1783 the *Gentleman's Magazine,* advertising some of its reprinted volumes, insisted that "the Parliamentary Proceedings . . . will be found amply recorded, and stated with the strictest regard to truth."[128] By 1783 Johnson had long given up any direct interest in the *Gentleman's Magazine,* and he was not consulted by the management about its promotional schemes.

Obviously Johnson's debates have no real historical accuracy, even though they always had some factual basis. They are, rather, imaginative essays with moralistic undertones, characteristic of the mature prose of the *Rambler.* Nor can the debates be regarded any longer as containing a political bias in favor of the Tories. Cave always intended to be impartial in his reports of public matters, and Johnson was employed to carry out his wishes. The notion that he incorporated his prejudices in the debates, promulgated largely by Murphy's report of Johnson's taking "care that the whig dogs should not have the best of it," is fallacious.[129] The significance of the debates as Johnson's most important contribution to the *Gentleman's Magazine* is dependent, thus, not on the fact or lack of historical veracity, but rather on their literary and philosophical quality. His achievement was the reshaping of scanty facts available to him so that they became the unmistakable expressions of his own attitudes. Yet even historians and biographers were convinced that they were reading genuine parliamentary reports. As expressions of Johnson's talent and personality, furthermore, the debates provide an important insight into his capacity to reason well. His grand rhetoric and splendid command of the language mirror his ability to grasp concepts clearly and to express himself on a host of military, economic, and political subjects, domestic and foreign. His aptitude for writing lucidly and fluently on almost any subject is especially evident in the composition of the debates, which always combine a tone of authority and self-assurance with literary excellence.

Shortly after Johnson began to write the *Parliamentary Debates,* he abridged and edited for the *Gentleman's Magazine* one of the debates of 1657, a version of which had been published in 1660; but he used as his main source the *Memorials* of Bulstrode Whitelocke, keeper of the Great Seal in Cromwell's time. To justify his task Johnson speculated that the original speeches had been taken down in shorthand and printed with resulting inaccuracies that he intended to rectify. He found the task painful but necessary and important; and as he fabricated speeches for the ten members of the Committee and recorded Cromwell's reply, he chided the reporter for carelessness and the printers for "negligence and ignorance."[130] Legislative proceedings, thus, engaged much of Johnson's editorial attention, but it may be assumed that as before he was less interested in them than was Cave. This belief is supported by a letter of 1742 to the bookseller in which Johnson implied his indifference, if not reluctance, toward Cave's design for a historical account of parliamentary proceedings. Its intention was to amplify the debates published in the *Gentleman's Magazine.* "I think," Johnson wrote, "our work ought to partake of the spirit of history which is contrary to minute exactness, and of the regularity of a journal which is inconsistent with spirit."[131] The very contradictions which he foresaw in this kind of fusion of history and journalism explain why he failed to go ahead with it. As an added obstacle, probably, the scope of the undertaking was too extensive for Cave at this time.

But Cave's ambitious scheme for dealing with parliamentary matters ultimately did come to fruition with the publication in 1769 of *The Debates of the House of Commons From the Year 1667 to the Year 1694,* which had been collected by Anchitell Grey, a member of Parliament. The proposals were announced in the *Gentleman's Magazine* as early as 1745, and the unqualified statement made in *The Autobiography of Sylvanus Urban* that Johnson composed them is worth considering.[132] Johnson, of course, would have been useful to Cave for these proposals because of his availability and his recent experience with debates. Once again, elements of style and attitude may lead to a resolution. The characteristic balance is evident in such phrasing as: "Every man of fortune in the kingdom must surely desire to view the gradations of these memorable events, to trace revolutions to their causes, and to know to what names the nation is indebted for its honour, and its liberty." Or: ". . . the reader is led forward from day to day, and from question to question, and enjoys the view of all the variations of that uncertain time; observes the birth, the progress, the maturity of designs, sees the colours of party change before him, and patriotism sink in one year, and rise in another." In addition, the concepts of *revolution, honour, liberty, patriotism,* and changes of political fortune are commonly found throughout Johnson's writings.

Like Johnson, the author of the proposals is interested in the quality of writing: ". . . the artless and concise manner of expression, without circumlocution, or the embellishment which even an extempore discourse might admit." As though he is describing one of the aims of the contemporary Lilliputian debates, the author applauds because Grey did "not conceal the ability and the spirit of the speaker." Comparably, attention is drawn to the realism with which the reader is induced "to consider himself present in this active and honourable assembly, partaking the ardour and anxiety of the unbiassed Englishman, and resenting the subtleties and evasions of his opponent." If Johnson himself did not always successfully inject drama and verisimilitude into his own debates, he approved of these touches, which are found to be an admirable part of Grey's reports. There are further hints that Johnson wrote the proposals in the allusions to Grey's authoritativeness:

Thus no objection can be made to this work in point of authority, which in former collections may be much doubted, because they appear to have been drawn up for publication, and might, therefore be intended for the service of a party; and because the writers were either unknown, or for the most part obliged to receive their information from others.[133]

Coming so soon after Johnson's dissociation from the current debates, the statement is unusually provocative. While on the surface it formally invites the confidence of readers, it also seems like a remarkably open confession of the techniques employed by Guthrie, Cave, and Johnson. Cave, certainly, had nothing to lose, since interest in the Lilliputian debates was dying and he was beginning to exploit other matters. For Johnson, the statement would serve as veiled confession.

On the other hand, segments of the proposals are less convincing. It is hard to believe, for instance, that Johnson would have let pass an unwieldy sentence like this one:

At a time, therefore, when the history of our own country appears to be so far the prevailing object of literary curiosity, that not only three or four several editions, now publishing on this subject in folio, find reception, but annuities are settled to promote another yet in embryo, it is hoped that this proposal, which has a particular tendency to its amplification and advancement, will not fail of encouragement.

Only haste enforced by a printer's deadline could account for this syntax, which is strained even though formidable traces of the familiar undulations persist. In the main, however, the overtones are sufficiently Johnsonian to make one conclude that Cave probably gave him a draft of the proposals which he then reworked quickly in their present form.

After Johnson ceased writing the debates in 1743, Dr. John Hawkesworth probably continued them through 1745,[134] and procedural reports appeared sporadically in 1746. Although Cave assured the Lords they had been suspended in that year, both he and Astley published undisguised accounts of Lovat's trial by the Lords in March, 1747. Hill suspected Cave was protecting Johnson in denying any person in his employ had taken notes for him. Nichols conjectured that Johnson, because of Cave's appearance before the Lords, ended his major editorial activity on the *Gentleman's Magazine* in 1747, but that he offered occasional assistance thereafter.[135] A better reason for Johnson's termination of extensive journalistic activities at this time, of course, is that by 1747 he was fully occupied with compiling materials for the *Dictionary*.

CHAPTER II

"THE DIGNITY OF LITERATURE":
JOURNALISTIC ASSOCIATES

I

NO MAN, we are told, "had a higher notion of the dignity of literature than Johnson, or was more determined in maintaining the respect which he justly considered as due to it. . . . [O]nce when he dined in a numerous company of booksellers, where the room being small, the head of the table, at which he sat, was almost close to the fire, he persevered in suffering a great deal of inconvenience from the heat, rather than quit his place, and let one of them sit above him." Goldsmith similarly had a notion of the dignity of literature, once complaining because a nobleman took no more notice of him than if he had been "an ordinary man." Although Boswell found this attitude indicative of Goldsmith's "diverting simplicity," Johnson agreed that Goldsmith's literary position as an author entitled him to a respect that money and family position alone would not warrant.[1]

Before attaining this respect, however, both Johnson and Goldsmith served arduous apprenticeships in Grub Street, discovering for themselves the hardships and insecurity of journalism. With the broad-scale publication of newspapers and magazines in the early eighteenth century, publishers were becoming absorbed in the competition of a large new branch of commerce. In satisfying public taste, journalism became rowdy and personal; name-calling and sensationalism became part of an accepted pattern. Many of the same readers who seized upon the periodicals for their lurid contents were hypocritically censorious of both publishers and writers, but especially of the latter, whom they blamed as reprobates incapable or undesirous of a respectable existence. Although this charge was frequently justified, attempts to ameliorate a degrading social situation were belated.

London was filled with literary adventurers who had failed in their aspirations and who were in desperate need of employment, or who regarded journalism as a stepping stone to serious writing. Publishers, thus, had no difficulty in procuring competent hacks at minute wages. Politicians were no less alert than the publishers to the enormous value of the press in furthering their personal aims. Party writing rapidly became a common source of income for the Grub Street hacks, whether they were subsidized by the ministry or opposition forces. Under the banner of a "free press" both sides resorted to name-calling of the vilest kind.[2] Walpole's unlimited budget allowed the establishment of numerous periodicals dedicated to the praise of his government and the slander of the opposition. The opposition for its part, though not having Walpole's resources, found many outlets for returning the abuse. English readers took in the publications of both sides with interest, and when the enjoyment had worn off impartially condemned both sides. The publishers and politicians were mainly culpable, but their writers and printers were the scapegoats, suffering abuse and even legal prosecution.[3] A respectable observer like David Hume noted that writing failed to enjoy the esteem in England that it did in France. The cause he attributed to the "factious barbarians of London" who practiced the craft. English literary taste he extravagantly regarded as decayed and depraved, and the country "so sunk in stupidity and barbarism and faction that you may as well think of Lapland for an author."[4]

The degraded, sensational tone of English journalism, in general, contributed heavily to its disrepute, whether social or moral or economic.

> St. James's Chronicle alarms the town,
> And in four columns scandal marches down.

So wrote Arthur Murphy in his satire *The Examiner* (1761), and though his complaint is a personal one, his lines represent enlightened censure of the press in the eighteenth century. But journalists had their apologists, among them James Ralph, who justified what he called "the authour's sin of venality" by tracing the roots of that sin directly to the publishers and to society. "Instead of reproaching authours for living by their labours," he commented, "we ought to reproach ourselves for allowing them no means to live." The complaint is actualized when we compare Ralph's generalizations with the conditions suffered by Johnson and his early colleagues. Ralph went on to say, "Thus, there is no difference between the writer in his garret, and the slave in the mines. . . . The compiler must compile; the composer must compose on; sick or well; in spirit or out; whether furnished with matter or not; till, by the joint pressure of labour, penury, and sorrow, he has worn out his parts, his constitution, and all the little stock of reputation he had acquired among *the Trade*."[5]

The garret image is a popular one in the eighteenth century to denote the execrable conditions endured by authors—Johnson used it in the *Rambler,* Nos. 117, 161. Goldsmith, whose empirically bitter knowledge of English journalism left him little occasion for illusion, wrote to Robert Bryanton (August 14, 1758): "Well, now I am down, where the devil *is I?* Oh Gods! Gods! here in garret, writing for bread, and expecting to be dunned for a milkscore!" Another time he said: "Let such as have not got a passport from nature be content with happiness, and leave the poet the unrivalled possession of his misery, his garret, and his fame."[6] Although Goldsmith, like Ralph, eloquently censured economic inequalities, it should be acknowledged that the profligate habits of many authors (Savage, Goldsmith, Johnson, and countless others providing excellent illustrations) were at times also responsible for their difficulties. Nevertheless, indebtedness was caused by inadequate income and other economic factors as much as by wastefulness. With a conclusion reminiscent of Ralph's, Goldsmith provides a justification for the low status of eighteenth-century writers and an indictment of the social attitudes to which it was largely attributable.

The poet's poverty is a standing topic of contempt. His writing for bread is an unpardonable offence. Perhaps of all mankind an author in these times is used most hardly. We keep him poor, and yet revile his poverty. Like angry parents who correct their children till they cry; and then correct them for crying, we reproach him for living by his wit, and yet allow him no other means to live.

His taking refuge in garrets and cellars has of late been violently objected to him, and that by men who I dare hope are more apt to pity than insult his distress. Is poverty the writer's fault? No doubt he knows how to prefer a bottle of champagne to the nectar of the neighboring alehouse, or a venison pasty to a plate of potatoes. Want of delicacy is not in him, but in us, who deny him the opportunity of making an elegant choice.[7]

In an equally reasonable though more philosophical tone, Goldsmith iterated his belief in public responsibility and affirmed his faith in the value of authorship, contending for a significant relationship between extensive literary endeavors and a nation's "spirit of freedom."[8]

The minor eighteenth-century writer has frequently been ridiculed as a misfit incapable of earning his livelihood in some more stable occupation. Even more generally he is regarded as a weakling cleverly duped by the nefarious bookseller. A great deal has been said of the machinations of the Trade and much of what has been said, regrettably, is true. At the beginning of the century, when publishing conditions were at their worst, John Locke made this observation in a letter to Anthony Collins:

> Books seem to me to be pestilent things, and infect all that trade in them; that is, all but one sort of men, with something very perverse and brutal. Printers, binders, sellers, and others that make a trade and gain out of them, have universally so odd a turn and corruption of mind, that they have a way of dealing peculiar to themselves, and not conformed to the good of society, and that general fairness that cements mankind.[9]

Despite improving conditions, of course, many of those engaged in various aspects of the Trade continued to merit censure such as Locke's. Not all publishers, however, were villains; nor were all authors—even of the lesser sort—systematically bled by them. Publishing standards were still unsettled and reading habits not yet sufficiently reliable to assure the ultimate success of the Trade. Publication was expensive and printed matter was assessed accordingly. Following the age-old precept of economics, the publishers paid their employees—writers and printers—as little as the traffic would bear in order to earn the highest possible profits for themselves.[10]

The average author was in a difficult position because he could not afford to wait. The royalty system had not yet been conceived; customarily, authors sold their copyright entirely at the outset of a transaction. Yet risks were common to both writer and bookseller; an author having received a small outright payment stood to lose if, over a period of years, his work became a marketable success; on the other hand, booksellers frequently purchased works which proved to have no commercial value. It should be noted, however, that on occasion scrupulous booksellers voluntarily made additional payments to authors whose works had turned out to be unexpectedly successful.[11]

Though the Trade was very well organized, it was not so wholly monopolistic as is often charged.[12] Despite the exclusiveness of established booksellers, new booksellers appeared independently from time to time and succeeded. Authors in theory had the option of holding out for the highest bidders and publishers of bidding for the best authors. Even in journalism it was possible for a writer to live by the pen without demeaning his talents or his integrity. Johnson proved this in his first ten years in London, although he was obliged to compromise to a degree. On the whole, the more enlightened business men engaged in publication won the high regard of their writers, Johnson among them. In a rather specialized instance concerning the operation of the Clarendon Press—a university institution —Johnson once recommended an increase in publishers' profits. Boswell presented Johnson's comments in vindication of "that respectable body of men, the booksellers of London, from vulgar reflections, as if their profits were exorbitant, when, in truth, Dr. Johnson has here allowed them more than they usually demand."[13]

The impression which emerges from a study of contemporary attitudes is that real economic independence was possible for only authors of first-rate talents, like Johnson. The ranks below were largely dependent upon the inconsistent benevolence of the booksellers. One pamphleteer points out, "Writers of real abilities need not be slaves to booksellers, unless the most profligate morals and habitual indiscretion conspire to make them drag such a galling chain. In this case they are not slaves as authors, but as men."[14] Another writer, Catherine Macaulay, urged that authors should obtain economic independence, citing Pope as the exemplary figure who had been able to rise above the whims of patrons and booksellers.[15] Optimistic as such statements may be, they are clearly limited to the artist, denying any substantial hope to the artisan writing for scraps and bread. It must have been just such a person who wailed, "My Lord, it is now twelve a clock, and I want a dinner; and, alas! I doubt my bookseller will not trust me with a shilling, without mort-

gaging these my papers into his hands for the sum aforesaid."[16] Later,
Pope himself was to write in the *Epistle to Dr. Arbuthnot* of a similar
author, who

> Rhymes are he wakes, and prints before term ends,
> Obliged by hunger, and requests of friends.

Without presenting an unduly charitable view of eighteenth-
century booksellers, we should reflect that not all of them were
inherently rascals; for there is reason to believe that, in spite of their
aggressiveness and acquisitiveness, many had a sense of public and
literary duty. Johnson's relations with the booksellers, of course, are
a conspicuous instance of this. One contemporary, anonymous pamphleteer attempted to give a balanced appraisal of eighteenth-century
authorship, offering his answers to two commonly voiced complaints
against booksellers: "First, *that you are not always sufficiently ready
to print all the works of authors;* and secondly, *that you do not give
them a sufficient encouragement,* but pocket all, or most of the profit
of their labours to yourselves." The first charge he concluded to be
without basis. To the second charge he replied that the author is at
liberty to bargain to his own advantage. In the course of his argument
this pamphleteer ascribed a certain amount of blame to the booksellers. He decided, nevertheless, that on the whole the booksellers
worked for the advantage of the authors as well as themselves. One
of his statements merits serious, if skeptical, consideration.

> Besides, Gentlemen, I must do you still further justice in the following
> remark, which all authors are, or at least ought to be acquainted with,
> *viz.* that, perhaps, one third of the books disposed of is not sold for
> ready money; and that two thirds, if not three fourths of those you put
> off are exchanged among yourselves for others, which would have no
> sale at all, were they not thus pushed and dispersed abroad by members
> of your Society, whose particular interest it is so to render copies that lie
> in obscurity more universal. Is, then, the good success of a work, in this
> case, to be solely ascribed to an author's merit; or, rather, is it not prin-
> cipally, if not wholly owing to the bookseller's vigilance, care, and industry,
> who disposes of it to the best advantage?[17]

His censure of the booksellers is restrained, thus suggesting that he
was probably employed by the Society of Booksellers to counteract
some of the numerous complaints against them. Under any circumstance, the reasonable tone of the pamphlet is a refreshing antidote to

the reams of vituperative writing of the period and gives us an attitude toward booksellers which anticipates Johnson's.

When Johnson became a member of Cave's staff in 1738, many of those with whom he was most intimate were lowly, often dissolute, hacks whose sole aim in writing was to earn money for food and lodging. Aspiring to a more elevated goal than most, he nonetheless suffered the same deprivations. After the publication of the *Life of Savage* in 1744, Cave entertained Johnson in his house. But when another caller came, Johnson "skulked" behind a screen where he was "sent a plate of victuals," because his "dress was so shabby that he durst not make his appearance."[18] Association with such men as Moses Browne, John Duick, Richard Savage, William Collins, Samuel Boyse, and even Cave (despite Johnson's loyal admiration) in the wretched environment of Grub Street imbued him with a permanent sympathy. He often spoke of them with scorn because of their moral failings, and yet he always evinced the deepest regret for their kind of existence. From the Grub Street period came the sympathetic inspiration for numerous of the authorial topics which he developed in the *Rambler, Idler, Universal Visiter, English Poets,* and in his conversation. But not all of Cave's staff were literary vagabonds. The *Gentleman's Magazine* could not have achieved its eminence without a core of substantial, reliable authors, among them Elizabeth Carter, Thomas Birch, John Hawkesworth, and John Hawkins, whose presence helped Johnson to realize that he was not necessarily doomed to a life of literary futility. Distinction must be made between the journalists who merely provided reading for daily perusal and the talented writers of permanent literature like Johnson, Goldsmith, Fielding, and Smollett. Such notable figures played a dual role in English literary history, contributing to the periodicals as a matter of daily necessity, but also writing works of lasting value.

Johnson thus witnessed the coming of age of professional authorship during the course of his journalistic and literary career. That abuse and bad taste abounded is very evident. But what is much more important is that gradual, substantial improvement made possible the ultimate dignity of authorship as a profession in eighteenth-century England. Those connected with the public press found themselves in a strongly competitive enterprise in which finally quality rather than abuse became the principle of survival. With a public literary market which made the private benevolence of patronage and subscription-sales anachronistic, writers and booksellers found it profitable to defer to the maturing interests of mass readers. For a period of fourteen years (1735-1749) they even attempted a formal consolidation of their cause through the operation of a Society for the Encouragement of Learning.[19] Although the process of achieving dignity was a slow one and offensive literary and journalistic practices never completely vanished, the improvement throughout the century is gratifying. Concurrently, writers gained appreciable rewards in increased salaries, copyright security, and professional respect. Johnson, among others, was influential in achieving these gains, his attainment of a lofty goal from the humble beginnings at St. John's Gate being one of the major salutary influences on English journalism and literature.

II

Edward Cave influenced Johnson more than any other single figure in this period, for it was he who provided Johnson with a literary foothold during his critical formative years. Neither Cave nor Johnson was an easy man to get along with; and yet, despite occasional quarrels, they maintained a congenial relationship until Cave's death in 1754. Cave, who seems to have treated most of his writers rather imperiously, paid tribute to Johnson's talents and personality by according him unusual respect.[20]

Cave was born in Newton, Warwickshire, on Feburary 27, 1692, the son of a Rugby cobbler. Following a short period of schooling in Rugby, terminated because of unruly conduct, he became assistant collector of excise in Rugby and then an employee of a London timber merchant. Next he was bound to Freeman Collins, a London printer and deputy alderman. He was suited to the printing trade because, according to Johnson, it was one "for which men were formerly qualified by a literary education."[21] Cave must have been skillful in his new occupation because in 1714 Collins placed him, then a twenty-two-year-old apprentice, in charge of the *Norwich Courant, or Weekly Packet*. Cave married and at the end of his apprenticeship returned to London where he committed himself to the Tories; in 1717 or 1718 he became a writer for *Mist's Journal,* for which Defoe was then also writing.

Not long thereafter Cave was enabled, through the influence of his wife, to procure employment in the London postoffice. This was advantageous because he now had access to country newspapers from which he extracted news for at least one London newspaper—perhaps *Mist's*—for a guinea a week. This kind of practice was not uncommon among eighteenth-century postal clerks. Later Cave performed a similar news service for country newspapers, selling them intelligence which he extracted from London papers.

Unfortunately for Cave, one of his clients, Robert Raikes of the *Gloucester Journal,* brought before the bar of the House of Commons in 1727 on a charge of printing parliamentary proceedings in breach of privilege, disclosed Cave as his news source. Raikes, Cave, and several other newspapermen accused of the same violation were found guilty, placed in custody for a short time, reprimanded and fined. Cave, said Johnson, was "treated with great harshness and severity, but, declining their questions, by pleading his oath of secrecy, was at last dismissed." All but Raikes, who was excused because of illness, were, according to the official account, compelled to beg forgiveness of the House on their knees.[22] Despite his irregularity, Cave retained his postal position until his retirement because of ill health in 1745, only two years before he was again in trouble with Parliament for the commission of a like offense.

In 1731 he purchased the printing office at St. John's Gate that was to become the famous home of the *Gentleman's Magazine* for the next fifty years, but he was too shrewd and active a business man to confine himself to any single venture. Thus, while he published the magazine with the assistance of his brother-in-law David Henry, he engaged in other minor printing undertakings. He also had a part in the invention of a speedometer and was financially interested in Lewis Paul's spinning machine in Birmingham. Fond of scientific experimentation, Cave offered prizes for perpetual motion devices and publicized Franklin's electrical experiments.[23] His varied interests brought him considerable wealth, no small part of which was the result of his ability to attract assistance and associates—like Johnson and Birch—who could help him carry out his plans. Of one of Cave's schemes, the poetry contest, Johnson wrote in a tone both tolerantly contemptuous and admiring. "[B]eing but newly acquainted with wealth, and thinking the influence of fifty pounds extremely great, he expected the first authors of the kingdom to appear as competitors." Cave was surprised when only obscure poets competed for the prize and "the universities and several private men" refused to serve as judges. But Cave's "wider accquaintance with the world soon cured him of his astonishment, as of so many other prejudices and errors." Cave never acquired a social polish, and in general conversation his subjects were mundane, usually relating to the *Gentleman's Magazine*. Johnson was not blind to Cave's faults, which were most pronounced in his "chilness of mind." The bookseller's colleagues found him at times annoyingly deliberate in his decisions and narrow in his range of interests. Underlying his reserve, however, were persistence, loyalty, and even generosity.

To Johnson, one of those "who best knew him," Cave was a good friend; and though Johnson liked to hold himself socially above booksellers, he entertained Cave in his house on an equal footing with his more select friends.[24] Two years after Cave's death Johnson wrote to Elizabeth Carter (on January 14, 1756): "Poor dear Cave I owed him much, for to him I owe that I have known you. He died, I am afraid, unexpectedly to himself, yet surely unburthened with any great crime, and for the positive duties of religion, I have yet no right to condemn him for neglect."[25] And yet if Cave's own religious life was not as exemplary as Johnson wished it had been, the pages of the *Gentleman's Magazine* during his editorship are reflective of his religious toleration. By comparison with many of his fellow booksellers, Cave was humane in his treatment of his workers. He drove them, and himself as well; but he provided them with an opportunity to live, however poorly, by their pens. The *Gentleman's Magazine* was the first miscellany in England to enjoy enduring success and certainly one of the first to give fairly durable employment to non-political journalists; Cave helped enormously to open journalism as a new enterprise in the first half of the eighteenth century.

He gathered about him a group of writers, many of them mediocre, who formed the nucleus of the *Gentleman's Magazine*. When Johnson was about to begin his journalistic employment, Cave displayed his hacks in a Clerkenwell alehouse in an effort to impress his new author. The leading writer of this nondescript and undistinguished company was probably Moses Browne, a pen-cutter and poet, and ultimately an ordained Presbyterian minister. A facile writer, Browne was frequently a contributor of poetry to the *Gentleman's Magazine* and a competitor and judge in Cave's poetical contests. Pope, who failed to see Browne's poetic merits, was overruled by the other judges when in 1735 he voted against awarding a prize to Browne.[26] This obscure versifier was much indebted to Cave, who in 1739 produced a volume of his *Poems on Various Subjects,* a number of which had been awarded prizes. In an address to the reader Browne wrote:

> Having entertained a very early love of poetry, and since made it, at leisure intervals, an innocent amusement of my life, I had (in a perfect obscurity) published some pieces, in which I was so happy to please several persons of unquestionable taste, some of whom had even been competitors with me in the prize-poems, proposed under very encouraging rewards, (and which were equitably and honourably distributed by the proposer.)[27]

Johnson, apparently, was not among those who encouraged Browne's inferior performances. Even if he had found it expedient to praise them, it is not likely that, in 1739, his recommendations would have counted for much. Eulogies of Browne in this volume were composed, however, by such shadowy figures as John Duick, Henry Price, Richard Yate, John Ward, and John Bancks, none of whom were of sufficient importance to be included in the *Lives of the English Poets.* Not only did Browne immodestly include their laudatory verse, but he in his turn dedicated poems to Savage, Duick, Birch, and Cave. Browne's *Poems on Various Subjects* served the further purpose of answering Cave's detractors. In response to the complaints of a group of correspondents that Cave revised their verses as he saw fit, Browne answered with a lampoon, *The Reading Ballad.* The *London Magazine,* said Browne of another skirmish, engaged against "Mr. Urban and his party, in a most scandalous manner; . . . merely upon account of his success in the prize verses." As an additional gesture of gratitude Browne also included a tribute to Cave's editorial abilities in the lines *To Sylvanus Urban, on his Monthly Lucubrations.*[28]

Cave thought well enough of Browne as a contributor and judge to defer to him on occasion. For example, he inscribed a plate in the translation of Du Halde's *Description of China* "To Moses Browne," and when the poet was offended by this unseemly famili-

arity, Cave appeased him by commissioning an engraver to alter the
line, having it read, "To *Mr.* Moses Browne."[29] Among other things,
Browne translated Luther's hymn *Es ist nicht schwer ein Christ zu
sein,* and composed a poetic *Essay on the Universe.* A book of verse
meditations, *Sunday Thoughts,* Johnson liked so little that he ironically proposed a companion volume, *Monday Thoughts.*[30] Closer
rapport was later established between Browne and Johnson, largely
because of a mutual interest in Isaac Walton. Johnson admitted that
he had once intended an edition of Walton's *Lives,* although as late
as 1774 he declined to participate in a similar project because Lord
Hailes had already undertaken it.[31] When Browne brought forth his
first edition (1750) of *The Compleat Angler,* he wrote in the preface: "At the instigation of an ingenious and learned friend, whose
judgment of men and books is sufficiently established, by his writings, in the opinion of the world, I undertook this employment." In
a footnote he identified the friend as "Mr. Samuel Johnson, who may
probably, on another occasion, oblige the publick with the life of
Walton." Again, in another edition (1759), Browne acknowledged
his debt to "a very ingenious and learned friend," now identified
in a note as "Mr. Samuel Johnson, author of the folio Dictionary of
the English language."

A few of the other early contributors to the *Gentleman's Magazine*
may be noted briefly. John Duick, another inferior poet and pen-
cutter, was related to Browne, and like him he was a pious Presbyterian. In Duick's house in Clerkenwell Green, reported the candid,
observant Thomas Marryat, "I could find no other book than a Bible
and Dr. Watts' hymns. Squalid poverty appeared there in its most
offensive form of filth and dirt among his numerous progeny."[32]
Foster Webb, before he died of tuberculosis at the age of twenty-
two, was a translator of classics and composer of enigmatic verses.
John Smith, who also died young, wrote religious essays. John
Canton, who contributed poetry and papers on philosophical and
religious subjects, was a competent enough scientist to be recognized
by the Royal Society. William Rider, later ordained, wrote verses.
Adam Calamy, an attorney by profession and "a consistent protes-
tant," wrote on theology and politics. From the academy of John
Eames in Moorfields came the writings of unidentified young men,

who were training to be dissenting ministers, on "mathematics and other branches of science and polite literature."[33] And even John Hawkins, who in his youth visited St. John's Gate frequently, was writing for the *Gentleman's Magazine* as early as March, 1739, when Johnson was already pretty well committed to his journalistic career.[34]

Samuel Boyse, a degenerate wastrel though a more talented poet than the others previously mentioned, came to Cave's attention in 1740, following publication of *Deity,* his imitation of Pope's *Essay on Man.* Cave had rejected the poem, but between 1741 and 1743 Boyse contributed poetry to the *Gentleman's Magazine* over the signatures "Y" and "Alcaeus." Boyse, who also achieved minor fame with his modernization of Chaucer (1741) and *Albion's Triumph* (1743), was favored by the high literary regard of patrons in Scotland and of Pope, Fielding, and the Reverend James Hervey in England.[35] Fielding, though he expressed little hope for its success, reviewed *Deity* favorably in the *Champion* (February 12, 1740) and then, nine years later, referred to it again in *Tom Jones* (Bk. VII, Ch. I), quoting the identical lines from the poem which he had used earlier in the review. Undoubtedly owing to the enthusiasm of Fielding and Hervey for its moral tone and for its physico-theological theme of the divine attributes, *Deity* came to three editions by 1752. It was frequently anthologized in the eighteenth and nineteenth centuries.

The elevated, theological quality of Boyse's poetry had no reflection in his personal life, which was made up of a series of sordid incidents, all stemming from his looseness and extravagance. The son of a dissenting Irish cleric, he was educated in Dublin and Glasgow, coming to London after his Scottish literary patrons failed to reform him. His first wife became a prostitute and he a beggar. When money occasionally came into his hands, Boyse was irrationally profligate, squandering it on rich foods. Friends would purchase a dinner for him and he would refuse to eat his roast beef without ketchup.[36] Johnson's opinion of him was uncomplimentary. "By addicting himself to low vices, among which were gluttony and extravagance [Johnson told Nichols], Boyse rendered himself so contemptible and wretched, that he frequently was without the least subsistence for days together."[37] His shirt was so often in pawn that he improvised cuffs and collars from paper. "In this plight," Shiels reported, "he frequently appeared abroad, with the additional inconvenience of want of breeches," covered only by a greatcoat.[38] Johnson stated that he once collected money to redeem Boyse's clothing from a pawnbroker. On those occasions when he had no clothing, Boyse wrote in bed, his head and arms through a hole in the blanket. It was with the knowledge of drudges like Boyse that Johnson later discoursed philosophically and with disillusionment, as in *Rambler*, No. 14, on the chasm that too often separated an author's conduct from his work.

Boyse once sent Cave a pitiful letter in which he begged for a half-guinea. "I humbly intreat your answer," he pleaded, "having not tasted any thing since Tuesday evening I came here [Crown Coffee House, Grocer's Alley]; and my coat will be taken off my back for the charge of the bed, so that I must go into prison naked; which is too shocking for me to think of."[39] Cave rescued him; thereupon Boyse addressed some Latin lines to his employer ending *Ex gehennâ debitoriâ, vulgò domo spongiatoriâ.* The publisher probably did not lose by his generosity for Boyse, who could write verses almost as rapidly as prose, produced poetry for which Cave "paid him by the [long] hundred lines," as Johnson recalled.[40] Almost equally rapid as a translator, Boyse received threepence a line for a number of Chaucer's tales which he modernized. He also translated a few Dutch and French authors, and appears to have had some musical and artistic ability. Boyse died a pauper in May, 1749, and was buried in common ground. According to one narrator he had been run over by a coach while drunk; according to another he had died in bed of starvation, pen in hand. Among his contemporaries who had less regard for his moralistic-literary abilities than either Fielding or Hervey, Boyse achieved notoriety. The satirist Archibald Campbell, for instance, has left a sketch of Boyse in his *Sale of Authors*.[41] Johnson had as unfavorable an opinion of Boyse's poetic abilities as of his moral character. He once "was asked, which was the best poet, Boyse or Derrick? When he sternly replied, 'How can I appreciate the difference between a flea and a louse?' "[42]

William Guthrie was another of the *Gentleman's Magazine* fraternity. Johnson believed that though he lacked "a great regular fund

of knowledge," he compensated for this deficiency through his reading and writing and merited a lasting biographical memorial.[43]
Guthrie was born in Scotland in 1708, the son of an Episcopalian
minister. Coming to London in 1730 to make his living as a writer,
he gained valued political experience as author of the *Parliamentary
Debates,* in consequence of which he ultimately became a propa-
gandist for the Whigs. For his services the Pelham government gave
him a yearly pension of £200; and indeed, so influential and unscrupulous a party writer had he been that the Bute administration
renewed his pension in 1762 in order to keep him quiet.[44] In his letter
of application to Bute on June 3, 1762, a prime example of boldness,
he said: "Your Lordship may possibly now suspect that *I am an
author by profession:* you are not deceived; and will be less so, if you
believe that I am disposed to serve his Majesty under your Lordship's
*future patronage and protection, with greater zeal if possible than
ever."*[45] In 1763 Guthrie published his first book, a *Complete List of
the English Peerage.* This he followed with several histories of England, Scotland, and the world, and with translations from Quintilian
and Cicero.

But of all the writers with whom Johnson associated when he was
an employee of the *Gentleman's Magazine,* none left a more profound impression upon him than Richard Savage, whom he could
have met in the fall of 1737 or early in 1738,[46] and to none was he
more loyal and sympathetic. In Savage Johnson saw the tragedy of
dissipation and wasted talents, championing him because of a humanitarian belief that he had been sorely wronged and that his family
had abandoned him. But he probably also shared at this time Savage's
rebellious political attitudes. In the spring of 1739 Savage probably
was his closest friend, offering to him companionship and brilliant
conversation, social requisites which never failed to sustain Johnson
in his many crises. Hawkins has attempted to account for the strange
relationship by theorizing that Johnson was attracted to people at
opposite poles from him. Despite Savage's degeneracy, Hawkins
wrote, he was on the exterior an accomplished gentleman who impressed Johnson with his social finesse and the story of his noble
birth.[47]

Johnson believed Savage when he told him and, indeed, anyone else who would listen, that he was born in 1697, the illegitimate son of Lady Macclesfield (who was separated from her husband because of adultery) and the Earl Rivers. Despite serious discrepancies in this story no one has ever succeeded in disproving it. He claimed that his mother abandoned him when he was an infant, and that after a brief education he became apprentice to a shoemaker. Then he discovered his mother's identity, but she would not acknowledge him. Turning to poetry and drama as the source of his livelihood, Savage was under the patronage of Sir Richard Steele, who succeeded in involving him in his many debts. A marriage was almost effected between Savage and Steele's natural daughter, but a quarrel terminated the match. Savage fell upon evil days during which he was often without bed and board, roaming the streets and composing verses in his mind until he could borrow pen and paper to jot them down. At the same time he was taking a malicious—if not mistakenly righteous—delight in publicizing his mother's perfidy. In 1727 he became embroiled in a tavern fight, as a result of which one man was killed and a woman wounded. Tried and found guilty, Savage was saved from the death penalty and released only by the intervention of Lord Tyrconnel, Aaron Hill, perhaps the Countess of Hertford, and others. Consequently he took advantage of the new notoriety to leech off his many friends. One of his early patrons was Pope, who sent him five guineas when he was in prison on the murder charge. Pope, who admired Savage's poetry, later employed him to procure information about various candidates for dunces and praised him in the *Dunciad*. Savage repaid this enthusiasm with an interest in Pope's poetry.[48]

The *Gentleman's Magazine,* to which Savage contributed poetry, probably brought Johnson and Savage together, the latter at this time wearing shoes with holes and a gold-lace trimmed cloak. Through Johnson or Cave, Savage now also met Elizabeth Carter, to whom he showed devoted admiration.[49] Cave's attitude toward Savage is not clear; some commentators speculate that they were on cordial terms and others that they were not. His erratic conduct, at any rate, was not calculated to invite Cave's trust, for Savage apparently sold the same poems to Cave and John Wilford of the *London Magazine*.[50] Johnson and Savage wandered around St. James, Grosvenor, and Westminster Squares at night, consorting with beggars and thieves (though there is nothing to substantiate hints that Savage led Johnson into moral irregularities)[51] and discoursing on international politics and the unequal distribution of wealth and fame. Any opinion about Johnson from John Wilkes must be suspect. But he theorized, interestingly if uncharitably, that Johnson and Savage were politically compatible, that they "were contented—in the open air—to growl at the moon, and Whigs, and Walpole, and the house of Brunswick."[52] From some of these rambles Johnson probably added to his store for many future *Rambler* and *Idler* reflections on authorship. Both men were so impoverished that they could not sit in taverns or get lodgings, and between them they could not raise fourpence halfpenny.[53] But they were always in excellent spirits. The question arises as to where Johnson's wife was during this period. One plausible suggestion is that she and Johnson were temporarily separated as a result of a quarrel or because of their poverty, and that she resided with friends.[54]

Savage was in desperate straits in 1739, for upon the death of Queen Caroline Walpole suspended the state pension he had been receiving. A group of friends headed by Pope raised enough money to send him to Swansea, away from the temptations of the city. Savage "left London in July, 1739, having taken leave with great tenderness of his friends, and parted from [Johnson] with tears in his eyes."[55] The poet continued to be profligate, abusing the hospitality he was accorded wherever he went. Finally, after alienating even Pope, Savage was imprisoned for debt in Bristol and died a pauper on August 1, 1743.

For all of his detestation of moral weakness, Johnson was tolerant of Savage's faults; nor, indeed, is his warm friendship with the poet strange when we remember other rakish men of the world with whom he was friendly—Henry Hervey, Boswell, and Beauclerk, among others. Johnson was well aware of Savage's faults of hypocrisy, untrustworthiness, pettiness, profligacy, and self-indulgence. He knew that Savage had false pride, that he was an opportunist, and that he could be virulent toward friends as well as enemies. Knowing all this, Johnson was fond of him, for he also recognized virtues. Savage, indeed, was not so black as many contemporary censors painted him. Thus, while his detractors eagerly publicized his excesses and shortcomings, they remained silent about any moral attributes they knew him to possess. One of his unpublished letters to Birch (September, 1734), for instance, reveals a modesty so inconsistent with the usual stories about him that it is worth quoting:

> Among the poetry of last month [in *G.M.*, IV (1734), 447], there are two very idle things—one of 'em downright obscene (tho' intended for the double entendre) concerning Mr. Cibber's verses on two ladies dancing; the inserting of the real names of those ladies is also monstrous; nor is it an excuse to say that it is copied from a newspaper; or that the other magazine [*L.M.*, III (1734), 444] has done the same—The second paper of verses (occasioned by reading some rhymes of Sir Walter Raleigh's) is really so very nasty, that they made my stomach quite squeamish; nor could I possibly read them out—I cannot imagine that either of 'em could be admitted there thro' Mr. Kimber's consent.[56]

Johnson, who witnessed both the vices and the virtues, wrote:

> This, at least, must be allowed him, that he always preserved a strong sense of the dignity, the beauty, and the necessity of virtue, and that he never contributed deliberately to spread corruption amongst mankind. His actions, which were generally precipitate, were often blameable; but his writing, being the productions of study, uniformly tended to the exaltation of the mind, and the propagation of morality and piety.[57]

This, on the surface, may appear oddly unlike the Johnson who inflexibly insisted that a man's life must be as exemplary as his writings. Yet there is no inconsistency when we consider Savage's letter to Birch and Johnson's motives of pity, sympathy, self-identification, and above all the conclusion of *Rambler*, No. 60. "If we owe regard to the memory of the dead, there is yet more respect to be paid to knowledge, to virtue, and to truth." Few people were more familiar with Savage than Johnson was. Knowing well and intimately the force of human weakness, he also knew well the force of friendship; and in a time of need, Savage was a good friend.

Johnson's tribute, the pamphlet *Life of Savage* which James Roberts printed in 1744 and which ultimately was incorporated with the *English Poets,* was his vindication of his late friend. One critic has praised him for the remarkable delicacy with which he treated Savage, attributing to the biography a sincere sympathy devoid of pedantic morality.[58] Although the *Life* gave Johnson an opportunity to defend Savage, his own financial needs also made its composition essential. He wrote the forty-eight octavo pages in the short space of a day and one-half or two days; Cave paid him (December 14, 1743) fifteen guineas for the copyright.[59] Because of its lurid details, Savage's life was fair game for the hack writers. Prior to Johnson's biography at least two short accounts had appeared, one in 1724 and one in 1727. His misfortunes and claims, furthermore, were widely circulated topics of London gossip. Nine years after Johnson's biography, there appeared another as from Cibber's pen. Like the life of Boyse, it was written by Shiels, who borrowed material from Johnson's work.[60] The laudatory introduction obviously refers to Johnson, "a gentleman, who knew [Savage] intimately, capable to distinguish between his follies, and those good qualities which were often concealed from the bulk of mankind by the abjectness of his condition."[61] Shiels was mistaken in asserting that the unnamed biographer had written the life several years after Savage's death, since in reality Johnson allowed less than a year to elapse. The *Life of Savage* brought Johnson much attention, including that of Sir Joshua Reynolds whom the biography moved deeply. This, at long distance, was the first connection between the two, for Reynolds did not know Johnson at the time he read the life in 1752 and probably did not meet him until 1756.[62]

William Collins, another poet with whom Johnson associated in the Grub Street period, was more reputable and more favorably renowned than Savage. In the *English Poets,* Johnson described Collins as a penurious "literary adventurer" who, because of vacillation and poverty, brought few of his numerous projects to fruition. "A man doubtful of his dinner, or trembling at a creditor, is not much disposed to abstracted meditation or remote inquiries."[63] He recalled that Collins had contributed verses to the *Gentleman's Magazine* in 1739, while he was yet a student at Winchester. Collins took a degree at Oxford in 1743 and then came to London in 1744 about the time the *Life of Savage* was published. From their cordial relationship Johnson was able to form a sympathetic judgment of Collins' personality. Even before writing the *English Poets,* Johnson contributed a sketch of Collins to the *Poetical Calendar,* the editors of which acknowledged that it came from "a gentleman, deservedly eminent in the republic of letters, who knew [Collins] intimately well."[64] In the summary, which Johnson included in the *English*

Poets, he wrote that the poet's "morals were pure, and his opinions pious." He admitted that after "a long continuance of poverty and long habits of dissipation . . . and long association with fortuitous companions," Collins' life was far from blameless. Yet Johnson regarded him as a man with a strong moral sense whose "faults had nothing of malignity or design, but proceeded from some unexpected pressure, or casual temptation." The resemblances between this evaluation and that of Savage are typical of Johnson's compassionate nature and his willingness to judge a person by his best qualities. Somewhat shortsighted about Collins' poetic abilities, Johnson was less concerned with his artistry than with the tragedy of his wasted life, his madness, and his poverty. Once he visited Collins while a bailiff besieged his lodgings for the payment of a debt, and in numerous letters to Joseph Warton, Collins' closest friend, Johnson inquired solicitously about the latter's health.[65]

Admiring among other qualities Collins' learning and imagination, Johnson nevertheless spoke slightingly of his "now and then odes" and considered him a poet of unfulfilled talents. He showed promise in his allegories but was never successful in his quest of beauty in "the grandeur of wildness," nor in avoiding harshness of diction and obsolescence. "As men are often esteemed who cannot be loved, so the poetry of Collins may sometimes extort praise when it gives little pleasure." That is Johnson's avowed opinion of Collins' poetry, but it may well be that some of his own later oriental themes in the *Rambler* are partially attributable to Collins. For example, Collins' *Eclogue II,* "Hassan; or, the Camel Driver," is a conventional poem in heroic couplets dealing with the evil consequences of acquisitive desires, a favorite subject of Johnson. While the theme and oriental locale are commonplaces of eighteenth-century moralizing, Johnson probably went to those works closest at hand, Collins' among them. His attraction to orientalism, as in the *Rambler* and *Rasselas,* is good evidence that he would not have found Collins uncongenial.

A composite picture of many of these early colleagues and their way of life would be one of unalleviated squalor, misery, and degradation, reminiscent of Hogarth's portrayal of "The Distrest Poet." But Cave also brought to the Gate writers whose lives were more admirable. One such writer was Mark Akenside, who contributed verses to the *Gentleman's Magazine* between 1737 and 1739. Johnson apparently did not know Akenside personally, but that did not prevent him from forming a contemptuous opinion of his "clamours for liberty." He considered Akenside an undistinguished poet, though superior to Gray and Mason. Johnson protested that he could not read through the *Pleasures of the Imagination* and that his odes in general, of which "nothing favourable can be said," were dull and unreadable.[66]

Perhaps most eminent among Johnson's associates in his early years on the *Gentleman's Magazine* was the whiggish Dr. Thomas Birch (1705-1766) who, though born of Quaker parents in Clerkenwell, became an Anglican divine. Birch was one of Cave's editorial advisers and occasional judge of his poetry contests. As editor and friend, Birch frequently rendered service to Savage by conveying his contributions to Cave and perhaps transmitting assignments from him.[67] Johnson apparently came to know Birch in 1738 when he was editing the *General Dictionary, Historical and Critical.* And at this time he inscribed the Greek epigram to him.[68] Later, in 1756, Johnson reviewed Birch's *History of the Royal Society* for the *Literary Magazine.* He regarded Birch as a dull writer but a good conversationalist. "Tom is a lively rogue; he remembers a great deal, and can tell many pleasant stories; but a pen is to Tom a torpedo, the touch of it benumbs his hand and his brain: Tom can talk; but he is no writer."[69] Johnson valued Birch as a friend and scholar.

Another contributor to the *Gentleman's Magazine,* familiar to its readers as "Eliza," was Elizabeth Carter (1717-1806), translator of Crousaz's *Examen.* She was later to become a *Rambler* enthusiast and contributor. Cave, who was a friend of her father, a clergyman, began printing her poetry in 1734, when she was only seventeen. In 1738 he published an anonymous edition of her verses, most of which had appeared in the *Gentleman's Magazine.* Of this unusual woman Sir Egerton Brydges wrote that "her learning was sound, deep, and critical; her knowledge general, and her taste pure and classical."[70] She was thoroughly steeped in Greek, but she also had a command of Latin and Hebrew. In addition she had compiled a manuscript dictionary of Arabic, and knew a variety of modern languages. The principal work of Miss Carter, whose versatility extended to history and astronomy, was her translation of Epictetus.[71] Apparently attracted by her unusual attainments, Johnson was always kind to Miss Carter. He celebrated her talents in a Greek epigram and recommended that she undertake a translation of Boethius' *De Consolatione Philosophiae.*[72]

Though Miss Carter was early impressed by Johnson, her father was contemptuous of his obscurity and attainments. A parental letter addressed to her on June 25, 1738, is supercilious and, in retrospect, amusing: "You mention Johnson; but that is a name with which I am utterly unacquainted. Neither his scholastic, critical, or poetical character ever reached my ears. I a little suspect his judgment, if he is very fond of Martial."[73] Any reputation which Johnson enjoyed after the publication of *London* on May 13, 1738, had not yet reached Mr. Carter's attention. Miss Carter was less conscious of the social barriers between Johnson and his elite friends than were some of her haughtier acquaintances. Several years later, in 1756, when his writings had been more widely acclaimed, he wrote to Miss Carter and her friend, Catherine Talbot, to encourage a benefit for his blind dependent, Anna Williams. Miss Talbot, who had contributed to the *Rambler,* then wrote to Miss Carter: "Before your letter came, I had been honored with one from Mr. Johnson himself, so highly polite and complimental that it infinitely distressed me. To answer it was impossible, to leave it unanswered rude. I sent at last somewhat between a note and a card. . . ."[74] Elizabeth Carter, on the other hand, felt no such arbitrary social scruples and remained Johnson's lifelong friend.[75]

One more acquaintance of the Grub Street days, with whom Johnson was to continue association, was Dr. John Hawkesworth (1715?-1773), who began contributing verses to the *Gentleman's Magazine* in 1741. It is generally believed that he wrote the *Parliamentary Debates* after Johnson left off. Ultimately he became an editor of the magazine and projected the *Adventurer,* in which he had Johnson's assistance. He was a close imitator of Johnson's style, and also his social intimate as a fellow member of the famous Ivy Lane Club.

From Cave and his circle we pass to one of Johnson's most remarkable acquaintances, who was known only by his pseudonym of George Psalmanazar, or as "the pious fraud." This strange man was a combination of saint and sinner, who has been remembered through his unverifiable *Memoirs* and the random comments of contemporaries.[76] Apparently he was born in southern France about 1679, of Roman Catholic parents. As a precocious student in Avignon he began to misrepresent himself, pretending that he was a victim of religious persecution. Then he posed as an Irish student of theology who, with a fluent command of Latin, dressed as a pilgrim and begged. At his father's urging, Psalmanazar traveled in Belgium, Holland, and Germany. For a time he was suspected of being a spy, but he cleared himself and served in a German regiment. Proving too frail for the army, he was dismissed but doggedly reënlisted for a short time. Then he pretended that he was a Japanese, and in this disguise assumed the name of the Biblical Shalmaneser (II *Kings* XVII. 3), which became Psalmanazar in English. He permitted an English cleric, Alexander Innes, who discovered the fraud and abetted him in it, to "convert" him to the Church of England, while he was still on the Continent. Then, thoroughly convincing in his oriental role and living an abstemious, pious life, he arrived in England about 1703, to become the rage of London. At the behest of Innes he wrote in two months the *History of Formosa,* an absurd fabrication in which he invented for Formosa strange customs, an alphabet, and a language.[77] He received ten guineas for this book and an additional twelve guineas for revisions. So popular was Psalmanazar's creation that it went through two editions with its authenticity unchallenged.

He was even invited to study in Oxford, where he remained for six months, burning candles in his window that people would think he applied himself to his studies all night. As a reward for his conversion of Psalmanazar, Innes was made chaplain-general of the British forces in Portugal. Meanwhile, Psalmanazar became the subject of growing skepticism and attack. Locke, for intance, wondered "if poor Psalmanassar be really a convert from paganism (which I would be glad to be assured of)."[78] This was an ironical delay of justice, for once Innes left him Psalmanazar sought to earn an honest living.

After brief service as a clerk of a regiment dispatched to put down the Jacobite uprising of 1715, Psalmanazar taught for a short time and performed duties as a translator. In 1728, allegedly after reading Law's *Serious Call to a Devout and Holy Life* and Nelson's *Method of Devotion* (the first work was also an early source of inspiration for Johnson), Psalmanazar reformed and then began his *Memoirs*. As a result of an illness in the same year, he commenced the sustained use of laudanum. This learned man was fluent in languages, among them Hebrew, which he taught himself to speak with ease. Turning to literature and hack writing for a livelihood, he did an edition of the *Psalms*. But this was anticipated in 1736 by Dr. Hare, Bishop of Chichester, and Psalmanazar's version was not published. His chief publication was the *General History of Printing* (1732), in which he was associated with the printer Samuel Palmer. In 1742 or 1743 Psalmanazar was indexing the *State Papers of John Thurloe,* which Dr. Birch edited in seven folio volumes. Perhaps about this time, owing to the mutual acquaintance with Birch, Johnson met Psalmanazar. Another circumstance that could have brought them together was Psalmanazar's participation, between 1735 and 1744, in the compiling of the *Universal History,* for both knew many of the same booksellers.[79]

Late in life Johnson admitted that Psalmanazar was one of the men he used to seek out the most, sitting with him in the alehouse on Old Street, where he had also met the "metaphysical tailor," the uncle of the poet John Hoole. To Psalmanazar's credit, Johnson thought him the best man he ever knew and discoursed with him on subjects of "religion and learning." So much did Johnson revere his piety that he would "as soon think of contradicting a bishop." In his *Prayers and Meditations,* Johnson commended the uniformity of Psalmanazar's life, with apparent reference to his morality.[80] Johnson knew him to have been an imposter, but accepted him as repentant. Certainly Psalmanazar himself made no attempt to conceal his previous waywardness. He made an anonymous confession in the *Complete System of Geography* (to which he contributed the essay on Formosa), and he stated in his introduction to his *Memoirs* that the volume was "the last will and testament of me as a poor sinner and worthless creature commonly known by the assumed name of George Psalmanazar." Again confessing his deceptions, he asked for a common, unmarked grave.[81] Like most of the "scoundrels" whom Johnson, as Adam Smith said, patronized,[82] Psalmanazar had self-evident frailties. But evil and malice were not among them. When he died shortly before the momentous meeting of Boswell and Johnson in 1763 in Tom Davies' parlor, the brief obituary in the *Gentleman's Magazine* avoided explicit mention of his former notoriety: "Mr. Psalmanazar, in Ironmonger-row, aged 84, well known for many ingenious performances in different parts of literature."[83] Psalmanazar's frauds belonged to a colorful past and now London was charitably content to let him fade into the obscurity he desired. For Johnson it was enough that Psalmanazar had become a good man.

Comparison between Johnson and most of his early London acquaintances is obviously unfair. The impact of his talent and the force of his personality obscured the accomplishments of even the reputable figures with whom he associated. Johnson needed always to be central in any group, whether adjudicating, dogmatizing, or enchanting, and others were always willing to let him dominate. Even as a writer for a magazine, where anonymity was one of the rewards of literature, Johnson became a well-known personality. Remembering his journalistic days and companions, writing and talking about them, Johnson became an unofficial historian of Grub Street. Exposed to the humility of poverty and squalor, Johnson never succumbed to them. It is, indeed, remarkable how well he survived in Grub Street and then left it an immeasurable distance behind him. It is, perhaps, equally remarkable that his literary triumphs are founded upon his journalistic lessons there.

CHAPTER III

THE GRUB STREET HISTORIAN: THE *LITERARY MAGAZINE* AND OTHER JOURNALS

WITH a substantial reputation based upon the *Rambler,* two major poems, *London* and *The Vanity of Human Wishes,* and the drama *Irene,* Johnson was well known in English literary circles after the middle of the eighteenth century. He was, furthermore, recognized for his undertaking of the *Dictionary,* even though it was not to appear until 1755. Thanks to his labors for Cave and the *Gentleman's Magazine,* Johnson's name had become familiar among London booksellers and authors, who knew that if he were once enlisted he could be relied upon to produce better than competent essays and reviews. Writers of quality were scarce enough in Grub Street so that Johnson was in frequent demand by miscellaneous journals for prefaces, original essays, and book reviews. Occasionally he was asked to take over an editorship, as with the *Literary Magazine,* which proved to be one of his most important journalistic ventures; and, frequently, he was induced to make contributions because of friendship, as with Christopher Smart's *Universal Visiter.* Whatever the occasion, however, Johnson found writing a chore. Toward the end of his life he commented, "I allow you may have pleasure from writing, after it is over, if you have written well; but you don't go willingly to it again." Despite an easygoing attitude toward financial matters, Johnson took a practical view of his writing talents. He maintained that composition is "all work, and my inducement to it is not love of fame, but the want of money, which is the only motive to writing that I know of." Such a materialistic impulse made it simple for him to forego sentimentality and insist upon compensation for his efforts. This practical trait is illustrated by Hawkins' report that Johnson "was never greedy of money, but without money could not be stimulated to write. I have been told by a clergyman . . . with whom he had long been acquainted, that, being to preach on a particular occasion, he applied to Johnson for help. 'I will write a sermon for thee,' said Johnson, 'but thou must pay me for it.' " Whether he wrote sermons or journalistic pieces, Johnson was equally steadfast in his belief that "no man but a blockhead ever wrote, except for money."[1] Once he gave up his duties on the *Gentleman's Magazine,* he never again relied upon a periodical (excluding, perhaps, the *Rambler* and the *Idler*) for his principal source of revenue. His contributions to the *Student,* the *Universal Visiter,* the *Literary Magazine,* the *London Chronicle,* and the *Daily Gazetteer* were supplementary to major literary undertakings, such as the *Dictionary* or the edition of Shakespeare.

I

THE *Literary Magazine*

In 1756 English literary journalism was thriving, with the *Monthly Review* firmly rooted since 1749 and the *Critical Review* offering spirited competition since February, 1756. Determined to take advantage of mass interest in books, the printer William Faden and the publisher-bookseller J. Richardson began still another periodical, the *Literary Magazine, and Universal Review* (titled once, in January, 1758, the *Literary and Anti-Gallican Magazine*), which they issued in twenty-seven numbers between May, 1756, and July, 1758. But they avoided an excessive show of rivalry by organizing the *Literary Magazine* as a miscellany with a substantial section of book reviews. Faden was in general charge of editorial details, and his most competent writer of essays and reviews between May, 1756, and July, 1757, was Johnson, who at the same time served as an editor. A long-standing acquaintance of Johnson and his occasional creditor, Faden had printed the *Rambler* and was later to be co-publisher of the *Universal Chronicle,* in which the *Idler* appeared. He was perhaps the printer of the *Literary Magazine,* but if he had any proprietary interest beyond publishing the first number it has been concealed effectively.[2] The printer, whose address was Wine Office Court, Fleet Street, was also connected with the publication of John Newbery's *Public Ledger,* Goldsmith's *Bee,* and Arthur Murphy's *Gray's-Inn Journal* (which Johnson reviewed in the first number of the magazine).[3] Despite the publishing experience of the founders, with whom Newbery may have been associated,[4] the *Literary Magazine* apparently failed to attract a profitably wide audience, for either the ownership changed hands or publishing arrangements were altered. The first volume was printed for Richardson, of Paternoster Row; the second (which begins with the tenth number, February, 1757) and the third (which begins with the twenty-first number, January, 1758) for John Wilkie, publisher and bookseller of St. Paul's Church Yard.

Those who instituted the *Literary Magazine,* thus, were professionals in their crafts, and they sought out other professionals to help them make a success of their venture. Though Faden was nominally editor, it is not likely that he, as an active printer, had the requisite time for sole editorial responsibility. Johnson among others, therefore, became affiliated with the *Literary Magazine* under circumstances which may be hypothesized, though verifiable evidence is regrettably limited. Hawkins, who was aware that Johnson wrote essays as well as reviews, stated only that "he assumed or submitted to the office of a reviewer, as it is called, for the publisher of a monthly collection, intituled 'The Literary Magazine,' of which one Faden, a printer was the editor."[5] Hawkins, thus, was uncertain whether Johnson came to the publication voluntarily or because of necessity. Undoubtedly, Johnson was asked to join the staff of the *Literary Magazine* because Faden was acquainted with his editorial ability and experience. (There had been no previous relationship between Richardson and Johnson.) A fact probably also known to Faden was that Johnson had personal editorial aspirations. For many years, indeed until he achieved a measure of financial security, Johnson looked almost automatically to journalism as a way of supplementing his resources. As recently as the spring of 1755, when the *Dictionary* was nearing publication, he had given serious consideration to the possibility of editing a *Bibliothèque,* a review journal.[6] The idea of a literary periodical was thus congenial, and Faden must have prevailed upon him not only to take charge of the literary department, but to be an editor as well.[7] The man who had devoted a large part of seven or more years to the editorship of the *Gentleman's Magazine* had invaluable knowledge to apply to the features of a new miscellany whose design was very much like Cave's. It may be imagined that Johnson was consulted as the principles of the *Literary Magazine* were being formulated, if he did not actually create the scheme himself, and that before long he found his anticipated share of the work extended.

Neither Boswell nor Murphy is any more helpful than Hawkins about the specific nature of Johnson's duties and about the salaries paid him and his fellow contributors. Yet it may be assumed that Johnson needed the income at this time, for he was between major projects—the *Dictionary* had been completed and the edition of Shakespeare, for which proposals were printed in 1756, was being contemplated. As a matter of fact, the *Literary Magazine* work comprises but a part of his activities; during 1756-57 he was also writing dedications and articles for the *Universal Visiter* and the *London Chronicle*. Meanwhile, his social life went on as usual. The *Literary Magazine*

engrossed but little of Johnson's time. He resigned himself to indolence, took no exercise, rose about two, and then received the visits of his friends. Authors, long since forgotten, waited on him as their oracle, and he gave responses in the chair of criticism. He listened to the complaints of, the schemes, and the hopes and fears, of a crowd of inferior writers, "who," he said, in the words of Roger Ascham, "lived *men knew not how, and died obscure, men marked not when.*" He believed that he could give a better history of Grub-street than any man living.[8]

Judged from this account, Johnson was completely at his ease; yet, in actuality, his fortunes were very low. Only one year after the publication of the *Dictionary,* he was arrested as a common debtor and had to be rescued by Samuel Richardson. In addition to his London debts, he was still under obligation to the Levetts of Lichfield for a £12 mortgage on the Johnson home, contracted by himself and his mother in 1740. This he did not pay until 1757.[9]

Even though Johnson did not devote much of his creative energy to the *Literary Magazine,* he was invested with more responsibility than Hawkins or Murphy suspected. More than a mere reviewer or writer of occasional essays, he was an editor, an important part of his tasks being supervisory.[10] His editorial role is implicit in a letter to the Oxonian law professor Robert Chambers on July 31, 1756, concerning a contribution to the magazine by the latter. The letter is of additional interest in that it reveals Johnson's consistent desire for journalistic anonymity. He wrote:

Dear Sir

Your Life came indeed too late for the month, but we suffered no inconvenience from the delay, because we had more materials than room. I have sent it already to the press, unread, for the next month, and am much obliged to you for doing it. I will contrive to find you more work. If you could send us any performances from Oxford they would be of great advantage to us. I wish you could add something to the printed accounts of any events that happen among you. I shall take care to send you the monthly [number?] gratis, if you contribute to it. But you must not tell that I have any thing in it. For though it is known conjecturally I would not have it made certain.[11]

Further, it appears that he must have had a hand in the editing and possibly the writing of the *Historical Memoirs,* a department given over to editorial commentary on domestic and foreign political occurrences. This was the kind of work to which Cave had assigned him in connection with the Lilliputian debates, and the signs of Johnson's editorial management will be worth considering. As an editor, then, he probably supervised literary and political matters, and also arranged for the procurement of articles.

There is tangible evidence that the proprietors or editors thought highly of Johnson, at least during the period of his connection with the *Literary Magazine.* The review of his Shakespeare proposals which appeared in No. 13 (May, 1757, pp. 177-180) is unusually laudatory, as even the reviewer admitted, for a work which had not been published (though it was still being promised for Christmas).

He who pretends to give an edition of Shakespeare, should have a mind as comprehensive as that of his author; he should be possessed of an elevation of genius and a strength of imagination, which will enable him to spring away at once, and follow our wonderful poet in his most daring flights; he should have a quick discernment into the operations of the passions, and all the workings of the human mind; he should be a master of history foreign and domestic, ancient and modern; he should be acquainted with the ideas and customs of the old Romans, the old Britons, and almost all the states in Europe; and he likewise should have an insight into all the various departments of human life, and of all the foibles, humours, and manners peculiar to each rank. That the future editor of Shakespeare is possessed of these qualifications, I believe, is well known to all who have seen his admirable essays in the *Rambler.*

The review, probably written by Murphy,[12] must have had the approbation of Faden and his colleagues. The extravagant praise would have been less surprising had it been applied to a work already published. Attached to mere proposals, it has a tone of intimacy, as though, indeed, the person writing it were familiar with Johnson's erudition. While much of the eulogy could have been motivated by an appreciation of the *Rambler,* or the Drury-Lane *Prologue,* to both of which the reviewer alludes, objective criticism is much less evident than praise which is excessive for the occasion. This subjectivism must have been apparent to the reviewer also, who added for authority that "Mr. Johnson is well known to be perfectly acquainted with the rise and progress of English literature, and the various provincial dialects, and peculiar modes of phraseology, which were used by contemporary writers, and which Shakespeare has interwoven into his diction." The recognition stated in these claims a year after Johnson had begun to work for the *Literary Magazine* indicates that he enjoyed the continuing high regard of the proprietors.

Because of Johnson's customary reticence about his journalism, the record of his contributions to the *Literary Magazine* is incomplete. Whatever importance is to be attached to this work today, Johnson himself was casual about it, as may be inferred from a letter to Charles Burney, dated March 8, 1758. "Since the Life of Brown I have been a little engaged, from time to time in the *Literary Magazine,* but not very lately." The implication, thus, is that he regarded the magazine as only part-time employment. But by 1758 he was less reluctant to acknowledge his association with the magazine than when he had written to Chambers. Apparently in response to an inquiry, Johnson told Burney: "I have not the collection by me, and therefore cannot draw out a catalogue of my own parts, but will do it, and send it. Do not buy them, for I will gather all those that have anything of mine in them, and send them to Mrs. Burney, as a small token of gratitude for the regard which she is pleased to bestow upon me."[13] If there ever was such a list, then, it was merely in marked numbers of the *Literary Magazine* which Johnson sent to the Burneys. Boswell attributed to him the preface, at least five essays, and twenty-five reviews, although he probably did more. At any rate, Johnson's connection with the *Literary Magazine* was not long a secret

in literary London. William Kenrick, who for years feuded publicly
with Johnson, charged him with making "several efforts to assume a
kind of dictatorship over a certain periodical review, interfering on
subjects of which he was consummately ignorant."[14] Although Kenrick exaggerated in this allusion, undoubtedly to the *Literary Magazine,* there is no question of Johnson's range, which in fact partially
typifies the variety of the *Literary Magazine.* His essays were primarily political in content, and his reviews, representative of the
reading tastes of the latter half of the century, were of books en-
compassing subjects from morality to mechanics and science. Yet,
if his span was comprehensive, it was no more so than that which he
had projected for his own *Bibliothèque.*

As his first public assignment, Johnson was given the writing of
the preliminary address *To the Public* (No. 1, pp. iii-iv), and the
pattern which he had set himself in the *Gentleman's Magazine* he
now followed in his descriptive introduction to the *Literary Magazine.* Obviously mindful of his start in London journalism, Johnson
wrote that "the well-deserved popularity of the first undertaking of
this kind, has now made it almost necessary to prefix the name of
'magazine.' " The old violence was gone, however, and Johnson
substituted dignity (though touches of irony were not wanting).
To support his promise of exactness and variety, he announced "a
selection has been made of men qualified for the different parts of
the work, and each has the employment assigned him, which he is
supposed most able to discharge." Among those whose expert services
were solicited were the poet-dramatist-journalist Arthur Murphy, the
journalist Griffith Jones, Chambers, and perhaps Goldsmith.[15]

In describing the projected departments of the new journal,
Johnson was speaking with the objective voice of an editorial employee, though there is in the preface a limited relationship between
his claims for the *Literary Magazine* and his personal feelings about
the ephemeral contents of most periodicals. For instance, he wrote
of the journal's aim of recording "every remarkable event, extraordinary casualty, uncommon performance, or striking novelty"
that happened in England. Most of the details which qualified under
this statement came to be incorporated in a regular department known
as the *Chronological Diary,* and in the customary reports of deaths,
births, marriages, military promotions, and market news. But Johnson

also added with characteristic disdain that the *Literary Magazine* would apply its "care to the discovery of truth, with very little reliance on the daily historians." The claim, it might be noted, was more accurate than its fulfillment. He also conceded the needs of "a paper designed for general perusal." Thus, "the elegant trifles of literature, the wild strains of fancy, the pleasing amusements of harmless wit, shall therefore be considered as necessary to our collection." One can guess that Johnson was anticipating such articles as those "On the Inconveniencies and Disorders Arising from Strait Lacing in Stays," on manufacturing processes, bee keeping, curing epilepsy by firing a gun, the use of potatoes as an inexpensive food, and the like. Except for the book reviews which appeared regularly in the first volume, "the elegant trifles of literature" were many and worthwhile belletristic essays few. The most notable of the latter were reprintings of the *Connoisseur,* the *World,* the *Monitor,* the *Idler,* No. 6 (May, 1758) and No. 15 (July, 1758), and Faden's *Westminster Journal.* The occasional original pieces on the arts dealt with such hackneyed subjects as *Some Thoughts on the Origin of Painting,* heavily satiric *Canons of Criticism,* a *Letter on Criticism, An Essay on the Form and Structure of the Ancient Theatres,* a *History of the English Language,* attacks on and vindications of Garrick's talent. Somewhat more significant was a criticism of the censorship imposed by the Presbytery of Scotland on John Home's tragedy *Douglas,* with a defense of the play by David Hume (March, 1757).[16] Music and poetry of mixed quality also appeared each month, and the "harmless wit" was represented in vulgar prose and verse.

But the *Literary Magazine,* according to Johnson, had its serious side also, including "some inquiries into the history of nature, which has hitherto been treated as if mankind were afraid of exhausting it." Essays on sea cows, elephants, and other esoteric creatures, with elaborate engravings were prominent, as were essays on physiology. More important, however, were the political articles which appeared to be the major concern of the *Literary Magazine.* In an echo of his earlier *Debates,* Johnson cited the magazine's intention of reporting parliamentary procedures. Especially pertinent here is the veiled confession of his practice while he worked for Cave.

The chief political object of an Englishman's attention must be the great Council of the Nation, and we shall therefore register all public proceedings with particular care. We shall not attempt to give any regular series of debates, or to amuse our readers with senatorial rhetoric. *The speeches inserted in other papers have been long known to be fictitious, and produced sometimes by men who never heard the debate, nor had any authentic information.* [Italics are mine.] We have no intention to impose thus grossly on our readers, and shall therefore give the arguments used in the discussion of every question, and add, when they can be obtained, the names of the speakers.

Actually, parliamentary reports appeared in the *Literary Magazine* infrequently and in various manners—as direct quotations of official correspondence, apparently from authorized sources, and as parts of the *Chronological Diary* and *Historical Memoirs*. Unlike the earlier Lilliputian debates, these were soberly factual. The main political stress of the *Literary Magazine* fell on foreign affairs, its anti-French attitudes being pronounced and articles on Anglo-French colonial aspirations numerous. The other topic of continuing interest was Prussia's wars in Europe. Supplementing these matters were illustrations: maps of various sectors in Britain's world sphere were regular features of the monthly numbers; and a picture of "St. George destroying Universal Monarchy in the Character of France" preceded volume II. As an aid to its readers in this period of shifting European politics, the *Literary Magazine* published "An Alphabetical List of the Sovereign Princes in Europe" (No. 2, p. 100). That Johnson wrote several articles on British colonialism and Prussian militarism has been generally accepted, and they will be discussed in a subsequent section. It is also very likely that in his editorial capacity he was responsible for further writing—either through the editing of essays composed by others or through compositions of his own. These conjectural matters will be taken up as a part of the discussion of Johnson's political compositions for the *Literary Magazine*.

Not since his services for the *Gentleman's Magazine* had Johnson examined political questions in his journalistic writings, but the political essays which he composed for the *Literary Magazine* are indicative of his continuing grasp of current affairs and of his extensive reading. Independent and bold of judgment, they effectively negate the popular error that Johnson was an undeviating conformist. Two of the essays are strong attacks on British colonial policy combined with a censorious view of Anglo-French conduct in America. The first is *An Introduction to the Political State of Great Britain* (No. 1, pp. 1-9), a summation of Britain's political fortunes from the reign of Elizabeth to the year 1756, in the course of which he described his nation's many wars and the rise to power of the Netherlands and France. The essay culminated with a description of the war in America between England and France. Unsparing of Britain's failures in America, he made numerous indictments, including the inability of venal British traders to compete with the French, the military incompetence of Braddock,[17] a series of indecisive monarchs since James I. The second essay is *Observations on the Present State of Affairs* (No. 4, pp. 161-165), a consideration of the war in America, with severe criticism of French and English colonialism.

Throughout these essays, it is apparent that political happenings provide the subject matter for Johnson but that his comments have more lasting and penetrating values, some of which are broadly humanitarian and some politically philosophical; but still others, it must be observed, are frankly personal, such as his distrust of Charles II's Catholicism. Thus, in both the *Political State of Great Britain* and the *Present State of Affairs* he repudiated the French and the British for their mistreatment of the Indians. The fact that he regarded all savages as inferior beings did not encourage him to tolerate abuse of them. The British, he wrote in the *Political State,* "continue to shew every day by new proofs, that no people can be great who have ceased to be virtuous." By the same token, he objected to colonialism as a form of political expedience devoid of moral incentive. "We seem to have snatched [the American colonies] into our hands, upon no very just principles of policy, only because every state, according to a prejudice of long continuance, concludes itself more powerful as its territories become larger." This principle of aggrandizement which he damned in nations he also damned in individuals. As the British government ruthlessly extended her borders, her traders fattened their purses, defying the colonial governor when it was advantageous. The same thought was to appear many years later in *Taxation no Tyranny,* where Johnson termed "sons of enterprise" those colonists who "with, or without the consent of their countrymen or governours, went out to see what better regions they could occupy, and in what place, by conquest or treaty, they could gain a habitation . . . if they conquered, they conquered for themselves."[18] To a man as highly civilized as Johnson, colonialism meant a barbaric existence which could be justified only by the desire for gain or escape from misfortune. Although he mentions only the first in the *Political State,* the second must be considered as one of the personal reasons for his detesting migration. As he wrote in the *Life of Savage,* men go to "the remotest corners of the world, to avoid those hardships which they suffer or fear in their native place."[19] In this connection, his characteristically antipathetic attitude toward the New World is illuminating. Canada he regarded as "a cold, uncomfortable, uninviting region, from which nothing but furs and fish were to be had, and where the new inhabitants could only pass a laborious and necessitous life in perpetual regret of the deliciousness and plenty of their native country."[20]

In his *Present State of Affairs,* Johnson continued to belabor British colonial policy, but he also extended his remarks to a criticism of the French. He bluntly accused both nations of setting material or military gain before social interest, like two highwaymen quarreling for "the spoils of a passenger." Both nations, he concluded, were deluding their citizens about the causes of the American war, which had nothing to do with social good. Hidden in a "mist of controversy," "those whom the truth will not favour, will not step voluntarily forth to tell it, and where there are many agents, it is easy for every single action to be concealed." The French, whom he considered superior colonists, had achieved their excellence by ignoring the rights of other nations. Living under an absolute form of government in which debate was not tolerated, "they have no wish but for conquest, of which they justly consider riches as the consequence." But the British love of independence (as he remarked in the *Political State*), inviting an excessive practice of *laissez-faire,* brought its own, contrary ills in making the state subordinate to the individual. Although Johnson deplored despotism he advocated, as always, the restraint upon personal actions inherent in a large, unified order which operated for the benefit of the many. Rather than hasten "through by-paths to private profit," individuals should coöperate "in one great scheme." Somewhere between the extremes of absolutism and total freedom lay Johnson's ideal government. And it was an ideal which he could apply to colonial ventures as well as to domestic rule.

These two essays, comparable in places to the cogent reasoning and balance of the *Rambler,* vindicate Boswell's contention that Johnson's political character "has been misrepresented as abjectly submissive to power."[21] They are consistent with his respect for the delegated authority by which national actions are carried out and with his reserving for the people a right to examine and criticize the efficiency of those decisions which affect their well-being. Few men of his day could have been less abjectly submissive than Johnson to rash or willful authority, nor more respectful of its proper use. Perhaps, however, he was too forthright; for though a continuation of the *Present State* was promised readers of the *Literary Magazine,* none was ever published.

But colonialism was an absorbing topic for Englishmen in 1756, and the *Literary Magazine* had more to say about it than had been printed in the *Political State* and the *Present State.* Johnson, obviously steeped in the subject, was the magazine's chief political commentator. To him, therefore, probably went the task of continuing the flow of colonial observations, either in essays of his own or in editorial advice to others. Stimulating as is the search for hidden essays by Johnson, it is to be pursued with caution. A style as individualized as his frequently lent itself to imitation, and to state positively that an unacknowledged piece was written by him can be a disservice. Occasionally, however, a hint is turned up which fosters interesting speculation. One such hint is to be found in the now rare volume XIV, which John Stockdale and George Robinson added in 1788 to Hawkins' edition of Johnson's works. They reprinted from the June, 1756, *Literary Magazine* (No. 2, pp. 66-67) *Observations on the Foregoing Letter* as Johnson's response to *A Letter from a French Refugee in America to his Friend a Gentleman in England,* in the same number. Either because of skepticism or indifference to a minor journalistic essay, Johnsonians until recently have been content to take no further note of the *Observations on the Letter.*[22] Considered now in the light of Johnson's editorial position on the *Literary Magazine,* the two political essays already discussed, and characteristic attitudes, it warrants discussion.

The *Letter,* signed "Gallo-Anglus," is concerned with various complaints of the American colonists against the treatment they were receiving from England. The *Observations on the Letter* is a considerably more patriotic commentary than either the *Political State* or the *Present State.* But implicit in it, again, is the hostility to colonialism observable elsewhere in Johnson's writings. "Gallo-Anglus," for instance, had objected that beggars and idlers were being sent to America, colonialism thus serving as a means of removing undesirable citizens from England. Denying that beggary or idleness could be remedied by exile, the author of the *Observations* agreed that "the number, whom misery, terror and want drive into America, is already too great." "To free ourselves from beggars and strollers by sending them to America, is to cure an ulcer by cutting off the limb." Consistent with Johnson's opinions, then, the view here is that colonialism is too often a device for punishment or for the spurious obliteration of ills which require social action.

At the same time, however, the *Observations on the Letter* expresses irritation at "Gallo-Anglus' " reluctance to use America as a market for British goods.

If the American colonies can support themselves against their enemies, to what do they owe that strength, but to the protection of England, and how can they repay it but by contributing to the wealth of that country which protected them in their helpless state, on condition that they should obey her laws, and promote her interest.

This is the same kind of reasoning which Johnson later developed in his political pamphlets, especially *Taxation no Tyranny,* of which the *Observations* is in places a seeming anticipation. Colonies "are governed by English laws, entitled to English dignities, regulated by English counsels, and protected by English arms; and it seems to follow, by consequence not easily avoided, that they are subject to English government, and chargeable by English taxation."[23] Also familiar as one of Johnson's beliefs is the displeasure expressed by the author of the *Observations* regarding governmental restrictions, for they "always produce discontent and an habitual violation of laws, and, perhaps, seldom contribute much to the end proposed. But whether wise or not they may be undoubtedly just." The tone and attitude of this statement are so frequently enunciated throughout Johnson's conversations and writings that supporting quotations are unnecessary.[24] The opinions in the *Observations on the Letter*—patriotic toward England and paternalistic toward the Colonies—should not be interpreted as a contradiction of the thoughts expressed in the two previous essays. All three are concerned with colonial problems, but with different aspects of them. The first two, honestly critical of political and military ineptness, represent Johnson's concept of the democratic process, in which all citizens have the right and duty of questioning the follies of authority. The third, a summary examination of the responsibilities of English subjects—as he insisted upon regarding all persons of British birth, regardless of their place of residence—disseminates familiar convictions which Johnson cherished, especially in his middle and late years. On the basis of content, then, and the further evidence which may be deduced from Johnson's activities for the *Literary Magazine,* the acceptance of the *Observations on the Letter* as his appears justified.

Erroneous conclusions could be drawn from the testimony of Johnson and Murphy that the former did not give much of his time to the *Literary Magazine,* because Johnson when he worked was capable of diversified and prodigious effort. The rapidity with which he wrote for periodicals and adapted himself to new situations probably made the labors he performed seem less taxing to him than they would to others. Nor can his journalistic work be measured only by the compositions of his own pen. There is no way of knowing how much editorial advice he gave and how much editing or rewriting he did on the pieces of others. Yet, remembering how he reworked some of Guthrie's *Parliamentary Debates* in the *Gentleman's Magazine,* one supposes his experiences would have been utilized and therefore seeks signs of comparable activity among the political items of the *Literary Magazine.* The most probable area of his editorial interest would have been the *Historical Memoirs,* a regular department of observations on public affairs. Except for extracts, in the first number, of official correspondence from Whitehall, the *Historical Memoirs* was devoted mainly to foreign matters. In the first three numbers, especially, much space was given to the hostility in America between England and France. In other numbers England's treaties with European powers and Prussian militarism were prominent parts of the *Historical Memoirs.* The fact that Johnson wrote essays on these topics would seem to assure his competence as the editorial spokesman of the *Literary Magazine*. For the most part, however, the *Historical Memoirs* is sufficiently neutral in style to make one believe that it was the collaborative effort of several hands. That Johnson aided in the selection of material for it is likely but undemonstrable. That he actually wrote portions of it is similarly an attractive possibility, though wanting factual confirmation. Nevertheless, at least one section of the *Historical Memoirs* (No. 3, pp. 153-156) contains remarks so strikingly Johnsonian in attitude and style that it is worth reproducing for consideration.

In our last we laid before the public some important facts, which paved the way for our enemies to excite in our friendly Indians in North America that jealousy of our proceedings, which has so easily inclined them to take up the hatchet against us.

While the French have been endeavouring by every artifice that human policy could suggest to establish an interest among them, our Governors there, trusting to the increasing strength of the rising colonies, or perhaps having an eye only to their present gain, have for a series of years past taken no care to cultivate new friendships with the ancient inhabitants, nor has the government been at much expence to cement the old.

A people, therefore, thus neglected by one foreign nation, and courted by another, could not remain for ever in doubt to which side to join their force. War was both their pride and their profession; and they saw this additional motive to determine their choice, that the French were in general poor, active, and enterprising;[25] the English wealthy, laborious, and peaceable; hence they could not but conclude that as the spoils would be greater by warring against the latter; the hazard in obtaining those spoils would also be less.

These sentiments of the savages, so favourable to the views of France, and so artfully instilled, the enemy took every opportunity to improve; and soon formed projects of making trials how far this new doctrine would operate upon minds who had no idea of the advantages of property otherwise than by the present enjoyment of it: . . .

Again, though there can be no certainty that this passage is by Johnson, outward evidence favors the ascription. The stylistic test— without launching into tedious analysis—is provocative, especially of the use of antitheses, balance, and triplets, favorite devices found in the *Rambler*. On the other hand, there are some signs of haste as though Johnson (if he were the author) were not at his best. Nor would one expect him to be in a periodical essay dashed off under the pressure of a deadline. Most satisfying for speculation is the nature of the contents, which substantially reiterate what he had to say in the *Political State* and the *Present State*. The only discrepancy is that the alienation of the Indians is blamed on the French alone, while the English are placed in the virtuous position of being their friends. The author, it may be assumed, deliberately ignored the mistreatment of the Indians of which the British traders were accused in another essay. The *Historical Memoirs* under consideration contains special pleading which would not benefit from a strict adherence to accuracy. Whatever Johnson's real opinion might have been, he was expressing the editorial convictions of the magazine. For the journalistic purpose at hand this practice is no more surprising than his fabrications of the *Debates*.

Colonialism was but one aspect of English militarism for the *Literary Magazine*'s news and articles. At home, fear of a French invasion and a suddenly acute realization of the inadequacy of domestic defense resulted in the controversial Militia Bill of 1756. On the Continent, England hoped to supplement her own troops with foreign mercenaries through negotiations with Russia and Hesse Cassel. Meanwhile, the martial activities of Frederick the Great, affecting the European balance of power, were of major concern to the British. The *Literary Magazine* followed these momentous events in a steady succession of reports, many of them in the *Historical Memoirs,* and others in separate articles. That Johnson was well informed about these military matters is evident from his essays.

Like many topics about which he wrote during his journalistic career, these concerned with militarism were close to his own interests, personally and philosophically. "Every man," he once remarked, "thinks meanly of himself for not having been a soldier, or not having been at sea." This void in his own experience he nearly filled when he was conscripted for the London militia, "the trained bands" of the local defense. He did not serve, but he took a serious view of the responsibility, providing himself with a musket and sword. He enjoyed discussing the technicalities of firearms and gunpowder, and watching military maneuvers at close range. Nevertheless, the realities of military life were abhorrent to him. And though at times he fancied the glory which befell generals and admirals, he was pained by the living conditions, low pay, and dangers of common soldiers. But he also detested the immorality which he ascribed to them. In *Idler,* No. 21, he held "the most contemptible of all human stations, that of a soldier in time of peace." Soldiers as a whole, he said in *Marmor Norfolciense,* are a "pestiferous brood" guilty of "corruption, rapine, pollution, and devastation." War was to him "the last of remedies, 'cuncta prius tentanda,' " and "all lawful expedients must be used to avoid it." *Falkland's Islands,* in which he made this observation, was for Adam Smith an impressive pamphlet, "as it displayed in such forcible language, the madness of modern wars."[26]

"But surely war has its laws," Johnson maintained in *Rambler,* No. 79, "and ought to be conducted with some regard to the universal interest of man." Perhaps the only instance of "universal interest" in Johnson's ethic which would justify war was the protection of one's shores against invasion. As an advocate of nationalism and the defense of England by Englishmen, he gave limited approval in the *Literary Magazine* to Pitt's Militia Bill (No. 2, pp. 57-64), from which he quoted and found good in its "fundamental parts."[27] The act provided for the drafting of men between the ages of eighteen and fifty, and the exemption of militia officers, peers, university residents, office clerks, seamen, local government officials, and "papists, quakers, or men laboring under bodily infirmity." Johnson was for exempting also surgeons and attorneys. As usual, he thought of public issues in terms of his private morality. When he came to the clause of the Militia Bill setting the punishment for drunkenness, therefore, he proposed more severe discipline than the stocks and forfeiture of pay. Distrusting the use of liquor by himself and others, Johnson was at this time abstaining totally.[28] Implicit in his recommendation, thus, is a self-righteous attitude which caused him to expect of others the same kinds of denials which he imposed upon himself.

Most pertinent for the modern reader of Johnson's observations on the Militia Bill, however, is his repugnance of the provisions causing conscriptees to take an oath of allegiance to the king. Appalled by any suspicion of rebellion or disaffection toward the royal family, Johnson maintained that the oath would increase no man's loyalty, and might even stimulate doubts. The mere taking of an oath, he averred, is no assurance of loyalty, which cannot be forced. A loyal citizen gives his allegiance through choice and conscience. Oaths have only the purpose of exacting overt conformity, insistence upon this meaningless ritual inviting irreligion. "The frequent imposition of oaths has almost ruined the morals of this unhappy nation, and of a nation without morals it is of small importance who shall be king." There was, in fact, never any question in Johnson's mind that an oath must be taken reverentially. In the *Dictionary,* for instance, he defined it as "an affirmation, negation, or promise, corroborated by the attestation of the Divine Being." On at least one occasion, furthermore, he asserted that the sanction of an oath was binding, that it compelled truthfulness because of its sacred nature. But he was not always this convinced that an oath must elicit awe from the participant. Even as he questioned the validity of military oaths, he said, "To oblige people to take oaths as to the disputed right [of the Stuart succession], is wrong. I know not whether I could take them: but I do not blame those who do." And Elijah Fenton's "refusing to qualify himself for publick employment by the oaths required" Johnson called "perverseness of integrity."[29] In short, he was transigent on the subject. An oath taken under compulsion was a violation of religious principle and its essence was thus enervated. On the other hand, an oath taken voluntarily upon a truly meaningful or elevated occasion guaranteed observance without any external prompting. The flexibility of Johnson's opinion, however, was intended for others. As he said, "what is fit for Hephaestion is not fit for Alexander." He himself would never take an oath whose spirit he did not intend to keep, nor would he take an oath if he could not subscribe to the occasion which provoked it.

Disapproving the oath demanded in the Militia Bill, he proposed as an alternative to "let the officers who must be supposed to know the state of their own counties choose those whom the government may trust without an oath." He objected that the provisions of the bill forcing men to swear to the size of their estates was an affront to respectable Englishmen. While appearing to illustrate thus a certain democratic regard for the rights of individuals, he at the same time asserted, with dubious logic, that respected landowners would make respected officers in the field.

The regulation of military rank in the national army, by the gradations of property, is rational and just. The man who hazards most has most right to be trusted, and men willingly obey in the field those whom they are accustomed to respect in all other places.

More than mere naïveté, such an attitude was the outgrowth of a rooted, traditional respect for the gentry which blinded him to military exigencies. It was the opinion of one who believed unalterably that property is "a great principle in society."[30]

The same patriotic spirit which drew Johnson's approval for substantial portions of the Militia Bill caused him to repudiate in the *Literary Magazine* (No. 3, pp. 113-121) England's treaties with Russia and Hesse Cassel. Owing to native distaste for a large standing army and to a vulnerable geographical position which made this bias impractical, England frequently during the eighteenth century had the humiliating necessity of soliciting foreign troops for her defense and for her Continental military objectives. So motivated, her ministers negotiated the treaties with Russia and Hesse Cassel in 1755, placing a large number of troops at the disposal of England in Europe. The Russian treaty was never put into operation; but in 1756, under the threat of a French invasion, mercenaries from Hesse and Hanover were brought to England for her defense.[31] The Militia Bill might have resolved the embarrassment of foreign assistance, but it was overwhelmingly defeated by the Lords after the Commons had passed it.

Johnson, who objected to this outside help and recommended instead passage of the Militia Bill, took the critical view that the English were deluding themselves about the possibility of saving money where arms were concerned. The words which he once quoted as Pulteney's[32] appear to sum up his own skepticism about treaties as

the artillery of our enemies, to which we have nothing to oppose; they are weapons of which we know not the use, and which we can only escape by not coming within their reach. I know not by what fatality it is, that to treat and be cheated, are, with regard to Britons, words of the same signification.

Arguing that the exchequer was paying money to mercenaries for the protection of England, and that economy under such a condition was impossible, Johnson questioned the motives of the ministry in committing the country to the treaties with Russia and Hesse Cassel.

What honours our ministers and negotiators may expect to be paid to their wisdom it is hard to determine, for the demands of vanity are not easily estimated. They should consider before they call too loudly for encomiums, that they live in an age when the power of gold is no longer a secret, and in which no man finds much difficulty in making a bargain with bounty in his hand.

Were invasion to come, Johnson reasoned, it would come by sea; therefore, ships and sailors were required more than land troops. Even more significant as a representation of his political philosophy was his contention that the protection of England was a responsibility of Englishmen for which they were equipped with "strength, and skill, and courage equal to the best of the nations of the continent." Fired with this strong conviction, he went on to say:

We have long been without the need of arms by our good fortune, and long without the use by our negligence, so long that the practice and almost the name of our old trained-bands is forgotten.[33] But the story of ancient times will tell us, that the trained-bands were once able to maintain the quiet and safety of their country, and reason without history will inform us, that those men are most likely to fight bravely, or at least obstinately, who fight for their own houses and farms, for their own wives and children.

Proud and energetic as he is here, Johnson must have visualized himself shouldering his musket, a staunch defender of England. And it must be admitted, for all the incongruity of the image, that he could undoubtedly have worked himself into a properly aggressive frame of mind for such a satisfying venture as beating off foreign hordes.

From a journalistic point of view, the years 1756-57 offered remarkably exciting fare, because warlike activities invariably seize the public imagination. Colonialism, local defense, and foreign alliances gave periodicals like the *Literary Magazine* much to capitalize upon. But these were, after all, general and even impersonal matters of national policy. Fortuitously, however, there were dramatic issues which could be translated into more personal terms, and a dynamic figure who activated much of the drama. Under the leadership of Frederick the Great (1712-1786), Prussia was beginning to emerge as a first-rate European power. In 1756 began the Seven Years' War in which he, with only England as an ally, was opposed by a powerful union of European nations, including Austria, France, Russia,

Saxony, Sweden, and the Holy Roman Empire.[34] Intimately affected by Frederick's aspirations, thus, English readers closely followed reports of his campaigns. The *Literary Magazine* acknowledged this curiosity by devoting to news about Frederick and Prussia's wars a portion of the *Historical Memoirs* in September, 1756, and then, beginning with the October number, making the *Historical Memoirs* virtually a department of Prussian news.

To provide a critical background for these contemporary reports, Johnson in November began a "profile" on Frederick, entitled *Memoirs of the King of Prussia.* Covering the period from his ascension to the throne in 1740 to 1745, the article appeared in three successive numbers of the magazine, each installment serving as a leading essay; and it was reprinted several times in subsequent years.[35] Although the *Memoirs* obviously was written to help fulfill the magazine's aim of posting its readers upon events and people of importance, it had for Johnson the additional value of practice in biography. It is reminiscent of his association with the *Gentleman's Magazine* in at least two respects: For one, Johnson probably availed himself of materials he had gathered about fifteen years earlier while writing the *Debates,* in one of which he had recorded at length the parliamentary rhetoric on England's attitude toward the Queen of Hungary.[36] In the account of Frederick, Johnson extensively details the Prussian campaign against Hungary and gives a generally full and authoritative discussion of the quarrelsome relations between the two rulers. The second and more important refraction of Johnson's days with the *Gentleman's Magazine* is that the *Memoirs* constitutes a journalistic biography.

It is subtly divisible according to three premises: personal (biographical), public (political and military), psychological and moralistic (Johnson's subjective commentary interlarded with the first two matters). Although Johnson is comprehensive about Frederick's public career, regarding it as common knowledge he is often reluctant to discuss it except as it symbolizes the Prussian's personality. To describe battles, for instance, "would be tedious and useless." Nor would there be any need to exploit particulars which would be taken up periodically in the *Historical Memoirs* or were already recorded in history. As a biographer, however, Johnson was concerned with discovering everything possible about Frederick's background and inner nature, and with evaluating his findings. The biography thus has mere passing interest for its historical content, but genuine significance for Johnson's psychological and moralistic asides. The biographical technique, intermingling general and particular details, is consequently similar to that which he had employed in his earlier lives and is perhaps more polished.

In order to understand Frederick, Johnson at first explores the relationship between father (Frederick William I) and son. "In every performance, perhaps in every great character, part is the gift of nature, part the contribution of accident, and part, very often not the greatest part, the effect of voluntary election, and regular design." Oppressed by a cruel, tyrannical father, but endowed with acute talents, Frederick, according to Johnson, combined the gifts of heredity and will to condition himself for his future kingly role. His study of the Prussian led Johnson into numerous reflections, not only on tyranny, but on the education of princes, on intellectual attainments, and even on the worthlessness of Voltaire as a historian,[37] and the corruption of professional soldiers. Of these subjects, Johnson had most to say about Frederick's mathematical-artistic accomplishments and his respect for learning, even as he had centered attention upon intellectualism, wherever possible, in the *Gentleman's Magazine*. Always attracted to the study of law, Johnson digressed admiringly upon the enlightenment which made Frederick the compiler of a new body of law in a single volume, the *Code Frédérique*, as it was known; and he observed that the Prussian was "always propense toward the side of mercy." Frederick's opposition to duelling and his preference for having personal insults or injuries arbitrated was for Johnson another source of satisfaction.[38]

The humanitarian side of Frederick's life did, indeed, seem to Johnson wholly admirable. Despite his generosity in admitting this, however, he was profoundly disturbed by negative traits which nearly overshadow the positive in the *Memoirs*. As an example, Johnson questioned Frederick's professions of religious toleration, having "reason to doubt, whether this toleration is the effect of charity or indifference." No matter how eulogistic Johnson was of the Prussian's inner traits and capabilities, he never allowed himself to overlook the fact that his subject was an aggressive warrior whose protests of peacefulness were not to be trusted. Openly and satirically dubious of any "constructive" war, Johnson said: "Princes have this remaining of humanity, that they think themselves obliged not to make war without a reason. Their reasons are, indeed, not always very satisfactory." Frederick's motives, he felt, were of self interest. And "like Caesar . . . he conquered as he advanced." Johnson illustrated this untrustworthiness in discussing the Pragmatic Sanction, which Frederick guaranteed to support, but instead "fell upon the Austrian territories, as upon a dead carcass." The invasion of Bohemia was likewise an instance of unreliable conduct. Bitter as these charges are, they are less damaging than Johnson's accusations of brutality and impiety toward invaded people and insinuations of cowardice on the battlefield. Johnson, however, was not always well informed, for the reflections upon Frederick's courage appear to be historically groundless. Nevertheless, Johnson developed the facts as he thought them to be. Fleeing from the Austrians and returning to the safety of Berlin, Frederick forbade all public mention of the campaign. The censorship provoked Johnson to an angry comment, characteristic of his libertarianism, against undue suppression of any kind. It takes no strong imagination to infer his contempt in reporting that George II ordered in a similar spirit that "none should mention his nephew [Frederick] with disrespect."

The *Memoirs of the King of Prussia* may be regarded as unusually trenchant in consideration of the alliance between England and Prussia. It is, further, an effective crystallization of the views on wars of political intrigue which Johnson had condemned in other statements, in the *Literary Magazine* and elsewhere. Drawn as a sinister, ruthless militarist whose scholarship only partially humanized him, Frederick gave Johnson an excuse to reveal his own forthright liberal instincts, and to continue his animadversions upon English opportunism. Independent and outspoken as always, Johnson appears here as the conscientious apostle of the English people.

The political essays in the *Literary Magazine* were not so much a new kind of journalistic endeavor for Johnson as they were an extension of work he had already done for the *Gentleman's Magazine*. Broadly comparable to the *Parliamentary Debates* and the biographies, his efforts—and certainly this is true of the *Memoirs* of Frederick—are equal to most of the things which he wrote for the *Gentleman's Magazine.* One can only guess why he terminated his connection with the *Literary Magazine,* yet there are clues. Contrary to expectation, he seems to have exerted less influence upon the proprietors in literary matters, which were properly his concern, than in political. During the existence of the magazine, they sporadically published literary essays, few of which were of a quality likely to be acceptable to Johnson. The book review section started promisingly enough, and then it was permitted to lapse, even before his last contribution in July, 1757. All but about three of his own reviews appeared before the end of 1756; then, except for the important reviews of Jonas Hanway and Soame Jenyns between May and July, 1757, Johnson ceased to function as a reviewer. The second and third volumes of the *Literary Magazine* are similarly indicative of the sagging cultural spirit of the magazine. This diminution of reviews after the first volume constitutes the only observable alteration in the original plan of the *Literary Magazine.* But this significant change, reëmphasizing the miscellany's special attitude toward politics and religion,[39] occurred while Johnson was still holding a responsible position. Meanwhile, though contemptuous of news reports and limited in his regard for history, he had to write both. Giving ample proof of his political understanding, he nevertheless did not concentrate willingly on temporal matters. The magazine's intensified focus on prejudiced, non-literary articles therefore perhaps represents an editorial policy to which he objected.

There may have been other reasons for his withdrawal: perhaps he foresaw that the magazine—largely second-rate in quality and partisan—was creating a self-destructive limitation; perhaps he was engaged in other projects; perhaps he had differences of opinion over financial policy. Is there, furthermore, a hint that Johnson himself had fallen out of favor with the proprietors? In January, 1758 (pp. 6-8), the *Literary Magazine* published a *Poetical Scale* for scoring the merits of poets from Chaucer to Hughes. Among the eighteenth-century names—including Steele, Addison, Prior, Swift, Pope, Thomson—that of Samuel Johnson is prominently missing. The omission is at best a most surprising one, after *London* and the

Vanity of Human Wishes, and the glowing review of the Shakespeare proposals. The *Poetical Scale* is helpful not only in establishing a contemporary critical attitude toward Johnson, but in assessing his later relationship with the magazine. At one time the article was attributed to him and he denied authorship, adding with an emphasis implicit in the written words: "I fancy it was put in after I had quitted that work [the *Literary Magazine*]; for I not only did not write it, but do not remember it."[40] Of course, there cannot be ignored the possibility that the editors of the magazine accepted the review of the proposals and the *Poetical Scale* for their separate merits, without regard for personal feeling. But periodicals like the *Literary Magazine* were not customarily judicial, impartial forums, and circumstantially it appears that the earlier associations were strained and some kind of alienation or disaffection caused Johnson's voluntary separation from his editorial friends. Whatever the cause, Johnson could ill afford to give up his employment, and he certainly delayed as little as possible the inauguration of the *Idler,* which probably gave him a comparable source of income.

II

THE *Student*

English literary journalism of the mid-eighteenth century was concentrated in London, but infrequently attempts were made to establish periodicals in the provinces. The enterprising John Newbery foresaw the prestige of publishing in the university cities, and as a result he affiliated with John Barrett of Oxford to inaugurate in January, 1750, the *Student; or the Oxford Monthly Miscellany,* a sixpenny magazine devoted to polite literature. It presented a variety of poetry and essays on morality, history, and criticism, while eschewing politics. The first five numbers of the *Student,* bearing the names of Newbery and Barrett, appeared to emanate from both London and Oxford. Then, in June, J. Merrill was named as the Cambridge publisher, and the subtitle was enlarged to the *Oxford and Cambridge Monthly Miscellany.* Beginning with the sixth number, also, Christopher Smart became the principal contributor.[41] Others who wrote for the magazine were Johnson, Thomas Warton (the younger), Richard Rolt, Bonnell Thornton, and George Colman (the elder).

The journalistic associations formed in this connection were to be continued for Johnson.[42]

About the time he was writing his sole article for the *Student,* a biography of Francis Cheynel, Johnson importuned Newbery for money.[43] While this may be taken as evidence of his practical financial concerns, destitution was not the sole reason for his contributing to the *Student.* He was a sympathetic friend of Smart, who in his turn spoke highly of the *Rambler,* lauded it in the *Student* in 1750, and perhaps even borrowed from it.[44] In 1763 Johnson still evinced a paternal affection for the mad poet, who, according to the famous anecdote, "insisted on people praying with him; and I'd as lief pray with Kit Smart as any one else. Another charge was, that he did not love clean linen; and I have no passion for it."[45] And even though Johnson could hope for no large emolument, he was glad to assist Smart in the promotion of the *Student.* Despite its short life—the last number appeared in July, 1751—it was a meritorious publication.

Enhancing the quality of the *Student* in 1751 was Johnson's *Life of Dr. Francis Cheynel* (1608-1665), details of which he drew extensively from Anthony Wood and Edmund Calamy. This biography began in No. 7 and extended through three consecutive issues; it varied in length from nine pages in the first part to three pages in the last, which was signed "S. J——n." The *Life of Cheynel* differed in at least one important respect from the biographies which he had written for the *Gentleman's Magazine:* whereas those had been essentially eulogistic, that of Cheynel is censorious, expressive of Johnson's displeasure with Cheynel's revolutionary activities. Even as he was to take exception in the *Literary Magazine* to Frederick's career because of his own political bias, he now turned his pen against Cheynel because of his religious scruples. A study of this article, indeed, illuminates Johnson's attitude toward the Church of England on the one hand and toward dissenters on the other. About this religious zealot Johnson wrote that he "had qualities, which employed in a good cause, would give him some claim to distinction." But associated as he was with the Puritan uprising, Cheynel gave Johnson little basis for compliment, his name surviving in history only because of its association with the more illustrious

ones of Henry Hammond and William Chillingworth.[46] Of a very
uncertain temper, which Johnson considered deplorable, Cheynel was
denied his bachelor of divinity degree by Oxford because of a quarrel
over predestination. Cheynel was nevertheless permitted to preach.
He next fell out with Archbishop Laud, and at the height of the
controversy over the need for episcopacy, he declared himself a
Presbyterian. Always contentious, Cheynel became active at the outset
of the Civil War. In 1649 he engaged in embarrassing disputes in
Oxford over the source from which Presbyterian ministers derived
their right to preach. He became president of St. John's College although, Johnson asserted, he was not worthy of the position. When
the incumbent offered some objection Cheynel, "with his usual cool-
ness and modesty, took possession of the lodgings by breaking open
the doors." Cheynel continued hostile to opposition and persecuted
non-Presbyterians at Oxford until 1650, when he left the presidency
and retired to Sussex.

As an attack upon Cheynel and seventeenth-century Presbyterianism, the biography would appear to be oddly out of place in
an eighteenth-century literary journal, or at best justifiable as a
piece of Oxford history. While the latter reason certainly should not
be discounted, there were more immediate and subjective causes for
its publication. One should consider, for instance, that the Puritan
spirit became revitalized in the Methodist movement (which also
originated in Oxford), offering a considerably more vital religious
leadership to the middle classes than did the Church of England,
whose influence had been weakened under the Walpole administration. And though the Presbyterians were no longer militant, their
church was undergoing significant developments of doctrine, keeping
their issues alive for inquiring minds.[47] The two creeds, thus, were
attracting wide notice which champions of the Church of England,
like Johnson, hoped to counteract. In the spirit of toleration, Johnson
avoided explicit attacks upon contemporary dissenting groups. As a
historical biographer, however, he had the opportunity to muster
objective evidence against the nonconformity he deplored. The *Life
of Cheynel* has an analogical function, therefore, setting forth historical reasons for questioning dissent; and an exploration of its key
premises illustrates Johnson's own orthodox position.

Presbyterianism, especially that practiced currently in Scotland, always irritated him, so that even in the *Dictionary* he exemplified "presbytery" with an unflattering quotation from John Cleveland. He described Samuel Butler's Presbyterian Justice as one "who, in the confidence of legal authority and the rage of zealous ignorance ranges the country." When he was asked where John Knox was buried, he hoped "in the high-way. I have been looking at his reformations."[48] A trinitarian, furthermore, Johnson could not but be offended by the unitarianism which the Presbyterians espoused. And their "darling doctrine of predestination," as he called it in the Cheynel biography, he held once to be "a part of the clamour of the times." Discussion of this topic vexed him.[49] To him Presbyterianism represented the violation of authority and hierarchy. He argued in the *Life of Cheynel* as he had frequently elsewhere, "as authority is necessary to instruction, whoever endeavours to destroy subordination . . . defeats at once the institution." Ecclesiastical hierarchy, rejected by the Presbyterians, was especially dear to him. Profoundly reverential of this dogma, he paid unusual homage to Anglican dignitaries in whom he saw it represented, discoursed fluently on the theory of hierarchy, and praised Waller's stand against the abolition of episcopacy.[50] Related to Johnson's rational approval of subordination is his attitude toward toleration and persecution. "I am afraid," he said, "there is no other way of ascertaining the truth, but by persecution on the one hand and enduring it on the other." In the same vein he asserted, "Every man has a right to utter what he thinks truth, and every other man has a right to knock him down for it. Martyrdom is the test."[51] The final determination of the degree to which toleration might be allowed was dependent upon the good of the State and Church. Under the compulsion of a choice, the individual must always give way to the institution.

Yet Johnson believed "all denominations of Christians have really little difference in point of doctrine, though they may vary widely in external forms."[52] The pronouncement is nevertheless deceptively liberal, for he had decided opinions about these "external forms." One of them concerned the nature of Presbyterian sermons, which he thought in the *Life of Cheynel* empty and vociferous by comparison with the liturgy of the Church of England. The issue, again,

is less historical than personal, for Johnson is objecting to religious enthusiasm in general. Significantly, he worked in an unfavorable allusion to Methodists "and enthusiasts of all kinds."
Another objectionable feature of Presbyterian worship for him was
the ritual prayer which gave more sanctification to Parliament and
the army than to the King, and which omitted the Lord's prayer.
For this reason, among others, he admitted a preference for Catholicism. The Presbyterians, he said, "have no publick worship: they have
no form of prayer in which they know they are to join. They go to
hear a man pray, and are to judge whether they will join with him."
Abominating what seemed to him an undisciplined and individualized
ritual, he thus agreed to listen privately to a Presbyterian prayer but
would not give sanction by his presence to the assemblage.[53]

While Johnson was not remarkably flexible in his religion, he was
nevertheless capable of making allowances. Hence, he had acknowledged that Cheynel's intrinsic merit was not to be measured by the
limitations of his creed. He evinced the greatest respect for the moral
character of Herman Boerhaave, even though the scientist had exercised a strong influence over the Scottish Presbyterians, and of
Zachariah Mudge, who for a time had been a dissenter. The *Life of
Cheynel,* unfortunately, does not reveal this transigent aspect of
Johnson's personality. As a document philosophically important to
an understanding of Johnson's sense of ecclesiastical and secular
propriety, it is, rather, typical of his predilection for taking sides in
controversies and of his orthodox desire to preserve an established
order. Indeed, he denounced any kind of public upheaval motivated
by emotional rather than rational considerations. Whether concerned
with religious or political enthusiasm, he detested violent change as
a reflection of irresponsible, rabble-minded activity. His feeling for
Cheynel as for Milton was based on his own veneration for depend-
able British institutions and mores. To invoke radical change, especially when the new order was not demonstrably better than the old
and when the new was achieved as a result of mass action, was to
invite Johnson's abhorrence.

For many years he was silent about his authorship of this biography.
But one day in 1773, in Edinburgh, Sir David Dalrymple "told him,
he had discovered the Life of *Cheynel,* in the *Student,* to be his.—

Johnson. 'No one else knows it.' "[54] Perhaps he had become ashamed
of an attack upon a Christian denomination. But equally significant
was his usual persistence in believing that newspapers and magazines
were literary corruptions and that journalism was an undignified
trade. It is no surprise, therefore, that in his writings for periodicals
like the *Gentleman's Magazine,* the *Literary Magazine,* and even the
Rambler (allowing for the convention of the time), Johnson made
every effort to remain anonymous. With rare exceptions, as in the
Life of Cheynel, he preferred to withhold his signature from all but
non-journalistic writings. His first full signature had appeared in
1749 on the title page of the *Vanity of Human Wishes.*

III

THE *Universal Visiter*

Johnson renewed his professional association with Smart when the
unfortunate poet became one of the founders of the *Universal Visiter,
and Monthly Memorialist,* another sixpenny miscellany, which had
a run of twelve numbers in 1756. Typifying eighteenth-century magazines, the *Universal Visiter* was a catch-all of politics, news, vital
statistics, belles-lettres, poetry, and music. Its aim, however, was
preponderantly and affectedly literary. Adorning the title page is
an engraving of an author contemplating five busts: Chaucer, Spenser, Shakespeare, Waller, and Dryden. Beneath are appropriately
laudatory verses, while the magazine's motto is drawn from Chaucer's
description of the Clerk of Oxford. The literary matter, alternating
between light and serious, includes essays on Chaucer, Spenser,
Shakespeare (by Smart), Philips, and Pope (by Johnson). Moralizing
allegories, satirical essays on authorship, and reprints from the *Connoisseur* and the *World* bespeak the influence of the belletristic
tradition. The poetry is of the usual order of eulogies, anacreontics,
and pastorals. The most notable example of poetry originating in the
Universal Visiter is Smart's *Forty-Second Psalm* (October, pp. 471-
474), which also appeared in the *Literary Magazine* (May, 1757,
p. 205). But there are also poems by Colley Cibber and Richard
Rolt. Pope figures prominently through imitations of his poetry,
numerous allusions to him, and Johnson's essay on his epitaphs.
Each issue contains the *Theatrical Diary,* a historically useful calendar

of current Drury Lane productions in which the players are named occasionally. Interspersed among these literary performances are political articles on European militarism, Minorca, Admiral Byng, the militia bill, and the like, as in the *Literary Magazine* and other miscellanies. These pieces were written by Rolt and infrequently by Smart, or they were derived from papers like the *Daily Advertiser* and the *London Gazette*.[55] Conventionally, the *Universal Visiter* assumed a nationalistic and anti-Catholic position. Like the *Literary Magazine* (September, 1756, p. 257), thus, it printed an argument for confining grants of public-house licenses to Protestants (September, pp. 416-422).

Today the *Universal Visiter* is important because of Smart's and Johnson's connection with it; but it has also become a literary curio as a result of the much publicized contract signed by its projectors: Smart and Rolt, the writers; Edmund Allen, a printer; and Thomas Gardner, a bookseller of Temple Bar. By the terms of this contract the writers were to furnish two-thirds of the copy and each was to receive one-fourth of the profits. Then comes the seemingly unusual clause, for the authors agreed that they would not undertake a similar journalistic activity during the life of the *Universal Visiter*, to which they bound their services for ninety-nine years. Should the venture be unprofitable for six months, however, any of the signers could dissolve the contract. For a long time Johnson, who had not seen the contract and whose knowledge was apparently only hearsay, was the sole authority for information about its unusual contents. Then, in 1928, the document was discovered and certain misconceptions perpetuated by Johnson were rectified.[56] For instance, he did not know about the proviso permitting termination of the agreement at the end of six profitless months. Nor did he seem to know that Smart and Rolt could—and did—assume other literary responsibilities, so long as they did not duplicate the *Visiter*. Probably inadvertently, through reliance upon his memory, Johnson distorted some of the essential clauses of the contract, although he remembered broad details. As far as he was concerned the transaction was an infamous one, and it elicited from him one of his few unfavorable opinions of the Trade. At the time he contributed to the *Universal Visiter*, Johnson claimed, he was in ignorance of the terms of the contract; but he was not in ignorance for long. "I hoped [Smart's] wits would soon return to him. Mine returned to me, and I wrote in 'The Universal Visitor' no longer."[57] When Johnson began his connection with the magazine, he did so at least in part as an act of friendship for Smart, whose senses were already failing him. During the first half of the year, Smart had sufficient command of himself, apparently, to continue with part of his burden; or perhaps earlier writings were being introduced into the magazine to fulfill his agreement. By the middle of the year, however, it must have become apparent to Johnson that Smart's situation was hopeless and he indignantly separated himself from the *Universal Visiter*.[58]

If talent alone had been the test of the *Universal Visiter*'s survival, then it should have been a successful periodical, for Garrick, Bishop Percy, and perhaps Dr. Burney, in addition to Johnson, Smart, and Rolt, contributed. But it may be assumed that administrative or economic difficulties beset the magazine. When the January number appeared on February 2, Smart was apparently in charge of the literary department and Rolt was responsible for the political news, as Johnson had been in the *Literary Magazine*. With a weighty editorial responsibility upon a man whose capacity for maintaining it was dubious, Rolt had to diversify his energies and write poetry and literary essays as well as his own political accounts. The outside contributions were helpful, of course, but they were not sufficient to support a journal capable of competing with others. Gardner obviously discovered the need for financial assistance, for though the *Universal Visiter* was first printed for him alone, he was soon joined by other publishers in the venture: B. Davey and H. Law, of Avemary Lane; Stanley Crowder and Henry Woodgate, of Paternoster Row; A[nne?] Dodd, of Temple Bar; and "the booksellers of Great Britain and Ireland."

The *Universal Visiter* was commendably temperate in its introductory statement:

> The following work will be conducted by a society of gentlemen, who, in a great measure, have made it the study of their lives, to aim at some degree of excellence in several branches of writing. . . . In this performance they hope to appear as politicians without party, historians without prejudice, philosophers without moroseness, critics without ill-nature, and as men of rational pleasure without wantonness.

There was some justice to these claims, for if the magazine was not absolutely impartial, as it stated it was, it was certainly more moderate than most. Despite its judiciousness, however, it was received with critical bad taste. The *Critical Review,* which also first began publication at this time, presented specimens from the first number, following this uncharitable observation:

This is a periodical pamphlet proposed to be continued monthly; it consists of several loose pieces in prose and verse, thrown together in the manner of a magazine; from which it differs in having fewer subjects, less variety, and half a sheet more of paper. . . . the *Visiter* is not the child of one father, but the offspring of a little community, the members whereof generously club their wits for public entertainment. . . . The following bagatelles we present for their curiosity; and readily allow them to be the compositions of a graduate in the University of Nonsense; . . .[59]

Stung by the affront to the new periodical and its authors, Smart or one of his coadjutors protested. Because of his infirmity, however, Smart was cruelly vulnerable, and the *Critical Review* was inspired to make an even harsher attack in which it paraphrased a line (156) from Pope's *Epistle to Dr. Arbuthnot.* "[The Critical Reviewers] have nothing to say to the Visiter, but that *they wage no war with Bedlam and the Mint.*"[60]

The outlook for the *Universal Visiter* could not have seemed promising to Johnson; yet he grudgingly lent his pen to the miscellany through May of 1756. Criticism such as that of the *Critical Review* would not have affected him, for he was accustomed to journalistic name-calling. At the same time, loyalty to his friend and the opportunity of earning a few guineas might have given him at least a lukewarm attraction to the new venture. The full extent of his writings must remain doubtful until the disclosure of more evidence than is presently available. But with a reasonable certainty, Johnson may be given credit for three essays between the March and May numbers of the *Universal Visiter: Further Thoughts on Agriculture* (March), *Reflections on the Present State of Literature* (April), and a *Dissertation on the Epitaphs Written by Pope* (May). Additionally, note must be taken of three other essays tenuously ascribed to him: *The Life and Writings of Chaucer* (January), *Reflections upon the State of Portugal* (February), and *The Rise, Progress, and Perfection of Architecture* (June). Hawkins, who had observed that the other contributors signed their compositions with the initials of their surnames, first assigned to Johnson all the pieces in the *Universal Visiter* subscribed with two asterisks. But of the six pieces so designated Boswell firmly rejected the last three.[61] A recent attempt to admit the questionable pieces to the canon must for want of substance be viewed cautiously. A Latin poem on page 142, *Nequicquam Danaen includit ahenea turris,* also bearing the two asterisks, has been denied as a product of Johnson's pen.[62] The most authoritative opinion, of course, is Boswell's, and his attributions will be taken up first.

Agriculture would seem an unlikely topic for Johnson, but in *Further Thoughts on Agriculture*[63] he treated it with his accustomed assurance and versatility, demonstrating that he could be as much at ease writing of agricultural economics as discussing a purely literary problem. He drew his immediate motivation from an article by Rolt in February (pp. 59-63), *Some Thoughts on Agriculture; both Ancient and Modern.* Here Rolt had maintained that "the labour of the farmer . . . is now the spring which sets the whole grand machine of commerce in motion." His opinion, further, was that the farmer was "in general too much disregarded among the politer kind of people in the present age," and that only in antiquity had he been properly honored. Although Rolt may have come upon this idea independently, it was not an unusual one. Nor would it be surprising to discover that he had probably consulted Johnson about it. In fact, almost four years earlier, in *Rambler,* No. 145, Johnson had anticipated Rolt partially, lamenting that the farmer was not honored by society in proportion to his accomplishments. At any rate, Johnson was sufficiently familiar with the subject to write *Further Thoughts* as though it were a continuation by the author of *Some Thoughts.* Hawkins, who carelessly overlooked the discrepancies of style in the two essays, was thus misled into attributing to Johnson "two or three letters . . . on the subject of agriculture."

In *Further Thoughts,* Johnson explained that the previous article dealt with the usefulness of agriculture and the present one with its necessity, reiterating that its importance should be acknowledged widely. Only an agriculturally sufficient country, he asserted, can achieve independence. Countries essentially dependent upon commerce may acquire riches, but they must rely upon traffic with other nations. He pointed out that nations like Spain, with mines to provide gold and silver, may starve for want of a sound agricultural economy. In England, Johnson saw the opportunity of achieving a real independence and stability, for the English soil and climate are ideal for the cultivation of edibles. Of course, he inelegantly went on to say, "I am far from intending to persuade my countrymen to quit all other employments to manure the ground." He did, however, wish to place due emphasis upon the importance of the land. Reasonably, he was striving for a fundamental balance. As there could be no ships without trees, there could be no real commerce without agriculture. Ten years later, in his *Considerations on the Corn Laws,* he pursued the need for complementing commerce with agriculture. Johnson's interest in agriculture, thus, was more than a mere fad or an expedient engendered by periodical employment. We are reminded that even though he was a city dweller, he understood the theory and practice of agriculture, from processing malt to thatching a roof.[64] In his Scottish travels, he keenly observed farm practices and commented on their inadequacies as well as on the conditions necessary to a successful agrarian community.[65] And if he had no respect for the moral character of farmers as individuals, he was deeply sympathetic toward the hardships they endured in their tenant-landlord relationships.[66]

Seldom did Johnson let pass an opportunity to protest against the hardships enforced by writing. In his poetry, in his periodical essays, in his conversations, he never tired of animadverting upon the insufficient rewards of professional authorship and the debasement of literature by incompetent hacks. His major serials, indeed, provide a store of angry reflections on the subject. By 1756, when he was forty-seven years old, he had not yet attained that financial security to which he was well entitled. His own poverty continued to haunt him not only as unhappy memories of the past but as the actualities of the present. And had he been able to forget his own experiences, an uneasy conscience would have kept Smart before him as a miserable symbol of an unfortunate social condition. Inevitably, therefore, Johnson made one of his papers for the *Universal Visiter* an attack upon the state of professional authorship. The leading article for April, presented as a letter to the magazine but identified in the

table of contents as *Reflections on the Present State of Literature,*
is comparable in length and contents to many of the *Rambler* essays
on authorship.[67] At the same time, it is more bitter in tone, as a
summation will indicate.

The opening lines from the Ninth Satire of Juvenal, used by
Johnson as motto, instantly afford a caustic revelation:

> *Scire velim, quare totiens mihi, Naevole, tristis*
> *Occurras, fronte obducta ceu Marsya victus.*[68]

Innocent enough in this isolated position, the passage is introductory
to what recently has been called "one of the most shocking poems
ever written."[69] The selection of the Ninth Satire was quite deliberate
as an exemplification of the charges Johnson intended to place
against indiscriminate authorship. Not only did he know thoroughly
the Third and Tenth Satires, which he had imitated, but all the others
as well. He should have liked to render additional satires by Juvenal,
except that some of them "were too gross for imitation."[70] The
significance of this exception must not be overlooked, for while he
never translated or imitated the Ninth Satire, the principals of whom
he was thinking typify the worst depravities of ancient Rome. And
while he never achieved the depth of Juvenal's scorn in his own
Reflections, he was giving subtle literary notice that he associated
the abnormalities of Naevolus and Virro—pervert and patron—with
the unregeneracy of contemporary hacks. Allowance must be made,
of course, for dramatic exaggeration; yet the anger and mockery
implicit here are characteristic of his general attitude toward the
subject.

"Literature," he seriously began, "is a kind of intellectual light,
which, like the light of the sun, may sometimes enable us to see what
we do not like; but who would wish to escape unpleasing objects by
condemning himself to perpetual darkness?" Then, as though he were
expressing confidence that the Juvenalian quotation would give
thoughtful readers a clue to his profoundly moral disapprobation,
he chose to discuss only the lighter, more amusing evils inherent in
professional authorship. A journalistic essay, after all, should entertain as well as instruct, and the occasion was less appropriate to
weighty indictment than to ridicule. Irony, thus, would be a palatable
means of calling attention to the sinister implications which lay very

near the surface, accessible to those who chose to make them so. While admitting the necessity of authorship, Johnson voiced one of his common objections, that those who are too incompetent or indolent to earn their livelihood otherwise frequently turn to writing. For them it is a means of escape from something less pleasant rather than a profession limited to those with a genuine passion and talent for writing. With farmers, sailors, tradesmen, and "ladies of the pen" adopting literature, hack writing had become so extensive that it was no longer confined to Grub Street or Moorfields.[71] "The great misery of writers proceeds from their multitudes." Were he "to form an adage of human misery, or fix the lowest point to which humanity could fall," he would use the life of an author as his standard. Savagely he wrote,

. . . like wolves in long winters, they are forced to prey on one another. The *Reviewers* and the *Critical Reviewers,* the *Remarkers* and *Examiners,* can satisfy their hunger only by devouring their brethren. . . . they are hungry, and hunger must be satisfied; and these savages, when their bellies are full, will fawn on those whom they now bite.

Throughout the essay, then—vigorously, banteringly, ironically, harshly—Johnson emphasized his displeasure with the undignified uses to which authorship was being put.

From the satire of the *Reflections* Johnson turned next to serious if sketchy literary criticism. The *Universal Visiter* printed in May (pp. 207-219) his *Dissertation on the Epitaphs Written by Pope,* an essay later added to the third collected edition of the *Idler* and to the biography of Pope in the *Lives of the English Poets.* Since *An Essay on Epitaphs,* published sixteen years earlier,[72] Johnson's enthusiasm for epitaph-writing had diminished perceptibly. Discussing the mode in general rather than the devices of any writer in particular, he had even complained in 1740 that "no critic of note" had investigated its possibilities. Because everyone, he had reasoned, might expect to be immortalized at some time in an epitaph, it would be fitting to know the genre in which people had always honored their dead. But when in the *Universal Visiter* he came to discuss Pope's practice, he no longer believed epitaphs sufficiently complex or distinctive to merit critical examination. "To define an epitaph is useless; every one knows that it is an inscription on a tomb."[73] Condescendingly, however, he agreed "to entertain the young students in poetry, with an examination of Pope's Epitaphs." For this purpose, at least, he was willing to set forth the fundamental characteristics of epitaphs. In spite of himself, therefore, his observations on the individual epitaphs of Pope constitute his critical judgment of the form.

In the *Essay* he had urged simplicity and such attractive representation that living persons would wish to imitate the subject. In the *Dissertation,* likewise, he proposed as the only restraining or modifying rule for an epitaph, "that it ought not to be longer than common beholders may be expected to have leisure and patience to peruse." Within this limitation he demanded the incorporation of obvious data, such as the names of the subjects. This was a detail of which both Pope and Cowley[74] were sometimes negligent. As for emulation, Johnson assumed an epitaph would be panegyrical and even allowed exaggeration. Eventually he arrived at the axiom, that "In lapidary inscriptions a man is not upon oath."[75] For the most part, Johnson passed judgment on literary failings to be avoided in literature generally rather than in epitaphs alone. Language was of special concern to Johnson, who complained, for instance, of the loose application of the word *sacred,* "which surely should never be applied in a serious composition, but where some reference may be made to a higher being, or where some duty is exacted or implied." Examples of redundancy and grammatical inadequacy also annoyed him, as in the epitaphs on Sir William Trumbull, John Gay, and Sir Godfrey Kneller. Nor did he approve, with respect to the memorial to James Craggs, the intermingling of Latin and English, which is like "the conversation of a foreigner, who tells part of his meaning by words, and conveys part by signs."[76] A comparable inconsistency to which he objected was the use of terminology "too mythological to be admitted into a Christian temple."

The only epitaph of which he approved, indeed, was that "On Mrs. Corbet, Who Died of a Cancer in her Breast." The reason is curiously autobiographical, for he seemed to discover in Mrs. Corbet traits applicable to his own wife. She

is a character not discriminated by any shining or eminent peculiarities, yet that which really makes, though not the splendour, the felicity of life, and that which every wise man will choose for his final and lasting companion in the languor of age, in the quiet of privacy, when he departs weary and disgusted from the ostentatious, the volatile, and the vain.

To these "domestic virtues" Pope's genius did justice; but in none of the other pieces would Johnson deem him successful. He regarded Pope's fourteen epitaphs as prosaic and imitative, containing "more repetitions than will easily be found in all the rest of his works." Contemptuously, he alluded to Pope's "sepulchral performances,"[77] and reproached him for the epitaph on himself, "in which he attempts to be jocular upon one of the few things that make wise men serious." An experienced epitaphist in his own right[78] and fearfully respectful of death, Johnson resented what seemed to him a series of unseemly or unskillful literary exercises.

If one could say confidently, as did Boswell, that Johnson wrote only these three essays for the *Universal Visiter,* then a troublesome bibliographical question could be avoided. The voice of Hawkins, however, is sometimes as commanding as that of Boswell; so we must remember that, in print at least, Hawkins was the first to note the symbols used by Johnson in lieu of a signature. It is possible that someone close to Johnson and familiar with the *Universal Visiter*—if not Johnson himself—mentioned the symbols and that Hawkins assumed all the pieces terminating with the double asterisks were by the same author. The assumption, no matter how logical, could not be strongly defended without other evidence, for the symbols might be regarded as a convenient typographical device for any writer choosing to avoid a signature as distinctive even as a mere initial. Certainly, Hawkins made no more than a desultory inspection of the magazine as compared with Boswell's obviously more careful perusal. Since Boswell was undoubtedly right in attributing the first three pieces, then why was he not equally correct in rejecting the last three?

Unfortunately—or fortunately, as the case may be—a third party desired to identify the writings not only of Johnson but of others connected with the magazine. Ann Gardner (presumably a relative of Thomas Gardner) made ascriptions in her own copy of the *Universal Visiter.* Because a discussion of that episode is now available,[79] it need not be detailed here. Of immediate significance, however, is the fact that she placed Johnson's name opposite each of the six essays in question, but did not so mark the Latin poem. What authority Ann Gardner had for her attributions may never be known, and there is no sign that her facts are any more acceptable than Hawkins'. But even in the absence of any justifiable basis for assuming her accuracy, one should hesitate to reject the three essays without further examination.

Of these three questionable pieces, only one concerns a literary problem. This is *Some Account of the Life and Writings of Chaucer,* which appeared in January (pp. 9-15). Spiritless and frequently banal, the essay would be no great accomplishment for even a lesser author than Johnson. Biographical details are treated in a cursory manner; for instance, it is noted that Chaucer "made an incredible progress in logic, rhetoric, poetry, philosophy, mathematics, and divinity" at Cambridge University. One may be sure that Johnson would have made particular observations on such accomplishments, which he had consistently prized in his own journalistic biographies; but the author of the *Account* is content to record a fact. Chaucer's character is summed up thus: "With regard to his person, he was reckoned one of the handsomest men of his time; his temper, not-withstanding the gaiety of some of his writings, was reserved and modest, his disposition was very amorous in his younger [*sic*], but as he advanced in years, prudent, religious, and philosophical." While the thought might be ascribed to Johnson, it might also be ascribed to anyone else, and the writing is hardly distinctive enough to support an attribution. Elsewhere, in fact, the writing and judg- ments are so hackneyed that Johnson's responsibility for them must be denied: Chaucer was "one of the greatest and most universal genius's that ever the world produced. . . . we shall find, that if not the greatest, he was, without controversy, the most universal genius that ever was." The examples could be multiplied. The essay is similarly deficient in literary criticism, the author of the *Account* speaking mainly and generally of the shorter poems. When he finally touches upon the *Canterbury Tales,* it is to dismiss it in two sen- tences as an example of comedy and as "a kind of dramatic per- formance."

Too slight to warrant further discussion, the essay is surely by some hand other than Johnson's. Not even his hastiest biographies—with the possible exception of the life of Roscommon in the *Gentleman's Magazine*—sink to this level of superficiality. Furthermore, there is no evidence that Johnson shared this biographer's intense admiration for Chaucer. As recently as 1755 he had committed himself publicly to the opinion that Chaucer "does not . . . appear to have deserved all the praise which he has received, or all the censure that he has suffered."[80] In the *Lives of the English Poets,* where he had the opportunity to express himself fully, he made only passing references to Chaucer, without indulging in praise. The booksellers' original concept of the *English Poets,* as a series from Chaucer to the eighteenth century, was modified for the exclusion of poets prior to Cowley. And though Johnson recommended four or five poets be included, Chaucer was not one of them. To be sure, he once projected a new edition of Chaucer's works and a life, but like so many of his projects this one never materialized.[81]

Instinct perhaps more than internal evidence prompts the rejection of *Reflections upon the State of Portugal* in the *Universal Visiter* of February, 1756 (pp. 67-73). Thinking of Johnson's political activity this same year for the *Literary Magazine,* one might be disposed to link the *Universal Visiter* article with the several others on international affairs for which he was responsible. But unscientific though such a declaration may be, the *Reflections* simply does not sound like Johnson. Briefly, it begins as a history of Portugal and its climate, after which it proceeds to observations on trade relations between Portugal and England. Regarding England as Portugal's most essential source of necessities, the essayist concludes trade between the two nations to be mutually advantageous. The *Reflections* appears to have a twofold function, for it at once challenges France and Spain for the trade of Portugal[82] and asserts that they are military threats to Portugal. Of the two claims, the first is the more realistic if not the more sincere.

The excessively pious assertions of friendship are particularly suspect. Certain extravagances or inconsistencies noted in connection with the *Literary Magazine* have a reasonable explanation: as an editor, Johnson was frequently carrying out a policy of the magazine with which he did not necessarily concur wholeheartedly. As a contributor to the *Universal Visiter,* however, he had no direct editorial obligation, and it may be assumed that he wrote according to the dictates of his own conscience. Thus, one finds this statement in the *Reflections:*

. . . where can Portugal, too weak to defend herself, look for an able and trusty ally? To no where but to Great Britain, which is the only nation that ever has been, can, or will be, the safe, trusty, and honourable supporter of Portugal. The English generously helped them in their emancipation from the Spanish yoke, and have protected them in it ever since.

These fulsome yearnings for amity[83] are completely at odds with Johnson's known attitude toward Portugal. Only three years later (1759), in the introduction to *The World Displayed,* he condemned the Portuguese colonial policy, finding Portuguese explorers guilty of barbarous practices among the natives and the country itself party to avariciousness, power-seeking, and corruption.[84] Stated without equivocation or exception, these accusations could hardly be regarded as an expression of the author of the *Reflections.* The piece in the *Universal Visiter,* furthermore, lacks any kind of stylistic distinctiveness. The grounds for admitting it into the Johnsonian canon are altogether too tenuous and some other author should receive credit for it.

Finally to be considered among the doubtful essays in the *Universal Visiter* is *The Rise, Progress, and Perfection of Architecture among the Ancients; with some Account of its Declension among the Goths, and Revival among the Moderns.* Mainly a factual summation of the problems noted in the title, this was the leading article in June, 1756 (pp. 255-258). Examined on its own merits and with reference to Johnson's architectural comments elsewhere, the article could not satisfactorily resolve the question of whether he was the author. As a periodical essay, it is competent but not distinctive enough in style to warrant a prudent attribution to him. Yet he had definite opinions about architecture and even wrote on the subject, though never in a manner which would encourage his identification as author of the *Universal Visiter* article. A study of it, however, does not lead to wholly negative conclusions, for a hitherto unrevealed source emerges as Ephraim Chambers' *Cyclopaedia: or, an Universal Dictionary of Arts and Sciences* (London, 1728). *The Rise of Architecture* is a close adaptation of definitions in the *Cyclopaedia* related to architecture. The initial clue is a deceptive one, for it brings the reader dangerously close to inferring Johnson's authorship. Illustrative of the term *architecture* in the first edition of the *Dictionary* (1755) is a condensation of Chambers' learned materials. Omitting the technical details, which had no pertinence for him, Johnson concentrated his *précis* on a historical sketch of architecture. At the end of the sketch he gave Chambers' name without mentioning the *Cyclopaedia*. Examination of Chambers' definitions of architecture, however, instantly determines the exact source of Johnson's illustration. Comparison of the *Dictionary* condensation with *The Rise of Architecture* next reveals that the latter piece covers substantially the same ground and also uses some of Chambers' terminology or paraphrases of it. To assume, therefore, that Johnson, still desirous of helping Smart, simply enlarged upon his own *Dictionary* gleanings would be understandable but erroneous.

The explanation will be facilitated by a summary of the *Universal Visiter* article, the opening paragraph of which gives the theme and exemplifies the style:

The liberal arts, such as architecture, sculpture, painting, and music, have had their happy ages, in which they have appeared with greater splendor, and cast a stronger light, as well as the sciences; but this was of no long duration, except in Greece, where they continued longer than in any other part of the world. However, I shall confine myself, at present, to the rise, progress, and perfection of architecture among the ancients; with some account of its declension and revival among the moderns.

The essayist then begins with the building of houses as a protection against the weather, proceeding next to the development of architecture from its utilitarian origins to its association with the other arts, "which introduced pomp, grandeur, and magnificence, that became highly laudable on many occasions; but they were soon strangely abused by luxury." Noting that there are three kinds of architecture—civil, military, and naval—the author takes up only the first. Sketchily, then, he describes ancient architecture from the time of the Tyrians, through the Biblical, Greek, and Roman periods. Following this, he discourses on Gothic architecture and concludes with admiration for Italy's return to the classical mode. This is of course a breathless review for an article only a few pages long; and while it is implicitly erudite, it could be the work of any literate layman. The *Cyclopaedia* was readily available, and a comparison between a few key passages in the *Cyclopaedia* and the *Universal Visiter* will show how dependent the writer in the latter was upon Chambers' important work:

Cyclopaedia	*Universal Visiter*
1.	**1.**
"Civil architecture, called also absolutely and by way of eminence *architecture,* is the art of contriving and executing commodious buildings for the uses of civil life."	"Architecture may be properly divided into three branches; civil, military, and naval: but I am now only speaking of the first [Chambers defines all three but expands only upon civil architecture]; which is the art of contriving and executing commodious buildings for the utility and ornament of civil life."
2.	**2.**
"Nature and necessity taught the first inhabitants of the earth to build themselves huts, tents, and cottages; from which in the course of time, they gradually advanced to more regular and stately habitations, with variety of ornaments, proportions, &c."	Houses at first "were erected only for convenience, to protect mankind against the inclemency of the weather. . . . But men were not long contented with conveniency alone: the workmen became more industrious and expert; whereby architecture called in other arts to its aid, which introduced pomp, grandeur, and magnificence, that became highly laudable on many occasions; but they were soon strangely abused by luxury."
3.	**3.**
"Authors distinguish between two kinds of *gothic* architecture; the one antient, the other modern.— The *antient* is that which the Goths brought with them from the north, in the fifth century: the edifices built in this manner were exceedingly massive, heavy and coarse. Those of the modern *gothic* run to the other extreme, being light, delicate, and rich to a fault."	"The ancient [Gothic architecture] is that which the Goths brought forth from the north, in the fifth century; being massy, heavy, and gross. The works of the modern Gothic stile were more light, easy, delicate, and of an astonishing boldness of workmanship; . . ."

In spirit, organization, and frequently even in language, the articles in the *Cyclopaedia* and the *Universal Visiter* are so closely related that there can be no question that the essayist of 1756 had Chambers' work before him while he was composing his piece. Other examples of similarity could be mentioned. For instance, both authors have something to say about the destruction caused by the Visigoths and about the artistry of the Trajan column. These matters, to be sure, had been established historically. But only a very remarkable coincidence could account for the sameness represented in the two articles. The chief difference stems from the respective purposes for which they were published. Chambers was striving for objectivity and terseness. The writer for the *Universal Visiter* was striving for literary coherence and narrative fluidity; consequently he omitted many of the details of technique and bibliography which a periodical audience would find dull, and he inflated other materials because of their greater interest.

The identification of passages in *The Rise of Architecture* with parallels in the *Cyclopaedia* momentarily complicates rather than simplifies the problem of authorship. Because of the characteristic "signature" at the close of the *Visiter* article and the use in the *Dictionary* of an illustration from the *Cyclopaedia,* the temptation to posit that Johnson borrowed from and enlarged upon a convenient source may be strong. But as has already been pointed out, the double asterisks by no means guarantee that each article so designated is by the same author. Even more significant is the matter of borrowing, for the line between plagiarism and expansion is very thin indeed. While *The Rise of Architecture* shows a few signs of independence, it is demonstrably so close to the *Cyclopaedia* that the charge of plagiarism would not be unjustified. This circumstance perhaps more than any other should serve to dissociate Johnson's name from *The Rise of Architecture.* Like any other writer—especially any other periodical writer—he had from time to time drawn upon printed sources. But not even in his essays for the *Gentleman's Magazine* had he failed to give some indication of indebtedness. Warning against reckless charges, he himself had said (in *Adventurer,* No. 95) that plagiarism is "one of the most reproachful, though, perhaps, not the most atrocious of literary crimes." And by

1756—when he had a solid literary reputation, when his connection with the *Universal Visiter* was undoubtedly known, and when his authorship of such a piece as *The Rise of Architecture* might have been guessed—his ethical sense as well as his public status would have made this virtually undisguised pilfering both ridiculous and abhorrent.

If Johnson did not write the article, then it may be wondered whether someone in his circle did. Although it need not have been written by an architect, the inclination is to search for someone with professional knowledge or interest. At least two of Johnson's contemporaries, both celebrated architects and authors, may be considered briefly. Not only were they recipients of Johnson's literary assistance, but their architectural careers touched in two instances. When John Gwynn (d. 1786) in 1755 declined the role of instructor of architectural drawing to the Prince of Wales (George III), William Chambers (1726-1796) accepted it. Both were unsuccessful contestants in the Blackfriars Bridge competition of 1759. Gwynn was described in 1760 as "till of late of another profession," but he had been writing about art and had been known as a draftsman as early as 1734.[85] Gwynn knew Johnson by at least 1759, and probably earlier. But there is no available evidence to link him to *The Rise of Architecture.*

A slightly stronger case can be made for Chambers. Returning to England in 1755 after studying Italian architecture, he probably met Johnson shortly thereafter.[86] He presented the manuscript of *Designs of Chinese Buildings, Furniture, Dresses, Machines, and Utensils* (1757), which Johnson not only saw and approved, but for which he also supplied three prefatory paragraphs.[87] When Johnson met him, he was merely a talented young man without any of the tangible accomplishments or reputation which ultimately were to assure his renown as architect of Somerset House and ridicule as author of the *Dissertation on Oriental Gardening.* In addition to his work in orientalism, Chambers was "collecting from the Writings of others, or from my own Observations . . . a series of sound precepts and good Designs" for civil architecture.[88] This laborious and important work first appeared in 1759 as an elaborate folio specimen of work in progress under the title *A Treatise on Civil Architecture,* which he published at his own expense.[89] Apart from a common interest in classical civil architecture, there is no reasonable basis for associating *The Rise of Architecture* and the *Treatise* with the same author. Historical details which appeared only in subsequent editions of the *Treatise* were incidental to Chambers' technical concerns. Furthermore, he consistently showed an indifference to Greek architecture for which he has been reproached; while the author of *The Rise of Architecture* asserted "the perfection of architecture must be ascribed to Greece, where we must still go as to the school of good taste in all the arts and sciences, if we desire to excel in any." Chambers, then, used the *Cyclopaedia,* but he also used a great many other sources.

Neither Gwynn nor Chambers bears any serious resemblance to the author of *The Rise of Architecture.* Even as Johnson must be barred from authorship almost automatically because of the taint of plagiarism, so should the two architects be excluded. Too skilled in their profession to require the assistance of a reference work, they would not have jeopardized their promising careers with such flagrant filching. Nor would Johnson have given friendship and aid and silently condoned a breach of ethics, if he had suspected the authorship of either. Perhaps continued searching will one day reveal the author of the *Visiter* article. For the moment, however, it may be stated confidently that neither Johnson nor his two friends were responsible. The truth may be that Johnson suggested an article to one of his obscure journalistic friends in an effort to discharge his own obligation to Smart. Aware of the extensive outline in the *Cyclopaedia,* this person could then have taken the convenient and not unusual course which resulted in *The Rise of Architecture.* But the proof of this must depend upon future investigation.

With his usual good judgment about Johnsonian matters, Boswell properly limited the essays in the *Universal Visiter* to the first three discussed above. Essentially, therefore, Johnson's direct association with the magazine affected only the three numbers from March through May, 1756. Yet there are services and influences which cannot be measured explicitly, and despite his gruff withdrawal from the periodical Johnson was one of those who steadied it for a time.

His chief benevolence, of course, was toward Smart, when he helped with his physical presence during the desperate months while there was still hope for Smart and the magazine. What editorial counsel was solicited from him and what he gave is still a mystery. But that he was asked and that he responded is a virtual certainty. Experienced, generous, and loyal, Johnson could not have been as close as he was to the *Universal Visiter* without some form of direct participation. Certain tangible signs of his influence may be deduced also from the contents of the magazine. Smart, who contributed to the January number *Some Thoughts on the English Language* (pp. 4-9) with the example of Johnson's philological accomplishments fresh in his mind, praised the *Dictionary* as "a work I look upon with equal pleasure and amazement, as I do upon St. Paul's cathedral; each the work of an *Englishman.*" Though, oddly, none of the *Rambler* essays were reprinted, the *Universal Visiter* carried a number of moralizing allegories and narratives which would have won Johnson's approval; for instance, *The Story of Ethelinda* (April, pp. 175-179), *The Story of Amintor,* by Garrick (May, pp. 231-236), and *The Old Woman of Redburn,* by Rolt (June, pp. 267-272). Also to be noted are pieces on the vicissitudes of authorship, a problem close to both Smart and Johnson. One is an unsigned epigram, *Advice to the Starving Poet* (July, p. 332). But considerably more substantial is an essay by Smart, *On the Multiplicity of Modern Authors* (March, pp. 135-137). Reminiscent in spirit and theme of Johnson's *Reflections on the Present State of Literature* and several of his *Rambler* papers, this is a satire upon the great number of writers. Their pettiness and immorality are characterized by their designations as species of fish, and even a periodical, *The Fishmongers Magazine: or, Mother Gunter's Critical Repository,* is invented for them. The signature is "S. Gelasimus," a name apparently borrowed from *Rambler,* No. 179. Johnson's "Gelasimus," likewise, is the frustrated man of learning. As Smart had been indebted to Johnson for assistance with the *Student,* he was now even more indebted. Circumstantial though these various tokens may be, they should be considered as likely clues of Johnson's relationship to Smart and the *Visiter.*

IV

THE *London Chronicle*

The *London Chronicle: or, Universal Evening Post* (1757-1823), the first of a number of British newspapers with "Chronicle" in the title, was published every Tuesday, Thursday, and Saturday, at twopence each number (the price was raised to twopence halfpenny in 1759 and to threepence in 1776), and attained a large circulation. Johnson wrote a preface, a review, and an obituary. Among other contributors were Boswell and Arthur Murphy. William Strahan was printer and part-owner, and a Mr. Spens was editor. Robert Dodsley was interested in the paper through the eleventh number, but he withdrew because of the scurrility of one of the features published despite his protests.[90] After Dodsley's complaint the editors modified their policies sufficiently for Boswell to observe that "it has all along been distinguished for good sense, accuracy, moderation, and delicacy." Boswell, however, was hardly a paragon of journalistic propriety in his own *London Chronicle* writings, which fall short of the claims he advanced, and his judgment should not be considered authoritative.[91] Nevertheless, a severe critic of newspapers like Johnson thought well enough of the *London Chronicle* to make it "the only newspaper he constantly took in."[92]

One of Dodsley's first acts on behalf of the paper was to procure Johnson's services for a *Preliminary Discourse*. Regardless of his later aversion to most newspapers,[93] Johnson accepted the commission and wrote the introduction, which occupied the three columns on the first page of the first number, Saturday, January 1, 1757. His stipend was a guinea or, as has been estimated, a little more than twopence a line.[94] Since the *Preliminary Discourse* is a puff for the *London Chronicle,* it follows a conventional pattern which does not make it more or less important than most specimens of this same genre. As an example of Johnson's journalistic duties, however, it has an intrinsic value that must be examined. Johnson himself conceded that such preliminary remarks as he was about to make were mere formalities. "Even those who profess to teach the way to happiness have multiplied our incumbrances, and the author of almost every book retards his instructions by a preface." In consideration of

The Grub Street Historian 137

Johnson's acknowledged ability and experience in this kind of writing, the conjecture may be made that he had a hand in the organization of the periodical, despite his unenthusiastic admission that it was an addition to other newspapers with which the public was "already rather wearied than satisfied."

Like many of his earlier prefaces to the *Gentleman's Magazine* and the *Literary Magazine*, the *Preliminary Discourse* functionally stated what was expected of it, the plan of the newspaper. If the *Discourse* may be said to have any distinguishing qualities, they are its literary superiority for this kind of composition and certain attitudes which have come to be identified with Johnson. The promises of moderation and accuracy were, of course, characteristic of Johnson; but they were also assertions made by all periodicals. Among other things, as in the *Gentleman's Magazine*, he engaged in the popular pastime of baiting party writers. He recognized a tendency of some to publish without regard for truth or decency, "proud of the hourly encrease of infamy, and ready to boast of all the contumelies that falsehood and slander may bring upon them, as new proofs of their zeal and fidelity. . . . With these heroes we have no ambition to be numbered."

Truth seems to fly from curiosity; and as many enquirers produce many narratives, whatever engages the public attention is immediately disguised by the embellishments of fiction. We pretend no peculiar power of disentangling contradiction, or denuding forgery. We have no settled correspondence with the Antipodes, nor maintain any spies in the cabinets of Princes. But as we shall always be conscious that our mistakes are involuntary, we shall watch the gradual discoveries of time, and retract whatever we have hastily and erroneously advanced.

Worth noting is the fact that Johnson seemingly divided his scorn between the Tories and the Whigs and sided with neither. The *London Chronicle*, he said, would have no part of political machinations, but would accept a dual responsibility of concentrating upon truth and attempting to raise the level of periodical writing. His feeling about party writing is consistent with his belief that political factions would "do any thing, no matter how odd or desperate, to gain their point; they'll catch hold of the red-hot end of a poker, sooner than not get possession of it."[95]

Varying his tone to complement his feelings about the problems as he enumerated them, Johnson ranged from slightly mocking to matter of fact and serious. Soberly, thus, he announced that the *London Chronicle* proposed to report upon foreign and domestic matters, grain and stock reports, and to be especially meticulous in the reporting of individualized news like births, deaths, and preferments. And with somewhat stronger feeling, fresh from his *Literary Magazine* experiences, he also stated the *Chronicle*'s intention of starting a "Literary Journal, or account of the labours and productions of the learned." The keynote again is moderation and judiciousness, applicable to a section of reviews that would fill a long-felt want in news periodicals. He could not, however, forbear the temptation to reflect briefly upon "other disturbers of human quiet, a numerous body of *reviewers* and *remarkers*," a phrase which he took almost directly from the *Reflections on the Present State of Literature* in the *Universal Visiter*. But he concluded temperately with the statement: "No man can modestly promise what he cannot ascertain. We hope for the praise of knowledge and discernment, but we claim only that of diligence and candor."

After the *Preliminary Discourse,* he wrote only two items for the *Chronicle,* one a review[96] and the other an obituary. The short memorial for the Reverend Zachariah Mudge (1694-1769)—Prebendary of Exeter and Vicar of St. Andrew's in Plymouth—who once preached a sermon especially that Johnson might hear him, was the final contribution to the *Chronicle*.[97] Even though the piece occupies the larger part of a single column, the editors apparently did not regard Mudge's death as offering unusual news interest, for the obituary appears in the midst of other personal reports undistinguished by headlines or any typographical device. Yet this erstwhile dissenter, we are told, was "idolised in the west, both for his excellence as a preacher and the uniform propriety of his private conduct."[98] Admired by many of the contemporary intellectuals, Mudge had influenced Reynolds' philosophical growth. Reynolds, who was devoted to the entire family, painted Mudge's portrait three times. He had once hoped to republish the clergyman's sermons with a memoir of him. Burke thought highly of Mudge as a Platonist. Johnson first met Mudge in 1762, while he and Reynolds were guests of his son, Dr. John Mudge, a well-known physician and surgeon whom Johnson consulted.[99]

The obituary, which Johnson showed Reynolds at the time he wrote it,[100] is typical of his concern for piety and strength of character. He is scanty of factual details, but he writes with an earnest conviction and an insight into personality indicative of his first-hand knowledge. Mudge's "principles, both of thought and action, were great and comprehensive," his quest for truth was steady and elevated. A learned man, he was also a good companion. "Though studious he was popular, though argumentative he was modest, though inflexible he was candid, and though metaphysical yet orthodox." Appreciative of his *Essay towards a New English Version of the Book of Psalms* (1744), Johnson was particularly aware of his preaching ability.

His discharge of parochial duties was exemplary. How his *Sermons* were composed may be learned from the excellent volume which he has given to the public;[101] but how they were delivered can be known only to those that heard them; for as he appeared in the pulpit words will not easily describe him. His delivery, though unconstrained, was not negligent, and though forcible was not turbulent; disdaining anxious nicety of emphasis, and laboured artifice of action, it captivated the hearer by its natural dignity, it roused the sluggish, and fixed the volatile; and detained the mind upon the subject without directing it to the speaker.

The obituary of the Reverend Mr. Mudge was obviously gratuitous, a gesture of friendship, since by 1769 Johnson, modestly affluent as a result of the yearly pension which he had been receiving since 1762, had almost given up writing for periodicals. His literary position, furthermore, enabled him to accept or reject periodical assignments virtually at will, and the Mudge testimonial could not have been very remunerative.

The brief essay gives an interesting view of Johnson as a critic of pulpit oratory. Not only did he listen attentively to the sermons of others, but he could also discourse knowingly on the styles of various popular preachers of the day. He could write sermons for some clergymen and give sound advice on their correct preparation to others, believing sermons an important branch of English literature.[102] Despite his generous memorial, privately he did not wholly approve of Mudge's sermons, considering them "good, but not practical. He grasps more sense than he can hold; he takes more corn than he can make into meal; he opens a wide prospect, but it is so distant, it is indistinct."[103] This criticism, however, was not directed solely against Mudge, for he regretted that the English had "no sermons addressed to the passions that are good for any thing." Expression, he insisted, should be simple in order that the congregation be reached. For this reason, he objected to the Anglican clergy's proclivity for ornamentation—"polished periods and glittering sentences flew over the heads of the common people, without any impression upon their hearts."[104] At least this much he admired of Methodism —its preachers knew how to invigorate their hearers.

V

THE *Daily Gazetteer* AND THE *London Gazette*

Among Johnson's diversified acquaintances was John Gwynn, the architect on whose behalf in 1759 he became embroiled in a controversy over the most adequate way to construct the proposed Blackfriars Bridge over the Thames in London. Gwynn submitted in a competition a set of plans calling for semi-circular arches. But he and another who favored semi-circular arches were defeated by Robert Mylne, a distinguished architect who had won a prize for architecture in Rome and who favored elliptical arches for the proposed bridge. As a result of the interest in the competition, there was an exchange of letters in the *Daily Gazetteer,* three of which Johnson wrote for Gwynn.[105] The heat of the disagreement was such that at its peak he resorted to innuendoes, arguing that the public could not help suspecting ulterior motives if the judges selected the weaker elliptical design. Furthermore, he reflected unkindly (in Letter II) on Mylne's European triumph, and warned him, "let it not be presumed that a prize granted at Rome, implies an irresistible degree of skill. The competition is only between boys, and the prize given to excite laudable industry, not to reward consummate excellence." Nor did he regard Rome as a reputable center of architectural studies, his reason being the degeneration of architecture there.

Inevitably, those close to Johnson began to speculate on his sources of technical information and his reasons for entering into the dispute. One contemporary impression was that he studied bridge construction carefully, if only for the occasion, before committing his ideas to print.[106] Another was that he had to go to an outside source for his mathematical information. Connected with this same opinion is the implication that he was especially harsh to Mylne because the architect had the misfortune to be a Scot. But this is not a tenable theory because Johnson and Mylne became friends after the competition.[107] It appears likely now that Johnson became involved in the quarrel primarily because of his friendship for Gwynn, under whose coaching he studied the subject carefully enough to write three effective letters. Shortly thereafter Johnson helped him revise a pamphlet, *Thoughts on the Coronation of George III* (1761); and then he wrote a dedication to Gwynn's *London and Westminster Improved* (1766). With this "fine lively rattling fellow" Johnson disputed about the merits of ornamental architecture, and he visited Oxford and Shrewsbury (of which Gwynn was a native) in his company.[108]

"In 1760," reports Boswell,[109] "[Johnson] wrote 'An Address of the Painters to George III, on his Accession to the Throne of these Kingdoms,' which no monarch ever ascended with more sincere congratulations from his people." This address, which appeared in the official *London Gazette* in 1761,[110] Boswell ascribed to Johnson on internal evidence. The first of a series in this number of the *Gazette* given over to adulations by various organizations and municipalities of the realm, the address takes up less than a column. Journalistic only because it appears in a newspaper, its chief significance lies in the fact that Johnson was elected to be the spokesman for those in the arts. His substantial reputation as well as his association with Gwynn, Chambers, Reynolds, and other practitioners of the arts undoubtedly made him an inevitable choice for this performance.

Formally panegyrical, it should not be expected to reveal much; yet one passage illuminates Johnson's personality and literary career:

> It is our happiness to live in the age, when our arts may hope for new advances towards perfection, assisted by the favor of a British King, of a monarch no less judicious to distinguish, than powerful to reward; who knows the usefulness and value of that skill, which delights the eye with beauty, but not corrupts the manners by unlawful passions, and which has been hitherto learned in foreign countries, for want of sufficient encouragement in our own.

Following his usual practice, Johnson introduces a moral note into esthetic matters while implicitly criticizing the absence of moral purpose in English letters. Then he concludes with the hope that the new king will "make the arts of elegance subservient to virtue and religion." Written without anticipation of future benefits, remarks such as these served nevertheless as useful links in the circumstances leading to the granting of the pension and augured well for his future meeting with the King.

Although Johnson wrote at random for a number of miscellaneous journals, his associations and contributions are a notable extension of the career he began with Cave on the *Gentleman's Magazine*. The later phase of his journalistic activities is, to be sure, an optimistic one, for Johnson was now able to see the fruitful beginnings of a significant literary course for himself outside of journalism. Between 1738 and 1745 he had no brighter immediate prospects than any other Grub Street journalist or editor. Later, however, sustained by his prospects, he could divorce himself from the deadly routine of continuous journalistic employment. He was formerly the valued adviser of one man, but now he was the adviser of many, materially demonstrating the lessons he had learned so painfully under Cave. He became friend as well as guide to those he assisted; but friendship was not enough, and he continued to labor under the pressures of financial necessity. At the same time, however, Johnson was able to add to his journalism lasting qualities, even as he had while he was an employee of the *Gentleman's Magazine*. So it is that we see in the pieces described in this chapter the development and maturing of ideas which culminated in works like the *Rambler* and the *English Poets*. For Johnson this was part of a progression from journalistic prefaces and hack work to belles-lettres and criticism. His later journalism is a further proof of his versatility. It was an enforced means of permitting him to discourse on such varied topics as authorship and epitaphs, and in such diversified areas as biographies, eulogies, and technology, politics and foreign affairs. For all of his reluctance to be the historian of Grub Street, he was eminently qualified for the role. Perhaps, indeed, it was this very reluctance that facilitated his removal from Grub Street to Parnassus.

THE

NUMB. 2.

UNIVERSAL CHRONICLE,
OR
WEEKLY GAZETTE.

To be Published every S A T U R D A Y, Price Two-Pence Half-Penny.

From SATURDAY, April 8, to SATURDAY, April 15, 1758.

The IDLER. No. 1.

Vacui sub umbra

Lufimus. Hor.

HOSE who attempt periodical Essays seem to be often stopped in the beginning, by the difficulty of finding a proper Title for their Work. Two Writers since the time of the Spectator, have assumed his Name, without any Pretensions to lawful Inheritance; an Effort was once made to revive the Tatler; and the strange appellations, by which Papers have been called, sufficiently show that the Authors were distressed, like the Natives of America, who sometimes come to the Europeans to beg a Name.

It will be easily believed of the *Idler*, that if his Title had required any search, he never would have found it. Every mode of life has its conveniencies. The *Idler*, who habituates himself to be satisfied with what he can most easily obtain, not only escapes labours which are often fruitless, but sometimes succeeds better than those who despise whatever is within their reach, and think every thing more valuable as it is harder to be acquired.

If similitude of manners be a motive to kindness, the *Idler* may flatter himself with universal Patronage. There is no single character under which such numbers are comprised. Every man is, or hopes to be, an *Idler*. Even those who seem to differ most from us are hastening to encrease our Fraternity; as Peace is the end of war, to be idle is the ultimate purpose of the Busy.

There is perhaps no Appellation by which a Writer can better denote his Kindred to the human Species. It has been found hard to describe Man by an adequate Definition. Some Philosophers have called him a reasonable Animal, but others have considered Reason as a Quality of which many Animals partake. He has been termed likewise a laughing Animal; but it is said that some Men have never laughed. Perhaps Man may be more properly distinguished as an Idle Animal; for there is no Man who is not sometimes Idle. It is at least a Definition from which none that shall find it in this Paper can be excepted; for who can be more idle than the Reader of the *Idler*?

That the Definition may be complete, Idleness must be not only the general, but the peculiar characteristic of Man; and perhaps he is the only Being that can properly be called Idle, that does by others what he might do himself, or sacrifices Duty or Pleasure to the Love of Ease.

Scarcely any Name can be imagined from which less envy or competition is to be dreaded. The *Idler* has no Rivals or Enemies. The Man of Business forgets him; the Man of Enterprize despises him; and though such as tread the same track of Life, fall commonly into jealousy and discord, *Idlers* are always found to associate in Peace, and he who is most famed for doing Nothing, is glad to meet another as Idle as himself.

What is to be expected from this paper, whether it will be uniform or various, learned or familiar, serious or gay, political or moral, continued or interrupted, it is hoped that no Reader will enquire. That the *Idler* has some scheme, cannot be doubted; for to form schemes is the *Idler*'s privilege. But tho' he has many projects in his head, he is sparing of communication, having observed, that his hearers are apt to remember what he forgets himself; that his tardiness of execution exposes him to the encroachments of those who catch a hint and fall to work, and that very specious Plans, after long contrivance and pompous displays, have subsided in weariness without a trial, and without miscarriage been blasted by derision.

Something the *Idler*'s Character may be supposed to promise. Those that are curious after diminutive History, who watch the Revolutions of Families, and the Rise and Fall of Characters either Male or Female, will hope to be gratified by this Paper; for the *Idler* is always inquisitive and seldom retentive. He that delights in Obloquy and Satire, and wishes to see Clouds gathering over every Reputation that dazzles him with its Brightness, will snatch up the *Idler*'s Essays with a beating Heart. The *Idler* is naturally censorious; those who attempt nothing themselves suppose every thing easily performed, and consider the unsuccessful always as criminal.

I think it necessary to give notice, that I make no contract, nor incur any obligation. If those who depend on the *Idler* for intelligence and entertainment, should suffer the disappointment which commonly follows such ill-placed expectations, they are to lay the blame only on themselves.

Yet Hope is not wholly to be cast away. The *Idler*, tho' sluggish, is yet alive, and may sometimes be stimulated to vigour and activity. He may then descend into profoundness, or tower into sublimity; for the diligence of an *Idler* is rapid and impetuous, as ponderous bodies forced into velocity move with violence proportionate to their weight.

But these violent exertions of intellect cannot be very frequent, and he will therefore gladly receive help from any Correspondent, who shall enable him to please without his own labour. He excludes no style, he prohibits no Subject; only let him that writes to the *Idler* remember, that his letters must not be long; no words ought to be squandered in declarations of esteem, or confessions of inability; conscious dulness has little right to be prolix, and praise is not so welcome to the *Idler* as quiet.

Monday, April 10.

Landshut, March 22.

THE King of Prussia, who arrived here the 17th, set out the 19th for Crissau, where the head quarters of his army will be established tomorrow. 30,000 Prussians are actually encamped between Breslau and the frontiers of Poland, in order to observe the motions of the Russians, who are marching towards this province.

Dantzick, March 21. In all probability some bloody scenes will be disclosed on the banks of the Vistula, where both the Russians and Prussians seem as if they designed to assemble their forces. The 24th instant a numerous corps of the former advanced as far as Thorn, under the Command of Prince Gallizin. On the other hand, a strong detachment of Marshal Lehwald's army has already made its appearance in the environs of Stolpe, where it seized on several posts, and seems to expect only a few regiments to form a grand enterprize.

Prague, March 29. The head quarters of the army were not moved the 23d, on account of the great quantity of snow that fell the preceding day, which retarded its operations. A body of 10,000 Prussians, commanded by General Fouquet, have driven the troops under General Jahnus out of the county of Glatz; and it is thought their view is to seize our magazine at Leutomyssel. The King of Prussia's motions in Silesia seem to have a design to attack our main army, and that he concerns himself very little about the progress of the Russians.

The body of troops under General Nadasti is to assemble in the Upper Silesia.

By letters which came to hand the 26th inst. we learn, that Marshal Count Daun's army has advanced towards Silesia, and that General Laudon is dead of a fever.

Berlin, March 30. We have received advice, that a detachment of five hundred Austrian hussars, being part of a body of troops posted in the Upper Lusatia, came a few days ago to Cotbus, and seized all the money they found there

Idler, No. 1, which appeared in No. 2, first page, of the *Universal Chronicle, or Weekly Gazette* (Saturday, April 15, 1758). From the copy in the Yale University Library.

CHAPTER IV

"THE ANXIOUS EMPLOYMENT OF A
PERIODICAL WRITER"

I

GENERAL CONSIDERATIONS

(a) *The Rambler*

IF PRIOR to 1750 the essays of Addison and Steele are supreme in Britain, those of Johnson—especially the *Rambler* papers—are foremost in the second half of the century. Even Macaulay, who thought Johnson's series inferior to Addison's, saw the importance of the *Rambler*. Not only are the essays valuable literary contributions, but they serve also as gauges of altering modes in serials after the *Tatler* and *Spectator*. The *Rambler* reveals how essays in the previous forty years had expanded from two-page folios, with two or three columns to the page, to six-page, single-column folios. Johnson developed a tone more serious, philosophical, and dignified than that of his predecessors;[1] yet his debt to them was considerable, and he especially admired Addison's technique. Both Addison and Steele, he was later to write, "taught, with great justness of argument and dignity of language, the most important duties and sublime truths." To this judgment should be added the well-known eulogy: "Whoever wishes to attain an English style, familiar but not coarse, and elegant but not ostentatious, must give his days and nights to the volumes of Addison."[2]

Johnson initiated the plan of the *Rambler* and wrote more than 200 of the 208 numbers which appeared semi-weekly between Tuesday, March 20, 1750, and Saturday, March 14, 1752. Hawkins and others assumed the *Rambler* had been undertaken for the alleviation of loneliness, melancholia, and the drudgery of the *Dictionary*. But Johnson, who was socially active in 1750, was less in need of a diversion than he was of funds—as he himself admitted—to discharge numerous obligations.[3] He had cut himself off from full-time employment on the *Gentleman's Magazine* three years earlier. Work on the *Dictionary*, at least until 1750, had proceeded so steadily that the definitions for the first three letters were printed off,[4] and his staff absorbed much of the advance money he had received. In addition he had committed himself to paying off the debt contracted in Lichfield. Poverty, thus, was a subject about which he could write with real authority in many of the *Rambler* papers.

John Payne, the bookseller of Paternoster Row who published the *Rambler,* paid Johnson two guineas a paper and a share of the profits as the papers were collected in book form. Johnson retained the copyright even after the expiration of the series but later sold it, perhaps to help meet the payments on his debt.[5] Cave, who printed the first two collected editions, was assigned by Johnson the rights to the second.[6] At the outset the *Rambler* had a disappointing sale, seldom exceeding five hundred copies for a single essay. Many eminent persons, according to Cave, placed the *Rambler* "in a rank equal, and some superior to the *Spectators* . . . but, notwithstanding such recommendation, whether the price of two-pence, or the unfavourable season of their first publication hinders the demand, no boast can be made of it."[7] In two letters to his patron, Philip Yorke, Dr. Birch likewise alluded to the poor sale. Johnson, he said, "designs to continue his *Rambler* till he has finished one year's course. He will then probably stop, for his bookseller complains of the want of encouragement, as he himself does of the want of assistance."[8] In spite of his discouraging prospects Johnson was able to continue the series for a full two years.

Consideration of the substantial bulk of Johnson's writings makes apology for his "indolence" hardly seem necessary. No apathetic man could have produced all but four and parts of three other *Rambler* papers, in addition to his work on the *Dictionary* and his contributions to the writings of others. Johnson's contributors to the *Rambler* were: Hester Mulso (Mrs. Chapone), four letters in No. 10; Catherine Talbot, No. 30 (signed "Sunday"); Samuel Richardson, No. 97, the only paper to have a large sale; Miss Carter, Nos. 44 and 100 (reprinted in her *Poems on Several Occasions*); Garrick, second letter in No. 15; Joseph Simpson (also of Lichfield), second letter (signed "Amicus") in No. 107.[9] Though he suffered from mental depression frequently, Johnson never failed to get the paper out on time. He wrote rapidly, as he did the *Parliamentary Debates,* and with dogged determination, often relying for topics on a commonplace book in which he had jotted ideas. At times the printer's boy waited while he dashed off a *Rambler;* nor did he trouble to reread what he had written.[10] Yet his performance is constant in its stately dignity, in its balance, in its reasoned discourses, and in its variety. Bishop Percy believed Johnson was so impaired by nearsightedness that he would mull over an entire subject in his mind and then, aided by his unusual memory, write the essay in its completed form, seldom employing a rough draft.[11] One of his idiosyncracies was to talk to himself as he composed. Many years later, in his biography of Pope, he made a statement which could well be applied to his own practice: "Of composition there are different methods. Some employ at once memory and invention, and, with little intermediate use of the pen, form and polish large masses by continued meditation, and write their productions only when, in their own opinion, they have completed them."[12]

The series ended suddenly three days before the death of his wife, although there is no recognizable connection between the two events. In No. 208, the concluding paper, Johnson wrote: "Time, which puts an end to all human pleasures and sorrows, has likewise concluded the labours of the Rambler. Having supported, for two years, the anxious employment of a periodical writer, and multiplied my essays to upwards of two hundred, I have now determined to desist." This statement, coupled with Birch's letter to Yorke and one from Cave to Richardson,[13] indicates that from the start Johnson and his publishers, in accordance with contemporary practice, intended to collect the *Rambler* in book form. The first collected edition came out early in 1752 in four volumes (Nos. 1-136), while the single essays were still appearing. In the summer the two remaining volumes were issued, with tables of contents and translated mottoes at the end of the sixth volume.[14] The anecdotes concerning Johnson's hasty composition have created the myth that he never revised, and it is true that he spent little time on the single essays. But that he polished very carefully for book republication is evident in the fourth edition of the *Rambler* (1756), the product of his final corrections.[15] While his ideas remained seemingly inflexible, Johnson simplified in a striving for exact diction. He applied the same diligence to the essays of his contributors, making changes in Richardson's and, to her displeasure, Miss Carter's.[16]

Collection in book form seems to have increased the popularity of the *Rambler.* The 1752 edition was being read in the American Colonies by 1756.[17] Twelve editions appeared during Johnson's lifetime, including one Scottish and one unauthorized Dublin edition. The English editions, Hawkins asserted, amounted to 12,500 sets; and, according to Alexander Donaldson, the Edinburgh bookseller, the Scottish edition had a substantial sale. By 1817 at least twenty editions had gone to Johnson's growing public.[18] Appearing almost simultaneously with the single London issues of the *Rambler* were the authorized Edinburgh numbers which, under the editorial direction of James Elphinston, were first placed on sale June 1, 1750, at one penny each. Elphinston's collected edition appeared between 1750 and 1752 in eight duodecimo volumes with translations of the mottoes, thirty-six of which Johnson used in his collected London editions and in which he felt free to make changes. And Elphinston, for his part, borrowed Johnson's translations to round out his remaining mottoes. Johnson had a high regard for Elphinston, despite his Scottish ancestry, and furnished him with copies of the *Rambler* and even corrections of previous numbers.[19]

The *Rambler* brought Johnson fame; but it also brought him adverse criticism, some of it because of the envy and malice of other writers. One enthusiastic admirer was Samuel Richardson, who even before he participated in the series guessed the identity of the author. In a letter to Cave on August 9, 1750, which is important as one of the earliest recognitions of Johnson's essay talents, Richardson lavishly praised the *Rambler* as a periodical superior even to the *Spectator,* and spoke of using his influence to win new readers. Cave in his response (August 23) admitted that although Johnson had intended to remain unnamed throughout the series, he had found anonymity impossible. David Garrick and several friends suspected Johnson's hand and soon revealed his authorship.[20] Additional praise came from the famous Miss Mulso, one of Johnson's correspondents and a member of the Richardson circle. She recommended to young ladies the reading of such serials as the *Rambler* and the *Adventurer*, as well as the *Spectator* and the *Guardian*, because they enlightened pleasantly.[21] Contemporary editors of periodicals likewise apprehended the qualities of the *Rambler*, if we are to judge from the glowing compliments of the *Daily Advertiser* and the *Student*.[22]

On the other side, Miss Carter and Miss Talbot quarreled with their socialite friends who had passed unfavorable judgments on the series. Discussing the objections, they revealed some of the major causes of public apathy. Miss Talbot felt that Johnson used too many "hard words," and that he was not discriminating enough in the selection of his correspondence. Following what was probably the attitude of London's *haut monde*, she regretted that Johnson devoted insufficient space to humor, clubs, and society, the "living manners of the times." His excessively heavy style, she thought, required the balance of a lighter touch. "Humor," unfortunately, "and the manners of the world are not [Johnson's] forte." Although she would have approved of a paper by Lord Chesterfield to enliven the series, she was sensibly fearful of broaching the subject to Johnson. As an alternative, she therefore begged Miss Carter to contribute a cheerful paper.[23] On September 7, 1751, Birch sent Yorke a *Rambler* on epistolary writing [No. 152, August 31], "that you may judge your self of the merits of that paper, and see how far the public is in the right in suffering it, (as I am told the fact is) to decline in the sale, which was never very considerable." Yorke concurred in Birch's oblique criticism, tersely replying September 10, "The Rambler you sent me is a mere collection of pretty phrases."[24]

Johnson's literary fame, especially in connection with the *Rambler*, made him one of the most satirized persons of his times. Even while the serial was appearing semi-weekly, coffee house wits were declaring that the papers were burdened with pedantries and moralizing judgments. To be sure, he had the loyal support of many of his friends, including that of Charlotte Lennox who smartly rebuked in the pages of the *Female Quixote* malicious and sophisticated carpings against the *Rambler*.[25] This, however, did not lessen the attacks. For instance, Archibald Campbell, a purser in the Scotch navy, doled out rough treatment in his introduction to *Lexiphanes*,[26] an obvious animadversion on Johnson. Campbell heavily insisted upon the resemblance of Johnson's characters to the Limousin scholar in Rabelais and to Lexiphanes in Lucian, and he depicted Johnson muttering unwieldy words and constructions in the "Lexiphanic style" which he claimed to have drawn from the *Rambler*. In a subsequent volume, Campbell, who by now apparently regretted his original position, complained that he had been misunderstood in *Lexiphanes*. He asserted in illogical terms that he had been making fun not of Johnson but of his imitators. Further, he averred, he was laughing not at these authors, but at "the low and trifling taste of the age in general."[27]

A more genial satirist was Bonnell Thornton, who had a clever knack for parody. He began an essay serial of twelve numbers, the first of which appeared on January 16, 1752, under the designation *Have at You All*, as a satire upon Fielding's *Covent-Garden Journal*. But after the second number Thornton expanded his derisive scope to such periodicals as Smart's *Midwife*, the *Gentleman's Magazine*, the *London Magazine*, the *Universal Spectator*, and Johnson's *Rambler*.[28] Another amusing consequence of fame was Dr. Birch's dark suspicion that Johnson might have been the author of a satirical paper, the *Impertinent*,

printed in the same form and for the same bookseller with the Rambler, which it greatly resembled in the style. But it so fully answered its title in the general opinion, that its existence, like that of the insects, called the Ephemera, was determined within one day, and on Thursday last [August 13, 1752] we were told by the publishers, that we should have no more of them. I have too good an opinion of Johnson to assign to him a piece of so much malignity as well as petulance; but the suspicion will not easily be removed till he gives the public that satisfaction, which he likewise owes to himself.[29]

If Johnson ever attempted to vindicate himself of the accusation, the record does not reveal it. Undoubtedly he deigned no such answer and the matter slid into obscurity. The only palpable significance of the affair is the extensiveness of Johnson's reputation, which won him such notoriety as well as laurels.

Arthur Murphy's long association with Johnson began as the result of a misunderstanding about a *Rambler* paper. In the summer of 1754 when he was contributing to the *Gray's-Inn Journal*, he translated for this periodical an essay which had appeared in a French *Journal Littéraire,* and only too late did he discover that he had retranslated a *Rambler* without either acknowledgment or permission. Calling upon Johnson to make his apologies—which were accepted—he found Johnson "covered with soot, like a chimney-sweeper, in a little room, as if he had been acting Lungs, in the Alchymist, *making aether.*"[30] Goldsmith was another who drew upon the *Rambler.* He borrowed the character of "Croaker" in the *Good-Natured Man,* which Johnson admired, from "Suspirius, the human screech owl" (*Rambler,* No. 59).[31] Goldsmith also presented a comic interlude in No. 5 of the *Bee,* describing the traveler who was given a place in a stagecoach because he had a copy of the *Rambler* in his pocket.

Female admirers were plentiful. Hannah More, who late in Johnson's life sought to lionize him, referred to him endearingly as that "*Idler,* that *Rambler*"; she ranted about a visit to "Dr. Johnson's *very own house;* yes, Abyssinia's Johnson! Dictionary's Johnson! Rambler's, Idler's and Irene's Johnson! Can you picture to yourself the palpitation of our hearts as we approached his mansion."[32] In a letter to the University recommending Johnson for a master of arts degree (February 4, 1755), the Chancellor of Oxford cited him for "having very eminently distinguished himself by the publication of a series of essays, excellently calculated to form the manners of the people, and in which the cause of religion and morality is every where maintained by the strongest powers of argument and language. . . ."[33] In 1763 Boswell venerated Johnson as "the authour of the *Rambler* and of *Rasselas*"; his friend Sir David Dalrymple considered Johnson "one of the best moral writers which England has produced."[34] As late as 1783 Johnson was still receiving and acknowledging requests for complimentary copies of the *Rambler.*[35] His fortunes, indeed, had improved considerably since his melancholy observation in *Rambler,* No. 208, that "I have never been much a favourite of the public."

Boswell has apologized for the *Rambler* on the grounds that, because it was the work almost exclusively of one man, it lacked variety.[36] That, however, is not an admissible criticism. While the essays cannot be said to abound in a large variety of styles and subjects, they do have a distinguished range, from the humor of "Suspirius" (No. 59) to the philosophy of a discourse on spring (No. 5); from the criticism of Milton (Nos. 88, 94, 139, 140) to a discussion of the miseries of authorship (*passim*); from the characters of "Mrs. Busy" (No. 138) and "Squire Bluster" (No. 142) to the misfortunes of "Misella" (Nos. 170, 171). No man, surely, need apologize for the limitations of the *Rambler*.

Although the contents were frequently scholarly and grave, they were always underscored by Johnson's broad understanding of human nature. When he chose, he could be as entertaining or as brittle as any contemporary satirist in ridiculing trivialities; and his lessons mingled morality with psychological perception and erudition.[37] Like any good journalist he learned to depict daily events and human affairs. So sharply illuminated were some of the *Rambler* characters, as an example, that a number of sensitive, presumably vulnerable, persons—including Garrick—fancied themselves the subjects of Johnson's caricatures.[38] His main concern, however, was ethical, and frequently he reserved Saturday's essays for appropriate themes, thus providing food for reflection over the sabbath.[39] The seriousness of his intention is best disclosed by the prayer he composed at the time of the first essay:

Almighty God, the giver of all good things, without whose help all labour is ineffectual, and without whose grace all wisdom is folly; grant, I beseech Thee, that in this my undertaking, thy Holy Spirit may not be withheld from me, but that I may promote thy glory, and the salvation both of myself and others; grant this, O Lord, for the sake of Jesus Christ, Amen.[40]

It is a fact that the *Rambler* has many commonplace truths; but, after all, Johnson was interested in those everyday truths that are related to the lives of average people rather than in novelties that find only rare application. His generally serious tone was probably accountable for his lack of immediate popularity, and for his gradual and lasting acquisition of enlightened readers. His writings were the earnest products of painful experience and deep reflection. Many of his ideas were exhibited in the *Rambler* for the first time: his love of London, the differences between personal and political liberty, his contempt for parental authority, his interest in realistic writing, his distrust of literary "rules," his censure of Milton and of the metaphysical poets.[41] By the end of the eighteenth century the *Rambler* was esteemed by many as his greatest work.[42]

(b) *The Adventurer*

Eight months after the cessation of the *Rambler,* John Hawkesworth as editor and principal writer offered to the British public a new series, the *Adventurer*. It appeared between Tuesday, November 7, 1752, and Saturday, March 9, 1754. Published twice weekly in a half-sheet folio, the *Adventurer* came finally to 140 numbers, perhaps twenty-nine of which Johnson wrote on a variety of literary and moral subjects. ("Do *you* know," asked Miss More, "I did not, that he wrote a quarter of the Adventurer?")[43] Similar in scope and contents to the *Rambler,* the *Adventurer* was the more popular in its own day, although it was never to attain importance in literary and journalistic history. The quality of the *Adventurer* is attributable to the distinctive essays of its contributors, but Hawkesworth himself was largely responsible for its popularity, thanks to his own allegorical, oriental, and domestic tales, which constituted about one-half of the entire series. In addition to the essays from Johnson, Hawkesworth published contributions from Joseph Warton, Miss Mulso, George Colman, the Reverend Richard Jago, Hamilton Boyle (Earl of Corke and Orrery), and perhaps Richard Bathurst and Bonnell Thornton. Hawkesworth purposely terminated the *Adventurer,* despite a large weekly sale, and then exploited it in book form. His decision was justified by four large editions in eight years, which assured his reputation and gave the proprietor, John Payne, a respectable profit.[44]

Inevitably the *Rambler* and *Adventurer* were closely compared, and implicit in some of the comments even before Johnson wrote for the *Adventurer* was the assumption of his participation. He did not contribute his first essay until March, 1753, but four months earlier a review had stated: "The *Rambler* being finished, another periodical paper has appeared, called the *Adventurer*. It is printed after the manner of the *Rambler,* and sold also at two-pence each number, published on Tuesdays and Saturdays."[45] Two months prior to Johnson's first essay, Miss Talbot seemed virtually certain of his connection with the series, and loyally sought contributions to lighten his load. On January 29, 1753, she expressed to Miss Carter her conviction that Johnson was responsible for "all the papers that are not marked A [still unidentified], as evidently as if I saw him through the keyhole with the pen in his hand." She predicted an immediate fashionable success for the *Adventurer,* which unlike the *Rambler* was blessed with ease of diction and humor.[46] Her mistake about the authorship is not surprising, for Hawkesworth—who had succeeded Johnson as composer of the *Parliamentary Debates* and as editor of the *Gentleman's Magazine*—was long a skillful imitator of the Johnsonian style.[47] His choice of format for the *Adventurer* was likewise obviously derivative. The resemblances moved Kenrick to comment, "The Rambler and the Adventurer, in their journey to the temple of Fame, were . . . obliged, like travellers that had but one horse between them, to ride and tie, from month to month occasionally."[48] While Hawkesworth and Johnson were for the most part good friends, the latter was annoyed by his pomposity and once called him a "coxcomb" made arrogant by success.[49]

In a letter to Joseph Warton (March 8, 1753) Johnson indicated how actively interested he was in the *Adventurer.* At the request of Hawkesworth and Payne, he invited the scholar to furnish each month an essay on criticism or literature for which he would receive two guineas. (Johnson likewise, as with the *Rambler,* was paid two guineas for each essay.) Others, he said, had already agreed to contribute imaginative pieces and "pictures of life." Johnson admitted writing as "one of the fraternity though I have no part in the paper beyond now and then a motto."[50] As a consequence, Warton's first essay, No. 49 (which, like all his *Adventurer* papers, he signed "Z"), appeared April 24, 1753. Later an agreement was fixed whereby Hawkesworth should write forty-six papers and Warton and Johnson twenty-three each.[51] Again, on March 8, 1754, only one day before the last *Adventurer* was published, Johnson wrote to Warton. Now he congratulated him on his distinguished essays. And, as evidence both of his high regard for Warton and his personal interest in the *Adventurer,* Johnson explained that he had caused Hawkesworth to acknowledge publicly Warton's part in the series.[52]

Johnson was reluctant to admit the extent of his essay contributions to the *Adventurer*. Perhaps he wished Hawkesworth to gain the advantage of favorable public reaction, or perhaps he was merely exercising his customary reticence about his journalism. At any rate, it took the prodding of Hill Boothby to make him acknowledge confidentially that he wrote all the essays signed "T" from No. 45 on. Another essay, No. 39 (March 20, 1753), a philosophical disquisition on sleep, may have been in part by Johnson, for it too was signed "T." The attribution of this essay, however, wants fuller confirmation, since, according to Boswell, Johnson's first was No. 45, dated April 10.[53] One reason for suspecting Johnson's hand in No. 39, aside from the characteristic signature, is the reference to Barretier, whose biography he had written for the *Gentleman's Magazine*. There are also four other *Adventurer* papers (Nos. 34, 41, 53, 62) signed "T" in a series written by the fictional "Misargyrus." These in the past have proved vexing because Boswell attributed them to Richard Bathurst, whose capacity for hating rogues and Whigs pleased Johnson.[54] But Powell has shown conclusively that Johnson was the author of two in the so-called "Misargyrus" series, Nos. 53 and 62, and from his evidence he has assumed that the other two, Nos. 34 and 41, are also Johnson's.

Like many of the *Rambler* essays, to which Johnson's *Adventurer* contributions were comparable in length, his essays in the later series were philosophical in tone, with frequent emphasis upon literary themes and the quest for human happiness. Those in the second category, especially, conformed to the elevated goal of the *Adventurer,* whose ultimate design, Payne told Dr. Birch, "is to promote the practice of piety and virtue upon the principles of Christianity; yet in such a manner that they, for whose benefit it is chiefly intended, may not be tempted to throw it aside."[55] But Johnson's *Adventurer* essays lacked the sustained interest of those of either the *Rambler* or the *Idler;* with infrequent exceptions, as in the narrative of the "Admirable Crichton" (No. 81), they tended to be even more abstract and general. Furthermore, they lacked the pleasant characterizations and the narrative letters of the *Rambler* and *Idler*. Johnson was often at his best when he was angered by the misfortunes of his fellow men. In the *Adventurer,* however, he seemed to have little of this kind of incentive. He wrote of the unhappiness and miseries of authorship;

but here he stated his opinions with less force and, perhaps, with less inspiration than in his two major serials. Probably because he wrote thus occasionally and without direct responsibility, Johnson failed to achieve the intensity and vigor he could muster when editors were dogging him personally. His essays in the *Adventurer* lack the deep understanding and sympathy which distinguish the *Rambler*.

(c) *The Idler*

The year 1758 found Johnson, as usual, in need of funds. The edition of Shakespeare was progressing slowly and it was certainly no more adequate a source of income than his contributions to miscellaneous periodicals during this time. Requiring employment, thus, he began the *Idler* series as a business venture. The first *Idler* appeared in the second number of the *Universal Chronicle, or Weekly Gazette,* on Saturday, April 15, 1758, and the subsequent essays continued regularly each week through April 5, 1760. John Payne, who was one of several successive owners of the *Universal Chronicle* (between May 6, 1758, and January 6, 1760),[56] had the distinction of publishing all three of Johnson's serials. The arrangement for publishing the *Idler* was one of mutual importance. Not only would Johnson benefit from a more extensive circulation (though it was not so extensive as might have been hoped) than he had attained with the *Rambler* and *Adventurer,* but he would also share in the profits of the *Universal Chronicle*.[57] For its part, the *Universal Chronicle* was to be enhanced by a dignity and literary tone rarely found in newspapers. Although the *Idler* was directed to a less sophisticated audience than were the previous serials, the essays contain valuable examples of the periodical essayist's art. They are uniformly shorter and brisker, lighter and less philosophical, yet nonetheless moral in theme and tone. They also deal with many literary problems. On the whole, however, the *Idler* essays, somewhat in the manner of modern newspaper "columns," are more topical than either the *Rambler* or *Adventurer* papers. Each issue of the *Universal Chronicle* contained eight pages, with Johnson's rapidly written essay the dominating feature. Week after week the *Idler* was printed on the first page in two or more columns of leaded type.[58]

At the outset Johnson remembered his previous difficulty in

selecting an appropriate designation for the *Rambler*,[59] and he now gave the title more attention, even devoting a part of the opening essay to this topic. He wished a name that would be truly distinctive, one that would not elicit a false appeal such as numerous imitators of Addison and Steele relied on. Operating from this typically independent premise, he decided that the *Idler* was a most satisfactory title, fitting not only his own character but that of the reader as well. As he whimsically chided, "who can be more idle than the reader of the *Idler?*" The serial was to provide a common ground for the meeting of minds. And yet, offering no ambitious promises or important projects, the author assumed the privilege of writing as the mood directed him. Without taking Johnson's prolegomenon too seriously, even the casual reader soon discovers for himself that the *Idler* was a much more responsible literary venture than the prefatory remarks might suggest; for even in them Johnson's implied principal aim was that of edification coupled with entertainment.

Of the 104 essays in the series, all but twelve were written by Johnson. The other known contributors were Thomas Warton (Nos. 33, 93, 96), Bennet Langton (No. 67), Sir Joshua Reynolds (Nos. 76, 79, 82), William Emerson [or Emonson] (No. 98), Bonnell Thornton (No. 15). The essays of unknown authorship are Nos. 9, 42, and 54. While the first collected edition was in the press, Reynolds' articles—his first literary efforts—were offprinted with new pagination and given to him by Johnson in appreciation. The weekly essays made a stir in the literary world, and they were frequently reprinted.[60] The reprints duly acknowledged by the borrowing periodicals were authorized, but there were also many pirated versions of the *Idler*. Johnson warned literary thieves in the *Universal Chronicle* (January 5, 1759) that he would not hesitate to discredit them and degrade their publications. Bishop Percy used one paper (No. 4), *Charities and Hospitals,* for a charity sermon, and his superiors insisted against his will that it be printed. In this dilemma Percy sent an emissary to Johnson, who assented to the pious duplicity with amused tolerance.[61] Charles Burney, who did not meet Johnson until 1760, early recognized the merits of both the *Rambler* and the *Idler;* he read the essays to his friends and praised them extravagantly.[62] Mrs. Piozzi, who was in the habit of drawing upon

Johnson's writings, made no exception of the *Idler* from which she quoted in 1786 during an Italian sojourn.[63] And in Scotland, where his friends were almost as numerous as the anti-Scottish anecdotes attributed to him, Johnson himself had the pleasure of sending a set of *Idler* essays to Donald Macqueen, an appreciative minister.[64]

With the completion of two years' essays, the *Idler* was discontinued serially and republished by Newbery in more lucrative book form. The first collected edition, of which 1,500 sets were printed, appeared in two volumes in October, 1761. There is a record of an arrangement between Newbery and Johnson, whereby Johnson was to receive two-thirds of the profits of the edition—a sum of £84, 2*s*. 4*d*.—and Newbery one-third—or £42, 1*s*. 2*d*. The sale was slow and, generally, the collected *Idler* never attained the popularity of the collected *Rambler,* going to only four editions in Johnson's lifetime.[65] The first edition contained only 103 essays because Johnson omitted No. 22, a presumably offensive misanthropic document in which he detailed the instruction given by a mother vulture to her young. She is quoted as calling man "a friend to vultures . . . the only beast who kills that which he does not devour, and this quality makes him so much a benefactor to our species." It has been surmised that Johnson wrote this essay in a fit of despair and that he later regretted it.[66] Subsequent editions of the *Idler* contained 104 essays, Johnson having written a new No. 22 on the stupidity and ineffectiveness of imprisoning debtors. In the 1783 and following editions of the *Idler* the original No. 22 was appended. The third edition (1767) contained three additional essays by Johnson: (1) *Essay on Epitaphs,* first printed in the *Gentleman's Magazine* for 1740 (pp. 593-596); (2) *Dissertation on the Epitaphs Written by Pope,* first printed in the *Universal Visiter* in 1756 (pp. 207-219) and later added to the biography of Pope in the *English Poets;* (3) *Bravery of the English Common Soldiers,* first printed in the first number (January, 1760, pp. 37-39) of Smollett's *British Magazine,*[67] probably as a token of Johnson's interest in the new venture.

The *Idler* has been noted for characterizations such as those of Jack Whirler [John Newbery, according to Goldsmith], Ned Drugget, Zachary Treacle, Betty Broom, and Dick Minim the critic. The accuracy with which he was able to give the illusion of delineating

particular individuals even while he was portraying types, once again
—as in the *Rambler* series—offended sensitive persons who fancied
they had been caricatured. But Johnson appreciated a joke, and even
though—if Mrs. Piozzi can be trusted—he tried to conceal signs of
his authorship, he portrayed himself (in No. 31) in the character
of "Sober."[68]

Sober is a man of strong desires and quick imagination, so exactly balanced
by the love of ease, that they can seldom stimulate him to any difficult
undertaking; . . . Mr. Sober's chief pleasure is conversation; there is no
end of his talk or his attention; . . . But there is one time at night when
he must go home, that his friends may sleep. . . . These are the moments
of which poor Sober trembles at the thought.

The resemblances between Johnson and "Sober," each with his extremes of conviviality and melancholy, are too congruous to be acci-
dental. Like Johnson, "Sober" was an amateur chemist, and he
played with scientific experiments to stave off mental despair. The
Persian student, Gelaleddin, in another *Idler* essay (No. 75), was
intended to represent Johnson at the beginning of his London career.
By means of this oriental figure Johnson was able to voice his own
disillusion and, also, his own realism; for the theme of this essay
is that the world is a cruel place for anyone who hopes to win his
way by intellectual attainments and wit alone. The self-portrait is
one of those all too rare Johnsonian pieces which combine mild
satire and charming candor. Probably anyone but Johnson would be
accused of either guilelessness or conceit in describing himself as
"a young man amiable in his manners and beautiful in his form, of
boundless curiosity, incessant diligence, and irresistible genius, of
quick apprehension and tenacious memory, accurate without narrow-
ness, and eager for novelty without inconstancy." Satirical of his
physical attributes, frank about the powers of his intelligence, Johnson here recorded a priceless autobiographical sketch.

The prototype for "Betty Broom" (Nos. 26, 29) came from the
"Ladies Charity School for Training Girls as Servants." The school
was founded in the first year of Queen Anne's reign, in the parish
of St. Sepulchre, under the auspices of the "Society for the Promotion
of Christian Knowledge." Johnson and Mrs. Anna Williams, his
blind dependent, were interested in its organization, and Mrs. Piozzi
became active in its operation. Mrs. Williams left her inheritance to

the school.[69] Observable in both of these essays, despite their matter-of-fact tone, is Johnson's unfailing compassion for the oppressed and the outcast. *Idler,* Nos. 26 and 29, is an effective indictment of the treatment generally accorded eighteenth-century servants, especially those who aspire to literary or intellectual improvement.

The light, often jocular, tone of this series could not always persist in the face of sorrow and melancholy. Sarah Johnson, his mother, was buried in Lichfield on January 23, 1759, and four days later he published his *Idler,* No. 41, to state his profound reaction.[70] The final paper also was a gloomy but religious meditation in which he questioned his own popularity and shrank from the finality of concluding the *Idler.* He observed the significance of the *Idler's* expiring during Easter week (Saturday, April 5, 1760), "which the Christian world has always set apart for the examination of the conscience, the review of life, the extinction of earthly desires, and the renovation of holy purposes. . . ." For all of Johnson's intention of concealing his own identity, he gave himself away as clearly as though he had signed his name to his final essay serial, in consequence of his gravity of tone, his pious sincerity, his statement of attitudes which had come to be recognized in his own wide circle of friends as typically Johnsonian.

Although Johnson had now concluded his career as an essay serialist, he was established as the dean of English journalists. The booksellers had complained that his writings were not profitable, and yet there is a likelihood that, encouraged by an increasing public demand for his essays, they urged him to undertake still another serial. That, at least, is the extremely interesting speculation that Dr. Birch recorded in a letter to Lord Hardwicke (October 25, 1760):

> Sam Johnson is in treaty with certain booksellers to supply three papers a week in the nature of essays like the Rambler, at the unusual rate (if my [information?] be true) of three guineas a paper. But I question whether even the temptation of so liberal a reward will awaken him from his natural indolence enough to fulfill his engagement. For when his *Rambler,* which came out but twice a week, was on foot, Cave, the proprietor, has told me, that the copy was seldom sent to the press till late in the night before the day of publication.[71]

Such a compact with the booksellers might, indeed, have been considered. Birch writes with convincing assurance, and he was close enough to Johnson to have access to this information. Though never completed, the negotiations show that despite their earlier misgivings the booksellers had come to regard Johnson as a good risk. His serial fame, especially as author of the *Rambler,* was to receive material recognition, if Birch is correct. Perhaps the increased stipend from the customary two guineas to three guineas a paper should not be considered extravagantly liberal, but the booksellers could give no more convincing indication of their respect and admiration. Speculative though this conclusion must be, the temptation to believe it is strong, and there is no doubt that by 1760 Johnson was preëminent as an essay serialist.

II

JOHNSON ON AUTHORSHIP

As the unofficial tutor and spokesman for authors in eighteenth-century England, Johnson often enunciated his feelings about their status and their professional problems, and nowhere did he express his views more cogently or more forcefully than in his essay serials.[72] There he stated his serious regard for the responsibilities of authorship. There too he sympathized with the Grub Street hacks over their economic misfortunes and at the same time condemned shoddy work. He denounced public fickleness and extolled independence. He decried the demands for trivia and the cheap, deliberate quest for fame. Never before or since has a literary figure plunged more wholeheartedly into an examination of the problems and miseries of authorship. Trenchant though Johnson frequently was, he never professed to be a crusader or reformer. He was, rather, a moral philosopher of letters. He realized from experience how chaotic and inequitable writing—especially journalism—was, and he hoped to fix attention on this profession and to exemplify by his own career the precepts he intended to teach. Both compassion and integrity vivify those essays concerned with literary matters.

His faith in the superior attributes of first-rate authors may be traced as far back as his poetic characterization of *The Young Author.* Imbued with a dualistic notion of the author as teacher and entertainer, as he indicated in *Rambler,* No. 3, and *Adventurer,* Nos. 137 and 138, he expected other writers to aim toward his own elevated goal. His expectation was not an immodest one, for though he may have been troubled frequently by a sense of psychological or temperamental inadequacy, he never had any doubts about his technical abilities as a writer. Nevertheless, he was overtly concerned with the moral value of his accomplishments, so that he could wonder in *Adventurer*, No. 137, whether his efforts had been "applied to a good and laudable purpose, or suffered to fume away in useless evaporations." The uncertainty of this nature which disturbed him throughout his life is poignantly observable, for instance, in his *Prayers and Meditations*. Implicit in his career—irrespective of outward assurance—is the humility with which he undertook important tasks, judging himself as he expected other writers to judge themselves, and candidly recognizing his own shortcomings. He admitted in No. 137 that, on the whole, people in his day read but little and then to be amused. Willing to concede that even the writer who composes merely to entertain is not wholly useless, he nevertheless protested that entertainment should not be his sole purpose. No. 137, in a way, was Johnson's public apology and modest tribute to himself, for he felt that in the *Adventurer* he had presented what was both useful and entertaining.

But writing was not merely an abstract lesson for Johnson, who insisted that a man's conduct must meet the standards set forth in his compositions. Once more Johnson was proposing a rule that he followed assiduously and that he had to justify in his associations with Savage and the other Grubeans. We may believe his pain in his noting (*Rambler*, No. 14) glaring inconsistencies between the life of the average writer and his writings. If a man is ethically better in his writings than in his conduct, it is because he finds teaching in the abstract easier than self-application. Here (as in *Adventurer*, No. 137) Johnson argued that we must at least propose the idea of perfection in order that we may have an ultimate goal. A writer who cannot live up to his own stated maxims in his everyday conduct would do well to write anonymously to avoid the danger of exposing his true character to a credulous public. Johnson could justifiably have written about himself as readily as about Milton, who, "in a letter to a learned stranger, by whom he had been visited, with great reason congratulates himself upon the conciousness of being found equal to his own character, and having preserved, in a private and familiar interview, that reputation which his works had procured him."

As a practical matter, Johnson insisted upon a high level of technical competence for authors. In *Adventurer*, No. 115, he wrote that their qualifications must include perfect knowledge of subject, mastery of language, "a style clear, pure, nervous, and expressive," with "the superaddition of elegance and imagery." Thus, even as he demanded of the literary critic a comprehensive knowledge of literature in general, he now demanded of all writers a comprehensive talent for rhetorical expression. Whether the writer is a literary critic or a creative artist, he must have above all things the ability to communicate, for the teacher who fails to convey his instruction serves a futile cause. Furthermore, Johnson appreciated the writer's need for a scholarly background; but in *Adventurer*, No. 85, he also decried the folly of drawing all experience from books. This to Johnson was an important consideration, which he still felt keenly almost thirty years later. "Knowledge of mankind indeed, less extensive than that of Addison, will show that to write and to live are very different." The thought reappears in the life of Milton, where he distinguishes between the secluded scholar and the man who has to face the world for his living.[73] For the best training Johnson recommended moderation and balance between intensive study and general reading. From his own experiences he also concluded that extemporaneous conversation would help a writer to gain facility with the pen. "[M]ethod is the excellence of writing, and unconstraint the grace of conversation." A superb conversationalist himself, Johnson had admitted in *Rambler*, No. 14, that writing is the more difficult medium. But too many capable writers and scholars, he had complained, are wanting in the refinements of parlor talk.

The writer will, of course, derive great satisfaction from his own skillful work, after the accomplished fact and perhaps even in anticipation of it. But for Johnson, as for most professional writers, the physical act of writing was an agony. Thus he complained in *Idler*, No. 102, that a man's business is seldom his pleasure, and that no one but an amateur would pretend to enjoy the creative process. Even under favorable circumstances, Johnson commented in *Adventurer*, No. 138, writing is painful. "Composition is, for the most part, an effort of slow diligence and steady perseverance, to which the mind is dragged by necessity or resolution, and from which the attention is every moment starting to more delightful amusements." Authors, continued Johnson, suffer in their struggle to find distinctive words. Indeed, suffering of spirit as well as of body is the essence of serious literature. This he implied in *Rambler,* No. 184, where he said that actual composition must begin from and proceed under stress; like life itself, authorship is the fruit of troubled uncertainty and chance. Johnson was perhaps more acutely conscious than most writers of physical and psychological strain, and he was disinclined to linger over his own compositions. He warned against haste, however, in *Rambler,* No. 169, as an obstacle to adequate writing. "One of the most pernicious effects of haste, is obscurity." And "[n]o vanity can more justly incur contempt and indignation than that which boasts of negligence and hurry." The ancients, modest and hard-working, were, he felt, superior writers. Men like Milton and Pope achieved supremacy by blotting frequently. But in Johnson's generation too many writers eager for praise were willing to rush hastily into print.

A constant source of irritation was the callous abuse of literary dignity by uncritical and inept persons who flooded the bookstalls with valueless writings. In *Idler,* No. 85, he observed, "few of those who fill the world with books have any pretensions to the hope either of pleasing or instructing. They have often no other task than to lay two books before them, out of which they compile a third, without any new materials of their own, and with very little application of judgment to those which former authors have supplied." Notwith-standing this cynical attitude Johnson admitted that some compila-tions, such as contain scattered bits of scientific information, are useful and even laudable if the material is properly collected and classified. Most compilations, unfortunately, are made with little care; even as "a corrupt society has many laws . . . an ignorant age has many books." Johnson's chief objection was to repetition and the consequent uselessness of the material gathered together. Writers who thus extract from others while pretending to be original authors, he said, are secondary and their influence—good or evil—is shortlived. Although writers cannot always be excellent, they can at least avoid causing mischief and should have an honest purpose.

These observations inevitably call up the larger problem of plagiarism, on which he discoursed in both the *Rambler* (No. 143) and the *Adventurer* (No. 95). This, of all literary accusations, he said, is the most dangerous and destructive. It is dangerous because there is always the reasonable possibility of coincidence, and it would be unfair to charge plagiarism simply because an author had duplicated a mood or a sentiment. Before condemning, the reader should take cognizance of the subject; for certain ideas like love and hate, greed and resentment, ambition and indolence are eternal and may be described innumerable times and in different ways. Man, as Johnson wisely pointed out in the *Adventurer,* has a relative paucity of basic emotions. Definitions of like things are bound to be similar, and descriptions of phenomena must have some resemblance. Two closely parallel passages in Virgil and Horace do not presuppose literary theft. If Cicero and Ovid made statements on the honor or victory belonging to common soldiers, that is no indication of plagiarism. Following this argument, in the *Rambler,* Johnson asserted that an author sometimes proves his good judgment and is not necessarily to be stigmatized as a plagiarist when he borrows from another. Yet Johnson did not condone real plagiarism, "one of the most reproachful, though, perhaps, not the most atrocious of literary crimes," as he described it in the *Adventurer;* or, as in his simple definition in the *Dictionary,* "Theft; literary adoption of the thoughts or works of another." His views on plagiarism tend to be abstract, for he attempts no concrete basis for finding fault. They are, nevertheless, notable for characteristic reasonableness and understanding.

Among a formidable array of prejudices one would have to give prominence to Johnson's loathing for dilettantism and ineptness in any form. He was particularly irritated by lady writers, even though a few of his most valued literary associates—notably Miss Mulso, Miss Carter, and Mrs. Lennox—thus appear to fall under his indictment. He was singularly intolerant of women who set themselves up in the professions—whether preaching or art or writing—in competition with men.[74] His unemancipated attitude, of course, was typical of the eighteenth century and much of the nineteenth and twentieth. But more important was his feeling toward those who wrote for social prestige in competition with authors in need of daily bread, or who had at least demonstrated peculiar talents for authorship. And ladies, according to Johnson and conventional standards, could have no more than a dilettante interest in letters. So it was that he was especially intolerant of women writers, although he would have admitted grudgingly that a few had superior attributes. In *Adventurer,* No. 115, as in *Idler,* No. 2, and in *The Present State of Literature,* Johnson expressed his dissatisfaction that women had taken up authorship, which like warfare had been considered a man's prerogative, until "the revolution of years has now produced a generation of Amazons of the pen."

Generously, however, he did not limit his condemnation of this "epidemical conspiracy for the destruction of paper" to women, observing that there were plenty of useless writers of both sexes. In *Rambler,* No. 145, as well as in *Adventurer,* No. 115, *Idler,* No. 2, and *The Present State of Literature,* he derided the widespread activities of the literary inept. "There is now no class of men without its authors [he wrote in the latter essay], from the peer to the thrasher; nor can the sons of literature be confined any longer to Grub Street or Moorfields; they are spread over all the town, and all the country, and fill every stage of habitation, from the cellar to the garret." His, he complained in the *Adventurer,* is an age of authors, "and he that beats the anvil or guides the plough, not content with supplying corporal necessities, amuses himself in the hours of leisure with providing intellectual pleasures for his countrymen." Comparable sentiments emerge from the other essays. In *Idler,* No. 2, thus, Johnson invited the contributions of only those who aspired to be professional writers and rejected the bad phrases of cooks, threshers, traders, and girls who were turning glibly to letters. As in his earlier essays, he was pleading that each person elevate himself in the calling for which he is best suited, that writing is a special skill not to be trespassed casually. As editor of the *Idler* Johnson intended to maintain the integrity and dignity of authorship.

As for the talented, serious writer, he must be more than an attractive moralist. He must also have a set of esthetic standards and an independent spirit that will make him impervious to the demands of a fickle public. To be most effective, as Johnson demonstrated in the life of the "Admirable Crichton" (*Adventurer,* No. 81), each person should recognize his own abilities and develop rather than under-rate or subvert them. They suffer the most who fail to live up to their own expectations; self-judgment, thus, is vital. In the absence of responsible criticism, he insisted similarly in *Rambler*, No. 23, the writer must be his own critic and guide. Not all writers, however, possess the ability to judge themselves. Many, he pointed out in *Adventurer*, No. 138, dream so ardently of success that they often blind themselves to their true function. And, as he said in *Rambler*, No. 21, the guilt of self-infatuation leads these deluded persons to admire their "juvenile compositions" and to be so smitten with the flow of their own words as to preclude any kind of effective self-criticism. The public, then, seeing the errors by which writers were trapped, were frequently justified in their harshness. Since a man is judged by his worst as well as his best performances, he should at least take cautionary measures. Johnson, who had a passion for anonymity in his periodical writings and respected it as a right, urged contributors (in *Rambler*, No. 56) to "observe the cautions of Swift, and write secretly in his own chamber, without communicating his design to his nearest friend, for the nearest friend will be pleased with an opportunity of laughing."[75] As a solution anonymity is not satisfactory, but Johnson regarded it as at least a partial means of frustrating capricious commentators.

At this midpoint in his literary career he was openly contemptuous of querulous critics. His own lessons, which had been dearly purchased, he wished to impress vigorously upon younger writers, thus warning, in *Rambler*, No. 21, that a "successful author is equally in danger of the diminution of his fame, whether he continues or ceases to write." The new author, unlike himself, frequently attempted to appease his most dangerous opponent, the professional critic. Sardonically Johnson suggested, in *Rambler*, No. 3, that use might be made of both claret and flattery. Whereas the tough *Rambler* rejected the authority of "the ministers of criticism," he was well aware that the less hardened author, being sensitive to attack and desiring to preserve his work, could not adequately withstand the critic's spleen. The critic's "purpose is to conquer; the author only hopes to escape." Too many critics, said Johnson, have faulty vision: either they look at everything too closely, as through a microscope; or more clearly but distantly as through a telescope. Seldom, as he frequently contended, is criticism fatal to the author who, if worthy, will answer arrogance with firmness of spirit. "No genius," he asserted in *Idler,* No. 60, "was ever blasted by the breaths of criticks."[76]

He delighted in singling out critics for his satire, especially because they abused their influence and molded untutored popular tastes to specious standards (*Idler,* No. 3). One of his most famous portrayals is that of Dick Minim (*Idler,* Nos. 60, 61), through whose depiction he brilliantly expressed his contempt for popular criticism. "Criticism is a study by which men grow important and formidable at a very small expense," and it is an easy approach toward early success. As Johnson often maintained, the real danger lies not in censoriousness but in the total absence of any kind of recognition, good or bad. This was an attitude which he had vivified in *Rambler,* No. 144, in his threefold classification of critics. Of the "Roarers," "Whisperers," and "Moderators," he had considered the last most pernicious, for they listen to all arguments, ever extenuating writers' faults but never denying them.[77] Minim, who as a rule was wise enough to attack none who might resist him, became famous by uttering all the accepted clichés pertaining to versification and by speaking learnedly of the defects of the traditionally accepted poets. Of all the writers examined, Milton alone proved thoroughly acceptable to Minim. To be sure, he accomplished nothing positive; but neither did he succeed in damaging anyone. For Johnson the two *Idler* essays served a dual purpose. They let him work off in amusing fashion his animus against critical superficiality which distorted public taste. And they gave him an outlet for his discontent with the trend of Milton worship, in anticipation of his more fully developed analysis in the *English Poets.*

Even as Johnson derided critics he also scorned mercurial popular taste and was superior to the whims of booksellers. He commented bitterly in *Idler,* No. 102, upon public inconstancy. If, upon the appearance of a new book, the author is feted and dined and footmen are deferential, "he may be sure that his work has been praised by some leader of literary fashion." If, on the other hand, an author fails to meet fashionable expectations, he is spurned by all. With a power of observation and a sympathy derived from personal experience, Johnson successfully recorded the futility and anguish to which the

professional author could expect to fall heir. In the same mood he
pretended, in *Idler,* No. 55, that he had a communication from an
aspiring young author who had studied natural history intensively for
many years before he began to write on that subject, and then only
to meet with rebuffs. The essay is at least partially autobiographical,
for like Johnson in his early London years the acolyte had offers from
neither booksellers nor patrons. Like his creator, Johnson, this author
was irascible. A bookseller offered to print the work if subscriptions
could be guaranteed. "I lost my patience, and gave him a kick; for
which he has indicted me." The incident is amusingly reminiscent of
the more celebrated one, when Johnson purportedly struck the bookseller Thomas Osborne. Johnson, who boasted of having "beat
many a fellow,"[78] also had little respect for the subscription method
of publication.

Among the authorial topics which could incite Johnson to belliger-
ence were what he considered unreasonable public demands for
novelty and foolish attempts by authors to satisfy them. Most essayists
select their subjects without discrimination, he asserted in *Rambler,*
No. 184, and thus earn a good deal of the criticism directed against
them. Under the pressure of providing novelty they are prey to all
kinds of error. Their judgment is confounded, their imagination is
unchecked. Johnson believed strongly in the neoclassical concept of
originality, but he bitterly resented innovation that was merely for
innovation's sake. Once again he found the critical arbiters of literary
style at fault, for it was they who insisted on novelty which had no
particular merits in its own right. Consequently a beginning series
like the *Idler,* he said in No. 3, which had the disadvantage of working in a field much plowed by predecessors, was "forced to peep into
neglected corners, to note the casual varieties of the same species,
and to recommend [itself] by minute industry and distinctions too
subtle for common eyes." The essayist's task is painfully and unnecessarily complicated by sluggish readers. Undiplomatically, though with
vigorous independence, Johnson lashes away at the many who freeze
"in perpetual inactivity, till some external impulse puts them in
motion; who awake in the morning, vacant of thought, with minds
gaping for the intellectual food which some kind essayist has been
accustomed to supply." What Johnson regarded as particularly de-

plorable was this tendency to let others think for them and to demand writings that were merely entertaining.

In the *Idler* he evinced an interest in contemporary political matters and even current events to a far greater degree than in his earlier essay serials. He might in the *Rambler,* as in No. 23, reveal his impatience with social foibles and trivia, but he made no attempt to associate them with any specific institutions or groups. On the whole, Johnson did not believe that opinions on evanescent affairs had any place in serious literature; but he was sensitive to the popular medium in which the *Idler* appeared, and—at least in part —he considered his weekly essay as little more than a journalistic enterprise. And whatever Johnson felt about the place of current events in literary composition, his prejudices were strong enough to make him welcome an opportunity to express them. His apparently sudden allusion, in *Idler,* No. 65, to "a scribbler for a party" as one of the "lowest of all human beings" is merely the reiteration of an attitude which he had already stated more than once in the *Gentleman's Magazine.* When Johnson drew his *Idler* materials from the news of the day, he often retorted with sly malice to the foibles of the citizenry. One item which appeared in the *London Chronicle,* for instance, attracted his mordant wit and gave him the opportunity to write a piece of vigorous satire. The newspaper had described the feat of a young woman, who on a wager, rode one thousand miles in one month.[79] In *Idler,* No. 6, Johnson ridiculed the interest given to this event and suggested that the courageous equestrienne had been ill-treated in being honored with flowers rather than guineas. Trivial though the occurrence is, it suggests that Johnson on occasion could turn his attention forcefully from the general to the particular.

A long-standing critic of the business of news gathering, he decried it as an insignificant occupation little better than party writing. Compilers of newspapers, he felt, were often incompetent and grasping, but their audiences hardly inspired elevation. He declared, in *Idler,* No. 30, that one "of the amusements of idleness is reading without the fatigue of close attention, and the world therefore swarms with writers whose wish is not to be studied, but to be read." News writers, he sneered in *Idler,* No. 7, are necessary "in a nation where much wealth produces much leisure, and one part of the people has

nothing to do but observe the lives and fortunes of the other." He
was horrified (in No. 30) by the outpourings of news scribblers as
well as by their lack of scruples and talents. Prepared to think the
worst, Johnson charged them with capitalizing on public sadism
through their exaggerated reports of violence and wars. His repugnance for such editorial malpractice was typical of that of a large
number of his contemporaries who felt that this frenzy of sensationalism warranted intelligent censure. Public morality was at such
a dismal ebb that Johnson was justified in saying, "I know not
whether more is to be dreaded from streets filled with soldiers accustomed to plunder, or from garrets filled with scribblers accustomed
to lie." Observing (in No. 7) the vast amounts of repetitions occur-
ring in the morning and evening news, Johnson made a practical
suggestion that the hordes of news writers affiliate and pool their
information. Unconsciously, and despite his cynicism, Johnson's proposal anticipates the sound practice of modern reporting.

High on his list of journalistic infamies was advertising, which he
termed in *Idler,* No. 40, a betrayal of the reader who did not expect
an advertisement in lieu of news. Nor did he think well of a com-
mercialized wandering from the majestic to the ridiculous, from the
depiction of war-clad Mohawks to advertisements of mustard, butter,
and razor straps. And yet, with an almost charming disregard for
strict consistency, Johnson himself was later to write a number of
advertisements, mainly political.[80] His own practice, to be sure,
was motivated by friendship in what he thought useful causes; in
characteristically humane fashion, he made his principles flexible
enough to accommodate special circumstances.

Several of the *Idler* papers were concerned with other problems
allied to his journalistic interests, among them, biography, history,
and translation. Johnson restated (in No. 84) his preference for
biography, which "is, of the various kinds of narrative writing, that
which is most eagerly read, and most readily applied to the purposes
of life."[81] His continuing interest in translation resulted in two *Idler*
essays (Nos. 68, 69) about the history of that literary mode. Among
the distinguished works which he admired and wished to preserve
in manuscript form, he wrote in No. 65, was Clarendon's *History*.
From Clarendon, Burnet, and other recent as well as ancient historians

Johnson had borrowed freely for many of the essays he wrote for the *Gentleman's Magazine.* Although in his works and in his conversation he frequently protested that the value of historical writing was far inferior to biographical, Johnson had an excellent knowledge of such writing.[82] His own practice is sufficient reason to believe that his expressed lack of interest in history must not be taken completely at face value.

Johnson's delayed literary success gave him considerable opportunity to think about the transience and insecurity of literary fame. Only singleness of purpose, as he knew, could sustain the author. "Fame," he said, "is a shuttlecock. If it be struck only at one end of the room, it will soon fall to the ground. To keep it up, it must be struck at both ends."[83] His attitude toward the quest for fame is complemented by frequent solemn remarks scattered throughout the *Rambler* and in *Idler,* No. 59. By the time Johnson had attained middle age, his literary reputation was firmly established. But he knew from stringent experience how difficult it is to rise above arrogant criticism and to crack public indifference. He was jealous of his hard-won fame, but he was also deeply sensitive to the struggles of other writers of merit who had not yet achieved recognition.

Fame as a writer's principal motivation, he exhorted in *Rambler,* No. 193, is dangerous because it leads to shallow opportunism. But any normal person desires approbation, and if he so regulates his own work as genuinely to merit applause, his desire for fame may come to a good end. Writers have long sought to build eternal monuments to themselves which are all too often inadequately founded. This we may note (and he repeats the idea in the *Idler*) in the libraries crowded with unknown and unread books. The writer should be willing to recognize his limitations, but, as Johnson asserted in *Rambler,* No. 25—and elsewhere—many excellent writers are ignored. The responsibility for this neglect is that of the public which, devoid of intellectual interests, will not read an author until his reputation has been fixed. But often, even thereafter, fame proves to be transient. Such declination Johnson regarded as justifiable—both in *Rambler,* No. 193, and *Idler,* No. 59—when prestige has been gained through servility or friendship; or, just as tenuously, through the appeal of subjects with contemporary rather than universal attraction.

The writer on topics of universal truth has permanent value. But "he that lays his labors out upon temporary subjects, easily finds readers, and quickly loses them; for what should make the book valued when the subject is no more?" This theme is almost an obsession with Johnson, whose insistence upon universality is characteristic of neo-classicism and his own practice. When he broke away from this doctrine, as he sometimes did in the *Idler,* he was less effective in the delineation of particular events and people than in the formulation of generalized truths which were moral and far-reaching in their intention. In *Rambler,* Nos. 3 and 21, Johnson emphasized that the only true test of merit is time, which will preserve superior writings against the carpings of critics.

Among the problems of authorship he thought often about independence. Self-sufficiency, in his opinion, even if accompanied by poverty, is infinitely superior to the degrading rewards of patronage. He was, to be sure, keenly aware of the power of material goods and of the comforts denied him because of his lack of affluence. Although poverty horrified him, as he demonstrated in the "Misargyrus" series, he never deluded himself into believing that riches were the answer to happiness. The speciousness which he attributed to purely materialistic goals is clear elsewhere, in the *Adventurer* (Nos. 102, 119, 120). He might write jestingly about the benefits of living in a garret, as in *Rambler,* No. 117; or allegorically about the debasement of patronage, as in *Rambler,* No. 91; or in varying degrees of humor and seriousness about authorship, as in *Rambler,* Nos. 21, 26, 27, 136, 145, 163, and 208. But whatever his tone, and despite the fact that he wrote numerous dedications on behalf of others, he maintained the most resolute scorn for patronage and the obsequiousness demanded by literary patrons. This was undoubtedly a part of the same native independence and pride which led him to write his classic denunciation of Chesterfield.[84] This matter, as well as his allusions in the *Dictionary* and his conversation, are familiar. A summation of the attitudes in the *Rambler,* although it alters nothing, provides a valuable impletion of his theories.

In No. 136 he attacked indiscriminate dedications, for "[t]o scatter praise or blame without regard to justice, is to destroy the distinction of good and evil." Some dedications, he acknowledged, are merited and some patrons deserve praise; but only when the motives of both patron and writer are commendable. "To encourage merit with praise is the great business of literature." His major concern, however, is with abuses, as in No. 21, where he protests that authors are hurt and limited by not having a free choice of subjects. Association with the great often causes a writer to be influenced because he wishes to please in exchange for favors rendered by patrons, who, he asserted in Nos. 26, 27, and 163, frequently propagate false hopes. In his final *Rambler*, No. 208, Johnson prided himself on not having stooped to attain patronage. He could not "boast that, in the progress of [his] undertaking, [he had] been animated by the rewards of the liberal, the caresses of the great, or the praises of the eminent." Likewise, in the preface to the *Dictionary*, he was to assert proudly, perhaps sadly, that he had written "without any patronage of the great; not in the soft obscurities of retirement, or under the shelter of academick bowers."

Perhaps Johnson had a tendency to dramatize the evils of patronage unwarrantably from his own unhappy experiences, and to intensify many of his attitudes toward authorship. The reality of his bitterness, however, is unquestionable, the empiricism of his beliefs and his consistent reflections resulting in brilliant, even profound, commentaries on writing conditions in his day. As for exaggerations, if such indeed exist, they are readily defensible. Literary license—as Johnson would agree—is always acceptable if it does not conceal the truth and if it is directed toward high purpose. As adviser and critic, Johnson was always constructive and his opinions ultimately accurate.

CHAPTER V

CRITIC OF THE LEARNED: JOHNSON
AS BOOK REVIEWER

I

JOHNSON'S description of his times as "an age of authors" is an apt one. In response to public demands for writings on all subjects, booksellers and printers and writers combined forces to keep an endless supply of reading material before their patrons. And as books multiplied, so did reviews and notices of books. These reports were indispensable for those who wished guidance in their reading, and for those who claimed literary taste but preferred the capsule synthesis to the whole work. One of the significant developments of eighteenth-century journalism, thus, was the periodical which featured book reviews. For the literary historian these journals provide useful data about the kinds of books read in the eighteenth century and the physical details incidental to their publication, such, for example, as names of publishers, prices, formats, and dates of publication. They offer also an insight into one more aspect of the employment to which literary men, both great and small, turned for supplementing their incomes.[1]

The crude beginnings of the British book review may be traced to a Continental publication, Denis de Sallo's *Journal des Sçavans* (1665), and to Henry Oldenburg's *Philosophical Transactions of the Royal Society* (1665). Slightly later but still archetypal in the nature of their reviews are journals like Jean Cornand de la Crose's *Universal Historical Bibliotheque* (1687). John Dunton's *Athenian Gazette* (1691), and Peter Motteux's *Gentleman's Journal* (1692). The first British literary journal in the eighteenth century was Michael de la Roche's *Memoirs of Literature* (1710), which carried literary news, reviews, and book notices; thereafter, reviews became a part of the British periodical tradition, though most of these review journals were short-lived.[2] The *Literary Journal* of Dublin (1744-1749), using the method of analysis and abundant quotation, deserves recognition for advancing the mode. But the first of the truly notable periodicals was the *Monthly Review* (1749-1844), initiated by Ralph Griffiths, which developed into a critical journal produced by distinguished contributors, after beginning as a collection of extracts. The chief rival of the *Monthly* was the *Critical Review* (1756-1817), begun by Smollett and Archibald Hamilton. The *Critical* supported the principles of the Tories and the Anglican Church, in opposition to the principles of the *Monthly*.[3] It was the latter journal which Johnson—a contributor to the *Critical*—censured once for lack of piety and which he believed inferior to the *Critical*. The *Monthly* and the *Critical* had common aims of completeness, timeliness, and critical objectivity (though this last point frequently may be disputed).

Basically more limited in appeal than other kinds of periodical offerings which were aimed at less intellectual readers, book reviewing nevertheless acquired vogue. Appearing both in journals exclusively literary and in those which allotted departments to literary matters, the earliest book reviews were presented in a manner primitive and even indiscriminate. Variety as well as quality was the standard of selection. In the late seventeenth and early eighteenth centuries reviews dealt with books and pamphlets on literature, science, theology, philosophy, witchcraft, medals, biography, and history. Nor did they necessarily limit themselves to current publications. Dr. Samuel Jebb, in his *Bibliotheca Literaria* (1722-1724), for instance, reported on obscure works which "are in a manner lost to the world, by reason of their being too small to be separately published." Books published on the Continent were also reviewed regularly for British readers.

The term "review" is a misnomer for the conceptual form; a more accurate designation would probably be "abstract" or "extract." Readers were at first left largely to their own abilities to formulate critical opinions. At the outset reviews were usually abstracts or copious specimens out of context, later becoming abstracts-extracts with some critical opinions, and finally critical opinions united with generous samplings. Originally, thus, skillful abridgment or digestion rather than critical acumen was the reviewer's responsibility. Even in 1757 Shebbeare was complaining about reviewers who presented mere specimens from the originals without critical guidance.[4] There is, in fact, much evidence that though review journals were widely read they were not universally admired. As Goldsmith tartly commented in 1759 in the *Present State of Polite Learning* (Ch. XI):

We have two literary reviews in London, with critical newspapers and magazines without number. The compilers of these resemble the commoners of Rome; they are all for levelling property, not by encreasing their own, but by diminishing that of others. . . . The most diminutive son of fame, or of famine, has his *we* and his *us*, his *firstlys* and his *secondlys* as methodical, as if bound in cow-hide and closed with clasps of brass. Were these Monthly Reviews and Magazines frothy, pert, or absurd, they might find some pardons; but to be dull and dronish, is an encroachment on the prerogative of a folio.

Not until the end of the century, with growing emphasis upon positive if not always constructive critical standards, do we finally see clear indications of the direction toward the great nineteenth-century journals like the *Edinburgh Review* and the *Quarterly Review*.

The eighteenth-century pattern is consistent and, on the whole, predictable. Generally the comments of the reviewer are prefatory to the extractions which compose the bulk of his review. For example he may offer a few sentences by way of reference to a well-known book that he suggests merits rereading. In other instances he may endorse a book because of its unusual contents: this is especially true if the work concerned deals with antiquity. The earliest kind of critical commentary is seldom more than a recommendation that the book be read, and the reviewer offers no particular evaluative reason. That most of the early reviews are implicitly laudatory suggests a practical association between the reviewers and the booksellers for the stimulation of sales. Booksellers, in fact, frequently had a direct financial interest in the publication of review journals. Beyond formal praise, the early reviewers are surprisingly timid about stating their own opinions; and often they quote some authority or well-known author about the subject in a book under review rather than rely upon their own judgment. With the advance of the century, however, and the growth of journals like the *Monthly* and *Critical*, criticism—or at least opinion—shares importance with extracts and paraphrase. Johnson's reviews are characteristic of the techniques evolved during the century, ranging from little more than notices combined with specimens to penetrating analyses of content and form.

II

At one time Johnson seriously considered editing a *Bibliothèque,* or review journal, proceeding so far as to study other periodicals and to invite contributions from Thomas Warton. Yet reviewing was a task for which he had no more fondness than for any of his Grub Street activities. Only on infrequent occasions, when he felt a strong conviction about a subject, did he attempt to make his reviews any more than the customary hack pieces of the day. "A man," he said, "will more easily write a sheet all his own, than read an octavo volume to get extracts." As Boswell suggests, Johnson was the rare individual who preferred writing original compositions to extracting from the works of others. For a task which he considered onerous, therefore, six guineas a sheet ("but not *communibus sheetibus*") was not an unusually generous rate of payment. "Pray, Sir," asked Boswell, "by a sheet of a review is it meant that it shall be all of the writer's own composition? or are extracts, made from a book reviewed, deducted?" To which Johnson replied from his experience, "No, Sir: it is a sheet, no matter of what."[5] Johnson quickly stifled his interrogator's notion that extraction from the work of others is simpler than original composition.

Johnson wrote a considerable number of reviews, the majority of them for the *Literary Magazine* shortly after the publication of the *Dictionary.* But he also reviewed works for the *Gentleman's Magazine,* the *London Chronicle,* and the *Critical Review.* For the greater part, he resorted to book reviewing only as a matter of practical necessity. When Sir Joshua Reynolds expressed surprise at the quantity of good writing which appeared in literary reviews, Johnson advised him, "those who write in them, write well, in order to be paid well." Fame, he insisted, was no motive.[6] Nor did he consider journalistic reviews consequential as a form of literary criticism. He once took only casual heed of a "notice in some paper" regarding the unauthorized *Beauties of Johnson* (1782), for he maintained that "he was accustomed to think little of newspapers."[7]

Curiously enough, one of Johnson's most substantial reviews was his first, which appeared in the *Gentleman's Magazine* in four installments between March and June, 1742.[8] His subject was the controversial Duchess of Marlborough, who had invited the hostility of many pamphleteers, but who also had her champions, among them Henry Fielding.[9] Johnson's review was of her memoirs which, after she had lost favor with Queen Anne and had been dismissed from the Court, she commissioned Nathaniel Hooke to write for a reported fee of £5,000. Indignant over the Duchess' disrespect for recent British monarchs, Johnson made no pretense of examining the book with detachment. His technique alternates between that of the essay serialist, expounding on the historico-literary subject of memoirs, and the journalistic biographer, concerned with inner details of personality, morality, and politics. Instead of the customarily meager critical or quasi-critical introduction followed by specimens, Johnson wrote an essay that combines literary polish and personal rancor. Anyone reading only the version of the review which appears in the Oxford edition of the *Works* would be misled by a seeming attitude of acceptance, for this is a reprint of the first installment only and omits important subsequent opinions. Both bland and objective, these introductory pages contain broad observations on memoirs in general and an almost casual summation of the Duchess of Marlborough's arguments. Only after a reading of the three following installments does one fully realize that the introduction is a delicately barbed piece of irony. Initially Johnson gives the impression that the attitudes stated are his own. He does not quote direct passages from the memoirs in the text, although he annotates his material from the memoirs as though to give support to what he is saying. Even later in the review, when he quotes he does so sparsely and discriminately. Furthermore, he gives no clues to the identity of the speaker, such as, "according to the Duchess," or "the Duchess states." Nor does he offer in the first installment more than inferential judgments about the quality of the book. Perhaps eighteenth-century readers, understanding that this was not acceptance but preliminary ironical feinting, were thus made eager to see the coming, explicit numbers.

In a manner that was to become familiar in the *Rambler, Ad-*

venturer, and *Idler,* Johnson made a leisurely approach to his particular subject. He began his essay with generalized observations about the writing of memoirs. Such compositions, he said, should appeal to our love of truth. And he assumed that those writing in self-defense, like the Duchess of Marlborough, are more likely to be objective "than the advocates which faction or interest have raised in their favour." At the same time he acknowledged that the writer of a memoir, motivated by self-interest, is tempted to disguise truth even though he does not consciously disseminate falsehoods. While memoirs may have an unusual historical value because of their contemporaneity, they must be examined with sufficient skepticism to refine acceptable data from distortions or half-truths. The burden of judiciously evaluating memoirs is upon the student of history, according to Johnson, and is a challenge to his skill and integrity. "Distrust quickens his discernment of different degrees of probability, animates his search after evidence, and, perhaps, heightens his pleasure at the discovery of truth; for truth, though not always obvious, is generally observable." The ambivalence of Johnson's position is unmistakable even in his generalized comments. He mingles irony with seriousness, and he is torn between a suspicion of the Duchess (which he elsewhere expressed in a more direct manner),[10] and an unwillingness to reject first-hand information.

Having made significant remarks on the historical value of memoirs, Johnson went on to more specific details about the epistolary documentation employed in the Marlborough work. At first glance he appeared to praise this method, asserting that through the use of letters the Duchess "has not only set the greatest part of the work above the danger of confutation, but has added to the entertainment of the reader, who has now the satisfaction of forming to himself the characters of the actors, and judging how nearly such, as have hitherto been given of them, agree with those which they now give of themselves." But his approval was edged with scorn as he pointed out that letters contain intimate details which could not be derived from general history. As though accusing the Duchess of prying, he observed that letter writers reveal themselves "in their private apartments, in their careless hours, and observe those actions in which they indulged their own inclinations, without any regard to censure or applause." With the passage of years Johnson amended his feeling, arriving at the conclusion that a "letter is a calm and deliberate performance in the cool of leisure, in the stillness of solitude, and surely no man sits down to depreciate by design his own character."[11] But in the journalistic review Johnson saw letters as a source of psychological perception, capable of revealing depths of personality and conduct. He saw them also as literary documents, and read them with a critical eye for such qualities of expression as purity, correctness, and naturalness.

Without openly interjecting his disagreement in the first number, Johnson dispassionately restated the severe criticisms which the Duchess had made of Kings Charles II and William III. The former she had charged with betrayal of his country and the latter with the lesser sins of "brutality and insolence," rapacity and tyranny. But when speaking of the accusations against William's queen, Mary, Johnson feelingly described her as "the beneficent, the pious, the celestial Queen Mary," and he deplored the shadow that had been cast upon her popular image. Indignantly he added:

What can be charged upon this delight of human kind? Nothing less than that she wanted bowels, and was insolent with her power, and that she was resentful and pertinacious in her resentment, that she descended to mean acts of revenge, when heavier vengeance was not in her power. That she was desirous of controuling where she had no authority, and backward to forgive, even when she had no real injury to complain of.

Johnson reminded his readers "that no virtue is without its weakness," and that Mary's esteemed character "hitherto, had this great advantage, that it has only been compared with those of kings." His admiration of Queen Anne (by whom he had been "touched" for his scrofula in 1712) is equally evident as he suggests that the letters cited by the Duchess would be no less valuable to her adherents than to her enemies. He alludes, furthermore, to her strength as a ruler in spite of the controlling Whig "party whose principles she detested."

The March installment, thus, is a subtly satiric review of the memoirs. In the succeeding numbers Johnson abandoned this indirect method and categorically denied the Duchess' premises, although his phraseology was still frequently ironic. In April, for instance, he returned to his previous contention that the memoirs would edify those who were not deeply concerned with truth, and he stated that the "spirit, humour, and language" were characteristic of the Duchess' contempt of dignity. Mary, he wrote, "did not want bowels, but boldness to disobey her husband." Anne he defended in the May number, praising her for "her sincerity and uprightness of heart." Here, also, he accused the Duchess of bitterness and malice for her assault on William and Mary. In the final number Johnson made a further spirited defense of William. His strongest protestations were against the defamation of Anne. "I have always heard it objected to the memory of Queen Anne," Johnson wrote, "that she indulged those who were about her in such liberties as first rendered them insolent to others, and at last insupportable to herself. This is a foible incident to good natured people, and was the grand failing of the House of Stuart." Johnson's contempt for the Duchess is everywhere apparent. In the first number he had said with ironical intention that her book was an intimate study of human nature, a reliable source of little-known historical details, and a creditable piece of writing, dignified and artfully simple. By the end of the review, however, he stated bluntly that it was a disgusting invasion of privacy. Moderate readers, he said, "know that princes have their foibles as mortals; but they know too, that it is the duty of good subjects to conceal them." He implied that the Duchess had lied and omitted evidence, and stated that she had "embarrassed one whole reign, influenced the greater part of another, and has occasioned much noise and disturbance ever since." The Duchess, as he said on a later occasion, "had not superior parts, but was a bold frontless woman, who knew how to make the most of her opportunities in life."[12]

Aside from the extensive repudiation of the Duchess and her charges, the review contains a useful exposition of Johnson's political views. A letter preceding the first number identified the piece not as a review but as an essay, which has no "intention to please or offend any party." Johnson did, indeed, remain aloof from politics until the final number, and there he gave up the idea of neutrality. In that number he insisted the letters used in the memoirs "can give pleasure only to the violent of both parties, I mean the *Jacobites* and the *furious Whigs*." His antipathy to the Whigs is familiar, with accusations of moral compromise and material corruption. His clear aversion to the Jacobites, however, and on the same grounds of extremism, offers an opportunity to modify exaggerated notions of his politics. While analyzing the Tory party which William called to his assistance for protection against Whig ambitions, Johnson pointed out that the Tories consisted of two diverse elements, extreme and moderate.

The *nominal Tories* were *Jacobites,* of loose principles, who took the oaths to a King *de facto,* that they might better serve their King *de jure.* The *real Tories* were such as determined to serve the new King upon their old principles. . . . the plain reason why the Tories were decried in that reign was, that the Whigs represented them all as Jacobites; and, on the other hand, the complying Jacobites all pretended to be Tories.

Deploring the compromised *"nominal Tories,"* the Jacobites, as much as he did the Whigs, Johnson was a *"real Tory"* loyal to the ruling family. His position was later clarified by Boswell, who likewise associated himself with genuine Toryism while condemning Jacobite disloyalty to the reigning family as "one of the worst consequences of the Revolution." Johnson, he declared, not believing in the principle of *jus divinum,* "is not properly a *Jacobite."* The right of monarchy, according to Johnson, is determined by "long possession, which ought not to be disturbed upon slight grounds." He intimated, further, that the removal of James II by revolution was justified. After the long tenure of the Hanoverians he believed that they had acquired the same rights to the throne as the Stuarts. "His difficulty is as to the right still in some measure belonging to that unfortunate family. In short, he is dubious; and he would not involve the nation in a civil war to restore the Stuarts."[13] Despite indications in the Marlborough review of his perhaps nostalgic leaning toward the Stuarts, he accepted the ruling monarch both *de facto* and *de jure.* If occasionally, as perhaps during his association with Savage, Johnson expressed revolutionary opinions, he was merely engaging in academic conversation out of temporary bitterness. His active principles are well stated in the review. He advocated moderation and allegiance, justifying the monarch in power as long as the reign was dedicated to the best interests of the people. Like Boswell, he admired "that reverence and affection for a sovereign which constitute loyalty." As a final expression of fidelity, he signed the review "Britannicus."

This first review, then, is valuable as an early revelation of Johnson's opinions about politics, morality, monarchy, and historiography, with its special emphasis on memoirs and epistolary documentation. Concerned with personalities essentially, it is more notable for vigorous independence than for profundity of thought. Yet, compared with most reviews of the day, Johnson's is a superior performance, rich in personal observations. It is unlike his later reviews, except for a few—as of Soame Jenyns and Jonas Hanway—in which he made the book being considered an excuse for developing his own opinions.

In his second and final review for the *Gentleman's Magazine,* and one of the last book reviews which he wrote, Johnson was again concerned with the house of Stuart. And again he weighed the validity of epistolary documentation. His review of a book of letters, collected and analyzed by William Tytler for the purpose of vindicating Queen Mary of Scotland of the accusation that she murdered her husband, appeared in 1760,[14] only two years before a Hanoverian king granted him a pension. Published long after Johnson had suspended an active connection with the miscellany, the review was probably a voluntary contribution motivated by personal conviction or prejudice. Although as evidence of his enthusiasm for Jacobitism it is no more conclusive than his study of the Duchess of Marlborough's memoirs, it is an almost equally impressive token of his Stuart sympathies. More specifically, it expresses his abhorrence of the injustice which he thought Mary had been accorded. Even years later he reproached the Scottish people for having allowed such injustice to a queen whom "every man of gallantry of spirit would have sacrificed his life for."[15] The epistolary evidence against Mary, he deduced, was fraudulent. Quoting Tytler's assertion, that " 'if [the letters] be genuine, the queen was guilty; and, if they be spurious, she was innocent,' " Johnson unhesitatingly concluded, "That the letters were forged, is now made so probable, that, perhaps, they will never more be cited as testimonies."

Arguing for liberty as "security from persecutions of power," he protested "that one should talk of it less, and use it better." He refused, furthermore, to defer to vulgar bias. "When an opinion has once become popular, very few are willing to oppose it. Idleness is more willing to credit than enquire; cowardice is afraid of controversy, and vanity of answer; and he that writes merely for sale is tempted to court purchasers by flattering the prejudices of the publick." The Tytler review is one more proof of his consistent faith in fair play, his logical clear-headedness, and his bold if partisan reasoning. He asserted that the letters "thus timorously and suspiciously communicated" were the sole evidence against Mary. And he commented also upon the insufficiency of witnesses to the truth of the letters as well as the unreliability of internal evidence. Although a substantial portion of the review consists of abstractions and quotations, Johnson interjected his own opinions freely, examining the alleged testimony with legalistic intensity. Much of his intention seems to have been a repudiation of Hume's and Robertson's anti-Stuart opinions, to which Tytler had also taken exception.

Although Johnson composed a scattering of book reviews during his Grub Street career, he wrote them sustainedly only in 1756 and 1757, when he was contributing editor of the *Literary Magazine*.[16] Financially straitened as usual, Johnson had the disagreeable task of writing at least twenty-five reviews in one year, in addition to other essays, on an astonishing variety of subjects: politics and public affairs, military matters, ethics, literature, antiquity, philosophy, science, geography, trade, and tea drinking. Many of the reviews, to be sure, are perfunctory, but the extensive area covered is evidence of a prodigious quantity of reading in preparation for the reviews, even though—by his own admission—he never read a book through. Johnson's modest statement of aims in the preliminary essay (*To the Public,* No. 1, pp. iii-iv) illuminates the standards to which he and his colleagues adhered. Refusing to make extravagant promises, he did guarantee just and candid notices, criticism when it was warranted, and careful selectivity of "the best and most important pieces . . . that we may sometimes influence the public voice, and hasten the popularity of a valuable work." Most of the books reviewed were, as Johnson commented, significant for their current interest. Despite the sketchy nature of many of his reviews, several others are worth more than passing interest today because of the full and independent manner in which he examined certain works.

A widely disputed political and military issue in England in 1756 was the case of Admiral John Byng (1704-1757), whose naval task force had failed on May 20, 1756, to lift the French siege of Minorca. Pamphleteers successfully stimulated popular resentment of a British defeat, and Byng was tried and found guilty of hesitant conduct against the French and of failure in his mission as a result of his own misjudgment. So publicized was the incident that opposite the front page of the *Literary Magazine,* No. 4 (July 15 to August 15, 1756), was printed an engraving of Byng which surmounted a scene of the disastrous naval battle. Beneath were these jeering lines:

> We have lately been told
> Of two Admirals bold,
> Who engag'd in a terrible Fight:
> They met after Noon,
> Which I think was too soon,
> As they both ran away before Night.

Incensed by the efforts to make Byng a public scapegoat, Johnson carried on an energetic defense in two subsequent numbers of the *Literary Magazine,* reviewing harshly partisan pamphlets to show that Byng had not received a fair hearing in the press or courts.[17] "To hear both parties, and to condemn no man without a trial are the unalterable laws of justice." But Byng, he insisted, condemned by public and governmental pressure "without any calm or candid examination," was being persecuted for a defeat that was the result of an inferior navy and the absence of essential land forces. "[S]ince the prosecution of Laud," he maintained, "no such zeal for vindictive justice has been ever shown." And he went on to demand, "That whatever be the fate of Byng, the justice of the nation ought to hunt out the men who lost Minorca." The death penalty was mandatory, and regardless of the efforts of influential friends and a few indignant and spirited commentators like Johnson, Byng was executed by a firing squad March 14, 1757, on the deck of his ship. The House of Lords sought to suppress discussion as much as possible, but without success; nor would Johnson be silenced, even after he had written his fruitless reviews, and he continued to deplore the matter.[18] Sharply critical of ministerial and military bungling, Johnson neither forgave nor forgot. Here is one more demonstration of his libertarianism, and of his boldness and independence of judgment, even in a futile cause.

When Soame Jenyns, one of the contributing wits of the *World,* brought forth his *Free Inquiry into the Nature and Origin of Evil*, he could not have anticipated the acrimonious and celebrated reaction of Johnson, who brilliantly demolished his position while establishing his own ethical philosophy.[19] That Johnson should have troubled to rebut Jenyns in a journalistic piece is in itself evidence of the importance which he attached to the matter. Based primarily upon Pope's *Epistles,* the *Free Inquiry* struck at Johnson's fundamentally gloomy philosophy and awakened his resentment. To arrive at a better understanding of Johnson's review, it is necessary to examine briefly some of Jenyns' underlying principles, to which Johnson was unequivocally opposed. An amiable, socially acceptable country gentleman, Jenyns (1704-1787) was a Deist until his late conversion in 1776. Glorifying things as they were and advocating submission, Jenyns—as has been said—represented the "official optimism" of the eighteenth century. He held that all evils are the result of "the necessity of their own natures." Naturally, he said, there are bound to be imperfections in the universe, such as pain, poverty, and toil. But they are all a part of man's lot and must be borne cheerfully. Every evil, he said, has some good; and thus following the dicta of Mandeville he naïvely termed ignorance an opiate that makes poverty endurable to those "born to poverty."[20]

But who, thundered Johnson, "is born to poverty?" The subject was one which filled him with the greatest compassion, so that he could once write to Boswell:

Poverty, my dear friend, is so great an evil, and pregnant with so much temptation, and so much misery, that I cannot but earnestly enjoin you to avoid it. Live on what you have; live if you can on less; do not borrow either for vanity or pleasure; the vanity will end in shame, and the pleasure in regret.[21]

Jenyns asserted that although poverty is "the want of riches," hope and reduction of fear compensate the poverty-stricken for their want of goods. Johnson, however, went to his own experiences to show that poverty is the "want of necessaries." "Life," he said, "must be seen before it can be known." Neither Jenyns nor Pope, he wrote, had endured poverty. Objecting to the thin optimism which supported a belief that charity could alleviate the miseries of poverty, he resented Jenyns' theory that pain is necessary to happiness, that our pleasure depends upon the sufferings of other creatures, and that poverty is necessary to balance the economic order of the universe. He resented, further, Jenyns' assumption that there are "Superior Beings" who may enjoy life by the miseries of others, and that men are mere puppets.

Both Jenyns and Johnson subscribed to the theory of subordination in the scale of created being; but Johnson—as has been pointed out—examined the question realistically and pragmatically, whereas Jenyns elected to be an elegant and impractical theorist. Such irrational optimism as Jenyns' in no way mitigated the poverty which Johnson had seen and shared. He dedicated himself in numerous of his essays, notably *Adventurer,* No. 111, and *Idler,* Nos. 22, 28, and 89, as well as in his long poems to exposing London's dreadful conditions. He knew at first hand the horrors of poverty, criminality and debtors' prisons. His view of Jenyns' problem was, indeed, clear and realistic. Always conscious of the inequity of economic class distinctions, he felt that because of the pains to be encountered everywhere in the world, one must strive to alleviate the sufferings of the lower classes. Thanks to this feeling which he expressed so profoundly in his long review, Johnson destroyed the arguments of Jenyns—a second-rate thinker, at best—although, paradoxically, he gave him an uneasy immortality.[22]

Remarkably rich in commentary, the Jenyns piece is atypical of eighteenth-century book reviews, which very seldom have a comparable flavor of reasoned and forceful original composition. In reviews of other ethical or philosophical subjects, as a matter of fact, Johnson himself is often disappointingly mechanical. Probably because of his reluctance to become entangled in a metaphysical subject, Johnson's review of Newton's *Four Letters* to Dr. Bentley—arguments in proof of a deity—is almost apathetic.[23] Aside from a generalized complaint about the obscurity of the work, Johnson has little desire to commit himself. His most illuminating comment is that the "principal question of these letters gives occasion to observe how even the mind of Newton gains ground gradually upon darkness." The body of the review is divided somewhat evenly between quotation and abstract, since Johnson is willing to share his obvious uncertainty with his readers. Yet he maintains his respect for the philosopher here and in his conversation, asserting "the superiority of Sir Isaac Newton over all foreign philosophers."[24] Metaphysical speculation was not Johnson's forte, and he was disinclined to draw out a specialized subject. Newton's works, however, were popular subjects for reviewers and Johnson, hence, probably felt impelled by journalistic competition to undertake a consideration of the *Four Letters*.

A more descriptive bit calculated to stimulate public interest is the review of an edition of Browne's *Christian Morals*, which, as it happened, Johnson himself had prepared.[25] He had written the life of Browne, with brief explanatory notes, in 1756 for inclusion at the end of the second edition of the *Christian Morals*, and in this review he merely described the work itself and presented samples of his commentary. In a notably terse manner he praised Browne for the vigor of his sentiments, the variety of his learning, and the force of his style. Beyond that, and with little criticism, Johnson gave almost two pages of direct quotation from his life of Browne. Thus, Johnson, an old hand at writing reviews and biographies of learned men, modestly and successfully withstood a natural temptation to puff up his own work. But the sketchy review, designed merely to call attention to a work of current publication, has no intrinsic merit.

A personal bias is more overt in his review of Elizabeth Harrison's *Miscellanies*, a collection from various non-conformist writers of pious or moralistic essays and poems. Not only did he call sympathetic attention to a work originally limited by subscription to a relatively narrow body of readers, but he also revealed his familiarity with this kind of specialized literature. In his brief critical introduction he commended the essayists in the collection who "seem generally to have imitated or tried to imitate the copiousness of Mrs. [Elizabeth] Rowe" (1674-1737). He was further gratified that the influence of this popular writer could be traced not only in moral themes but in "brightness of imagery." As for the poets in the collection, Johnson credited them with having in mind the example of Isaac Watts, "one of the first who taught the dissenters to write and speak like other men, by showing them that elegance might consist with piety." This was a sentiment which he reiterated in his life of Watts in the *English Poets*. Then come eleven columns of direct quotation as samples of the religious pieces which Johnson found so worthy of study and emulation. In a manner typical of his conventionalism he chided, however gently, departures from the tenets of the Anglican Church even while giving wholehearted praise to the blameless morality of the authors. His prose, which shows a simple firmness and dignified sincerity not often evident in his other reviews, and his sympathetic comments warrant Boswell's judgment that this review "gives an eminent proof at once of his orthodoxy and candour."[26] Lacking though the piece is in depth of critical commentary, it is a valuable complement to our knowledge of Johnson's inner life.

No man was more loyal to his friends than Johnson, and no man was less capable of confusing friendship with literary integrity, as he demonstrated frequently in oral judgments on the literary productions of acquaintances. When his friend of almost two decades, Thomas Birch, acting in his secretarial capacity brought forth a *History of the Royal Society,* Johnson took on an official manner for the *Literary Magazine* to discuss a work which he obviously declined to recommend strongly. The resulting review, therefore, is interesting for its geniality coupled with firmness and restraint.[27] Although Johnson was openly disturbed by the *History's* excessively meticulous attention to detail, he forbore condemnation. "Many particularities are of importance to one man, though they appear trifling to another, and it is always more safe to admit copiousness than to affect brevity." As if his objective summary were not sufficient proof of the tedious but laborious work, Johnson concluded the review with five columns of quotation and abstraction. In dealing with another institutional compilation, Johnson was free of personal considerations. While finding "many entertaining and many useful narratives and observations" in the *Philosophical Transactions* for 1755,[28] Johnson wished "that the editors of these papers would have some regard to the purity of our language . . . and yet more to the sacrosanctity of religion, which seems treated with too little reverence when it is represented as hypothetical and controvertible, that all mankind proceeded from one original." The opinion is so characteristic as to obviate comment. Antiquarianism, about whose value Johnson had mixed feelings, drew his attention briefly during a review of Keith's

Catalogue of Scottish Bishops.[29] Apparently as ponderous in scope as
the two preceding works reviewed, the *Catalogue,* Johnson suggested,
"will give great pleasure to those who are studious of the *Scotish*
ecclesiastical antiquities, which the author, an antient bishop of the
church of *Scotland,* appears to have studied with great diligence."
What grounds Johnson had for this optimism is debatable. The number of readers who would have taken pleasure in the catalogue of
names and dates, illustrated by several columns of arid quotations,
must have been few indeed. Yet—and this is mere conjecture—the
fact that the Scottish bishops were loyal to the Stuarts may well have
disposed Johnson in favor of the *Catalogue.*

Arthur Murphy, who had met Johnson only two years previously in
consequence of a misunderstanding over a *Rambler* essay which he
reproduced without permission, brought forth in 1756 a collected
edition of the *Gray's-Inn Journal.* The serial was printed by Faden,
a sponsor of the *Literary Magazine,* and published by P. Vaillant.
No one, certainly, was better qualified than Johnson to review a collection of periodical essays; yet in his half-column introduction he
gave only slight acknowledgment of the significance of this literary
form which had virtually come to be identified with him as its
master. Nor is there any indication in this review of the mutual
esteem which eventually solidified the friendship between Johnson
and Murphy.[30] Although the paucity of Johnson's observations is
disappointing, what little he does say is consistent with his well-
established attitudes about serial writing. Weekly essays, as he felt
about his own serials, are in themselves unimportant, and any significance which adheres to them becomes fixed only through the
unifying agency of book publication. Regarded as weekly ephemera,
therefore, the individual essays are little better than trivial. Johnson
was amused by the "sprightliness and humour" of some of Murphy's
writings; but the serious essay serialist, he implied, must eschew
topical writing that is not designed to take its place in history. The
only worthwhile subjects are permanent and universal, and in dealing
with them Murphy was frequently successful. As far as Johnson's
own practice went—and this he expected of other serious essayists—
periodicals achieve lasting literary merit only insofar as their writers
strive to record and exemplify moral truths for all ages. Entertainment has its immediate value, but it should be considered secondary.

Infrequently during the course of writing reviews for the *Literary Magazine,* Johnson had the opportunity to compose literary criticism. To one piece in particular, Joseph Warton's *Essay on Pope,* he gave an extended notice, and it continues to have value today as a kind of prologue to his own critical biography of Pope in the *English Poets.*[31] That the criticisms of Pope by Warton and Johnson are consistent with a trend that had begun even before 1756, has been demonstrated.[32] But the review is also a reminder that Johnson thought long and fundamentally about such literary figures, and that when he was finally commissioned to write the *English Poets* he embodied in it the fruits of a lifetime of reading and speculation. Warton, an acquaintance and fellow contributor to the *Adventurer,* generally had Johnson's praise in the review as an exemplar of critical moderation, and occasionally his censure for deficiencies in critical method. For the most part Johnson found himself in agreement with Warton's learned judgments. He approved, for instance, because Warton "very justly censures" the pastorals, which fail to represent real life; "for there is in them a mixture of Grecian and English, of ancient and modern images. Windsor is coupled with Hybla, and Thames with Pactolus." But when Warton proposed unacceptable evaluations, Johnson quickly made his own position clear. He denied, for instance, that the imagery of Theocritus, which Pope imitated, was superior in terms of wildness, delicacy, and novelty.[33] This proved to be but a minor basis of contention, because Johnson agreed with Warton's statement that Pope's pastorals contain nothing new and "that their chief beauty consists in their correct and musical versification, which has so influenced the English ear, as to render every moderate rhymer harmonious."

Everywhere throughout the review are instances of Johnson's independence of literary judgment, as when he takes Warton to task for stating that the *Essay on Criticism* "was first written in prose." In a kindly, digressive rebuke Johnson cautioned Warton against the danger of relying upon or propagating hearsay evidence. The mild scolding would probably have been more appropriate in one of the *Rambler* papers than in a book review, but Johnson was not to be limited by literary convention; for him the time was always ripe for moral exhortation, especially upon such a favorite subject as this. Lest a negative impression be carried away from the review, however, Johnson advised that he intended "to kindle, not to extinguish curiosity" about Warton's work, which he recommended for its information and its "literary moderation." Although the above statements represent Johnson's personal attitudes, they are largely interspersed or intermingled with the customary body of abstractions (there is very little direct quotation). Almost every point set forth by Warton is enlarged or criticized by Johnson, evidence of a greater display of interest in his subject than he shows in many of his other reviews.

With the appearance of Charlotte Lennox's translation of *Sully's Memoirs,* Johnson once again had the opportunity to do a literary service for a friend. On several occasions throughout his literary career he had given her material assistance in her own writings, and she became his admirer and champion. In a brief review for the *Literary Magazine,* Johnson stated his high praise of her translation.[34] Forcefully he observed

. . . that those memoirs contain an account of that time in which France first began to assume her superiority in Europe; that they exhibit a nation torn with factions, and plundered by tax-gatherers, rescued by a great king and an honest minister. There can be no age or people to which such a history may not be useful and pleasing, but it must more particularly invite the attention of those who like us are now labouring with the same distresses, and whose duty it is to endeavour at the same relief.

Once again Johnson digresses from his role as reviewer, the obvious political analogy giving him an opportunity to voice clearly and distinctly his discontent with the British administraton. But he does not ignore the literary aspects of the translation, which he commends for ease and elegance.

Valuable commentary upon translation as a literary genre emerges from Johnson's review of Polybius translated by Hampton.[35] Aware that translations were not generally appreciated, Johnson intended to amend the slight. He acknowledged that "translations into the prose of a living language must be laid aside whenever the language changes." But a good translation, such as Hampton's, may have a long life, particularly since the English language gives promise of durability. The difficulty besetting any translator, of imbuing the spirit of the native language with the spontaneity of originality, "Mr. Hampton seems to have [met] in a degree of which there are few examples." Although Johnson, who favored periodic annotation for books dealing with past ages,[36] felt Hampton had not entirely fulfilled his obligation, he also felt notes could "easily be supplied by an inferior hand." Following less than a column of critical commentary, Johnson concluded his review with about four columns of direct quotation regarding Hannibal's march on Gaul. His praise of Hampton was unusual, since he generally looked upon translation as an inferior auxiliary "for people who cannot read the original."[37] As for literary usage, he found translation to be especially limited. "You may translate books of science exactly. You may also translate history, in so far as it is not embellished with oratory, which is poetical." But poetry, he insisted, cannot be translated.[38] Hampton, of course, earned Johnson's encomiums by adhering to prose.

From praise of Hampton, Johnson moves readily in the same number of the *Literary Magazine* to condemnation of another English writer dealing with a classical subject. He harshly reviewed Thomas Blackwell's study of Augustan times as the restatement of an old theme, the product for the most part of pedestrian, uninformative grubbing.[39] Unusually severe and extensive in his comments—for we would normally expect him to dismiss unoriginality with a few curt sentences rather than protract and belabor an inferior work as he does—Johnson does not explain his real dissatisfaction. A clue, however, appears in the final paragraph, where—in an epithet almost identical with one he later applied to Mark Akenside—he accused Blackwell of affecting "a furious and unnecessary zeal for liberty"[40] and innovation. By reference to Johnson's well-reasoned opinions on liberty and subordination, we may infer the cause of his impatience with the story of the Roman downfall. The necessity of change for improvement in the public welfare he never denied; but change brought about through violence and rebellion he abhorred. A personal philosophy, thus, even more than considerations of scholarship and historical contribution engendered this assault upon Blackwell. With his customary acumen, Boswell reflected: "In his review of the 'Memoirs of the Court of Augustus,' he had the resolution to think and speak from his own mind, regardless of the cant transmitted from age to age, in praise of the ancient Romans."[41]

Versatility and range, which highlight Johnson's contributions to the *Literary Magazine,* were the necessary equipment of any London reviewer in the eighteenth century. Among the numerous subjects in which he browsed were geography, natural science, and trade, matters with which he had also familiarized himself while he was writing copy for Cave. In a leading review in the *Literary Magazine,* Johnson considered Russel's *Natural History of Aleppo,* an account of the climate, people, products, and diseases of Aleppo.[42] Johnson's criticism consists of no more than a brief introductory statement in which he finds the author neither better nor worse than any other writer, with regard to history and style. Tolerantly he accepted Russel's organization of materials, even though he would have preferred the expansion of some parts and the contraction of others. Apparently counting upon a widespread current interest in exoticism (Russel reported that Aleppo was inhabited by Arabic-speaking Turks, Greeks, Armenians, Syrians, Maronites, and Jews), Johnson followed his noncommittal critique with almost six pages summarizing the contents of the *Natural History.* He remained skeptical of oriental influences, however, and when the Reverend John Hussey was about to depart to Aleppo (1778), Johnson gave him advice that a clergyman hardly required: "Let no opportunities of vice corrupt you; let no bad examples seduce you; let the blindness of Mahometans confirm you in Christianity."[43]

Judging by the quantity of books about far-off places, distant lands had a strongly romantic as well as commercial appeal for the average insular Briton of the eighteenth century. One such book was Patrick Browne's history of Jamaica, which Johnson praised for its accuracy while complaining about its excesses of inclusion.[44] He implied that he had read widely in the literature of natural history, his impatience being that of one whose time was being taken up unnecessarily with long familiar matters. This attitude, coupled with bland but vague literary allusions to natural history of the past and to Sir Hans Sloane's *Voyage to the Islands of Madera, etc.,* lends an undeniably authoritative tone to the review, even though he did not pause to expand his notions. "Natural history," wrote Johnson, "is above most other compositions subject to repetition; every man is fond of the country that he inhabits, and is willing to multiply its products, and celebrate its fertility." The historian should feel obliged to write about what is distinctive or not commonly known. Having delivered himself of an almost pedantic statement of principles for the benefit of other writers of natural history as well as for the immediate readers of the *Literary Magazine,* Johnson dutifully presented about nineteen columns of direct quotation. In reading Johnson's reviews, one cannot fail to be impressed with his masterly competence in stating neat generalizations. With the best reviewers of his day, Johnson well knew that his function largely was to preface copious illustrations from the works of others. Essentially a critic, however, he was reluctant to be a mere paraphraser, and he succeeded frequently in writing statements on general literary principles. His urbanity and critical judgment, circumscribed by space limitations and audience appeal though they necessarily were, enlivened many a dull series of abstractions or quotations. True to his own theory of selection, he excerpted from Browne numerous illustrations of vegetation and animal-life indigenous to Jamaica which must have astonished British readers. The subject considered, incidentally, anticipates and authenticates his later reviews of Dr. Grainger's poem *Sugar Cane,* which were to appear in the *London Chronicle* and *Critical Review.*

Continuing to demonstrate his interest in remote places, though he himself had not left England up to that time (1756), Johnson vicariously explored Scilly with William Borlase.[45] Reflecting his own interest in Britain's foreign trade, six or seven pages of direct quotation deal with descriptions of the picturesque country, its inhabitants, and customs. As a literary review, however, Johnson's contribution here is not satisfying. He noted merely that "This is one of the most pleasing and elegant pieces of local enquiry that our country has produced." Even as the restless advances of European explorers were forcing English attention to improbable pinpoints on maps, so political events were shaping a frequently unwelcome recognition of the growing importance of America in the world sphere. Appalled that an area of such cultural and physical primitivism could become the focus of an Anglo-French war, Johnson was yet grudgingly impelled to admit the destiny of the new land. Cynically he predicted that the Americans would "in time learn their own importance, and . . . be incited to attempt something more than the chase of beavers, when they are once convinced that something more may be performed." Hence, his review of a book by Lewis Evans on the Middle Colonies is an invaluable complement to the political essays, already discussed in the *Literary Magazine* and one more means of exposing his American antipathies.[46] For the student of Johnson's political attitudes, as well as of his reviews, this is a revealing piece.

Evans afforded Johnson an opportunity to digress upon matters that had long troubled him. His conclusion "upon these pompous paragraphs" of Evans' book supports the more overt opinion of his political essays, that Britain had committed herself to an unfortunate war and foreign policy. Johnson conceded the great value to Britain of the lands along the Ohio for which she and France were contending, but he believed the Colonies were being populated at the expense of the homeland. "We have at home more land than we can cultivate, and more materials than we manufacture; by proper regulations we may employ all our people, and give every man his chance of rising to the full enjoyment of all the pleasures and advantages of a civilized and learned country." He thought that the reports of raw silk, allegedly copious along the Ohio, were false lures leading to the "dreadful desarts" of North America. Johnson, in fact, had an exaggerated notion of the great quantities of silk available. Sericulture had been exploited in the Southern Colonies since the seventeenth century under royal mandate and bounty, but with indifferent success. Some experimentation, to be sure, took place in the Northern Colonies during Johnson's lifetime, but until the nineteenth century American silk production was on the whole meager and generally confined to Virginia, Georgia, and then Louisiana. Johnson's contempt for any traffic in luxuries and its attendant evils, however, is more notable here than his misconceptions about economic geography. His remarks serve to emphasize similar complaints which he made about the tea trade; they serve also as a reflection of his general abhorrence of poverty as well as of his beliefs in a higher economic standard for Britain herself.

Finally, in his review, Johnson was little concerned that the

American colonies will break off their dependence on England. . . . Every man and every society is entitled to all the happiness that can be enjoyed with the security of the whole community. From this general claim the Americans ought not to be excluded, but let us not be frightened by their threats; they must yet be dependent, and if they forsake us, or be forsaken by us [they] must fall into the hands of France.

With a curious inconsistency he initially referred to the Americans as though they had no national affinity with the British; yet in his conclusion he was for granting them "the security of the whole community" of Great Britain. Nor was he above specious argument when he considered migration to the Colonies exile to a "trackless" and "dreadful" desert. For Johnson residence anywhere outside of England would have been in fact calamitous. Of Evans' book as a literary accomplishment he was less eloquent, although he slyly inserted a few words of anti-American sentiment: "The map is engraved with sufficient beauty, and the treatise written with such elegance as the subject admits though not without some mixtures of the American dialect, a trace of corruption to which every language widely diffused must always be exposed."

Applying the same grave tone to works of practical science as he did to those on ethics and politics, Johnson reviewed Home's book on bleaching for readers of the *Literary Magazine*.[47] He was surprisingly tolerant of a treatise which was notable only for its utility in describing one of the "lower arts." Johnson's only serious complaint was that Home failed to use a terminology sufficiently clear for the layman and that he used Scotticisms. "The performance is indeed rather useful than pleasing, sometimes obscured by the use of terms, which none but bleachers understand, and sometimes made unpleasing to an English ear, by words and phrases never uttered on this side of the Tweed." Johnson, however, was inclined to excuse these faults on the grounds that "the author wrote for his countrymen, and his business was rather to instruct than delight." The review has some minor interest for showing one more facet of Johnson's versatility, but his introductory comments shed considerably less light on the subject than do the several pages of abstraction and extraction. He wrote more illuminatingly, as though the subject had a greater immediacy for him, when reviewing Stephen Hales' proposals for the distillation of sea water, "another of the labours spent in the service of mankind."[48] Dr. Hales (1677-1761), an Anglican clergyman, was a prominent physiologist and "pneumatic chemist." His varied interests extended to botanical experiments in the fermentation and distillation of vegetable substances. Fully aware of the importance of Hales' process to a sea-faring nation, Johnson judiciously praised the inventor's ability and modesty. He evinced familiarity with Hales' problems, especially that concerned with the ventilation of slave and transport ships. At least, the skepticism which Johnson occasionally voiced has the tone of authority, as though he had at some time looked into the subject. His critical remarks and reasonable questioning, however, were subordinated as usual to the quotations which comprise the main body of the review.

A tripartite review in the *Literary Magazine* of a scientific investigation of medicinal properties of water by Dr. Charles Lucas now has more interest because of Johnson's asides on liberty and orthography than because of the original subject. Cited as "a strong proof of his patriotick spirit," the review is a stirring denunciation of the political forces who engineered Lucas' exile from Ireland because of his efforts to eliminate corruption from government.[49]

[T]hey drove him from his native country by a proclamation, in which they charged him with crimes of which they never intended to be called to the proof, and oppressed him by methods equally irresistible by guilt and innocence.

Let the man thus driven into exile for having been the friend of his country be received in every other place as a confessor of liberty, and let the tools of power be taught in time that they may rob but cannot impoverish.

The appraisal of the contents (Johnson's feeling was that the subject was treated diligently) would be almost anticlimactic, were it not for his views on orthography, a problem which he had recently attended to in the *Dictionary*. As a part of his concern about regularized spelling, Johnson's comments have a genuine value. He regarded the "new mode of spelling" which disfigured Lucas' pages a "perpetual and glaring affectation" repulsive to readers. Innovation was in itself bad; but to fail—as Lucas had—to provide an improved substitute, and even to commit errors unjustified by "the laws of analogous derivation," were in Johnson's opinion indeed deplorable. His observations merit comparison with those in the plan of the *Dictionary*, where he proposed "to make no innovation without a reason sufficient to balance the inconvenience of change." Here, likewise, he held that "[a]ll change is of itself an evil, which ought not to be hazarded but for evident advantage."[50] Similarly he recorded in his other writings, such as the essay serials and the *English Poets,* distrust of the odd or unique. One of the keys to Johnson's philosophy is his detestation of singularity or exhibitionism in any form, for to him the old and the soundly established principles were comfortable and good; innovation, except on rare occasions when it could be justified as contributing to the public welfare, was the disruptive product of specious, upstart thinking. "There is in human nature," he said, "a general inclination to make people stare; and every wise man has himself to cure of it, and does cure himself. If you wish to make people stare by doing better than others, why, make them stare till they stare their eyes out."[51]

Sometimes Johnson in his book reviews welcomed an opportunity to turn from gravity to whimsy. An ideal circumstance offered itself when Jonas Hanway, an eccentric traveler and philanthropist, and a commissioner of the Navy for twenty years, produced an odd work about a journey through England in which he deplored the widespread consumption of tea. The book, as a matter of fact, was privately distributed; but Johnson could not resist exposing it to the readers of the *Literary Magazine* in two notices, which he wrote, as Boswell said, *con amore.*[52] In some of his wittiest satire, Johnson bludgeoned Hanway for both his argumentation and faulty grammar. He admitted that Hanway could "expect little justice from the author of this extract, a hardened and shameless tea-drinker, who has for twenty years diluted his meals with only the infusion of this fascinating plant, whose kettle has scarcely time to cool, who with tea muses the evening, with tea solaces the midnight, and with tea welcomes the morning." When Hanway "proceeds in the pathetic strain, to tell the ladies how, by drinking tea they injure their health, and what is yet more dear, their beauty," Johnson gallantly reflects upon the eternity of female attractiveness. To Hanway's complaint that tea drinking is wasteful of time, Johnson answers that idleness is a mark of their entire era, and that tea is merely an excuse for conviviality, its drinkers being "brought together not by the tea, but the tea table." The only arguments of Hanway's to which he did not take exception and which, indeed, he supported seriously were sociological and moralistic: loss of life in the perilous voyage to China, and the huge sums of money spent in illicit tea trading. He also concurred in a serious vein with Hanway's circuitous condemnation of alcoholic liquors; but he refused to accept the traveler's fears that tea destroyed health, beauty, and energy. Angered by Johnson's attitude, Hanway wrote a sharp retort, which appeared in the *Gazetteer,* May 26, 1757. This certainly did not help his cause; for, slyly sardonic, Johnson again attacked him, the only time in his life indeed "when he condescended to oppose any thing that was written against him."[53] His fencing with Hanway combines facetiously intellectual byplay with a well-reasoned consideration of social implications, though the former predominates. With affected innocence, Johnson asked what he had done to offend and restated his previous points. Thereafter Hanway had the good sense to remain silent.

When Johnson terminated his association with the *Literary Magazine* in 1757, he also virtually terminated his career as a reviewer. But in 1763 and 1764, apparently motivated by his acquaintance with the authors, he wrote three reviews of poems for the *Critical Review* and one for the *London Chronicle.* That he should write for these two periodicals when he was near the height of his career was undoubtedly a matter of choice, for he had positive opinions about the *Critical Review* as contrasted with his disapproving view of the *Monthly* (both of which he seems to have read with some regularity, as he did the *Chronicle*), and he was present at the birth of the *London Chronicle,* whose *Preliminary Discourse* of 1757 he had written. The *Critical Review,* which was founded by Archibald Hamilton under Smollett's editorship, Johnson approved of because of its Tory, Anglican proclivities; while its chief rival the *Monthly,* which took a more liberal position in matters of politics and religion, he distrusted. Despite his suspicions of the *Monthly,* however, he mistakenly contended that both it and the *Critical* were impartial in their reviews. "The Critical Reviewers," he said, "often review without reading the books through; but lay hold of a topick, and write chiefly from their own minds. The Monthly Reviewers are duller men, and are glad to read the books through."[54] As a book reviewer Johnson was in principle much closer to the policies and attitudes of the *Critical* than to those of the *Monthly:* he seldom read a book through, and he was certainly not a dull man. His best reviews are those in which he also wrote chiefly from his own mind. He valued critical commentary and original statement more than slavish extraction, and if the situation seemed to warrant the asides, he used the books under review as a kind of shelter for his complementary ideas.

For Johnson the ideal literary review was one that unhesitatingly took up a position as a cultural and social force, exercising its responsibility by a firm and appropriate bias in the selection of materials and by judicious presentation of commentary. As a matter of fact, such individuality was widespread but not always beneficial as Johnson would wish it to be. One of the most common offenses of reviewers, according to Boswell, was their reckless amputations of books for illustrative purposes. Another was their violation of objectivity to facilitate imposing their own attitudes upon review articles.[55] Not above departing from objectivity in his own reviews, especially in the accounts of Jenyns and Hanway, Johnson interjected opinions which are nevertheless profitable. Though his affinity for the *Critical* was manifested in review techniques, politics, and religion, and though he showed his further respect for the *Critical* by terming its contents "ingenious and . . . well expressed,"[56] he frowned upon any author's making overtures to the editors. Thus Lyttleton, he said, was out of order "for returning thanks to the Critical Reviewers, for having kindly commended his *Dialogues of the Dead*. Such acknowledgements . . . never can be proper, since they must be paid either for flattery or for justice."[57]

Johnson's first contribution to the *Critical Review* was a discussion in 1763 of *Telemachus,* a dull poetic mask (set to music in 1765 by Philip Hayes) dealing with "The contention between pleasure and virtue, a struggle which will always be continued while the present system of nature shall subsist."[58] The author was the Reverend George Graham (d. 1767), a dramatist and an assistant master at Eton where the boys called him "Gronkey." Graham is probably less remembered today for his *Telemachus* than for insulting Goldsmith in Johnson's amused presence during a bibulous evening.[59] The moralistic theme of the mask was one of interest to Johnson during his lifetime, and it predisposed him to a favorable opinion of a mediocre poem. Common though he knew this idea of a struggle between ethical opposites to be as a literary subject, Johnson nevertheless vindicated Graham's choice of topic because of its universal implications. A rather extravagant implied comparison with Shakespeare's use of fantasy is not justified by several pages of extracts— weak blank verse and ode forms. But the bias in selecting lines demonstrative of the triumph of virtue over pleasure helps to explain Johnson's approval. The approval, it should be remarked, hinges upon the propriety of the mythological and pastoral elements of Graham's poem; Johnson in the *Rambler,* the *English Poets,* and his discussion of the *Tempest* (by implication, also, with regard to *A Midsummer Night's Dream*) accepted such fanciful devices only after satisfying himself that they had both moral and esthetic utility. Perhaps Johnson anticipated the skepticism with which many readers would greet the poem; so he ascribed to it a quality of subtlety which would be less refutable than tangible components. He recommended "the fertility of imagination, the depth of sentiment, and the knowledge of passion, which are occasionally displayed, to the observation of those readers who have skill to discern, and delicacy to taste them." The review of *Telemachus* is characteristic of Johnson's predilection for literature with an intellectual and moralistic basis, even though he does not neglect esthetic considerations. That Johnson's regard for *Telemachus* was more than mere fancy or the conventional praise of a reviewer is implicit in his enjoining Boswell twice in later years to get for him a shilling edition of the work from the press of Andrew and Robert Foulis, the "Elzevirs of Glagow."[60]

Another of Johnson's reviews in the *Critical* is the brief notice of Goldsmith's *The Traveller,* which consists in the introductory paragraph of a quotation from the poet's "elegant dedication to his brother."[61] The second paragraph is an almost equally noncommittal allusion to Goldsmith's concern with degrees and excesses of happiness. After several pages of quotations, Johnson concluded: "Such is the poem, on which we now congratulate the public, as on a production to which, since the death of Pope, it will not be easy to find any thing equal." Once again Johnson strained for analogy, for neither the extremely meager critical commentary in which he praised Goldsmith as "a just estimator of comparative kindness," nor the specimens warrant the comparison with Pope. Even so, Johnson restrained himself from excessive exploitation of his well-known friendship with Goldsmith. Despite his frequent ridicule of Goldsmith, Johnson felt warmly toward him and helped him when he was in trouble. There is a story that when Goldsmith was arrested by his landlady for debt and Newbery would not advance him money, Johnson sold the *Vicar of Wakefield* for £60 to still the cries of his creditors. Although the *Vicar of Wakefield* was sold before the *Traveller,* the reluctant publisher did not print it until the success of the poem seemed to assure a successful sale of the novel. Johnson read the proof sheets of the *Traveller* and substituted several lines of his own, "not more than eighteen," as he subsequently admitted to Sir Joshua.[62] The notice in the *Critical Review* appeared at about the same time as the poem and contributed substantially to its favorable reception.[63]

Johnson's association with the *London Chronicle* has been discussed already, especially as it concerned the composition of the *Preliminary Discourse* and the obituary of the Reverend Mr. Mudge. In the former piece his attitude toward the common run of book reviewers is illuminating, for he held them to be "amongst other disturbers of human quiet" and, by his implication, excessively numerous. He wrote also of the *Chronicle*'s policies about "the labors of the learned" which were to provide the substance of a department called the "Literary Journal." The newspaper's reviewers would avoid pettiness and maliciousness, and would always be modest. "Our intention is not to preoccupy judgment by praise or censure, but to gratify curiosity by early intelligence, and to tell rather what our authors have attempted, than what they have performed." As for those authors guilty of raising false expectations through misleading titles, the *Chronicle* would expose them; "for though we write without intention to injure, we shall not be made parties to deceit."[64] On the whole, thus, the stated review aims of the *Chronicle* were characteristic of the period. Unfortunately, Johnson wrote but one review for the *London Chronicle* and his remarks in the discourse serve more practically as a standard for evaluating the reviews of other contributors to the newspaper. In July, 1764, he collaborated with Bishop Percy in a review of Dr. James Grainger's *Sugar Cane,* hints for planters in attenuated blank verse which had been published in the *London Chronicle* May 26. Aside from the three introductory paragraphs, which came from Johnson's pen, the review consists of but one brief paragraph prefatory to the tedious selections and a few summations. Percy was responsible for only the selection of the passages, which occupy the last two pages.[65] Later Johnson duplicated his own efforts when he wrote another review of the poem for the *Critical Review*.

Critical as always in his views of the New World, Johnson was nevertheless open minded and tolerant of its future possibilities. He wrote in the *Chronicle* that the traveler in a foreign land must orient his thinking to the distinctive features of that land. South America, for instance, should be considered "the habitation of uncivilized nations, remarkable only for their rudeness and simplicity," and devoid of a cultural heritage. The traveler in South America must prepare himself through "knowledge of nature, and copiousness of language, acuteness of observation, and facility of description." Johnson lauded Grainger for bringing to his utilitarian subject the qualifications of a philosopher and poet. Johnson seems deliberately to have refrained from making any literary judgments in this first review and, perhaps remorseful that he had not argued a stronger case for his friend's poem, he set about repairing the deficiency in a review for the *Critical* in October. The poor reception of *Sugar Cane* undoubtedly confirmed the need for words of literary praise.[66] Johnson urged the reader to discover for himself the richness of the poem's passions and imagination. No European, he said, could conceive for himself such profusion of tropical violence and tranquility as Grainger dealt with. "It is, indeed, a little extraordinary how regions so poetically striking, and so well known to the merchant, have been so little visited by the muse: and that . . . we have been destitute till now of [a significant] American poet." Not only was Johnson aware of the romantic tendencies in the poem, but he seems to have been attracted to them. In addition, he pointed to *Sugar Cane* as a good example of Virgilian imitation; and "although [Grainger] treads upon unclassic ground, yet [he] maintains a classical regularity." Grainger, he said, wrote with rising power and interest, and "as the *taedium* of reading increases, he makes the interest increase proportionably." In this sense he deemed Grainger superior to other Virgilian imitators such as Dyer and Philips. Further cause for Johnson's praise was the third book, in which Grainger dealt with "the celebration of Rum, which it is probable no other poet has dignified in verse before him," an essentially comic subject successfully treated "without sinking."

The extracts which we have given will enable the reader to judge for himself of the merits of this work. The poet had an untrodden country to clear; and, though he may not have entirely subdued the native rudeness of the soil, yet he certainly has opened a delightful tract for future civilization.

Much of the essay was given to extraction and abstraction, but Johnson interspersed a good deal of commentary to make this a much more entertaining and enlightening review than that in the *Chronicle*.

As later events demonstrated, however, Johnson was not revealing his true opinion of the poem's merit; his characteristic asides on topical and party writing and his literary comparison were merely a kind deception. One investigator, indeed, thinks Johnson was being "playful" when he wrote the three paragraphs in the *London Chronicle*;[67] and it is equally plausible that he was being charitable when he composed the subsequent review for the *Critical*. By means of an introduction from Grainger, Johnson met Bishop Percy in 1756; and Bishop Percy was annoyed that Johnson, who had liked other writings by Grainger, should ridicule *Sugar Cane*. Johnson and Boswell were frequently merry about the badness of Grainger's poetic effort. One story circulated that the poet, while reading the manuscript aloud, came to the line, "Say, shall I sing of Rats?" "No!" exploded Johnson.[68] "What," he grumbled, "could he make of a sugar-cane? One might as well write 'The Parsley-bed, a Poem'; or 'The Cabbage-garden, a Poem.'"[69]

As a book reviewer and commentator upon the craft, Johnson was versatile, impatient of mediocrity, and uncompromising in his moral principles. But above all, his reviews are lasting proof that there can be no division between what he regarded as his contributions to literature—such as the essays on language and Shakespeare, the *English Poets,* and even the essay serials—and what at first promised to be the merely casual, journalistic reviews. The nature of eighteenth-century book reviewing was such that it would, at first glance, appear vain to search out profundities of thought and gems of literary criticism. Yet Johnson, with his massive disdain for popular writing, succeeded often in liberating himself from the accepted circumscriptions of book reviewing to pronounce his own unambiguous views. Naturally, it is interesting to read Johnson's estimates of specific works and their authors, even though many of these books and many of these writers are virtually valueless today except as minuscular segments of eighteenth-century social, political, and ethical history. The modern value of his reviews, essentially, is that they have a very decided relationship to the entire body of his writing and thinking, since, like all of his contributions to journalism, they are splendidly integrated with his literature and philosophy. Similarly, his attitudes toward reviewing supplement his reflections on literature in general. For all of Johnson's reluctance to admit the relationship between his journalism and literature, the book reviews help to contradict him on this score and to demonstrate the growth of the earlier into the maturity of the later form. The contradiction is, indeed, to the honor rather than the abuse of Johnson.

CHAPTER VI

PIRACY, COPYRIGHT, AND THE ENCOURAGEMENT OF LEARNING

I

LEGAL recognition of literature as the personal property of an author or bookseller was sanctioned in England in 1709, the year in which Parliament created a copyright law known as "An Act for the Encouragement of Learning" (8 Anne, c. 19). The principal effect of the Act was official acknowledgment of authorship and publishing as legally protectable enterprises, and an attempt to end the literary freebooting which had flourished since the expiration of the Licensing Act of 1694. Literary thievery by rival authors and booksellers—particularly by booksellers, who were most likely to profit financially from literature—had grown into a common practice, despite the efforts of the Stationers Company. Pirates freely expropriated popular writings and reprinted them without permission or payment to their rightful owners. To combat this situation and to continue the publishing monopoly which they had come to look upon as their prerogative, the successful, strongly united booksellers—the Trade—sought legislation to contain the activities of their unscrupulous rivals. They felt legally and morally justified in insisting that once an author had sold his copy, their unqualified right to that copy was perpetual. Authors in the eighteenth century, indeed, were virtually the last to profit from their own works. The Act of 1709 was a partial solution to controversies about literary property, but it did not settle the question of whether copyright should be perpetual or limited.

With the expansion of education and the concurrently increased demands for "popular" literature, publishing became lucrative and the Trade a powerful enough organization to assure ready passage of the "Act for the Encouragement of Learning." Thanks to the grow-

The CASE *of the Booksellers Right to their* Copies, *or sole Power of Printing their respective Books, represented to the Parliament.*

UPON presumption that every one of Us, to whom an Author conveys a Copy, or, by whom a Book is first Printed, hath the sole Power of Printing that Book for ever after; We have always esteemed that Right a Just and Legal Property, and have therefore given great Sums of Money for Copies. Have serted them on our Wives at Marriage, on our Children at Death; and at this time many Widows and Orphans have no other Subsistence. And we will presume to say, that the Copies now in use, have cost the Present Possessors, exclusive of all Charge of Print and Paper, at least Fifty Thousand Pounds. And we conceive, this Property is the same with that of Houses and other Estates; because it is agreeable to both Common Law and true Reason, Which we will presume to set forth, as well as we can in so short a compass, as follows: *viz.*

According to COMMON LAW.

I. An Author is absolute Master of his own Writings; and may publish or destroy 'em as he sees fit. For no Man is bound to communicate his Knowledge to the World.

II. If an Author be Master of such Knowledge as to be capable of instructing the World, he has certainly a Right to choose the Hand by which he will convey his Work to the Publick.

III. The Bookseller to whom an Author conveys the Power of Printing his Work, has the sole Right of Printing it for ever, for these Reasons:

   1. The Conveyance of the Author. Seldom obtain'd but by Purchase.

   2. The Prime Occupator.

   3. By the Law, and Agreement of Booksellers.

   1. The Gift of an Author, who has the original indisputable Right of Publishing that Work, does undoubtedly give that Bookseller the Sole Power of Printing it the first time.

   2. The Bookseller, who is at the Expence of the first Edition, and takes the Risque of it, has a better Plea for continuing to Print it in future Editions, than another has.

   3. The By-Laws of the Company of Stationers, which have been several times confirmed as the Statute in that behalf requires, assign the sole Printing of a Book for ever to the prime Occupator.

Which By-Laws have been comply'd with and acquiesc'd in for at least 150 Years; a Term, we conceive, that amounts to a Pleadable Prescription.

According to REASON.

'Tis most common for a Bookseller to give an Author Money for his Copy; which the Author has undoubtedly a Right to ask; and with reason, because he must spend much time and Study in composing his Book, and can no other way secure to himself a Recompence.

Every Man that buys a Property is in all other Cases allow'd to enjoy it for ever.

A Bookseller very often loses by the first Edition of a Book, because of the slow Sale thro' its being unknown; which yet in time gains Reputation, and future Editions are profitable. In such case 'tis certainly reasonable that he who was the Loser by the First, should be the Gainer in the Future Impressions.

This Regularity in Property of Printing, is equally beneficial to every body exercising the Trade; the Poor and the Weak, that happen to be favour'd by an Author, enjoy the benefit of this Order as much as the Rich and Strong; whereby a Copy may be (and in Fact has often been) the Support of a Widow and Children.

The Expence preparatory to the Printing of a Book, that is to say, the Setting the Letters together is such, that nothing less than the Printing off and selling Five hundred, and in many cases a Thousand, will refund it. An Inconvenience that no other Trade is under: For in all other Manufactures the Workman can make as few as he pleases. As this was the reason of beginning the Order of Impropriation, it will for ever make the maintaining it necessary.

The Purpose of Books, which is the Instruction of Mankind, is altogether, as well pursued by the Observance of this Regularity, as it can be by the Breach of it, which Experience evinces: For Knowledge has been as well diffused hitherto, as it can be hereafter. And we will presume to say, that all the Books that are of general Use, are sold as cheap by the lawful Proprietors of the Copies, as they can be by Interlopers. Give us leave to instance in a few, *viz.* Bibles and Common-Prayer Books are sold cheaper in *England*, than in any other Parts of the World. Grammars, Dictionaries, and School-Books are as cheap as can be desired. *Littleton's* Dictionary is the cheapest Book in the World; and the Classicks *in usum Delphini*, as printed in *London*, out-do in Cheapness any thing printed in *Holland*, although that be reckoned the cheapest Place for Printing. The Antiquities of *Greece* Printed in *London*, with a Fifth Part added, is sold for two Thirds of the Price of the Latin Translation of it Printed in *Holland*; and indeed every Book that affords a numerous Sale, is printed as cheap in *England* as in any part of the World. And this too notwithstanding that Paper is at least a third Part dearer here than else where.

The most effectual way to secure to the Publick cheap Editions of Books, is to ascertain the Propriety of Copy; because that which enables a Bookseller to sell cheap, is the Printing a large Number at once: For as the greatest Charge in Printing is setting the Letters together; If he be secure that no body else can print the Book, he will venture to print off a much larger Number than with the danger of that Book being Printed by another, he durst do; whereby every single Copy costing him less than the smaller Number would, he can afford, and always does, to sell cheaper to the Publick. This in Fact is true in Bibles, Dictionaries, School-Books; And many others, which of late Years are printed on small Characters, and in large Numbers, and are thereby afforded to the Buyers at much lower Prices than formerly. But this Custom so happily begun, must be left off in all future Impressions, if this Act does not pass: For every body foreseeing that they shall have but a short time in the Profit of their Books will, to be sure, make as much as they can in that short time, and run as little risque as possible by large Impressions. We presume to affirm, that more Books have been printed on the small Characters, call'd *Small-Pica, Long-Primmer* and *Brevier*, within 40 Years past, than were done before from the Beginning of Printing. And as hereby the same matter is contained in one Sheet that used to be spread upon two or three, the Buyers are thereby accommodated with Books at half the Price they formerly paid. This Custom was begun under the Protection of the Statute in K. *Charles's* Reign, and is now become so general that nothing can break it but the Invasions of Interlopers. So that this double Convenience accrues to the Publick by protecting our Property, namely, Fair and well Printed Editions for the Gentry, and cheap Editions for the Populace: both which will be prevented by the Liberty.

Lest it should be suppos'd that we ask a Favour that is not granted in other Nations, give us leave to lay before you the State of the Case in other Countries.

This Custom of Impropriation of Copies is observ'd, in all Nations where Printing is Exercised, and we cannot doubt, that the Common Law protects it every where, since we see it no where invaded, and know very well that Copies are sold and Convey'd as Property in all Countries. But in those Parts, where narrow Jurisdictions have Independency in Civil Rights altho' subject to the same Sovereign, and a Book-seller of one Province may have no speedy remedy against a Book-seller, that Prints his Book in another Province, without having antecedently the Authority of the general Sovereign: It is necessary to have a general Inhibitory Privilege from the Sovereign. But altho' these Privileges or Patents are given for a Term of Years, yet since we see the same Family possess the Copy uninvaded even after the Expiration of the Patent we may justly suppose that the Right is continued by Common Law; and if it be asked why then is the Patent granted, it may be answer'd and we believe with great truth, that it serves only to ascertain the Penalty and Summarily to Punish Delinquents. And we are confirm'd in this Opinion by seeing that in *Holland*, where the greatest Liberty is Exercised, Copies are as frequently sold as elsewhere: Especially, we know that Mr. *Wetstein* of *Amsterdam* sold his Copies in Publick Auction not many Years ago, for several thousand Gilders, altho' all or most of the Books had been Extant alonger Term of Years, than the Patents ever bear.

The Liberty now set on foot of breaking thro' this ancient and reasonable Usage, is no way to be effectually restrained but by an Act of Parliament: For by Common Law a Bookseller can recover no more Cost than he can prove Damage; But 'tis impossible for him to prove the tenth, nay, perhaps the hundredth part of the Damage he suffers; because a thousand Counterfeit Copies may be dispersed into as many different Hands all over the Kingdom, and he not be able to prove the Sale of Ten: Besides, the Defendant is always a *Pauper*, and so the Plaintiff must lose his Costs of Suit. [No Man of Substance has been known to offend in this Particular; nor will any ever appear in it.] Wherefore the only Remedy the Common Law gives, is to confine a Beggar to the Rules of the King's-Bench or Fleet, and there he will continue the Evil Practice with Impunity. We therefore pray, that Confiscation of counterfeit Copies, be one of the Penalties to be inflicted on Offenders.

What is here declared, is the naked Truth, as we are ready to demonstrate, if required.

A plea by booksellers in an undated broadside for perpetual copyright. [B.M. 1887. b. 58 (3)]

More REASONS *Humbly Offer'd to the Honourable House of Commons, for the BILL for Encouraging Learning, and for Securing Property of
Copies of Books to the Rightful Owners thereof.*

THIS Honourable House, in its Great Wisdom and Justice, having always afforded Relief, by agreeing to New Laws, where the Old Ones have been defective, in all reasonable Cases; We cannot doubt, that in this, where that
most distinguishing Quality of Mankind [Learning] is so nearly concern'd,
the Honourable Members of it will fail to extend their usual Beneficence.

The Subject of our Request is, That You would be pleased to strengthen the Common
Law, in our Case, as preceding Parliaments have, in very many others, at divers times.
For whereas, by Common Law, we can recover no more Costs, than we can prove Damage; and the Damage we sustain, being always vastly more than we can prove; We
desire you will assign such Punishment upon Delinquents, as in Your Great Wisdom You
shall think fit.

We Hope, that we have the Common Law on our Side. We know that what
we desire, is what is granted by the Soveraign Power in all other Nations. And we
presume, that the Publick has never suffer'd Inconvenience by the Enjoyment of this
Right, which we have possess'd, by apparent Evidence, ever since the Encorporation of
the Trade: At least no Inconvenience has ever appear'd. For the reducing correct and
well-printed Sermons, into ill-printed Penny-Sheets, the best Effect of the New Liberty,
is, perhaps, by no means so great a Convenience, as to warrant a Liberty that will, in
the End, totally discourage Good Printing in this Nation; which is so well cultivated
among us of late Years, as to deserve the Protection of Authority. And that the continuance of this Liberty must necessarily discourage Good Printing, will appear very evident,
when 'tis consider'd, that the Printing a Book well, do's unavoidably require a very great
Expence of Money; when, at the same time, that very Book may be Printed Vilely, for
a Sixth Part of the Charge; which gives so great an advantage to a Counterfeiter, that
if the Practice be permitted to continue, no Bookseller must dare to Print a fair Edition
of any, tho' the most useful Book. And besides, an Author's Work is expos'd to mangled and corrupt Editions, which is the more fatal since the use of Printing; because the
Copies of a corrupt Edition, are vastly more multiplied by that Art, than it was possible
to be by Manuscripts.

As to the common Argument of Cheapness, we presume to say, that we do, in all Cases
that will admit of it, sell our Books as cheap as any Nation in the World: But it would
be unreasonable to require us to sell a Book, the Copy whereof cost us 50, 60, or 100 *l.*
as cheap as another Man do's one, whose Copy cost nothing. And it cannot be said, we
are Fools to give so much for a Copy, without saying also, that Authors are such to Spend
their whole Time, Years after Years, in composing a useful Book.

But it is said, That it is sufficient for us to enjoy a Term of Years in our Sole Right of
Printing. To this we Answer, That if we have a Right for Ten Years, we have a Right for
Ever. A Man's having possess'd a Property for Ten or Twenty Years, is in no other Instance
allow'd, a Reason for another to take it from him; and we hope it will not be in Ours. But
farther, the Reason assign'd for this Breach upon our Property, is Fallacious; for, whereas
'tis said, we get enough in the first Ten or Fourteen Years, to compensate all Charge and
Hazard: Upon Examination that will be often found untrue; for many excellent Books,
which cost the Authors many Years Labour, do not become so well known, as to make
a good vent, for Ten, nay Twenty Years, after Publication. Sir *Walter Raleigh's* Excellent History, did not become valu'd all his Life-time. The very Excellent Treatise, *The
Whole Duty of Man*, was hardly known for the first Three or Four Years, and yeilded no
Profit in its Sale for several Years after. Sir *Is. Newton's Princip. Math. Naturalis Philoso-
phiæ*, was at least Ten Years in gaining a knowledge in the World. And innumerable are
the Instances of Books, that lie unknown for many Years, altho' they are at last found
to be admirably useful to Mankind. And why, when a Book do's become known and
useful, the proper Proprietor may not have the Benefit of the Sale of it, we cannot see
any Reason.

If Books were as generally necessary, as Food and Raiment; or if the Holy
Scriptures, or other the most useful Books, were so loaded with Price, that the Poor could
not come at 'em, there might be Reason for this Plea: But in this Age, when Books
in general are a third Part at least, if not half in half, cheaper than they were a Hundred Years ago, and have been growing daily cheaper for these Fifty Years past, we
presume this Argument should not be now rais'd. And lest it should be said, that
this Reduction of Price is owing to the Liberty of late; give us leave to Answer, That
the greatest Instances of cheapness known in the World, the *Dictionaries*, and the *Dauphin
Classicks*, were brought to that State, under the Protection of an Act of Parliament, much
more severe to Offenders of it, than that we now ask.

A plea by booksellers in an undated broadside for perpetual copyright.
[B.M. 1887. b. 58 (6)]

ing patronage of the reading public, booksellers were in an ideal position to press their own financial claims. An unprecedented hunger for reading matter "tempted every one who was illuminated with the faintest rays of genius, to turn his mind to literary pursuits. Hence the number of authors hath daily increased, in proportion as readers have multiplied."[1] This amorphous public was financially a more satisfactory source of patronage for both authors and booksellers than were the former great patrons. The booksellers understood this and made every effort to assert their advantage even before the enactment of the historic legislation, utilizing broadsides and pamphlets in vehement protests against piracy. One of the earliest to complain against literary thievery was Daniel Defoe. By compelling authors to affix their names to their writings, Defoe argued, the law would assure them the right to their copy. Defoe strongly favored copyright legislation for the protection of authors, hoping thus for the elimination of piracy and for the encouragement of learning. "To print another man's copy," he wrote, "is much worse than robbing him on the highway."[2] Defoe, to be sure, was but one of many to protest thus against violations of literary property.[3] The plea for copyright as an incentive to learning became popular in the next seventy-five years, eventually enlisting the sympathies of thoughtful and rational writers like Johnson; and meanwhile failure to agree upon time limits of copyright precipitated many a bitter quarrel.

Early writers of broadsides consistently represented the legal claims of the booksellers to literary property as perpetual. As one pamphleteer said, the author has the sole right to his works, to "publish or destroy 'em as he sees fit. For no man is bound to communicate his knowledge to the world." The author is privileged to sell his copyright to a bookseller, he contended, and the bookseller then acquires the author's common-law right of perpetuity. The argument is founded upon a kind of economic reasoning as well as upon legality. If the bookseller takes the risk of publishing a work, according to this man, he should get the benefit of his venture over an indeterminate number of years. The benefit of this would also accrue to the public, since perpetual security would allow booksellers to market inexpensive editions.[4] What the writer failed to point out, however, and that aside from the moral implications of the situation, was that most authors were virtually obliged to sell their copyright because book-sellers were seldom willing to compromise for less than outright pur-chase of the literary property; and the purchase prices, with rare ex-ceptions, were parsimonious. The argument, furthermore, did not take into account the practical fact that pirates were able to thrive mainly because their editions were less expensive than those pro-duced by the copyholders.

As a consequence of numerous complaints, Parliament in the year 1709 finally took positive action upon a petition, by a committee rep-resenting some 5,000 London printers and bookbinders, to end liter-ary piracy.[5] Both Commons and Lords agreed that relief was neces-sary and provided a statute forbidding anyone to "print, reprint, or import, or cause to be printed, reprinted, or imported" writings with-out the consent of the proprietors. This law, "An Act for the En-couragement of Learning," provided severe penalties for violations. Offenses would result in the forfeiture of all copies of the pirated work in question and a fine of one penny for each sheet found in the possession of the offenders. The provisions, however, specifically al-lowed importing and selling in Great Britain works that had been printed abroad in Greek, Latin, or any other foreign language.[6] The inequity of this last proviso was advertised by Samuel Buckley, a printer and bookseller who undertook a Latin edition of Thuanus' *History* and then discovered that the Dutch booksellers were reprint-ing and selling this work in England much less expensively than he could. His only hope for protection, since the Act of 1709 failed to recognize this kind of situation, was a costly plea to Parliament for special legislation which would protect his interests through a limited period of copyright. He made his plea officially in 1734, and he also publicized his grievance. Buckley asserted that paper was cheaper in Holland because it was unaffected by the heavy taxes levied on paper imported into England from Holland. Actually, he complained with cause, the duty on imported paper was higher than on imported books. Buckley, who estimated that he had paid a tax of £750 on only the paper imported for his edition of Thuanus, pointed out that he was also obliged to give free copies, valued at 108 guineas, to nine designated libraries. The Dutch importers, of course, gave none. Con-sequently, he objected to the limitations of the Act of Anne and requested a fourteen-year copyright, which he finally received in 1739.[7]

Under the provisions of the Act, after April 10, 1710, authors of books already printed or booksellers who had purchased their copyright could claim exclusive possession of the copyright for an additional twenty-one years; authors of books printed after that date could have possession of copyright for fourteen years. If after fourteen years the author were still alive, he could renew his copyright for another fourteen years. This was a drastic curtailment of the Trade's claims to perpetual right. The law required, furthermore, that nine copies of each book were to be delivered to the warehouse keeper of the Stationers Company prior to publication for the use of specified libraries.[8] Authority to limit prices in England was vested in the Archbishop of Canterbury, the Lord Chancellor, the Bishop of London, the two Chief Justices, the Chief Baron, and the Vice-Chancellors of Oxford and Cambridge; in Scotland this authority was delegated to the Lord President, the Lord Justice General, the Lord Chief Baron, and the Rector of Edinburgh University. No parallel provision was made for Ireland.

The "Act for the Encouragement of Learning" was only mildly efficacious, even though it made literary piracy a criminal act. It did, however, create nominal checks on this kind of thievery. The booksellers themselves were not satisfied with the law, objecting to the brevity of the copyright period; and not until 1774 was there a general acceptance of the provisions of the Act. Meanwhile piracy continued. Only three years after passage of the legislation a self-designated Tory author decried the subterfuges employed by printers to escape prosecution:

> The great objection, is the scandalous practices of the pirate printers and their hawkers; which will be remov'd, when all printers are oblig'd to put their names, and register their presses: thus it will be as easy to come at 'em as at a figur'd coachman, or ticket-porter; and the offenders will have no way to escape the correction they deserve; which will at once put an end to that grievance, a crying one I own, and it is high time it should be redrest.[9]

The booksellers petitioned the House of Commons once again in March, 1735, this time for the overt purpose of seeking protection against infringements of the Act of Anne, particularly those brought about by importation of books from Ireland and Holland. But their ultimate purpose, it has been assumed, was to strengthen their property rights through revision of the Act.[10] They based their plea upon the publishing hazards resulting from foreign piracy, upon the laboriousness of authorship, and upon the great expense of publishing. They made no attempt at this time to attain perpetual copyright, although they did urge extension of the copyright period legalized by the Act. But suspicion of the Trade's motives, apparently, was sufficiently strong that the new bill more favorable to the booksellers which passed the Commons on May 1, 1735, never came to a final vote in the House of Lords. So fluid was the issue of perpetuity throughout the century and so far was it from resolution that a writer like Bishop William Warburton could plead for perpetual copyright in 1747 and, yet, reverse himself fifteen years later.[11]

It is ironical that in the many attempts by the booksellers to obtain virtual monopolies of printed matter, and despite their protests that they were acting in the interests of the authors as well as of themselves, the authors really counted for little. Since it was customary for booksellers to purchase the authors' copyright as an inseparable part of the copy to be published, the writers were practically excluded from any hope of financial gain after the initial transaction. The authors' option was highly limited. They could make the best possible bargain with the booksellers through outright sale of their copyright, or they could attempt publication of their own works. The latter, obviously, would be impractically expensive, and then they would have no adequate protection against piracy. The booksellers, thus, were interested mainly in self-aggrandizement, and most of their protests about authors' rights were secondary, if not downright subterfuge. Not all booksellers, to be sure, were so completely selfish, as is evident from Johnson's relations with these businessmen;[12] but there was a good deal of friction between authors and booksellers on this score.

Yet the need for an equitable relationship with their authors was impressed upon the practical booksellers, who of course desired to retain their monopolistic advantage. Banded together to share risks and expenses, and in public attestation of their good intentions, they formed in 1735 a Society for the Encouragement of Learning, "to assist authors in publication and to secure them the entire profits of their own works."[13] An advertisement appeared in the *Champion* on Tuesday, March 24, 1740/1, urging authors to patronize these booksellers and thus protect their literary rights. The advertisement is useful evidence that not all booksellers in the eighteenth century were corrupt in their intentions, and it helps clarify working relations between authors and booksellers. The members made quite clear the defensive nature of their position.

> The booksellers in general having the unhappiness to lie under the imputation of making properties of learned and ingenious men, and enriching themselves by the fruits of their studies and labours, whilst they allow them but scanty premiums, and make use of all artifices to deceive and impose upon them, to the great discouragement of learning and detriment to the publick, who are thereby deprived of many valuable pieces.— In order to remove these or any other prejudices, several booksellers have formed themselves in a society, and offer the following proposals to all whom it may concern.

They proposed a kind of editorial board for determining the selection of manuscripts and the prices to be paid. No restrictions were to be made with reference to subject matter, even on political topics, so long as they were "not offensive to good manners." The Society, sometimes known as the "New Conger," claimed strict impartiality, and guaranteed anonymity when it should be desired. They suggested, among other things, an alternative scheme whereby an author might retain copyright and share continually in the profits of the sale of his work, rather than sell his interest outright. The booksellers, further, guaranteed high quality typography and paper. For pieces too small to warrant individual publication, they proposed a twelve-penny miscellany, the *Publishers Magazine* (which, if ever published, is apparently no longer extant). The general agent for the booksellers was to be Thomas Osborne of Gray's Inn. On the surface, certainly, the majority of the Trade were interested in sound business relations with authors, a fact to which Johnson himself testified on more than one occasion. The advertisements suggest at least a formal desire to deal fairly with authors. Cave submitted *Irene* to the Society after having failed to sell it to John Gray the bookseller. The Society, however, was not interested. From the start the organization was doomed to failure. The booksellers, despite avowing eagerness "to make reprisals on such as shall invade their property," were not coöperative. They felt that in making concessions to authors, and in sharing their dividends with each other, they were losing a portion of their customary returns. As a result, the books of the Society were given only half-hearted promotion. And other members of the editorial board, James Thomson among them, were apathetic. In 1749 the Society quietly expired.

The London booksellers knew that their soundest insurance lay in legal sanctions, which they restlessly sought to amplify in their own behalf. Hence, they continued pamphleteering and in 1737 renewed their petition to Parliament, seeking if not literal perpetuity then a substantial extension of the Act of Anne. In support of their requests, the House of Commons prepared a bill holding that the earlier Act had failed to prevent piracy, which, indeed, had even increased.[14] The new proposal suggested stiffened penalties for infractions. Once again the House of Lords rejected fresh legislation, even though the 1737 bill would have increased the advantage of the authors more than that of the booksellers. The matter was permitted to expire again, perhaps because the new recommendation still had in it too many open indications of monopoly. At any rate, there the issue rested until 1739, when a new Act (George II, c. 36) became law on September 29. Although the copyright period was unaffected by the measure, piracy from abroad was challenged. With the specific interdiction against importing books reprinted abroad, the booksellers had achieved one of their major aims. In 1775 the Act was amended to endow the major universities and colleges of England and Scotland with perpetual copyright "in books given or bequeathed [them] for the advancement of useful learning and other purposes of education." The preferential intention of this measure (15 George III, c. 53) is apparent in the stipulation that such books were to be printed at the institutions' private presses; for only Oxford and Cambridge had private presses. (But even this perpetuity was cancelled by the Act of 1911.) The next notable change in the original copyright measure was introduced in 1814, when the copyright period for authors was extended to twenty-eight years, with provision for lifetime copyright extension if the authors were still alive at the end of the twenty-eight year period.[15]

Domestic piracies, we have noted, continued after the Act of 1739;

but under the threat of stringent penalties they became more hazardous and less profitable. Although the pressure of illicit European importations was now diminished, there was still little protection for English authors against unscrupulous Irish and American publishers.[16] Because under the English constitution the Irish Parliament was an indigenous body, the Irish legislators refused to acknowledge the legality of English enactments unless the Irish Parliament specifically endorsed them. For all practical purposes, hence, the parent "Act for the Encouragement of Learning" and its supplementary bills had no status in Ireland. Irish booksellers soon discovered that literary piracy could provide an effective part of their income, which they derived from both Irish and English sales. Not until the Act of Union of 1801 was there any real check on the piracy of English works in Ireland. Protection against American piracies was delayed even longer, for not until the United States adopted an international copyright law in 1891 was there even a degree of adequate restraint.

II

The very nature of magazine publication in the eighteenth century was an invitation to piracy. The *Gentleman's Magazine* and the *London Magazine,* to name the two most prominent periodicals in the first half of the eighteenth century, depended as much upon extraction and abstraction from other periodicals as upon original essays. Not until Johnson began to write for the *Gentleman's Magazine* did that publication reveal any genuine distinction in its original articles. The magazines of the day consisted largely of digested articles likely to provoke interest. The *Gentleman's Magazine,* more reputable than most, scrupulously noted the sources from which it reprinted pieces, although it did not pay for the privilege. No legal issue was ever made of such unauthorized borrowings because rival editors could always retaliate in kind, and it would have been mutually destructive to halt the custom. The life expectancy of most periodicals, furthermore, was notably short; and the contents, which generally were considered non-literary public property, could be expropriated virtually at will. Wholesale borrowing became a more serious matter when it affected literary articles like the *Idler,* for even though the single papers appeared in a newspaper, the author could rightly hold them to be individual, creative compositions. Yet little practical recourse could be had against piracy until their appearance in collected form. At best, Johnson could advertise in the *Universal Chronicle* to deplore the reprehensibility of "borrowing" without authority. But that even he hoped his scolding advertisement would be a deterrent is questionable.

From his earliest days in Grub Street, Johnson had ample occasion to consider the complications of piracy and copyright, and to formulate opinions. Among his first assignments for the *Gentleman's Magazine* were the prefaces attacking rival journals, especially the *London Magazine,* for their larcenous intentions. During the ensuing years *Rasselas* and many numbers of the *Rambler* and *Idler* were pirated. He had a shrewd enough perception of the value of the single *Rambler* papers to retain copyright during the course of the series, although he later sold this interest, probably out of a need for ready cash. Hawkins claimed he had papers that indicated Johnson's retention of the copyright until the conclusion of the series.[17] The single numbers attracted few purchasers and Johnson, probably not hopeful of an extensive book sale, was willing to relinquish the copyright at the time the series was collected in book form. Minor acts of piracy, unintentional though several may have been, were committed upon the *Rambler,* even by such intimates as Arthur Murphy, Thomas Davies, Goldsmith, and Mrs. Piozzi. These borrowings of whole or partial essays were in most cases, to be sure, not serious. Nor, for that matter, would it have been very practical to enforce legal protection of copyright for single papers while they appeared regularly each week. As a material consideration, indeed, the expropriated essays enhanced the value of the collected *Rambler* papers. Regarding even the willful piracy of the Dublin booksellers who brought out one unauthorized edition of the *Rambler* during his lifetime, Johnson must have felt as strong a sense of flattery as of injury. The reproduction of many of the *Idler* papers by various journals, even if unauthorized, must also have been considered a certain advantage for later book sales as well as a tribute to the author's popularity or merit.

Until collection in book form these papers, as far as copyright value was concerned, were almost as ephemeral as the day's news. As has been suggested, such unauthorized reprinting of single essays was

simply an accepted custom which Johnson himself followed as editor
of the *Gentleman's Magazine*. With the formal resentment and assurance of an established author, however, Johnson in a *Universal Chronicle* advertisement (January 5, 1759) sternly announced that the proprietors of the newspaper had lost all patience with pirates of the *Idler*.
"They have already seen [*Idler*] essays, for which a very large price is
paid, transferred, with the most shameless rapacity, into the weekly
or monthly compilations, and their right, at least for the present, alien-
ated from them before they could themselves be said to enjoy it."
Although, he went on ironically, there would be no more resentment
for past injuries, the future would hold no such leniency. "Whoever
shall, without our leave, lay the hand of rapine upon our papers, is to
expect that we shall vindicate our due, by the means which justice
prescribes, and which are warranted by the immemorial prescriptions
of honourable trade." In effect the *Universal Chronicle* promised to
treat the pilferers in kind, to degrade their copies "from the pomp of
wide margin and diffuse typography, contract them into a narrow
space and sell them at an humble price." And when the newspaper
proprietors had recouped their losses, they would direct the profits of
their punitive thievery "to the Magdalens; for we know not who can
be more properly taxed for the support of penitent prostitutes, than
prostitutes in whom there yet appears neither penitence nor shame."
That this elaborate complaint was not merely a Johnsonian crotchet
is substantially demonstrated by the protest of James Ralph, who in
the preceding year had objected to the inadequate protection which
the law gave authors. Yet Boswell at this time tended to dismiss the
matter airily. Impressed by the "high estimation" enjoyed by the
Idler, Boswell recorded his awareness of this notorious piracy. But
he considered it small matter, "in which there is, perhaps, more pomp
of words than the occasion demanded."[18] There is, probably, a certain
basis for his judgment, but in consideration of his later keen interest
in the copyright controversy it is here almost annoyingly superficial.
In all likelihood, however, Boswell associated the importance of
copyright with book publication rather than with the output of the
periodical press, even when productions like the *Idler* were at
stake.

At a time when the copyright question was most fluid, and despite his strictures against piratical booksellers, Johnson found himself embroiled as an accused offender in a copyright argument. Cave in June, 1739, printed an extract from the popular, controversial *Four Sermons,* a pamphlet written by the Reverend Joseph Trapp (1679-1747).[19] Minor pamphleteer, poet, and translator, Trapp was scoffed at by Pope and Swift, though Johnson once recommended his *Praelectione Poeticae* as part of an ideal educational program. The *Four Sermons* was directed against Enthusiasm and, more specifically, against George Whitefield, the Methodist preacher.[20] Although the editors advertised that they intended to continue the abridgment in subsequent numbers, the work never went beyond the June issue. The matter, obscure and somewhat conjectural, must be resolved through a footnote to *Considerations* which Johnson made on the *Four Sermons* and which were published posthumously in the *Gentleman's Magazine.*[21] Both Cave and Johnson, the note suggests, were apparently fearful of running afoul of the copyright law. (There is, of course, the further likelihood that Cave had no desire to become deeply entangled in a theological dispute centering on Prayer Book reform and Enthusiasm.) Technically there were no legal grounds for such fear in 1739, the question of abridgment not having been treated in the copyright act of 1709 nor its immediate revisions, and test suits not yet having been submitted for judicial opinions. Yet in view of the still unsettled atmosphere around copyright and both Cave's and Johnson's undoubted familiarity with the dangers involved, the fact probably is that Trapp's bookseller threatened them with court action. Cave, an astute, cautious business man, must have seen little advantage to incurring such risk on behalf of a debated work whose popularity was no reflection of its literary or theological importance. He was willing to take unusual risks, but only for publications of greater significance like the *Parliamentary Debates.* It was also one thing to expropriate ephemeral articles from the daily and weekly press, but another to reprint substantial parts of a "literary" production that had been entered in the Stationers Register and was covered by copyright. The printing of extractions from larger works was a popularly sanctioned method of literary reviewing, whose ostensible purpose was, at least partially, to present critical evaluations. Cave's purpose, on the other hand, had no relation to literary reviewing or criticism. Since legal precedent was not to be made of such cases until at least 1761, he had no reason to suspect that his position would have been readily tenable in a court of law. An editorial menial in 1739, Johnson himself, presumably, was prevailed upon to compose his spirited support of abridgments as a matter of expediency. Nevertheless, Johnson throughout his career held to the main points of his first views on excision and copyright. Later judicial opinion justified the conclusions of the *Considerations,* his first writing on the law.[22]

In paragraphs 29 and 30 of the *Considerations,* Johnson summarized his basic argument, maintaining "that we have not printed the complainant's copy, but abridged it. . . . This will need no proof, since it will appear, upon comparing the two books, that we have reduced thirty-seven pages to thirteen of the same print." His posthumous remarks on abridgments, and copyright in general, exhibit his lifelong moderate attitude toward literary property and freedom of the press. Johnson contended that the individual who purchased the manuscript copy of a book purchased only the right to print and sell it, but had no legal or moral right to make changes of expansion or abridgment without the author's consent. The purchaser of the single, printed book—the reader—had on the other hand "the right of making such use of it as he shall think most convenient, either for his own improvement or amusement, or the benefit or entertainment of mankind." Johnson admitted that this right frequently was disadvantageous to both author and bookseller, but he would not have withheld it any more than he would have withheld the right to criticize. His "reputation, as an author, is at the mercy of the reader, who lies under no other obligations to do me justice than those of religion and morality." The abridger, he advised satirically in *Rambler,* No. 145, "must not be rashly doomed to annihilation." On another occasion, more seriously, Johnson revealed his good opinion of skillful abridgment as a literary accomplishment.[23] Arguing now from the premise that the contraction of a work is related to the critical prerogative, Johnson continued: "Thus every book, when it falls into the hands of the reader, is liable to be examined, confuted, censured, translated, and abridged; any of which may destroy the credit of the author, or hinder the sale of the book."[24] His implication, thus, was that abridgment did not really fall within the jurisdiction of the courts, but was a matter of essential critical right. Being practical, however, Johnson also concluded that abridgment was legally defensible, inferring his belief from the unauthorized liberties which had been taken with the histories of Burnet and Clarendon.

The design of an abridgment is, to benefit mankind by facilitating the attainment of knowledge; and by contracting arguments, relations, or descriptions, into a narrow compass, to convey instruction in the easiest method, without fatiguing the attention, burdening the memory, or impairing the health of the student. . . . By this method the original author becomes, perhaps of less value, and the proprietor's profits are diminished; . . . so a tedious volume may, no less lawfully, be abridged, because it is better that the proprietors should suffer some damage, than that the acquisition of knowledge should be obstructed with unnecessary difficulties, and the valuable hours of thousands thrown away.

His seeming indifference to authors' rights was not typical unless we associate it with a trace of Johnsonian cynicism toward hack writers or unnecessarily verbose writers. But much more consonant with his concern over the public good, Johnson's views on abridgments correspond closely with the practice he followed in his literary reviews. By copious extractions from the works under review, he gave his readers generous timesaving samples of the originals. This interest in condensation, it might be added, is a natural corollary of his personal reading habits. Johnson had a capacity for finding the essential ingredients of books without reading any of them from cover to cover, a fetish which he abhorred. Even as a young man, it was reported of him, "He had a peculiar facility in seizing at once what was valuable in any book, without submitting to the labour of perusing it from beginning to end." As he himself said, "A book may be good for nothing; or there may be only one thing in it worth knowing; are we to read it all through?"[25] He would subscribe to abridgments as well as to literary reviews on this principle, that it is a waste of time and energy to concentrate on the trivial. Not many readers have the knack of isolating key ideas without thoroughgoing perusal, but Johnson had the knack and he was willing to apply it for the benefit of his periodical readers. His entire attitude toward abridgments reflects the broad view of a journalist skilled in the techniques of his craft and of a man impatient of superficialities. Also it was a convenient theory, since it was useful in the type of work he was doing.

Late in life Johnson amended his opinion of 1739. On August

20, 1773, in Scotland, "[Boswell] said printing an abridgment of a work was allowed, which was only cutting the horns and tail off the cow. Johnson. 'No, sir, 'tis making the cow have a calf.' "[26] The implication here is that an abridgment is not synonymous with the original work but is rather a byproduct of that work and, thus, a new work belonging to the abridger. By 1773 Johnson, as a widely published author, would have been affected financially by the indiscriminate abridgment of his important work, for others could then have promoted the abbreviated versions of his books and thus lessened the sales of the originals. In 1739, when he was just beginning, he had nothing to lose. As an editor, indeed, it was to his and his employer's advantage to print full abridgments without initial expense to themselves. The 1773 statement, on the other hand, is the evocation of a mature, experienced theorist with a different financial interest. At the same time, however, and without belaboring the significance of Johnson's epigrammatic retort, it appears indicative of his frequent practice of exploiting a situation for the expression of a witticism, even at the seeming expense of his own convictions. Although here he has obviously tempered his feelings about abridgments, he has not demonstrably altered his original theory nor, indeed, has he rendered any value judgment. Here, it will be noted, he avoids taking into account the author's position. Through playful emendation of Boswell's quip, Johnson really has enlarged his own attitude. He does not ask for limitations on the right of abridgment, but he now suggests that an abridgment is a new work.

Similarly Justice Willes in 1769 had recognized "Bonâ fide imitations, translations, and abridgments . . . as new works."[27] Four years later, however, in Scotland, Lord Hailes was to complain that booksellers through their abridgments limit the common-law right of authors, his point seemingly being that an abridgment is not a new product at all, but the reworking of an old one.[28] In a tone reminiscent of Lord Hailes', Boswell, who had thought Johnson's *Considerations* was "a very ingenious defence of the right of abridging an authour's work, without being held as infringing his property," favored strict limitation of this freedom.[29]

The first case of abridgment to be tested in the British courts was that of *Dodsley versus Kinnersley* in 1761, a case especially pertinent here because it dealt with one of Johnson's own works. Robert Dodsley, the bookseller, had applied for an injunction to restrain the defendant from publishing an abridgment of *Rasselas* in the *Grand Magazine of Magazines,* arguing that his injury was sustained as a result of Kinnersley's extracting the narrative portions rather than the moral lessons of *Rasselas.* But the injunction was not granted because Sir Thomas Clarke, Master of the Rolls, did not agree that Johnson's novel had been injured by the abstraction of less than one-tenth of its contents. He suggested, indeed, that abridgment might serve as advertisement for a work, as when the *London Chronicle* began to publish extracts from *Rasselas* on April 20, 1759 (one day after its publication was advertised).[30] Although the case of *Dodsley versus Kinnersley* thus established a precedent which was supported by later judicial opinions, subsequent decisions were not always consistent with this one. In the eighteenth century the general legal opinion was that a true abridgment, to be acceptable under law, must be an independent labor resulting from critical thought (an opinion that Johnson would readily concur in). The abridger was expected to preserve the substance of the literary work as well as reduce its size.[31] The tendency in the nineteenth and twentieth centuries has been to deny the legality of abridging copyrighted works without previous authorization.

Johnson's early concern with abridgment anticipated his reflections upon the broader subject of copyright that was to absorb much of his attention late in his career. His constant belief that a written work is for the benefit of the people and should be given the widest possible circulation made him impatient with unduly selfish control of literary property.[32] Johnson believed an author and his heirs should have the full financial benefits of literary property. Yet he disapproved of unreasonably long periods of copyright, considering at various times that limits of fifty, sixty, or one hundred years were adequate.[33] Despite the "Act for the Encouragement of Learning" of 1709, which definitely restricted copyright to a total of twenty-eight years in the author's lifetime, many authors and booksellers continued to challenge this restriction in favor of perpetuity and virtual monopoly. Their claims were strengthened in 1769 by a court decision in the case of *Millar versus Taylor,* which favored perpetual

copyright. But any binding legal claims to perpetuity were finally jetti-
soned in 1774, in the now famous law case of *Donaldson versus
Becket,* when the judges in the House of Lords denied the existence
of perpetual copyright in a published work. This was an opinion
concurred in by Johnson.

Alexander Donaldson was a Scotch bookseller who in 1763 opened
a shop in London for the sale of cheap editions of popular works.
Defending his right to operate against the powerful monopoly of
London booksellers controlling English copyright, Donaldson published pamphlets in which he defied the assumptions of a common-
law principle of perpetuity. However materialistic his intention, he
argued in reasoned and convincing terms against perpetuity as a
monopolistic evil which operated as a detriment "to the advancement
of learning."[34] After minor and inconclusive legal skirmishes in
which the London booksellers sought to establish their claims for
perpetual ownership, they won a temporary victory in the case of
Millar versus Taylor, three judges voting against one in favor of
perpetuity. For the first time in twelve years the Court of King's
Bench was split in a decision.[35] Although Robert Taylor (a London
bookseller who had brought out an unauthorized edition of the
Seasons in 1763) discontinued his part in the litigation, Donaldson
overtly ignored the decision by selling in England a large number of
copies of Thomson's *Seasons* which he had printed in Edinburgh.

The copyright was claimed by the bookseller Thomas Becket and
fourteen partners who had purchased it from the estate of the bookseller Andrew Millar in 1769 for £505; Millar had originally purchased the copyright of *Summer* in 1729, and of the remaining poems
of the *Seasons* in 1738. Donaldson had been excluded from any
possibility of sharing in the ownership of the *Seasons.* After his exclusion from the joint transaction which followed Millar's death in
1768, Donaldson firmly maintained his right to sell Thomson's poem
on the grounds that the estate had not had legal copyright claims
upon it, since the term under Anne had expired.

Donaldson found considerable moral support among anonymous
pamphleteers who resented this monopolistic stranglehold as much
as he did. One of them, who deplored the abuses of inferior craftsmanship contingent upon "an absolute monopoly established in

books," insisted that twenty-one or twenty-eight years should be a sufficient length of time for the author or his heirs.[36] The London booksellers, however, considered themselves firmly entrenched, legally and financially. Becket and his partners, therefore, filed suit in 1771 for an injunction to restrain Donaldson from further printing and selling the *Seasons.* Meanwhile, the Court of Session in Scotland heard the case of *Hinton versus Donaldson* (1773), and decided in favor of limited copyright contrary to the decision of 1769 in England. To nullify completely the findings in *Millar versus Taylor,* the House of Lords, to which Donaldson appealed his case, ruled in his favor in 1774. Thus it restored the letter of the Act of Anne and completely disposed of any possible legal claims to perpetuity. Literary monopolies were then ended in England, except for those granted to schools like Oxford, Cambridge, and Eton.[37]

Johnson had long followed the copyright struggle with interest. His friend Arthur Murphy was one of Donaldson's counsels in the classic case of 1774; Boswell, a counsel in *Hinton versus Donaldson,* argued against perpetuity (Johnson was displeased with the reasoning of the judges);[38] and Johnson had discussed the copyright question with his friends. As early as 1763 he had thought Donaldson was injuring the London booksellers, "for whom [Johnson] uniformly expressed much regard," by invading their rights. He pointedly supported the contention of the London booksellers, commenting that Donaldson "is a fellow who takes advantage of the law to injure his brethren." The booksellers in a practical sense, he felt, were justified by usage—despite the specific terms of the Act of Anne—in assuming perpetuity when they purchased copyright. But he took a moderate position, even at the cost of appearing self-contradictory, and suggested, at this time, sixty years as an adequate period.[39] Despite his loyalty to the Trade, Johnson often expressed himself explicitly against perpetual copyright, especially in letters to Boswell and Strahan in 1774, and indicated that no other position was morally or socially defensible. At times, to be sure, he stated his attitude almost laconically. In January, 1774, for instance, Johnson wrote to Boswell merely, "The question of literary property is this day before the Lords. Murphy drew up the appellants' [Donaldson's] case, that is, the plea against perpetual right. I have not seen it, nor heard the decision.

I would not have the right perpetual." On the whole, however, Johnson was one of the few important English authors to take an active interest in this subject, being "zealous against a perpetuity," as is especially evident in his letter of March 7, 1774, to Strahan. Walpole took fleeting note of the problem. Some other writers are Hume, who in judiciously evaluating the pros and cons of the legal situation leaned toward perpetuity, and Mrs. Macaulay, who fulminated in behalf of perpetuity. Murphy and Boswell had a legalistic concern, but Boswell went even further to make many random reflections against perpetual right.[40] The booksellers, of course, were generally more aggressive than the authors.

Johnson differed only on a philosophical plane from the opinion of Sir William Blackstone, the great legal authority of the eighteenth century and fellow Pembrokean, whom he admired. Blackstone assumed that an author retained exclusive possession of his manuscript, but that once it was published he could no longer claim proprietary rights except for those privileges accorded him under the statute of Queen Anne. After expiration of the legal privileges provided by the copyright act, Blackstone thought, the author's published work becomes a piece of public property. Under his interpretation of the law, therefore—the interpretation finally validated by the English court in 1774—ownership was a matter of temporary occupancy or proprietary right. Johnson admitted the practical necessity of this ruling; but he did not believe the principle of occupancy to be innately just, thinking each author had a "metaphysical," permanent claim to his work.

. . . a right, as it were, of creation, which should from its nature be perpetual; but the consent of nations is against it, and indeed reason and the interests of learning are against it; for were it to be perpetual, no book, however useful, could be universally diffused amongst mankind, should the proprietor take it into his head to restrict its circulation. No book could have the advantage of being edited with notes, however necessary to its elucidation, should the proprietor perversely oppose it. For the general good of the world, therefore, whatever valuable work has once been created by an authour, and issued out by him, should be understood as no longer in his power, but as belonging to the publick; at the same time the authour is entitled to an adequate reward. This he should have by an exclusive right to his work for a considerable number of years.[41]

Johnson's reasonable position, therefore, is one of compromise between individual and public, between moral right and social expediency. His realistic assumptions for literary property, as in his more specific comments on abridgment, are here attuned to the greatest good of society, coinciding with his general belief—and Blackstone's—that once published a piece of literature may no longer serve a private purpose. That Johnson nevertheless entertained respect for the creative talents of the author is implicit in the above quotation. But every man, both Johnson and Blackstone believed, must submit to some inconveniences in order to enjoy the benefits of society. This is a notion that recurs frequently in the *Rambler,* the *Idler,* and other of Johnson's writings, and is widely shared even by more liberal contemporary thinkers.[42] In keeping with his principle that the common good is paramount, therefore, Johnson opposed perpetual private ownership, proposing instead to make written works available as public property after a specified period of copyright. His care for the public will be recognized as the same doctrine which he applied to abridgments.

William Strahan, a leading London bookseller, asked David Hume, James Beattie, William Robertson, and other writers, Johnson apparently among them, for letters that he might use in an appeal on behalf of the booksellers of London against the finding in *Donaldson versus Becket*; and a number of these letters were presented to the House of Commons on May 13, 1774.[43] Hume, Robertson, and Beattie were with the small minority who favored perpetuity; but privately even Hume intimated that his sympathy was merely a friendly gesture on behalf of his publishers, who had treated him well but whose fears and convictions he did not really share. Johnson did not waver in his theoretical opposition to perpetuity, and it is not likely that the letter he wrote was read to the legislators, since he was unsympathetic to the cause of the booksellers. His letter to Strahan is presented in full because it so admirably summarizes his representative opinions in the protracted and important controversy, and because it is an indication of how clearly he had reflected upon it. In 1774 the reasoned conclusions which were heard with deep respect were substantially the same as those which he had uttered eleven years earlier in casual conversation, with respect to limited copyright. His first thought had been the adequacy of sixty or one-hundred years of copyright possession; now, in his concise notes to Strahan, he was proposing fifty-one years:

Sir

I will tell you in a few words, what is, in my opinion, the most desirable state of copyright or literary property.

The authour has a natural and peculiar right to the profits of his own work.

But as every man who claims the protection of society, must purchase it by resigning some part of his natural right, the author must recede from so much of his claim, as shall be deemed injurious or inconvenient to society.

It is inconvenient to society that an useful book should become perpetual and exclusive property.

The judgement of the Lords was therefore legally and politically right.

But the authour's enjoyment of his natural right might without any inconvenience be protracted beyond the term settled by the statute. And it is, I think, to be desired.

1. That an authour should retain during his life the sole right of printing and selling his work.

This is agreeable to moral right, and not inconvenient to the publick, for who will be so diligent as the authour to improve the book, or who can know so well how to improve it?

2. That the authour be allowed, as by the present act, to alienate his right only for fourteen years.

A shorter time would not procure a sufficient price, and a longer would cut off all hope of future profit, and consequently all solicitude for correction or addition.

3. That when after fourteen years the copy shall revert to the authour, he be allowed to alienate it again only for seven years at a time.

After fourteen years the value of the work will be known, and it will be no longer bought at hazard. Seven years of possession will therefore have an assignable price. It is proper that the authour be always incited to polish and improve his work, by that prospect of accruing interest which those shorter periods of alienation will afford him.

4. That after the authour's death his work should continue an exclusive property capable of bequest and inheritance, and of conveyance by gift or sale for thirty years.

By these regulations a book may continue the property of the authour or of those who claim from him, about fifty years, a term sufficient to reward the writer without any loss to the publick. In fifty years far the greater number of books are forgotten and annihilated, and it is for the advantage of learning that those which fifty years have not destroyed should become *bona communia,* to be used by every scholar as he shall think best.

In fifty years every book begins to require notes either to explain forgotten allusions and obsolete words; or to subjoin those discoveries which have been made by the gradual advancement of knowledge; or to correct those mistakes which time may have discovered.

Such notes cannot be written to any useful purpose without the text, and the text will frequently be refused while it is any man's property.

I am Sir your humble servant,

March 7, 1774   Sam: Johnson[44]

This letter was the sincere, lucid expression of a man who had known the uncertainty of Grub Street and the defenseless economic position of writers. But it was also the expression of a man who was intimate with the current arguments of legal and lay minds concerning the nature of literary property, and of one who saw the broad aspects of literature, knowing that good writing should be a cultural heritage of the majority of the people as well as a source of income for a writer or his immediate heirs. Johnson, it will be noted, concentrates at least as much attention upon social benefit as he does upon the profit motive.

Following the decision in *Donaldson versus Becket,* with booksellers scrambling to reprint popular works, Johnson was commissioned to prepare his edition of *English Poets.* "The poets were selected by the several booksellers who had the honorary copy right, which is still [in 1791] preserved among them by mutual compact, notwithstanding the decision of the House of Lords against the perpetuity of literary property." According to Edward Dilly, "about forty of the most respectable booksellers of London" pooled their resources to challenge "the little trifling edition" of poets—consisting of their works and biographies—which was produced by the Martins of Edinburgh and sold by Bell in London. The poor format and inaccurate texts were given by Dilly as reasons for the new edition, but so also was "the idea of an invasion of what we call our literary property."[45] It is reasonable to assume that these forty booksellers "of consequence" were more interested in challenging the upstart Scottish booksellers and in taking financial advantage of the works which they formerly had been able to monopolize more effectively than they were in providing the public with an "elegant" edition. Clearly, they intended to cling to their former property by offering their own edition in competition with that of the rival booksellers. In 1777, consequently, the London booksellers commissioned Johnson to write a series of lives of poets, to which would be added their works. Curiously, thus, Johnson in effect violated his own theoretical condemnation of literary perpetuity.

In the same year that he was invited to prepare the *English Poets,* Johnson was called upon to intercede for Charlotte Lennox against a threatened copyright violation. Mrs. Lennox's concern for her literary property becomes evident in the midst of a letter to Johnson (June 17, 1777) proposing that he come to her house to eat gooseberry tarts. As casually as though she were still talking about household trivia, she makes this transition:

Mr. Lennox is so desirous of recovering his property out of the hands of the booksellers, that he gives me leave to take any measures that shall be judged proper—it will be necessary to have the advice of some gentleman of the law, I am not known to Mr. Murphy, but if you will be so good to mention my affairs to him, and let me know where he lives, I will call upon him.[46]

It has been conjectured—and with reasonable cause—that Mr. Lennox's "property" is obviously his wife's work, which had been excluded under the decision of 1774 from perpetual copyright. The work in question is undoubtedly Mrs. Lennox's translation of *Sully's Memoirs,* which Johnson had reviewed favorably in 1756 upon its publication.[47] As she later notified Johnson, she had offered a revised edition of the *Memoirs* to James Dodsley and his partners near the conclusion of the initial copyright period; but they declined to purchase it, and prepared instead to bring out an unauthorized version. Hence, she sought the legal assistance of Arthur Murphy, who had proved his competence in copyright matters during the case of *Donaldson versus Becket.* The popularity of her work had already encouraged the piratical publication of two inexpensive Scottish editions, and now she was apparently determined to stand firm against further encroachment.

That she was not fully successful, however, is evident from the appearance of two editions of the *Memoirs* in 1778, both printed by Dodsley, Rivington, and their partners. Although the evidence is oblique, the motives behind this dual publication become reasonably clear from a letter which Mrs. Lennox addressed to Johnson May 29, 1778.

. . . I saw Mr. Dodsley yesterday, and he told me they had printed another edition of Sully's Memoirs—I apprehend they had no right to do this without my consent, it is more than fourteen years since that book was first published; and about a year ago I offered to give them my corrected copy for a reasonable consideration, which Dodsley in the name of the partners refused—and now they have reprinted it without consulting me although by the late decision concerning literary property the copy is mine—I am advised to publish it for myself in numbers, and if the partners expect to sell another edition, I have some reason to hope that I may have success by publishing it in this same manner, as the purchase will be so much easier—but I must be speedy, for Dodsley owned the book was almost ready—it will be necessary I suppose to draw up a little address to the publick explaining my reasons for publishing Sully myself, and in this manner—this favor I earnestly entreat of you. . . .[48]

The curious circumstance of two editions of the *Memoirs* issued by the same publishers in the same year thus seems to be explainable. Through her forthright action, and through the additional prompting of Mr. Lennox, Murphy, and Johnson, Mrs. Lennox would appear to have protected in some measure the title to her literary property and, probably, to have received the "reasonable consideration" which she had sought in the previous year. To induce Dodsley to bring out her own edition in 1778—as she apparently did—when his "was almost ready," she must surely have mustered a strong case for herself. Whether Johnson actually drew up an explanatory address to the public is not known today, although a subsequent letter raises the possibility that he urged a token edition of 150 copies of the *Memoirs.*[49] Mrs. Lennox, at any rate, certainly profited from the intercession of Johnson whose high regard for her was unfailing. "Three such women [as Elizabeth Carter, Hannah More, and Fanny Burney]," he assured Boswell, "are not to be found: I know not where I could find a fourth, except Mrs. Lennox, who is superior to them all."[50]

The copyright question was important to the hack writers of Grub Street as well as to reputable authors. Those small writers who produced books were given a degree of legal protection against pirates, although this protection did not go very far. They were able to share in some of the gains of cheap reprinting when copyrights expired under the provisions of the "Act for the Encouragement of Learning," for the resulting expanding markets gave them employment in editing, writing prefaces, and related tasks. Other Grubeans suffered because of the Act, since previously they had profited by working for unscrupulous literary pirates. The Act, while not entirely effective, did have some restrictive compulsion and piracy therefore became a risky trade. With his roots in Grub Street, Johnson was keenly aware of the effects of the copyright law upon authorship. He devoted much thought to the problem and reasoned soundly upon it, his opinions upon copyright being firmly based upon his extensive interests in scholarship, law, and journalism.

CHAPTER VII

JOHNSON ON A FREE PRESS

I

THE RISE of English journalism in the seventeenth century brought with it critical problems allied to freedom of the press. As the nearest approach to the expression of popular attitudes, journalism undertook the obligation of reporting on affairs of state and church for general readers. In the seventeenth century, however, neither secular nor ecclesiastical leaders were inclined to surrender controls on the numerous hack writers in English journalism. Political and religious unease, fear of seditious writings, jealousy of autocratic powers, and grave skepticism of the responsibility of the commoners were considered sufficient grounds for restraining freedom of expression and of the press. Growing public interest in contemporary affairs made total suppression impossible, but as long as some form of absolute rule existed, effective restrictions were enforceable. Yet many newspapers and pamphlets disputed established authority by flouting censorship. The new-found voice of the people was not to be silenced easily, and popular opposition views were widely circulated despite energetic attempts to enforce the licensing measures of the second half of the century. Fearless, radical libertarians like Milton were too rare, and progress, though it was made in the struggle for freedom of expression and opinion, was slow.

Eighteenth-century philosophical concepts of human liberties were intimately related to freedom of the press. But the notion that freedom could have a practical as well as a theoretical manifestation was often approached with caution, if not indeed with reluctance. Although sympathy with the populace's right to freedom of opinion—and hence of the press—grew appreciably during the century, an intellectual minority clung tenaciously to the proposition that individual representation must be equated with mob rule. Even moderate thinkers like Johnson agreed to the necessity of freedom, whether in ordinary conduct or in the press. But because of a basic suspicion of the irresponsibility of the commoners, the "rabble," Johnson and others like him—Hume, Goldsmith, Smollett, Horace Walpole— maintained that an uncontrolled populace, stirred to opposition, would tend toward revolution and anarchy. Any insistence upon individual rights leading to the overthrow of a benevolent established order is wrong, according to this view, for the whole is more important than the individual.

While supporting this typical attitude which prevailed in England almost to the time of the French Revolution, men like Johnson, Hume, and Goldsmith placed all their faith in a paternalistic government. They assumed first of all that the *status quo,* granted that it is a felicitous one, must not be jeopardized. They assumed next that the established order would provide maximum benefits for the individual. Should rulers with despotic intentions attempt to impose undue limitations, they argued, then the people would justifiably rise to protect themselves and their society against subservience. The parliamentary system, according to this contention, a sound medium between repressive monarchy and feared democracy, was the form of government most conducive to liberty.

On the surface such striving for an equipoise may seem almost illiberal as compared with twentieth-century democratic theories. But for the privilege of living in a civilized society, even today, the individual must expect to make reasonable concessions, being willing at times to subordinate his convenience to the convenience of the whole. "Freedom without limitation is a chimera."[1] When we speak of liberty in the eighteenth century, we speak in terms of degrees. On the one hand there was the natural rights theory of Locke and Rousseau for maximum liberty, manifested in the liberalism of Wilkes, Paine, and the later John Stuart Mill. On the other hand there were the appeals for limited liberty by Johnson, Hume, and Goldsmith. Those whose distrust of mobs and veneration of traditionalism led them to favor moderation did not deny the right of freedom in the press and in other activities. They insisted, however, that freedom without arbitrary limitations of some kind would be abused. At least until the expiration of the Licensing Act in 1694, many exponents of curtailed liberty hoped to limit the press prior to publication and thus reduce unfavorable criticism. Blackstone, summarizing the state of English law in mid-eighteenth century, approved in theory of an uncensored press; yet at the same time he certified an effective legal restraint, after publication, by sanctioning severe punishments for abuses. Obviously, fear of harsh discipline could be almost as cogent a deterrent as an absolute prohibition.

II

"I would rather trust my money to a man who has no hands, and so a physical impossibility to steal, than to a man of the most honest principles."[2] These words in the year before his death are the essence of Johnson's philosophy of a free press and of the inseparable problem of human liberty, two eighteenth-century issues that were to provide much of the groundwork of future liberalism in Europe and America. Thus he summed up his typical distrust of democratic privilege and his insistence that rulers apply prerogatives for the good of the many. Essentially Johnson believed that human rights must be respected but closely defined by a humane, authoritarian government legislating for the best interests of the people. No revolutionary group, he believed, could achieve this purpose because revolutionists are the rabble and the rabble are necessarily irresponsible. By the same token he believed that an unrestrained press is dominated by selfish masses whose interest is in the individual rather than in the social group. Inevitably capricious, such a press, in Johnson's opinion, can produce only sedition and disorder. And such disorder, he felt, must lead from benevolence to tyranny. He believed the government must impose certain restraints and that the press must obey them, if order is to be maintained.

To comprehend Johnson's views on freedom of the press we must comprehend his attitude toward human liberty and the scope that he would accord it. His thoughts were always tempered by veneration for the established authority of the state, which to him was the only justifiable guardian of citizens' rights. The individualism of popular government he decried as a step toward anarchy and chaos. In an age of order Johnson insisted upon the absolute order that he believed could be maintained only by the rigidly centralized control of a monarch and his parliament. This insistence was not out of an arbitrary worship of monarchial rule but out of a feeling that man's survival and happiness can result only from an enforced regimen.

It is essential to recall that Johnson's fearful view of democracy is typical of an idea prevalent in the eighteenth century prior to the French Revolution. According to this notion, the principle of individual representation was equated with mob rule, which Johnson dreaded would magnify the advantage of the individual above the good of the whole. Although he was aware that some English rulers might attempt tyrannical breaches of liberty, his general faith in monarchy led him to minimize such peril. Indeed, he even implied that freedom was permitted in England to such an extensive degree as to provoke danger of licentiousness. His distinctions in the *Dictionary* illuminate this point, for he defines *liberty* as "exemption from tyranny or inordinate government," and *licentiousness* (by which he means the same as *license*) as "boundless liberty; contempt of just restraint."[3] Despite his apprehension of the masses, Johnson contended that they so cherished their existent liberties as to render ineffectual any attempted serious limitations of their rights.

His entire attitude presupposed that government and public expression in England were as liberal and as free as they could possibly be for the greatest beneficence of the many. Like any careful observer of society, Johnson saw the parallel between a free government and a free press. And like any careful observer of society he saw the need for transigence. It has long been a common error to present him as an absolutist on social problems. Far from such inflexibility, Johnson recognized the essentiality of liberty to man's gregarious state. He differed from more liberal thinkers of his day only in degree. All admitted the value of a certain amount of restraint in government and in the press. But because of his reaction against the masses, Johnson insisted particularly upon imposition of curbs and careful enforcement. Nevertheless he resented extremes of authoritarian rule even as he resented extremes of democracy.

Johnson was not alone in advocating a quiescent form of English government. Goldsmith and Hume, for instance, held that the parliamentary system, by offering a happy medium between democracy and monarchy, was the form of government most conducive to liberty.

With a conservatism like Johnson's, Goldsmith suspiciously declared: "[E]very step . . . the constitution takes towards a democratic form, every diminution of the legal authority, is, in fact, a diminution of the subject's freedom; but every attempt to render the government more popular not only impairs natural liberty, but even will at last dissolve the political constitution."[4] Johnson, then, was but one of a group of distinguished moderate thinkers who abhorred the excesses to which lack of restraints could lead.

In his own day he had acquired in some circles a notoriety for intolerance and opposition to liberty. "What!" observed John Wilkes, "does *he* talk of liberty? *Liberty* is as ridiculous in *his* mouth as *Religion in mine.*"[5] Another contemporary, Joseph Baretti, admired Johnson but shared this notion of his lack of tolerance.[6] Yet at various times in his career Johnson praised the liberal condition of British freedom and insisted that its existence was important to the continued public welfare. On the occasion that invited Wilkes' contemptuous remark, Johnson had commented: "[I]t would be a wrong thing to deprive the small landholders of the privilege of assessing themselves for making and repairing the high roads; *it was destroying a certain portion of liberty, without a good reason, which was always a bad thing.*" In this statement is Johnson's clear perception of a need for respecting the rights of the commoners and of the state's function as an agent of the people. Compared with such champions of the populace as the flamboyant Wilkes, Paine, and others, Johnson is representative of a political caution which he drew from classical philosophers. In them, as in Johnson, a prudent, searching spirit always rebuked radical departures from established authority; but it also generally stimulated rather than negated the principle of human liberty in society. Plato, for instance, in advocating a strong ruler had said the people must have a certain degree of liberty or the state becomes despotic and the leaders self-seekers, contrary to the purpose of communal society.[7] Aristotle, who saw the necessity of sacrificing certain personal rights for the good of the commonwealth, considered liberty characteristic of a democracy.[8] Even Machiavelli alluded to the "golden age," when "everyone is free to hold and to defend his own opinion."[9]

During a conversation on toleration in 1773, Johnson revealed admirably his concept of liberty and its function in society. Liberty to him was a kind of grant extended by a beneficent government to its citizens. Within limits fixed by legislation that was in turn circumscribed by the political and social necessity operative for society as a whole, Johnson would accord the people relative, not absolute, freedom. Despite his mistrust of individualism, he reveals some flexibility in establishing the bounds of individual freedom. Even in so doing, however, he qualifies his attitude by reference to the "bad tendency" test, which our society has long since rejected.

Every society has a right to preserve publick peace and order, and therefore has a good right to prohibit the propagation of opinions which have a dangerous tendency. To say the magistrate has this right, is using an inadequate word: it is the society for which the magistrate is agent. He may be morally or theologically wrong in restraining the propagation of opinions which he thinks dangerous, but he is politically right. . . . Every man has a right to liberty of conscience, and with that the magistrate cannot interfere. People confound liberty of thinking with liberty of talking; nay with liberty of preaching. Every man has a physical right to think as he pleases; for it cannot be discovered how he thinks. He has not a moral right; for he ought to inform himself and think justly. But, Sir, no member of society has a right to teach any doctrine contrary to what that society holds to be true. The magistrate, I say, may be wrong in what he thinks: but, while he thinks himself right, he may, and ought to enforce what he thinks.[10]

In effect, then, Johnson argued that every man has the liberty to think as he pleases but not to act as he pleases, if his proposed action is not consonant with public good. The same idea he incorporated with this theory of a free press; the writer may be permitted to express only those ideas which authority has deemed good for the citizenry.

Because of gratification with the current state of British liberty, Johnson was inclined to brand quests for additional privileges as marks of immaturity. Furthermore, he frequently associated such dissatisfaction with the uncultivated and unknowing hordes of the "rabble." Of the letters of George Lyttelton, who advocated reform in parliament and an unrestrained press for reporting public matters, Johnson noted that they "have something of that indistinct and headstrong ardour for liberty which a man of genius always catches when he enters the world, and always suffers to cool as he passes forward."[11] Even more harshly did he view Mark Akenside's activities on behalf of liberty, attributing to his efforts the qualities of irresponsibility. Akenside, as he had also written of Thomas Blackwell, "certainly retained an unnecessary and outrageous zeal for what he called and thought liberty." Such zeal Johnson associated with a desire for selfish gain, and he was convinced that it led to the twin evils of innovation and anarchy. Extravagant concepts of liberty were for Johnson marked by "an impetuous eagerness to subvert and confound, with very little care what shall be established."[12] Despite his personal dislike for Sir Robert Walpole, Johnson did not join those who accused the prime minister of restricting liberty within the nation. On the contrary, he wrote: "At this time a long course of opposition to Sir Robert Walpole had filled the nation with clamours for liberty, of which no man felt the want, and with care for liberty, which was not in danger."[13] And in reviewing Tytler's vindication of Queen Mary, he had expressed a similar opinion. Not only did Johnson rebuke those who pursued a will-o'-the-wisp in liberty, but he also generalized, "It has been observed that they who most loudly clamour for liberty do not most liberally grant it." And "how is it that we hear the loudest yelps for liberty among the drivers of Negroes?"[14]

The demands of the people for liberty, whether in government or in journalism, Johnson regarded as the nugatory caprice of adolescents. "The notion of liberty," he wrote, "amuses the people of England, and helps to keep off the *taedium vitae*. When a butcher tells you that his heart bleeds for his country, he has, in fact, no uneasy feeling."[15] Johnson's utter contempt for the participation in government of the "rabble"—as he consistently termed the masses—parallels his scorn of their demands for a liberated press. In either case he suspected the citizenry would forget the prior claim of the state and turn unrestricted liberty to their individual, selfish uses. His attitude of superiority and distrust becomes particularly apparent in those political tracts dedicated to his attacks on John Wilkes, Junius, and the American colonists.[16] In each instance he reasserted his suspicion of the degree to which the commoners could be trusted. Particularly did he rebuke those whom he considered opportunistic scoundrels taking refuge in patriotism and hypocritically demanding exorbitant democratic privileges.[17] In the same tracts, furthermore, he strongly implied criticism of the press whose news writers abused their privileges and thus evinced their irresponsibility. Johnson's orderly sensibilities were offended by what he considered extravagant attacks upon the established, necessary system. He thought that John Wilkes had mesmerized the mobs into supporting him during the Middlesex elections by holding out to them extravagant promises of liberty. But Johnson refused to believe that any issue of English liberty was at stake; instead, he felt, Wilkes had resorted to a cheaply emotional display to enhance his own power and notoriety. Junius' popularity he could not vindicate, holding the anonymous pamphleteer to be an idol of the masses in an unadmirable cause. The defection of the American colonists, Johnson contended, was typical of that of any mob dazzled by a glittering bauble labeled "Liberty," even though they had no true conception of the meaning of the term. In making his strictures, Johnson allied himself with an ever narrowing intellectual minority.[18] Johnson's minority position is emphasized by the flood of anonymous pamphlets denouncing the prosecution of Wilkes.[19] Although many are, of course, by paid anti-administration writers, they serve to illustrate growing discontent with an arbitrary government and insistence upon greater individual liberty. It was for fear of ultimate violence that Johnson was so implacably opposed to the disquieting influence of Wilkes and Junius and the American rebellion. At best he could but deplore such disruptive activities, for to Johnson any disruption of established order was a violation of every notion of civilized society.

III

Basic to Johnson's concept of human rights is his belief that man's liberty is a social grant from the government which protects and represents him. But he also believed, at least implicitly, in a contractual relationship between the governed and the governing force. Hence he condemned oaths of allegiance as completely irrelevant, for loyalty must come by mutual consent and respect, not by compulsion. And for the same reason he insisted that Englishmen "intrusted with liberty" should be permitted to bear arms voluntarily for the defense of their country.[20] Stemming from this view is his hierarchical principle of authority, involving benevolent rule by a superior with voluntary subordination by an inferior. That is, he saw society as a necessary framework for the protection and maximum happiness of man. And no society may exist, Johnson was careful to emphasize, if individual whim is permitted to dictate the operation of that society. For the good of the many, therefore, there must be absolute if enlightened authority. "In sovereignty there are no gradations. . . . There must, in every society, be some power or other, from which there is no appeal." To the argument "Liberty is the birthright of man, and where obedience is compelled there is no liberty," Johnson replied, "Government is necessary to man, and where obedience is not compelled there is no government."[21] Motivated by these same precepts, Johnson sternly insisted absolute freedom of the press to be impossible. Since he had already established in his own mind the fallibility of individual representation in public matters, he was equally convinced of the dangerous folly of individual unrestrained expression, whether in speech, in writing, or in the pulpit. He maintained that the individual must always subordinate himself to the will of the state which has justly defined his maximum good; and by the same principle, that he must accept the reasonable proscriptions of the acknowledged heads of state.

Johnson was at one with much of the intellectual temper of his century in this insistence upon subordination—though in varying degrees—for mutual protection. He shared his belief with such diversified philosophers as Adam Smith, David Hume, and even John Locke, who had conceded that despite a condition of maximum liberty, due authority must be acknowledged.[22] There was, thus, a general belief in this period, joined in by Johnson, that in view of the essentiality of government, all men must be willing to forego certain of their rights and suffer certain inconveniences in exchange for the advantages of living in society.[23]

Johnson was not so jealous of the powers of the monarchy that he blinded himself to the dangers of despotism and tyranny. But because he did not believe that mankind would tolerate unusual subjugation, he assured himself that they would act as a check upon any overly ambitious rulers. "There is a remedy in human nature against tyranny, that will keep us safe under every form of government."[24]

"Kings change their laws," he stated in his poem *To Posterity* (1739), and "kingdoms change their kings." Or, as he wrote on another occasion, "let the tools of power be taught in time that they may rob but cannot impoverish."[25] Thus he respected mass opinion when it would serve to deny those undue attempts at repressions that were contrary to the moral right of the many. So remote was he from fearing British tyranny that throughout his writings and conversations he reasserted his conviction that the English government exercised too little authority and that a certain degree of compulsion is a necessary condition of government.[26] He reflected, indeed, that tyranny is encouraged by unreasonable demands for liberty; heads of states tend to impose excessive restrictions when discontent threatens their rule.

With considerable misgiving Johnson observed that the people of his day no longer had any reverence for government. Because of increasing circulation of money which was bringing about economic power in the middle classes, "subordination is sadly broken down in this age. No man, now, has the same authority his father had—except a gaoler."[27] These views led him to an abhorrence of any kind of opposition, which he associated with an unintelligent fear of power by a seditious, factious rabble.[28] No one, he said, is "more an enemy to public peace, than he who fills weak heads with imaginary claims, and breaks the series of civil subordination, by inciting the lower classes of mankind to encroach upon the higher."[29] For reasons like these Johnson held Milton's love of independence in the same low esteem as that of the American colonists, charging to both an unreasonable fear of authority rather than a true desire for liberty.[30]

Against all foes of subordination Johnson was unflagging in his determined belief that subordination of personal liberty is the chief means of attaining human happiness and prosperity, and that equality is an impossible condition because it will lead to brutishness.[31] As opposition to established forms of government, he maintained, "is always loudest, a majority of the rabble will be for opposition."[32] That constituted government must exist and thrive against all dissent, he hypothesized in the statement: "If the possibility of abuse be an argument against authority, no authority ever can be established: if the actual abuse destroys its legality, there is no legal government in the world."[33]

IV

As a journalist Johnson had many opportunities to witness the application of contemporary theories of liberty relating to the press and to utter his own opinions. The entire period was a test of how free a press may be and ultimately provided the modern criteria for liberty of the press. Significantly there was little if any question that a relatively free press is both the essential and moral right of the people. Johnson himself did not deny this. The issue in the eighteenth century was not of whether the press should be free, but of the maximum limits of its freedom. Johnson strongly favored restrictions in accordance with his principle of subordination. He vehemently denounced the extremes of press liberty suggested, for instance, by Milton in *Areopagitica,* or by the American colonists.[34]

The struggle for free expression was an ancient one, but one that in England did not actually acquire widespread support until the Revolution of 1688. Despite the impetus of this uprising, a full century was to pass before freedom of the press became a workable concept, in Fox's Libel Act of 1792. John Locke's enunciation of the principles of human liberty with his emphasis upon the rights of the common man was much more theoretical than applied. Not until Edmund Burke protested against George III's attempted abuses of human rights were the people as a whole to become keenly appreciative of the value of a representative government and press.[35] In Johnson's day, the now mature attitude was developing, that "self-government and a free press are inseparable."[36] And to this notion Johnson took forceful exception.

When Johnson began to write for the *Gentleman's Magazine* in 1738, he saw many evidences of agitation for a free press. Yet the agitation, owing to relatively limited and self-interested private enterprise, was sporadic. Despite a growing reading public which stimulated private ownership of newspapers, political patrons continued influential in the control of news organs. Although licensing regulations had long since expired, the government was able to use devices as restrictive as censorship. Parliament contributed to the restraints by heavily penalizing news writers and publishers who committed breaches of privilege. The outlook for a free press, however, was not entirely bleak. Recognition of proprietary rights of authors under the Copyright Act of 1709 was at least a minor step forward in liberating the press. Then there were early individual spokesmen for a free press, including Defoe, Swift, and Addison, who had attacked the Stamp Act of 1712 as a deliberate restraint of the press.[37] Another factor was the spirited if undignified "paper war" which flared between the Walpole subsidized journals and their dissidents. An active nucleus of opposition newspapers voicing criticism of the government emphasized the function of a free press in a free society.[38]

At the outset of his journalistic career, Johnson found praise-worthy an example of "liberty without licentiousness, . . . freedom of speech without neglect of decency."[39] And as early as 1744, in his introductory essay to the *Harleian Miscellany,* he asserted his belief in the existence of a free press in England. Pamphlets on political and religious subjects were possible only in a country where liberty of the press flourished. They "would never have appeared under arbitrary governments, where every man lulls himself in indolence under calamities, of which he cannot promote the redress, or thinks it prudent to conceal the uneasiness, of which he cannot complain without danger." In England, he added, every man had "boundless liberty" to "write his own thoughts."[40] Here we see once more John-son's consistent belief in the generous absence of restraint, both in government and in journalism, which for him constituted a broad degree of liberty. The passage is significant, also, in revealing his perception that statesmen are the servants of the people and may be criticized by the press within reasonable limits to prevent abuse of authority. Such an attitude is indicative of an open-minded if cir-cumspect temper that avoids extremes of freedom or tyranny, an inquiring spirit that is always typical of Johnson. But he also carried his theory into practice and on several journalistic occasions took issue with the government for its actions.[41]

Certainly Johnson was aware that the press was far from being absolutely free. His connection with the *Parliamentary Debates* is substantial proof that he himself was exposed to government censor-ship.[42] But as the introduction to the *Harleian Miscellany* indicates, he assumed a condition of *adequate* press freedom in England. Be-cause he was not merely an idle theorist of subordination to the state but an actual practitioner, Johnson saw no virtue in the absence of all restraints. Consistently he deemed absolute liberty less essential to the well-being of mankind than obedience to acknowledged authority. For all of his dislike of the Walpole government, he was silent about the interdictions imposed upon the press by the ministry. His general feeling seems to have been that as long as he and other journalists were able to use any means, moderate if devious, of stating their objections to governmental abuses, then liberty of the press existed to a reasonable and necessary degree.

Outwardly Johnson's attitude toward freedom of the press has a curiously disinterested cast. But that is not because he felt it to be an unimportant matter. Rather, as his frequent allusions indicate, he considered it an indissoluble part of his entire philosophy of human liberties. His suspicion of popular government is not to be dissociated from his lack of faith in popular expression. He therefore felt implicitly that the British press was as free as it should be for the good of the citizenry. "Now, Sir, there is the liberty of the press, which you know is a constant topick. Suppose you and I and two hundred more were restrained from printing our thoughts: what then? What proportion would that restraint upon us bear to the private happiness of the nation?"[43] At the same time he urged the distinction between the universal or popular political liberty of the state and the private liberty of individuals. Of the former he spoke "with a rough contempt," maintaining that it has value only insofar as it brings about private liberty. The implication, of course, is that without a judicious political state the individual can enjoy no freedom at all, and restraints wisely applied for the benefit of the many will ultimately bring greater good than undisciplined independence. Meanwhile Boswell, fearing that Johnson's seeming indifference toward individual liberty would be mistaken for callousness, suggested that his attitude "was a kind of sophistry in which he delighted to indulge himself, in opposition to the extreme laxity for which it has been fashionable for too many to argue, when it is evident upon reflection, that the very essence of government is restraint." But Boswell in his zeal to show Johnson in the most liberal light failed to associate these remarks with the consistency of Johnson's political and philosophical doctrines of liberty and subordination.

Like many other rational thinkers of his day, Johnson suspected the motives of those who most vehemently sought for unrestrained press freedom, fearing the abuses which they might impose on the press for individual advantage, and the irresponsibility of their insistence on such a privilege. Thus in his discussion of Richard Savage's *Authour to be Let,* Johnson complained: "[T]he liberty of the press is a blessing when we are inclined to write against others, and a calamity when we find ourselves overborne by the multitude of our assailants."[44] In so earnestly deploring abuses of freedom of the press, Johnson was not unique in his day, being in such good company, for instance, as that of Henry Fielding and Horace Walpole and numerous other commentators.[45]

Fundamental to much of Johnson's doubt about the value of an unrestrained press as the organ of popular expression is his frequently pointed and stated scorn of professional news and party hack writers. In his prefaces to the *Gentleman's Magazine* and the *London Chronicle,* in his essay serials, in his *Reflections on the Present State of Literature* in the *Universal Visiter,* even while he lamented the unhappy lot of periodical writers, he denounced their venality and lack of ability. By transparent implication he repudiated the essentiality of freedom for a press that would encourage, even insist upon, the prostitution of writers' services. He was very much like Smollett's Mr. Bramble, who wrote to Dr. Lewis that "the liberty of the press is a term of great efficacy; and like that of the Protestant religion, has often served the purposes of sedition. . . . like every other privilege, it must be restrained within certain bounds."[46]

By the middle of the eighteenth century freedom of the press had become a celebrated issue. Demands in pamphlets and periodicals vouchsafed the support of the people and made inevitable not only official sanctions but official restraints. The most liberal exponents of a free press have always granted the need for some kind of restrictions; although, again it has been generally granted, the ideal is the least limitation.[47] Blackstone rejected censorship. He agreed that "liberty of the press is indeed essential to the nature of a free state: but this consists in laying no previous restraints upon publications, and not in freedom from censure for criminal matter when published."[48] The general thought of the day affirmed the need of a press that was free to criticize the government, but like Blackstone insisted that punishment after publication was necessary to prevent libelous abuse and vilification. Johnson, on the other hand, desired restrictive laws before publication, to preclude the danger of abuse. As a rule, however, few attempts were made to define the limits of the checks.

Duplicating his complete faith in parliamentary government and its obligation to give the citizenry any privileges which are not harmful to the state, Johnson protested against overly liberal concessions to the press for fear they would be abused. From his understanding of human nature Johnson had deduced that the people, refusing to bow to a despotic regime, would lend their support only to a benevolent government. On the same plane of reasoning he speculated that the rulers would of necessity not withhold any privileges of utterance which their consciences told them were the moral right of the people. Since the citizen owes absolute allegiance to the state, the magistrate ought to restrain "any one who attempts to teach . . . doctrines contrary to what the State approves."[49] Even as Johnson seriously considered the possibility and essentiality of a free state, so he considered the extent of the license that might be given to the press. He meditated that the ideal of a free press like that of a free government was being cleverly dangled before the people by the politicians as an irresistible if mysterious treasure. The worth of the treasure, Johnson felt, the people failed to comprehend. He commented ironically that he should dissuade the political leaders "from any direct attempt upon the liberty of the press, which is the darling of the common people, and therefore, cannot be attacked without immediate danger."[50]

Johnson examined the problem according to his own views on statecraft and conceded the existence of a dilemma. On the one hand he feared the danger that might arise if a despotic, arbitrary government imposed shackles on expression; on the other hand he feared the seditious harm that might be done if malcontents were permitted to write unchecked. Again, as in his political ideology, he denied the ability of the "rabble" to think and to speak for themselves. We must remember that he did not deny that they had this right morally; he simply did not think that they could administer this right except through the agency of a strong, benevolent, central authority. The best expression of his concern over this predicament occurs in his life of Milton. While examining *Areopagitica,* in which he found himself at odds with Milton's liberal, revolutionary opinion on the unlimited scope of free expression, Johnson revealed his irresolution. He wrote:

The danger of . . . unbounded liberty and the danger of bounding it have produced a problem in the science of government, which human understanding seems hitherto unable to solve. If nothing may be published but what civil authority shall have previously approved, power must always be the standard of truth; if every dreamer of innovations may propagate his projects, there can be no settlement; if every murmurer at government may diffuse discontent, there can be no peace; and if very skeptick in theology may teach his follies, there can be no religion.[51]

Although Johnson accepted Milton's principle that dictatorial suppression of opinions is evil, he nevertheless took the more practical, less theoretical stand best suited, in his opinion, to his times and country. Neither England nor any other country, by Johnson's implications, was yet ready for freedom of expression. He denied the efficacy of punishment after the crime; for such action, "though it may crush the author, promotes the book; and it seems not more reasonable to leave the right of printing unrestrained, because writers may be afterwards censured, than it would be to sleep with doors unbolted, because by our laws we can hang a thief."[52] This, then, serves as Johnson's answer to Blackstone, and to Milton, who almost a century and a half earlier had in a sense anticipated Blackstone, urging vigilance as to "how books demean themselves as well as men; and thereafter to confine, imprison, and do sharpest judgment on them as malefactors. . . . And yet on the other hand unless wariness be used, as good almost kill a man as kill a good book."[53]

The liberal theories of Milton were inimical to Johnson. At times Johnson appears to be conservative in the matter of a free press to a point little short of reaction. Yet at other times he is almost radical in denouncing violations of liberty. The answer involves no inconsistency by Johnson. Actually he was positive in his deference to reasonable authority but as firmly adverse to any acts which, according to his own lights, constituted oppression by that authority.

APPENDIX A

SOME FUGITIVE PIECES

JOHNSON'S secretiveness about his journalism and the generally fugitive nature of eighteenth-century periodicals have complicated the establishment of a final canon. Nevertheless, a good deal of scholarly detective work has expanded the canon to interesting dimensions, providing material for conjecture. Some of these attributions are significant enough to merit exploration.

Two letters in the *Daily Advertiser* supporting Cave in publishing quarrels have been assigned to Johnson on internal evidence of style and content. The first, a response on October 21, 1738, to the Reverend John Johnson's accusation of bad faith in the Sarpi translation, has been discussed in the first chapter. The second has to do with Cave's feud with the *London Magazine*. Nichols contended that a letter in the *Daily Advertiser* (April 13, 1739), in which Cave's competitors are identified only as "Rivals," was "by the same able hand" responsible for the *Appeal to the Publick* (March, 1739).[1] There is no preface to the *Gentleman's Magazine* for the year 1739 (barring the *Letter to Mr. Urban*), but the letter in the *Daily Advertiser*—along with the *Gentleman's Magazine* appeal and the address *To the Reader*—has a prefatory function. Though it is more restrained in some respects, the general similarity in tone and content between this letter and Johnson's various defenses of Cave against the owners of the *London Magazine* makes Nichols' attribution credible. As in the other pieces written for the same purpose, use was made of personal allusions. "It seems now," said the writer, "an established custom with the authors of the *Craftsman* and *White-Fryers Common Sense,* to conclude their papers with virulent reflections upon the compilers of the *Gentleman's Magazine*." The author of the letter then followed a pattern which was consistent with Johnson's claims for the superiority of the *Gentleman's Magazine* over the *London Magazine.* As proof of the former's primacy, he asked only that readers compare the two magazines. "I have found, upon an impartial and candid examination, that in the first part, which contains debates upon political subjects, Urban abounds in things, and his rivals in words; that he has a chain of arguments, and they a flow of periods; that their style is uniform and diffused; his, varied, concise, and energetic." The letter writer went on to deny that Cave had ever been guilty of partiality or suppression, and he maintained that "the great number of ingenious" original poems in the *Gentleman's Magazine* "give a shameful foil to the crude productions in the other, which usually exhibits such trash as schoolboys would be whipt for." He commended Cave further for encouraging poets through "large benefactions in prizes," and for ingeniously printing music. Generously the author conceded that both magazines had carefully drawn up historical materials. But again the laurels went to Cave, who, by adding maps "copied from the latest drafts, made an improvement of which his rivals themselves cannot deny the usefulness or merit." As final proof of Cave's superior ingenuity, the writer pointed out that he had printed important domestic transactions which had been overlooked by his competitors.

Although it is conceivable that Cave or one of his other workers wrote this letter, there is little likelihood that such was the case. Johnson had already demonstrated his usefulness in the writing of prefaces and essays identical in intention. His eagerness for the temporary security afforded by the *Gentleman's Magazine* and Cave's recognition of his talents for this kind of work contribute to the probability that he wrote the letter as one of the duties assigned him by Cave. There is also the internal evidence of style and phrasing, which are as surely Johnson's as any of his essays on the same subject in the *Gentleman's Magazine.*

An acceptable addition to the canon is the *Proposals* (September 24, 1744) for the *Publisher,* a miscellany, which has been attributed to Johnson and which the Johnson Club unanimously endorsed as Johnson's on the anniversary of his death in 1929.[2] This London miscellany of prose and verse, "a quasi-learned compilation of a kind not uncommon," was backed by James Crokatt, a bookseller. Crokatt was secretary or manager of the Society of Booksellers for Promoting

Learning, which sponsored the *Universal History* (1736-1765) in twenty-three volumes. He was also associated with Thomas Osborne in the publication of Dr. James' *Medicinal Dictionary* in three folio volumes and was part-owner of the *Daily Advertiser*. Crokatt, who said he undertook the *Publisher* to recover some of the losses he had suffered in his other publications, apparently failed to achieve his goal: the *Publisher* (the first number of which did not appear until 1745, with the proposals reprinted) went to only four numbers of sixty octavo pages each.[3]

Chapman has argued for adding the proposals to the canon because of the similarity in pattern between the *Publisher* and the *Harleian Miscellany,* descriptions of which Johnson wrote, and because the attitudes of the proposals are characteristically Johnsonian. In addition, the "Proposals are . . . nearer to Johnson's mature style than the *Account of the Harleian Library* or the *Introduction to the Harleian Miscellany."* The proposals do, indeed, bear emphatic resemblances to Johnson's style and to ideas on periodicals which he was to express later in the prefatory remarks to the *Literary Magazine* and the *London Chronicle.* The signs of his composition are unmistakable in the invitation for contributions from "young and timorous writers" who "may try their fortune with secrecy," and from those "whose character restrains them from an open pursuit of lighter amusements" and who may therefore "indulge their inclinations without danger of reproach." The proposals, furthermore, echo Johnson's concepts recently expressed in the *Introduction to the Harleian Miscellany* (1744) about the value of pamphlets and tracts. A plea is made in the proposals for the discovery of some method "of facilitating the publication of those [pieces] which are hidden from the world—because they are too small to appear single."

Joining others in an attempt to extend the Johnsonian canon, Alexander Chalmers attributed to Johnson three prefaces in the *Gentleman's Magazine* between 1751 and 1754, and several other pieces. Whether his evidence for most of them was more than circumstantial, this investigator is unable to say. He can confirm only that Chalmers recommended their consideration to Walesby, who was preparing an edition of Boswell's *Life of Johnson* (Oxford, 1826).[4] Like many other ascriptions, Chalmers' bear a resemblance to Johnson's own performances, but with a few exceptions their validity cannot be established at this time. For the sake of completeness and in the hope of encouraging further study, they are noted here briefly. Of the prefaces, it can be stated almost certainly that the first is not by Johnson. At the beginning of the volume for 1751, the writer presents remarks which have the outward characteristics of those written by Johnson in his prefaces since 1739. Eulogizing the originality of the *Gentleman's Magazine,* the writer triumphantly alludes to a "literary Bill of Mortality" which has affected a number of its principal imitators in the past year. Nine magazines "are since dead, most of them boasting of their increasing vigour, and the favour of the public, till their spirits were quite exhausted, and their bodies consigned to the Trunkmakers." One of the nine is Christopher Smart's *Student.* That Johnson would have brought public attention to his friend's inadequacy—especially since he himself had a part in the *Student*—would require absolute proof to be believable. While the style might be considered Johnsonian, it is more likely an imitation than his own. The other two prefaces come closer to Johnson. That for 1753 is somewhat calmer and more judicious. A sample follows:

It may, perhaps, be thought that we are yet in danger from the weariness which a long calm naturally causes, and the security which is too frequently the effect of success; but as our book has been long considered as the medium, thro' which men of learning and genius correspond with each other, our own labour naturally diminished as the merit of our collection encreased. . . . The favour of the publick, and the assistance of genius, which we have thus obtained, will ever be considered by us as an incitement, not only to perseverance but improvement, that we may still justify the zeal of our patrons, and not be disgraced by the praises that we receive.

And the preface for 1754 also has some Johnsonian echoes:

But our contempt of those, who, without our materials, are attempting to build upon our plan, is now mingled with pity. It is often the last effort of disappointed writers, whom the publick has rejected under every other appearance, and who hope that in a Magazine the contribution of others will supply the defects of their own inability. Ignorance, indeed, is no reproach to those whose opportunities of knowledge have been few. . . . Their misfortune, therefore, is greater than their fault; but yet admonition and example are lost upon them, and some are continually making the experiment, still solliciting for what they see we have obtained, and still believing success to be easy, because we have proved it to be possible.

The analyses of the prefaces in Chapter I obviate further discussion here. All that need be added is that evidence beyond style and tone is wanting, a case for Johnson's authorship of these prefaces therefore being dubious.

Chalmers made a safer attribution when he credited Johnson with the authorship of *Proposals for printing, by Subscription, Hugonis Grotii Adamus Exsul, Tragoedia,* by William Lauder. Printed in the *Gentleman's Magazine* (August, 1747, p. 404), this became substantially the preface which Johnson contributed to Lauder's *Essay on Milton's Use and Imitation of the Moderns, in his Paradise Lost* (1750).[5] A happier instance of Johnson's assistance to authors was the *Proposals* which he probably wrote for Anna Williams' *Essays in Prose and Verse,* and which appeared in the *Gentleman's Magazine* (September, 1750, p. 423 [misprint for 432]). A hint of Johnson's efforts on behalf of Miss Williams is observable in this statement: "I have been perswaded to suffer such Essays as I had formerly written, to be collected, and fitted, if they can be fitted, by the kindness of my friends, for the press. The candour of those that have always encouraged me, will, I hope, pardon the delays incident to a work which must be performed by other Eyes and other hands." The *Proposals* was included in the 1823 and 1825 (Oxford) editions of Johnson's *Works.* When Miss Williams' volume finally appeared in 1766 as *Miscellanies in Prose and Verse,* it was preceded by an advertisement written by Johnson and it contained several of his selections.

Finally, three other pieces ascribed by Chalmers should be noted. One, a criticism of Moore's *Gil Blas* in the *Gentleman's Magazine* (February, 1751, pp. 75-78), has been treated recently.[6] Another is the letter on fireworks in the *Gentleman's Magazine* (January, 1749, p. 8), signed "O.N." This is an attack upon public wastefulness and extravagance and has been included in Chalmers' and Walesby's editions of the *Works.* There appears to be no need for expatiating on the authenticity of this piece. And then, on the last page of the 1753 volume, there is a notice of Cave's death:

On *Thursday* the 10th of *Jan.* about one o'clock at noon, after a lingering illness of three years, died the ingenious and laborious Mr *Edward Cave,* the first projector of the *Magazine,* of which he lived to see three and twenty volumes successfully compleated, notwithstanding all the opposition that could be made by rival interests inflamed to malevolence by consciousness of piracy, and which the present proprietors hope to continue with the same spirit and the same superiority.

This and the two preceding items may very well be Johnson's, though again the attributions must be regarded as conjectural rather than absolute.

Although Johnson's relationship to the *Universal Chronicle* is commonly identified with the *Idler,* which appeared in it weekly, he possibly also wrote two introductory essays for the first number of the newspaper (April 8, 1758).[7] *Idler,* No. 1, was published in the second number (April 15). The evidence for Johnson's authorship of the two essays is slight, but arguments for their inclusion in the canon are convincing. The first piece is a preface for the *Universal Chronicle* and the second an essay on the subject *Of the Duty of a Journalist.*[8] They were not collected with the *Idler,* according to Hazen, because they were intended for a particular function and had no direct place in the essay serial.

His bases for acceptance are these: First of all, the style is characteristically Johnson's. Second, Johnson's publishing associates in the *Idler,* the same as those in the *Rambler,* knew his ability as a writer of prefaces, especially for the *Literary Magazine* and the *London Chronicle.* Logically they would have called upon him to render a similar service for the new paper. Third, the preface contains a discussion of contradictions in newspapers that significantly parallels the theme of *Idler,* No. 7. In the third paragraph of the preface we find this statement:

It is well known to all those whose curiosity hastens them to the earliest intelligence, that the same event is every week affirmed and denied; that the papers of the same day contradict each other; and that the mind is confused by opposite relations, or tortured with narrations of the same transactions transmitted, or pretended to be transmitted, from different places.

Hazen concludes Johnson developed *Idler,* No. 7, from his own prefatory remarks in the first number of the *Universal Chronicle.* Fourth, the bibliographical evidence is worth considering, for the two essays are related to the *Idler* typographically. Like each number of the *Idler,* they are set in leaded type on the first page to dominate the other contents of the paper, which are set in unleaded type. In using this format, the editor and compositor seem to have regarded the two essays as a part of the forthcoming *Idler*.

An additional point may be made of the fact that the introductory essays are analogous in organization and spirit to previous performances by Johnson: the preface is consistent with those he wrote for the *Literary Magazine* and the *London Chronicle*, and *Of the Duty of a Journalist* contains attitudes made familiar in the *Rambler* and the *Idler*. The preface, except for the revealing third paragraph, follows so closely the pattern of his prefaces for the *Literary Magazine* and the *London Chronicle* as to make dubious Hazen's claim for the superiority of the *Universal Chronicle* preface. There is little to distinguish the quality of the one from that of the others. At any rate, the plan is well enough known to obviate elaboration. The evaluation of a journalist is more interesting as a continuation of Johnson's long, earnest reflections on the subject. A journalist, the writer said, "is an historian, not indeed of the highest class, nor of the number of those whose works bestow immortality upon others or themselves; yet, like other historians, he distributes for a time reputation or infamy, regulates the opinion of the week, raises hopes and terrors, inflames or allays the violence of the people." In a temper characteristic of Johnson's the writer deplored the "violations of truth" committed by news writers capriciously or for the gratification of idle curiosity. The only business of the honest journalist is "to tell transactions of general importance, or uncontested notoriety, or by advertisements to promote private convenience without distubance of private quiet." The journalist's duty is not an exalted one, but it must be compatible with moral principles, and his information must be presented with utmost clarity for all classes of readers. The parallelism between these ideas and others examined earlier and Hazen's evidence make a strong case for the inclusion of the introductory essays in the journalistic canon.

That Johnson was the author of three essays previously attributed to Goldsmith is noted by Bishop Percy in a short collection of Johnson's writings.[9] On the flyleaf Percy wrote a list of additions, the first item of which was *The Weekly Correspondent in the first year of the Public Ledger*. This feature of the *Public Ledger*, for which

Goldsmith also wrote his famous *Chinese Letters,* was a series of three essays for December 2, 9, and 16, 1760. Although the third essay indicated that more would be forthcoming, none ever appeared. The second essay was reprinted in the *British Magazine* and from there incorporated with twenty-four other pieces in *Essays and Criticism by Dr. Goldsmith* (1798). Ever since publication of this volume the *Weekly Correspondent* has been attributed to Goldsmith; but on the basis of Percy's note and the style, Johnson has now been given credit for all three essays. Johnson and Goldsmith, thus, could have been associated as fellow journalists on the *Public Ledger,* Johnson then at the crest of his journalistic fortunes and Goldsmith still little more than a struggling hack. There is a possibility that they had become acquainted even earlier, in 1759.[10] Another colleague on the *Public Ledger* would have been Griffith Jones (1722-1786), the editor, who had worked with Johnson on the *Literary Magazine* and who was later his neighbor in Bolt Court.

Weekly Correspondent, No. I, contains a commentary on the public's fickleness toward authors, a recurrent source of irritation for Johnson and reminiscent of a number of his earlier essays in the *Gentleman's Magazine* and the *Rambler* serial. "A writer. . . does not engage his readers on equal terms; he presents himself to their notice, but they may neglect him without hazard. The most laboured performance of wit and learning is as easily thrown into the fire, as a taylor's bill. . . ." Equally typical is the contention that only posterity will assess the true worth of an author. But such judgment, unfortunately, is too belated and too leisurely to alleviate his despair. "It is much safer to lie concealed in nameless obscurity; and, instead of imploring posterity, to have this comfort in his disappointments, that none know them but himself."[11] No. II is a criticism of public extravagance, which, in the light of the magnificent coronation of George III, war had done nothing to diminish.[12] In No. III the author signed himself "Tom Stucco" and ironically claimed responsibility for building the Mansion House (1739-1753) and Blackfriars Bridge, while destroying Ludgate in the interests of civic improvement. The purpose of No. III, ostensibly, was to deride the constant destruction of landmarks. Though Johnson's hand is not so obvious in the last two essays (except for the interest in Blackfriars

Bridge) as in No. I, the evidence offers a reasonable basis for the belief that all three are of his authorship. McAdam conjectures that Johnson dropped the *Weekly Correspondent* after three issues in order that he might work more intensively on his edition of Shakespeare (which did not appear for another four years). He also believes that Johnson at least corrected and revised, if he did not write, the preliminary address for the *Public Ledger,* an introduction reminiscent of those for the *Literary Magazine* and the *London Chronicle.*

Among the multitude of Johnson's journalistic tasks was the writing of literary and political advertisements. He detested advertising— as he eloquently demonstrated in *Idler,* No. 40—because he felt that such commercialism was imposed upon unwilling and unwary readers;[13] but he could, under special circumstances, be persuaded to forego his principles temporarily to publicize a worthwhile project. His advertisements of literary matters have an affinity with his criticism, and therefore are of more than transient interest. In 1750 he wrote the prologue for Garrick's benefit performance of *Comus* for Milton's granddaughter, Elizabeth Foster, and also advertised the performance in a letter to the *General Advertiser* (April 4, 1750).[14] It was Johnson, indeed, who persuaded Garrick to give the performance. The attitude toward "our incomparable Milton" is perhaps more reverential than elsewhere in Johnson's writing, his generosity on Mrs. Foster's behalf compelling him to set aside some of the prejudices expressed later in the *Rambler* and the *English Poets.* If the advertisement is not notable as a piece of Milton criticism, it does bear an important relationship to Johnson's consistently expressed view in the essay serials about the uncertainty of fame and patronage. Many, he commented, "who would perhaps have contributed to starve [Milton] when alive, have heaped expensive pageants upon his grave. It must indeed be confessed, that this method of becoming known to posterity, with honour, is peculiar to the great, or at least to the wealthy."

Another advertisement now generally ascribed to Johnson is that of Ascham's *English Works,* which he helped James Bennett edit and bring forth in 1762. Johnson wrote the dedication to the Earl of Shaftesbury and the life of Ascham. But in addition, as an anonymous contributor to the *European Magazine* pointed out, he wrote the advertisement which was subjoined to *Proposals for Printing by Subscription the English Works of Ascham*. Characteristically he justified the value of "preserving or retrieving books which time has obscured or oversight neglected." That an author of such merit as Ascham "should fall into oblivion would be somewhat strange, if every nation did not afford instances and enquire what we have left behind in the progress of knowledge." Hazen states that the proposals with the advertisement were published late in January, 1758; and though the work itself is dated 1761, it was actually not published until January 7, 1762. Tom Davies asserted that Johnson, really the editor of the *Works,* undertook it to assist Bennett, an impoverished schoolmaster with a large family.[15]

John Newbery, who published the edition of Ascham's works, also brought out a collection of voyages and travels, *The World Displayed*. It is believed that Goldsmith and Smart were both then working for Newbery and compiled the materials.[16] Johnson wrote the introduction and an advertisement addressed *To the Public,* dated October 30, 1759, which thereafter appeared frequently in the *London Chronicle* and *Lloyd's Evening Post;* it was used again to advertise the second volume of the series and appeared as late as 1773 to publicize a new edition. "Curiosity is seldom so powerfully excited," he wrote, "or so amply gratified, as by faithful relations of voyages and travels. The different appearances of nature, and the various customs of men, the gradual discovery of the world, and the accidents and hardships of a naval life, all concur to fill the mind with expectation and with wonder." There is no more useful way of studying geography, he concluded, than through the narrations of journeys to distant places. Johnson had already undertaken geographical writing for Cave, with his accounts of Blake, Drake, the Amazons, and Du Halde. The advertisement announced that the first volume would be published December 1 and also listed the contents of the initial volume. True to promise, *The World Displayed* was published monthly between December 1, 1759, and July 1, 1761.[17]

An *Advertisement to the Re-publication of the Spectator, in 1776* is asserted by Powell to be among "other Johnsoniana of undoubted authenticity." The advertisement was reprinted in the *European*

Magazine from an unknown source. It praised the *Spectator* for its critical and moral precepts, for its elegance, inventiveness, and descriptions of manners, and for its employment of wit on behalf of truth. "It has now for more than half a century supplied the English nation, in a great measure, with principles of speculation, and rules of practice; and given Addison a claim to be numbered among the benefactors of mankind." The publishers, according to the advertisement, desired to make available to the public a handsome and readily portable edition. These observations were followed by conditions for publication which were apparently not by Johnson.[18] But the characteristic phrasing coupled with the admiration for Addison marks the advertisement as another of Johnson's journalistic contributions.

In the *Journey to the Western Islands* Johnson committed "an undesigned and involuntary injury" (as he himself termed it) to the Laird of Rasay, who had been one of his congenial Scottish hosts, by imputing to him an admission of the inferiority of his clan to the clan of Dunvegan. As soon as Johnson heard of the Laird's displeasure, he sent him a letter (May 6, 1775) via Boswell, in which he wrote apologetically that his meaning had been mistaken. "I only designed to express what I thought generally admitted—that the house of Rasay allowed the superiority of the house of Dunvegan. Even this I now find to be erroneous, and will therefore omit or retract it in the next edition." After this unusual show of humility, Johnson expressed his intention of inserting a correction in the Edinburgh newspapers, a mission which he entrusted to Boswell and which appeared as follows:

> The authour of the *Journey to the Western Islands,* having related that the M'Leods of Rasay acknowledge the chieftainship or superiority of the M'Leods of Sky, finds that he has been misinformed or mistaken. He means in a future edition to correct his errour, and wishes to be told of more, if more have been discovered.

The episode is remarkable as an indication of Johnson's character, especially of his sense of hospitality and his awareness of the sensitivity of others. The proud Laird must have recognized an honest slip on the part of Johnson, whose attitude toward the Rasay family in the *Journey* is uniformly complimentary; for, gratified by the letter, he later visited Johnson in his London home.[19] Despite his public avowals of chagrin, Johnson did not consider the incident important. Shortly thereafter (May 12) he wrote to Mrs. Thrale about the misunderstanding, and in his attitude at having offended the Scottish chief he combined amusement and mock alarm.[20] When the second edition of the *Journey* was published in the year after Johnson's death, the offending passage remained unchanged, but the publisher inserted Johnson's Edinburgh newspaper advertisement.[21]

Not only did Johnson write literary advertisements of one kind or another, but as a consequence of friendship, he became something of a political campaigner, vicariously to be sure, by assisting in or writing election advertisements for Henry Thrale. Thrale first employed Johnson's literary talents politically in the course of the parliamentary campaign for the seat from Southwark in the fall of 1765. On November 21 and the three subsequent days Thrale appealed for public support in the *Public Advertiser*. Proof sheets of the advertisement, with corrections in Johnson's hand, are still in existence. Once again, in 1768, Thrale requested Johnson's aid in the writing of political advertisements. Thrale's position for reëlection was strong, and Johnson wrote to Mrs. Thrale: "Though I do not perceive that there is any need of help, I shall write yet another advertisement, lest you might suspect that my complaisance had more of idleness than sincerity." He also offered to come to London from Oxford, if his help were further needed. During Thrale's successful 1774 campaign, Johnson again participated on his behalf by writing *The Patriot* and by drafting at least one campaign advertisement. In 1780, during Thrale's final and unsuccessful campaign, Johnson again wrote newspaper advertisements and gave other assistance.[22] No doubt he derived the same kind of pleasure from engaging thus in politics as from discoursing learnedly about other worldly affairs such, for instance, as the brewing business.

Parallel with these political advertisements is an attribution by Croker, which, if acceptable, would be equally reflective of Johnson's support of Thrale's political position.[23] On March 1, 1769, at a meeting of the electors of Southwark in the borough town hall, Sir Joseph Mawbey (1730-1798) became involved in a quarrel with Thrale, his parliamentary colleague since 1765 (and like him a distiller), over the requisition of troops to assist the regular civil guards of the Tower of London against the feared violence of mob action. His motive, apparently, was to arouse public indignation over Wilkes' imprisonment by calling attention to the imminence of an assault upon the prison. In a petition which the day before he had circularized for the additional troops, he included Thrale as one of the signers. Thrale, who was hostile to Wilkes and a political enemy of Sir Joseph, disclaimed approval of the petition. An article describing the heated borough meeting, at which Sir Joseph "took occasion to vindicate himself from some aspersions that had been propagated to his disadvantage," was printed in the *Gentleman's Magazine*. According to Croker, Johnson wrote the conclusion:

If therefore delicacy of situation, and fear of public resentment, were the motives that impelled Sir Joseph to do his duty against his opinion, let his excuse have its full effect; but when he regrets his cowardice of compliance, let him regret likewise the cowardice of calumny; and when he shrinks from vulgar resentment, let him not employ falsehood to cover his retreat.[24]

Croker was not quite accurate, for the lines quoted are the closing sentence of the next to final paragraph rather than the final paragraph. Croker assigned the sentence to Johnson solely on internal evidence. The *Gentleman's Magazine* article recommended triennial sessions of parliament, and Croker felt "Johnson's hatred of the whig septennial bill would naturally incline him" to this position; "and as, for Mr. Thrale's sake, he was obliged by the violence of the times, to adopt some popular topic, he would probably select that of triennial parliaments." This is meager evidence, to be sure, but the ascription has an authentically Johnsonian quality. Croker was correct about Johnson's scorn for the septennial measure, which he later stated trenchantly in the life of Addison.[25] Stylistic features, the parallel political attitudes, and Johnson's loyalty to Thrale are valid reasons for attributing the sentence to him.

The study of Johnson's work for the periodicals fittingly ends with the *Gentleman's Magazine* even as it had virtually begun there. In April, 1784 (pp. 260-262), there was published a short biography of Dr. Styan Thirlby (1692-1753), an erudite but unstable literary critic who was much admired by Johnson. The account in the magazine was the work of John Nichols, and he had drawn it up at the request of Johnson in 1782 for more information. When Johnson saw the proof sheets, according to Nichols, "he added to it nearly half of what is there printed." But the contribution was assimilated into Nichols' copy so that there is no sign of his authorship. Only this brief fragment from his notes remains: " 'What I can tell of Thirlby, I had from those who knew him; I never saw him in my life.' " Indirectly, however, there was a connection between them, for when Johnson was preparing his edition of Shakespeare he had access to one of Thirlby's books. Nichols subsequently expanded his biography for inclusion in the *Literary Anecdotes*.[26]

The fugitive journalistic pieces,[27] supplementing the more widely known compositions by Johnson, are reminders that he was never long free of writing for periodicals, whether because of his own financial needs or because of the bonds of friendship. Most of the pieces must also be recognized for the competence of their execution. Without exaggerating their intrinsic merit, one can see in them a clear link with his other journalistic performances and his more lasting writings.

APPENDIX B

THE JOURNALISTIC CANON

M ANY of the pieces listed below though not identified by Johnson have been attributed to him by Boswell and others on the basis of substantial internal evidence. These pieces are regarded as acceptable without question. Other attributions, more conjectural and not yet sufficiently conclusive but worth examining, are designated by a question mark. Reprints, generally, are not cited. Pertinent data are discussed in appropriate sections of the study above.

Adventurer (March 3 [?], 1753-March 2, 1754) [Ch. IV]:

Of the 140 essays, Johnson wrote Nos. 34 (?), 39 (?), 41 (?), 45, 50, 53, 58, 62, 67, 69, 74, 81, 84, 85, 92, 95, 99, 102, 107, 108, 111, 115, 119, 120, 126, 128, 131, 137, 138.

Birmingham Journal [Ch. I]:

Unidentified essays, 1732-1733. (?)

British Magazine [Ch. IV]:

"Bravery of the English Common Soldiers," I (Jan., 1760), 37-39. [Appended to the 3rd ed. (1767) of the *Idler*.]

Critical Review [Ch. V]:

"Telemachus. A Mask, by the Rev. George Graham," XV (April, 1763), 314-318.
"The Sugar-Cane, a Poem, by James Grainger," XVIII (Oct., 1764), 270-277.
"The Traveller, or a Prospect of Society, by Oliver Goldsmith," XVIII (Dec., 1764), 458-462.

Daily Advertiser [Ch. I and App. A]:

Letter answering the Rev. John Johnson with regard to the translation of Sarpi's *History of the Council of Trent* (Oct. 21, 1738). (?)
Letter on behalf of the *Gentleman's Magazine* (April 13, 1739). (?)

Daily Gazetteer [Ch. III]:

"Considerations on the Plans Offered for the Construction of Black-friars Bridge," three letters (Dec. 1, 8, 15, 1759).

Edinburgh Newspapers [App. A]:

Correction of a misinterpretation in the *Journey to the Western Islands* (May, 1775).

European Magazine [App. A]:

Attributed to Johnson a two-paragraph advertisement of proposals for publishing the *English Works of Ascham* (Jan., 1758), XVI (July, 1789), 4. [Advertisement is reproduced by Powell, *Life,* I, 550-551.]

Reprinted from an unknown source, an "Advertisement to the Republication of the Spectator, in 1776," XVI (July, 1789), 5.

General Advertiser [App. A]:

Advertisement, benefit performance of Milton's *Comus* (April 4, 1750).

Gentleman's Magazine [Chs. I, III, V, VI, and App. A]:

"Debates in the Senate of Magna Lilliputia." Johnson revised and wrote the parliamentary proceedings for the period Nov. 25, 1740, to Feb. 22, 1743. His essays were published in *G.M.* between July, 1741, and March, 1744. These include "Appendix to Capt. Lemuel Gulliver's Account of the Famous Empire of Lilliput," VIII (June, 1738), 283-287. (?) [Prior to Nov. 25, 1740, he had edited "Debates" written by Guthrie.]

"Ad Urbanum," VIII (March, 1738), 156.

"Ad Ricardum Savage," VIII (April, 1738), 210.

"Greek epigram to Elizabeth Carter," VIII (April, 1738), 210.

"To a Lady Who Spoke in Defence of Liberty," VIII (April, 1738), 211.

"Letter on Du Halde's History of China" [signed *Eubulus*], VIII (July, 1738), 365-366. (?)

"To Eliza Plucking Laurel," VIII (Aug., 1738), 429.

"To Lady Firebrace at Bury Assizes," VIII (Sept., 1738), 486.

"The Life of Father Paul Sarpi, Author of the *History of the Council of Trent:* For Printing a New Translation of Which, by *S. Johnson,* we have Publish'd Proposals," VIII (Nov., 1738), 581-583.

"On Thomas Birch," VIII (Dec., 1738), 654.

Advertisement of "Debates," VIII (supplement, 1738), 699. (?)

"Proposals for Printing by Subscription *Anagrammata Rediviva,*" VIII (supplement, 1738), 700. (?)

"To the Reader" (preface), VIII (1738), iii-iv.

"Letter to Mr. Urban," IX (Jan., 1739), 3-4.

"The Life of Dr. Herman Boerhaave, Late Professor of Physic in the University of Leyden in Holland," IX (Jan.-April, 1739), 37-38, 72-73, 114-116, 172-176.

"An Appeal to the Publick," IX (March, 1739), 111-112.

"To the Reader," IX (May, 1739), 223.

"To Posterity," IX (May and June, 1739), 269, 324.

"Considerations [by the late Dr. Samuel Johnson] on the Case of

Dr. T[rapp]'s Sermons, abridged by Mr. Cave, 1739." [Written in 1739. Pub. posthumously, LVII² (July, 1787), 555-557.]

"The Life of Admiral Blake," X (June, 1740), 301-307.

"The Life of Sir Francis Drake," X (Aug.-Oct., Dec. 1740), 389-396, 443-447, 509-515, 600-603; XI (Jan., 1741), 38-44.

"An Epitaph on Claudy Phillips," X (Sept., 1740), 464.

"An Essay on Epitaphs," X (Nov., 1740), 593-596.

"Epigrams from the *Greek Anthology*," X (Dec., 1740), 595.

"Some Account of the Life of John Philip Barretier," X (Dec., 1740), 612; XI (Feb., 1741), 87-88, 93; XII (May, 1742), 242-245.

"Preface," X (1740), iii-viii.

Abridged and edited "A Debate Between the Committee of the House of Commons in 1657, and O. Cromwell, upon the Humble Petition and Advice of the Parliament, by which he was desired to assume the Title of King," XI (Feb.-March, 1741), 93-100, 148-154.

Translation of "A Dissertation on the Amazons. From the History of the Amazons, written in French by the Abbé du Guyon," XI (April, 1741), 202-208.

"A Panegyric on Dr. Morin, by Mr. Fontenelle," XI (July, 1741), 375-377 [translation of Fontenelle's *Éloge de Morin*].

"Preface," XI (1741), iii.

"A review of the Account of the Conduct of the Dutchess of Marlborough [by Nathaniel Hooke]," XII (March-June, 1742), 128-131, 204-206, 256-258, 297-300.

"An Account of the Life of Peter Burman, the Late Professor of History, Poetry, &c. in the University of Leiden," XII (April, 1742), 206-210.

"Essay on the Description of China in Two Volumes Folio. From the French of Pere Du Halde," XII (June-July, Sept., 1742), 320-323, 353-357, 484-486. [Mainly extracts from the translation.]

"The Life of Dr. Sydenham," XII (Dec., 1742), 633-635.

"Proposals for Printing, by Subscription, the Two first Volumes of *Bibliotheca Harleiana*," XII (Dec., 1742), 636-639. [Advertisement of Vols. 3-4, XIII (Oct., 1743), p. 560.] (?)

"Foreign Histories," XII (Dec., 1742), 660-661; XVII (Nov., 1747), 546; XVIII (Nov., 1748), 526. (?)

"Preface," XII (1742), iii-iv.

"On the Dispute between Mr. Crousaz and Mr. Warburton, concerning Mr. Pope's Essay on Man," XIII (March, Nov., 1743), 152, 587-588.

"Friendship; an Ode," XIII (July, 1743), 376.

"Ad Lauram," XIII (July, 1743), 378.

"The Young Author," XIII (July, 1743), 378.

"Horatian *Ode* [I.22]," XIII (July, 1743), 380.

"Letter on Proposed Life of Savage," XIII (Aug., 1743), 416.

"Pope's verses *On his Grotto at Twickenham*," XIII (Oct., 1743), 550.

"Preface," XIII (1743), iii.

"Preface," XIV (1744), iii.

"Proposals for Publishing the Debates of the House of Commons, From the Year 1667 to the Year 1694. Collected by the Hon^able Anchitell Grey, Esq.," XV (March, 1745), 135-136. (?)

"Epitaph on Sir Thomas Hanmer," XVII (May, 1747), 239.

"To Miss [Carpenter] on her Giving the Author a Gold and Silk Net-Work Purse of her own Weaving," XVII (May, 1747), 239.

"Stella in Mourning," XVII (May, 1747), 239.

"The Winter's Walk," XVII (May, 1747), 240.

"An Ode," XVII (May, 1747), 240.

"To Lyce," XVII (May, 1747), 240.

"Proposals for printing, by Subscription *Hugonis Grotii Adamus Exsul Tragoedia,* by William Lauder, M.A.," XVII (Aug., 1747), 404.

"Life of the Earl of Roscommon," XVIII (May, 1748), 214-217.

"Letter on Fireworks," XIX (Jan., 1749), 8. (?)

Introduction to "Abridgement of a Voyage Round the World. . . . by George Anson," XIX (Sept., 1749), 393. (?)

"Proposals for printing by Subscription, *Essays in Verse and Prose.* By Anna Williams," XX (Sept., 1750), 423 [misprint for 432].

Theatrical criticism, 1751-1754: Moore, *Gil Blas,* XXI (Feb., 1751), 75-78; Mason, *Elfrida,* XXII (May, 1752), 224-227; Moore, *The Gamester,* XXIII (Feb., 1753), 59-61; Young, *The Brothers,* XXIII (March, 1753), 135-137; Morgan, *Philoclea,* XXIV (Feb. 1754), 81-84; Francis, *Constantine,* XXIV (April, 1754), 178-181. (?)

Unidentified contributions, XXI (1751). (?)

"Preface to Vol. XXI," XXI (1751), iii. (?)

Notice of Charlotte Lennox's *Female Quixote,* XXII (March, 1752), 146. (?) [Small, *Charlotte Ramsay Lennox,* pp. 78-79; *Life,* I, 367n.]

Translation of "Pope's *Messiah,*" XXII (April, 1752), 184.

"Preface" to the first *Index,* 1753.

"Preface to Vol. XXIII," XXIII (1753), iii. (?)

Notice of Cave's death, last page of *Index,* XXIII (1753). (?)

"An Account of the Life of the Late Mr. Edward Cave," XXIV (Feb., 1754), 55-58.

"Preface to Vol. XXIV," XXIV (1754), iii. (?)

"Account of a Book, Entitled, 'An Historical and Critical Enquiry into the Evidence Produced by the Earls of Moray and Morton, against Mary, Queen of Scots. With an Examination of the Rev. Dr. Robertson's Dissertation, and Mr. Hume's History, with Respect to that Evidence' [by William Tytler]," XXX (Oct., 1760), 453-456.

"An Account of the Detection of the Imposture in Cock-Lane," XXXII (Feb., 1762), 81.

Part of the "Historical Chronicle," XXXIX (March, 1769), 162. (?) [Vindication of Henry Thrale.]

"On the Death of Dr. Robert Levet," LIII (Aug., 1783), 695.

"Biographical Notice of Dr. Styan Thirlby" LIV¹ (April 1784), 260-262. [John Nichols' account enlarged by suggestions from Johnson.]

Literary Magazine, or Universal Review [Chs. III, V]:

I. Preface and Essays.

"To the Public," I ([No. 1] May, 1756), iii-iv.

"An Introduction to the Political State of Great-Britain," I ([No. 1] May, 1756), 1-9.

"The History of Minorca, extracted from the History written in the Form of Letters by Mr. Armstrong in 1740," I ([No. 1] May, 1756), 11-14. (?)

"The Militia Bill, with Remarks," I ([No. 2] June, 1756), 57-64.

"Observations on 'A Letter from a French Refugee in America to his Friend, a Gentleman in England,'" I ([No. 2] June, 1756), 66-67. (?)

"Observations on his Britannick Majesty's Treaties with the Empress of Russia and the Landgrave of Hesse Cassel," I ([No. 3] July, 1756), 113-121.

"Abstract of the Charge and Defence of Mr. A. Bower," I ([No. 3] July, 1756), 126 (*sic*)-133. (?)

"Historical Memoirs," I ([No. 3] July, 1756), 153-156; *et passim.* (?)

"Observations on the Present State of Affairs," I ([No. 4] Aug. 1756), 161-165.

"Memoirs of the King of Prussia," I ([No. 7] Nov., 1756), 327-333; ([No. 8] Dec., 1756), 383-390; ([No. 9] Jan., 1757), 439-442.

II. Reviews.

"An Authentic Account of the Present State of Lisbon. . . Extracted from a pamphlet intitled A Satirical Review of the Manifold False-hoods and Absurdities hitherto published concerning the Earthquake," I ([No. 1] May, 1756), 20-22. (?)

"The History of the Royal Society of London, by Thomas Birch," I ([No. 1] May, 1756), 30-32.

"The Gray's-Inn Journal, by Arthur Murphy," I ([No. 1] May, 1756), 32-35.

"An Essay on the Writings and Genius of Pope, by Joseph Warton," I ([No. 1] May, 1756), 35-38.

"The General History of Polybius, in Five Books. Translated from the Greek by Mr. [James] Hampton," I ([No. 1] May, 1756), 39-41.

"Memoirs of the Court of Augustus, by Thomas Blackwell," I ([No. 1] May, 1756), 41-42; ([No. 5] Sept.), 239-240.

"The Natural History of Aleppo, and Parts Adjacent, by Alexander Russel," I ([No. 2] June, 1756), 80-86.

"Four Letters from Sir Isaac Newton to Dr. Bentley, Containing some Arguments in Proof of a Deity," I ([No. 2] June, 1756), 89-91.

"Observations on the Ancient and Present State of the Islands of Scilly, by William Borlase," I ([No. 2] June, 1756), 91-97.

"Experiments on Bleaching, by Francis Home," I ([No. 3] July, 1756), 136-141.

"Christian Morals, by Sir Thomas Browne, of Norwich, M.D.," I ([No. 3] July, 1756), 141-143.

"An Account of a Useful Discovery to Distil. . . Sea-Water, by Stephen Hales," I ([No. 3] July, 1756), 143-145.

"An Essay on Waters, by Charles Lucas," I ([No. 4] Aug., 1756), 167-168; ([No. 5] Sept.), 225-229; ([No. 6] Oct.), 288-293.

"A Large New Catalogue of the Bishops of the Several Sees within the Kingdom of Scotland Down to the Year 1688, by Robert Keith," I ([No. 4] Aug., 1756), 171-176.

"The Civil and Natural History of Jamaica, by Patrick Browne," I ([No. 4] Aug., 1756), 176-185.

"An Impartial Account of the Invasion under William, Duke of Normandy, by Charles Parkin," I ([No. 4] Aug., 1756), 186-187. (?) See Ch. V, fn. 16.

"A Scheme for preventing a further increase of the National Debt," I ([No. 4] Aug., 1756), 188-190. (?)

"An Account of the Conferences held, and Treaties made, between Major-General Sir William Johnson, and the Chief Sachems and Warriors of the Mohawks, Onondagas, Cayugas, Senekas. . . .," I ([No. 4] Aug., 1756), 191-193. (?)

"Philosophical Transactions. Vol. XLIX. Part 1. For the Year 1755," I ([No. 4] Aug., 1756), 193-197.

"The Subtil Medium Proved, by R. Lovett," I ([No. 5] Sept., 1756), 231-234. (?)

"Observations on a Series of Electrical Experiments, by Dr. Hoadly and Mr. Wilson," I ([No. 5] Sept., 1756), 234-239. (?)

"Travels through Germany, Bohemia, Hungary, Switzerland, Italy and Lorrain, by John George Keysler," I ([No. 5] Sept., 1756), 240-247. (?)

"The Memoirs of the Duke de Sully, &c. Translated from the French by Charlotte Lennox," I ([No. 6] Oct., 1756), 281-282.

"Miscellanies on Moral and Religious Subjects, in Prose and Verse, by Elizabeth Harrison," I ([No. 6] Oct., 1756), 282-288.

"Geographical, Historical, Political, Philosophical and Mechanical Essays: the First Containing an Analysis of a General Map of the Middle British Colonies in America, by Lewis Evans," I ([No. 6] Oct., 1756), 293-299.

Pamphlets on the Byng case, I ([No. 6] Oct., 1756), 299-309; ([No. 7] Nov., 1756), 336-351 (*sic*).

Short notice of "A Journal of Eight Days Journey from Portsmouth to Kingston upon Thames, by Jonas Hanway," I ([No. 7] Nov., 1756), 335-342. Extended notice of the same work in II ([No. 13] May, 1757), 161-167. "Reply to a paper in the Gazetteer, May, 26, 1757," II ([No. 14] June, 1757), 253-256. [A continuation of the Hanway controversy.]

"The Cadet, a Military Treatise," I ([No. 7] Nov., 1756), 335 (*sic*).

"A Free Inquiry into the Nature and Origin of Evil, In Six Letters by Soame Jenyns," II ([No. 13] May, 1757, 171-175; ([No. 14] June, 1757), 251-253; ([No. 15] July, 1757), 301-306.

London Chronicle: Or, Universal Evening Post [Chs. III, V, and App. A]:

"Preliminary Discourse," I (Jan. 1, 1757), 1.

Reprint of Shakespeare "Proposals," I (April 12-14, 1757), 358-359, with introduction by Murphy. ["Proposals" first issued June 1, 1756.]

"To the Public," VI (Nov. 10-13, 1759), 459. [According to Hazen, *Prefaces*, p. 217*n.*, this advertisement of *The World Displayed* (1759-1761) was repeated in the *Chronicle* and *Lloyd's Evening Post* frequently after 1759. Powell (*Life*, I, 546) cites an appearance in the *Public Ledger* Jan. 14, 1760.]

Review of "The Sugar-Cane, a Poem, by James Grainger," XVI (July 3-5, 1764), 12; (July 5-7), 20; (July 7-10), 28.

"Obituary for the Rev. Zachariah Mudge, Prebendary of Exeter and Vicar of St. Andrew's, Plymouth," XXV (April 29-May 2, 1769), 410.

Concluding paragraph vindicating the late Dr. James of the charge of insanity made by his competitor, John Hawes, XLI (Feb. 20-22, 1777), 180. [A. T. Hazen, "Samuel Johnson and Dr. Robert James," *Bulletin of the Institute of the History of Medicine*, IV (1936), 455-465.] (?)

London Gazette [Ch. III]:

"The following Address of the Painters, Sculptors, and Architects, has been presented to His Majesty by the Right Honourable the Earl of Holdernesse, one of His Majesty's Principal Secretaries of State: Which Address His Majesty was pleased to receive very graciously," (Jan. 6-10, 1761), p. 1.

Monthly Melody: or Polite Amusement for Gentlemen and Ladies: being a Collection of Vocal and Instrumental Music Composed by Dr. Arne [App. A]:

"Dedication to His Royal Highness Prince Edward," (April 1, 1760), pp. i-ii. (?)

Museum [Ch. I]:

"To Miss [Carpenter] on her Playing upon the Harpsicord," II (Nov. 22, 1746), 178.

"On a Lady's Presenting a Sprig of Myrtle to a Gentleman," II (March 14, 1747), 429.

Public Advertiser (and other newspapers) [App. A]:

Revised advertisement in support of Thrale's candidacy for Parliament (Nov. 21, 22, 23, 25, 1765).

Subsequent campaign advertisements by Johnson appeared in the London newspapers March 3-7, 8, 1768; Oct. 3-4, 1774; Sept. 7, 1780; also Sept. 4, 6, 11 (?), 1780.

Public Ledger [App. A]:

Revised preliminary address to the public (1760). (?)
"Weekly Correspondent," Nos. I-III (Dec. 2, 9, 16, 1760).

Publisher [App. A]:

"Proposals for Printing every Fortnight, (Price Sixpence) *The Publisher* containing Miscellanies in Prose and Verse Collected by J. Crokatt, Bookseller."

Rambler (March 20, 1750-March 14, 1752) [Ch. IV]:

Of the 208 essays, Johnson wrote all except Nos. 30, 44, 97, 100, and parts of Nos. 10, 15, 107.

Student; or the Oxford [and Cambridge] Monthly Miscellany [Ch. III]:

"Life of Dr. Francis Cheynel," II (1751), 260-269, 290-294, 331-334.

[Payne's] Universal Chronicle, or Weekly Gazette [Ch. IV and App. A]:

"Preface," I (April 8, 1758). (?)
"Of the Duty of a Journalist," I (April 8, 1758). (?)
Idler (April 15, 1758-April 5, 1760): Of the 104 essays, Johnson wrote all but Nos. 9, 15, 33, 42, 54, 67, 76, 79, 82, 93, 96, 98.
Five "Observations" on the Seven Years' War, I (Aug. 19-Sept. 30, 1758), 160, 168, 176, 184, 208. (?)
Advertisement, II (Jan. 5, 1759).

Universal Visiter, and Monthly Memorialist, for the Year 1756 [Ch. III]:

"Some Account of the Life and Writings of Chaucer," No. 1 (Jan.), pp. 9-15. (?)
"Reflections upon the State of Portugal, from the Foundation of that Monarchy to the Present Time, Shewing its Connexions with the *European* Powers, particularly with Great-Britain," No. 1 (Feb.), pp. 67-73. (?)
"Further Thoughts on Agriculture," No. 3 (March), pp. 111-115.
"Reflections on the Present State of Literature," No. 4 (April), pp. 159-166.
"Dissertation on the Epitaphs Written by Pope," No. 5 (May), pp. 207-219.
"The Rise, Progress, and Perfection of Architecture among the Ancients; with some Account of its Declension among the Goths, and Revival among the Moderns," No. 6 (June), pp. 255-258. (?)

ABBREVIATED TITLES

Anecdotes	John Nichols, *Literary Anecdotes of the Eighteenth Century* (London, 1812-1815). 9 vols.
Bibliography	William P. Courtney and D. Nichol Smith, *A Bibliography of Samuel Johnson* (Oxford, 1915).
Catalogue	*A Catalogue of the Valuable Library of Books, of the Late Learned Samuel Johnson, Esq; LL.D.* Sold by auction February 16, 1785, by Mr. Christie in Pall Mall.
English Poets	Samuel Johnson, *Lives of the English Poets,* ed. George Birkbeck Hill (Oxford, 1905). 3 vols.
G.M.	*Gentleman's Magazine* (1731 ff.).
General Index, III	John Nichols, "The Rise and Progress of the Magazine," *Gentleman's Magazine General Index,* III, 1787-1818 (London, 1821), iii-lxxx.
Gleanings	Aleyn L. Reade, *Johnsonian Gleanings* (London, 1909-1952). 11 vols.
Hebrides	James Boswell, *A Tour to the Hebrides,* edd. Frederick A. Pottle and Charles H. Bennett (N.Y., 1936).
J.H.C.	*Journals of the House of Commons.*
J.H.L.	*Journals of the House of Lords.*
L.M.	*London Magazine* (1732 ff.).
Letters	*The Letters of Samuel Johnson,* ed. R. W. Chapman (Oxford, 1952). 3 vols.
Life	James Boswell, *The Life of Johnson,* edd. George Birkbeck Hill and L. F. Powell (Oxford, 1934; 1950). 6 vols.
Malahide Papers	*Private Papers of James Boswell from Malahide Castle,* edd. Geoffrey Scott and Frederick A. Pottle (Mt. Vernon, N.Y., 1928-1934). 18 vols.
Miscellanies	*Johnsonian Miscellanies,* ed. George Birkbeck Hill (Oxford, 1897). 2 vols.

Poems   *The Poems of Samuel Johnson,* edd. D.
                                Nichol Smith and Edward L. McAdam (Ox-
                                ford, 1941).

Prefaces   Allen T. Hazen, *Samuel Johnson's Prefaces
                                and Dedications* (New Haven, 1937).

Walpole's Correspondence   *The Yale Edition of Horace Walpole's Cor-
                                respondence,* ed. Wilmarth S. Lewis, *et al.*
                                (New Haven, 1937-1955).

Works   *The Works of Samuel Johnson, LL.D.,* ed.
                                Francis P. Walesby (Oxford, 1825). 11 vols.

NOTES

CHAPTER I

JOURNALISM AT ST. JOHN'S GATE

[1] *Gleanings,* V, 31 ff. For an indispensable treatment of Johnson's life to 1749, see J. L. Clifford, *Young Sam Johnson* (N.Y., 1955), pp. 109 ff.

[2] *Life,* I, 80n.

[3] *Gleanings,* V, 93.

[4] *Life,* I, 85; *Gleanings,* V, 94-95.

[5] *Idler,* No. 7; *English Poets,* II, 94.

[6] *Gleanings,* V, 93 ff.

[7] *Gleanings,* V, 97; *Life,* I, 87n.; *Letters, passim.* See also *Life,* III, 7; *Malahide Papers,* XI, 213-214; H. W. Liebert, "Dr. Johnson's First Book," *Yale University Library Gazette,* XXV (1950), 23-28; Arthur Sherbo, "Father Lobo's 'Voyage to Abyssinia' and 'Rambler' 204 and 205," *N&Q,* CXCVI (1951), 388; Clifford, p. 148.

[8] J. J. Brown, "Samuel Johnson and the First Roller-Spinning Machine," *MLR,* XLI (1946), 16-23. See Clifford, pp. 241-242.

[9] *Boswell's Note Book 1776-1777* (London, 1925). Boswell deleted the reference from the published *Life.*

[10] *Life,* I, 90.

[11] *Life,* I, 91; *G.M.,* IV (1734), 382, 560; V (1735), 41.

[12] John Hawkins, *The Life of Samuel Johnson,* 2nd ed. (London, 1787), p. 29. Boswell (*Life,* I, 92) also records Cave's answer of Dec. 2, but admits having no knowledge of further transactions between Cave and Johnson at this time.

[13] *Life,* I, 95n.

[14] *G.M.,* VI (1736), 360, 428.

[15] See Reade, "Gilbert Walmesley," *TLS,* XXXII (1933), 480; and Clifford, pp. 94-108. Also Johnson's life of Edmund Smith, *English Poets,* II, 20-21; *Hebrides,* p. 378; *Boswell's Letters,* ed. C. B. Tinker (Oxford, 1924), II, 310; *Miscellanies,* II, 416; Mme. D'Arblay, *Diary and Letters,* ed. Charlotte Barrett (London, 1893), IV, 23.

[16] Hawkins, p. 43; *Anecdotes,* VIII, 416; *Gleanings,* VI, 63, 64; X, 126.

[17] *Autobiography of Sylvanus Urban, G.M.,* I, ser. 4 (1856), 271.

[18] *Life,* I, 107; Clifford, p. 183.

[19] *Life,* I, 133. Because of Johnson's physical eccentricities, Gower declined Pope's recommendation that the author of *London* serve as his son's tutor (*Portraits by Sir Joshua Reynolds,* ed. F. W. Hilles [London, 1952], p. 70n.). Swift probably received the letter but was too ill to be concerned with Johnson's predicament. See Swift's *Correspondence,* ed. F. E. Ball (London, 1914), VI, 91n., 209-210; *Gleanings,* VI, 112-113.

[20] *G.M.,* XXIV (1754), 55-58; *Life,* I, 140n.-141n.

[21] *G.M.,* I (1731), 48.

[22] Walter Graham, *English Literary Periodicals* (N.Y., 1930), p. 150, notes significant miscellanies preceding *G.M.*

[23] *Sylvanus Urban, G.M.,* I (1856), 133. According to one account, Johnson received from Cave a yearly wage of £100 (*Prefaces,* p. xviin.).

[24] Nichols (*Anecdotes,* V, 27*n.*) suggested that in 1736 Johnson was a judge of the popular contest to which he had alluded in his Birmingham letter. See C. L. Carlson, "Edward Cave's Club, and its Project for a Literary Review," *PQ,* XVII (1938), 117-118; *G.M.,* V (1735), 726; "A Literary Competition," *TLS,* XXIX (1930), 256; Reade, "The Seatonian Prize at Cambridge," *N&Q,* CXC (1946), 68-69.

[25] *Life,* I, 112; III, 322; Carlson, *The First Magazine* (Providence, 1938), pp. 62-63.

[26] In his life of Cave, *G.M.,* XXIV (1754), 57; *Works,* VI, 431-432.

[27] Graham, p. 161. Boswell ultimately became one of the owners of *L.M.* Boswell's *Letters,* I, 183, 217; *Life,* I, 522.

[28] *L.M.,* VII (1738), 37, 100; *G.M.,* VIII (1738), 156.

[29] *G.M.,* VIII (1738), 156. A translation of these lines (not by Johnson) was printed in *G.M.* two months later (May, p. 268); another translation appeared in 1784, on the obverse of the title page, Pt. II. See *Poems,* pp. 100-102.

[30] *Life,* I, 115. In a letter to Cave (1738), Johnson alluded to *Ad Urbanum* as "my trifle." At this time he offered Cave *London* on behalf of a nameless, needy author. He praised Cave's generosity and humbly offered to "take the trouble of altering any stroke of satire which you may dislike" (*Letters,* I, 9-10 [No. 5]).

[31] *Sylvanus Urban, G.M.,* I (1856), 671-672.

[32] *Life,* I, 136-137; cf. *Gleanings,* VI, 120.

[33] *Life,* I, 532. Cf. III, 90; IV, 134; *Letters,* III, 212-213 [No. 1003]. See also *Life,* I, 135-136; *Anecdotes,* V, 27-28. In *A Defence of Mr. Kenrick's Review of Dr. Johnson's Shakespeare* (London, 1766), p. 12, William Kenrick raises the possibility that Johnson was still the editor in 1747 and after. Hawkins (p. 516*n.*) maintains that Johnson, to improve his qualifications as a translator, sought unsuccessfully to acquire a speaking knowledge of French at Slaughter's Coffee House, a gathering place for foreigners. But cf. *Life,* I, 115. Johnson described the material and spiritual impediments constantly dogging the author in his life of Pope, *English Poets,* III, 117. Undoubtedly he was thinking of his own struggles.

[34] Edmund Gosse, *A History of Eighteenth Century Literature* (N.Y., 1929), p. 284.

[35] Hawkins, p. 49.

[36] Hugh Kingsmill, *Samuel Johnson* (London, 1934), p. 38.

[37] *G.M.,* VIII (1738), iii; IX (1739), 111; *Works,* V, 345, 349. There is a notable similarity between the *G.M.* prefaces and those which Johnson wrote later for the *Literary Magazine* and *London Chronicle.* See App. A for a letter, possibly by Johnson, to the *Daily Advertiser,* April 13, 1739.

[38] *G.M.,* IX (1739), 223; cf. p. 92.

[39] *G.M.,* IX (1739), 3. Cf. his poem *The Young Author, G.M.,* XIII (1743), 378.

[40] *G.M.,* X (1740), iii-viii. See *Works,* V, 194-197; *Life,* II, 39-40; *English Poets,* II, 91 ff.

[41] See a *Dictionary of Greek and Roman Antiquities,* ed. W. Smith, W. Wayte, G. E. Marindin, 3rd ed. (London, 1890), I, 12-13; Gaston Boissier, *Tacite* (Paris, 1903), pp. 239-278; Emil Hübner, *De Senatus Populique Romani Actis* (Leipzig, 1859).

[42] *G.M.,* XI (1741), iii.

[43] *G.M.,* XII (1742), iii-iv; cf. 512, 569-570.

[44] *G.M.,* XIII (1743), iii.

[45] *G.M.,* XIV (1744), iii.

[46] This rare item has been reproduced by Powell, "An Addition to the Canon of Johnson's Writings," *Essays and Studies by Members of the English Association,* XXVIII (1942), 38-41. The attribution is Powell's.

[47] Clifford, pp. 250-252.

⁴⁸ L. L. Martz, *The Later Career of Tobias Smollett* (New Haven, 1942), pp. 1-4. Johnson's discussions of the Duchess of Marlborough and Queen Mary of Scotland are taken up in Ch. V, and his *Essay on Epitaphs* in Ch. III.

⁴⁹ The *Foreign Histories* are too routine to warrant analysis here. Those for 1742 and 1748 were attributed by Boswell solely on internal evidence. That for 1747 was suggested by an anonymous *G.M.* correspondent in 1794; *G.M.*, XII (1742), 660-661; XVII (1747), 546; XVIII (1748), 526; LXIV² (1794), 1001. See Arthur Sherbo, "Two Additions to the Johnson Canon," *JEGP*, LII (1953), 545-548. The letter on *Fireworks, G.M.*, XIX (1749), 8, also on current events, would (if it is by Johnson) offer a glimpse into his personal, cynical view of war. See *Bibliography*, p. 21.

⁵⁰ *G.M.*, X (1740), 612; XI (1741), 87-88, 93; XII (1742), 242-245; *Works*, VI, 376-391. John Croker, ed. *Boswell's Life of Johnson* (Boston 1832), I, 57n., claimed Elizabeth Carter corresponded with Barretier, who admired her work, and probably brought him to Johnson's attention.

⁵¹ *G.M.*, XII (1742), 206-210; *Works*, VI, 397-405; *Life*, I, 153. Cf. Pope's *Dunciad*, ed. James Sutherland (London, 1943), IV, 235-239; *Champion*, I (1739), 125.

⁵² *G.M.*, IX (1739), 37-38, 72-73, 114-116, 172-176; *Works*, VI, 270-292. See *Bibliography*, p. 10; W. L. Cross, *The History of Henry Fielding* (New Haven, 1918), III, 2, 16; *Transactions of the Royal Irish Academy*, X (1806), 231, 237. Boerhaave's writings were widely read in eighteenth-century translations and reviewed in numerous periodicals.

⁵³ *G.M.*, XI (1741), 375-377; *Works*, VI, 391-396; *General Index*, III, xxxin.

⁵⁴ *G.M.*, XII (1742), 633-635; *Works*, VI, 405-412. Cf. *Champion*, II (1740), 175-176.

⁵⁵ *G.M.*, VIII (1738), 581-583; *Works*, VI, 264-269.

⁵⁶ *G.M.*, X (1740), 301-307, 389-396, 443-447, 509-515, 600-603; XI (1741), 38-44; *Works*, VI, 293-309, 310-375. The life of Drake was advertised in *G.M.*, July, 1740, and began to appear the following month. An anonymous *Memorial against Sir Francis Drake* had appeared in July (p. 351), followed by editorial praise of Drake and a notice of Johnson's forthcoming biography. The *Memorial* might have precipitated Johnson's eulogy. See E. L. McAdam, Jr., "Johnson's Lives of Sarpi, Blake, and Drake," *PMLA*, LVIII (1943), 466-476.

⁵⁷ *Life*, II, 446.

⁵⁸ Cf. *English Poets*, II, 236.

⁵⁹ *English Poets*, III, 87.

⁶⁰ Cf. the essay on Burman, *Works*, VI, 405.

⁶¹ *Œuvres Complètes de Fonténelle* (Paris, 1818), I, 182-186. Johnson continued his interest in Fontenelle. See *Life*, III, 36, 247; *English Poets*, II, 160; *Miscellanies*, I, 417. Also A. T. Hazen, "Samuel Johnson and Dr. Robert James," *Bulletin of the Institute of the History of Medicine*, IV (1936), 455-465.

⁶² *G.M.*, XVIII (1748), 214-217; XIII (1743), 416. Cf. *English Poets*, I, 229-240; II, 321-440.

⁶³ *Life*, V, 240.

⁶⁴ The life of Boerhaave was reprinted in the *Universal Magazine* (Feb-March, 1752); *London Chronicle*, IV (1758), 570; *Annual Register*, I (1758), 245-247; James' *Medicinal Dictionary* (1743). See Hazen, "Samuel Johnson and Dr. Robert James," *loc. cit.;* W. K. Wimsatt, *The Prose Style of Samuel Johnson* (New Haven, 1941), pp. 123-124. For allusions to Boerhaave, see *Adventurer*, No. 85; *Life*, II, 372; *Hebrides*, p. 385; *Malahide Papers*, XIII, 241; Mrs. Thrale's *British Synonymy* (London, 1794), I, 279; *Thraliana*, ed. K. C. Balderston (Oxford, 1942), II, 1024. For public interest in the life of Sydenham, see R. W. Chapman with Hazen, "John-

sonian Bibliography," *Oxford Bibliographical Society Proceedings and Papers*, Vol. V, pt. III (Oxford, 1939), pp. 125-126; also *Life*, I, 38. On Barretier, see Hazen and E. L. McAdam, Jr., *A Catalogue of the First Editions of the Works of Samuel Johnson in the Library of Yale University 8 November to 30 December, 1935* (New Haven, 1935), p. 8. And on Blake and Drake, see McAdam, "A Johnson Pamphlet," *TLS*, XXXV (1936), 228; and "Johnson's Lives of Sarpi, Blake, and Drake," *loc. cit.*

[65] *G.M.*, XI (1741), 202-208; *Life*, I, 150; III, 300-302. Cf. *Idler*, No. 87.

[66] *G.M.*, VI (1736), 470; VIII (1738), 664 *(Register of Books)*; *Gleanings*, VI, 88n.-89n.

[67] *G.M.*, VIII (1738), 365-366; LV[1] (1785), 6n.; *Works*, VI, 1-4; *Bibliography*, pp. 162-164. Powell (*Life*, II, 483) thinks the letter is only partially by Johnson. Johnson could not decide whether the Chinese were "polite" or "barbarians" (*Life*, I, 89; III, 339).

[68] "As we are apt to look, either with an eye of contempt or surprise on the customs of other nations, which differ from our own, so we cannot help being pleased with any, which bear some degree of resemblance to those of our country." *G.M.*, X (1740), iii.

[69] *Life*, I, 136; IV, 30; II, 483; I, 157; II, 55; Isaac Disraeli, *Curiosities of Literature* (London, 1881), I, 47; *G.M.*, XII (1742), 320-323, 353-357, 484-486. One of the qualities of travel writing which Johnson insisted upon was truthfulness (*Life*, IV, 320).

[70] *Life*, II, 333, 377n.; III, 301-302.

[71] *Life*, I, 107; *G.M.*, VIII (1738), 581-583; *Works*, VI, 264-269.

[72] *Life*, I, 135; Hawkins, p. 64; *Anecdotes*, V, 27. This matter is detailed by Edward Ruhe, "The Two Samuel Johnsons," *N&Q*, n.s. I (1954), 432-435.

[73] See Ruhe, *loc. cit.*

[74] *Anecdotes*, V, 27-30; *Miscellanies*, II, 345; *General Index*, III, xvn., xxxix.

[75] *Life*, I, 137.

[76] *Life*, IV, 494-495; I, xiii; Chapman, "Johnsonian Bibliography," p. 124; Hazen, "Crousaz on Pope," *TLS*, XXXIV (1935), 704; Davidson Cook, "Crousaz on Pope," *TLS*, XXXIV (1935), 728; Hazen and McAdam, "First Editions of Samuel Johnson," *Yale University Library Gazette*, X (1936), 45-51; R. W. Chapman, "Crousaz on Pope," *RES*, n.s. I (1950), 57; *An Essay on Man*, ed. Maynard Mack (London and New Haven (1950, 1951), p. xxin.

[77] *A Commentary on Mr. Pope's Principles of Morality, or Essay on Man* (London [1741], 1742), pp. i-xx, trans. Johnson; Mack, pp. xix-xxii; R. W. Rogers, "Critiques of the Essay on Man in France and Germany 1736-1755, *ELH*, XV (1948), 176-193; *Dunciad*, IV, 198.

[78] *G. M.*, XIII (1743), 152, 587-588; *Works*, V, 202-205.

[79] See Clifford, pp. 204-205; J. H. Hagstrum, *Samuel Johnson's Literary Criticism* (Minneapolis, 1952), p. 159.

[80] See Francis Gallaway, *Reason, Rule, and Revolt in English Classicism* (N.Y., 1940), pp. 159 ff.; Mack, pp. xxxvi-xxxviii; Pope's "Moral Essays," in *Epistles to Several Persons*, ed. F. W. Bateson (London and New Haven, 1951), *passim*.

[81] *English Poets*, III, 174.

[82] *English Poets*, III, 164-169; *The Preface to the Preceptor*, *Works*, V, 202-205; *Life*, IV, 494-495.

[83] *General Index*, III, xlii. Carlson's attribution to Johnson of the introduction to an abstract of Anson's *Voyages*, XIX (1749), 393, is vague. Carlson's further suggestion (*The First Magazine*, pp. 22-23) that Johnson edited the life of Rienzi, XVI (1746), 3-6, 65-67, seems implausible. D. J. Greene proposes that Johnson contributed theatrical criticism to *G.M.* between 1751 and 1754: "Was Johnson Theatri-

cal Critic of the Gentleman's Magazine?", *RES*, n.s. III (1952), 158-161.

[84] *G.M.* XXXII (1762), 81.

[85] *G.M.*, XXXII (1762), 43-44.

[86] *The Letters of Horace Walpole*, ed. Mrs. Paget Toynbee (Oxford, 1903-1905), V, 169-171.

[87] *G.M.*, XXXII (1762), 339-340; XXXIII (1763), 144.

[88] Charles Churchill, *Poems* (London, 1763), pp. 216-217; *Miscellanies*, II, 354. Cf. *Life*, I, 418; Boswell's *Letters*, I, 13.

[89] *Life*, I, 405-406; II, 162-163, 179; III, 230, 268, 298, 349; IV, 294; V, 45; *Rasselas*, Ch. XXXI. As Fielding's Parson Adams said, "though I am not afraid of ghosts, I do not absolutely disbelieve them" (*Joseph Andrews*, Bk. III, Ch. II).

[90] The major source of bibliographical details and texts for this section is *Poems*, pp. 63 ff.

[91] *Life*, I, 136; *Gleanings*, VI, 154-155; X, 140.

[92] As did rival publications, such as *L.M.*, VIII (1739), 244; and others.

[93] *Life*, I, 50-52; Clifford, p. 76. When Johnson in 1736 drew up his own grammar school curriculum, he included the chief Latin writers and added the need for "a habit of expression" which "can only be acquired by a daily imitation of the best and correctest authours" (*Life*, I, 100).

[94] For analyses of the translations of Horace's ode and Pope's *Messiah*, I am indebted to Dr. George Luck and Dr. Lillian D. Bloom.

[95] *Life*, I, 61; *Poems*, pp. 86-92; Clifford, pp. 122-123.

[96] *Life*, I, 272.

[97] *Life*, I, 179.

[98] *Life*, I, 243; IV, 137.

[99] S. C. Roberts, *"On the Death of Dr. Robert Levet*—A Note on the Text," *RES*, III (1927), 442-445.

[100] *English Poets*, III, 441; II, 53; *Life*, I, 403.

[101] Clifford, pp. 78-79; *Poems*, pp. 97-100.

[102] Clifford, p. 123.

[103] *Poems*, pp. 126-127.

[104] Henry Hervey Aston, *A Sermon Preached at the Cathedral Church of Saint Paul*, ed. J. L. Clifford (Los Angeles, 1955); L. F. Powell, "Dr. Johnson and a Friend," *London Daily Times* (Nov. 25, 1938), pp. 15-16; *Life*, V, 483-484.

[105] *Poems*, pp. 119 ff.; Clifford, p. 306.

[106] *Life*, I, 179-180; *Poems*, pp. 123-124.

[107] *J.H.L.*, XXVII (1747), 107-109.

[108] *L.M.*, VII (1738), 237 ff.

[109] *G.M.*, VIII (supplement, 1738), 700; IX (1739), 699; *L.M.*, XI (1742), facing title page. As a precaution, however, Cave in Aug., 1738, had placed the designation "jun." after his name on the title page, to place responsibility—if necessary—on a mythical nephew. He continued the practice until 1752 (*G.M.*, I [1856], 670).

[110] *Life*, II, 52; I, 116-118; *Malahide Papers*, VII, 175; *G.M.*, I (1856), 671.

[111] *Life*, I, 136; *Gleanings*, VI, 88.

[112] *G.M.*, VIII (1738), 283-287; *Life*, I, 502; B. B. Hoover, *Samuel Johnson's Parliamentary Reporting* (Berkeley and Los Angeles, 1953), pp. 144-145. Croker had also attributed the "Appendix" to Johnson (*G.M.*, I [1856], 671).

[113] *Miscellanies*, I, 287, 452.

[114] *Life*, II, 319; IV, 61; *English Poets*, III, 38, 63. Boswell does not say there was *no* evidence that Johnson harbored a grudge against Swift, but that there was not *sufficient* evidence. Regarding Johnson's attitude after 1739, Boswell's qualification should not be ignored. As a lawyer, he respected evidence; and Johnson believed

"men hate more steadily than they love" (*Life,* III, 150). "The value of any story," he said, "depends on its being true" (*Life,* II, 433); and he denied "the efficacy of ridicule for the discovery of truth" (*English Poets,* III, 413; cf. *Miscellanies,* I, 452).

[115] *G.M.,* VIII (supplement, 1738), 699, 700; I (1856), 672; Hoover, pp. 181-184. The following Feb. there appeared in *G.M.,* IX, 55-59, an anonymous article, *Truth Asserted, or a Demonstration that the Relations in Mr. Gulliver's Voyages are no Fictions.*

[116] Gay's *Fables;* see *English Poets,* II, 274, 283.

[117] *Gleanings,* VI, 117 ff.; Clifford, pp. 222 ff.

[118] *Life,* I, 150.

[119] For this and some of the subsequent judgments about the creative quality of Johnson's *Debates,* I am indebted to Hoover, *passim.*

[120] See Hill, "App. A," *Life,* I, 510-511.

[121] *Ibid.,* I, 506-508; Hawkins, p. 122; *Miscellanies,* I, 379.

[122] Hawkins, p. 99.

[123] [Nichols], *G.M.,* LIV^2 (1784), 891; *Anecdotes,* V, 15. But it has been pointed out that others wrote the reports with at least equal rapidity (*G.M.,* I [1856], 671*n.*).

[124] Hawkins, p. 123. Probably, however, Hawkins exaggerated when he said the circulation rose to 15,000 copies a month (Carlson, pp. 62-63 and *n.*).

[125] *Miscellanies,* II, 342; Hawkins, p. 129; *Life,* I, 505. Cf. Smollett, *The History of England* (Oxford, 1828), III, 52-57, and Johnson, *Works,* X, 434 ff. Hoover, p. 34, places the Foote dinner in the 1760's.

[126] *G.M.,* XIII (1743), 59; *Bibliography,* p. 6. Clifford (pp. 263-264) cites waning public interest and added editorial obligations, as well as a painful conscience, among Johnson's reasons for giving up the debates.

[127] *Miscellanies,* I, 378-379; Hawkins, pp. 125-128; *Ancedotes,* V, 15.

[128] *General Index, III,* lxi.

[129] Hoover, Ch. III.

[130] *G.M.,* XI (1741), 93-100, 148-154. See *Prefaces,* pp. 248-249; Hazen and McAdam, *A Catalogue of an Exhibition of First Editions,* p. 6. I have found no evidence for Hoover's assertion (p. 157) that Johnson derived the Cromwell debate from Anchitell Grey's notes. Although it is possible, there is a curious inconsistency between the strong reprovals for the inaccuracies of this debate and the equally strong admiration for the accuracy of Grey's *Debates of the House of Commons* (see below). Reputedly Grey was a careful reporter.

[131] *Life,* I, 155.

[132] *G.M.,* XV (1745), 135-136; I (1856), 677*n.* Hoover (p. 158) speculates that Grey's *Debates* were the culmination of the "historical design" alluded to by Johnson.

[133] Grey took careful notes on the debates, most of which he attended. When he used information given him by members of Parliament, he generally named them.

[134] Hawkins, p. 132; cf. *General Index, III,* xli ff.

[135] *Life,* I, 505. Nichols asserts Johnson was making "some occasional contributions to the magazine" in 1751, but he does not identify them (*General Index, III,* xlvii). Se fn. 81 and App. B. After Cave's death in 1754 Johnson gave occasional assistance, presumably editorial advice, to the new editors (Nichols, p. lvi). Among the contributors to *G.M.* at this time were Sir John Hill, Dr. James, Christopher Smart, Ephraim Chambers, John Newbery. As late as 1784 Johnson assisted Nichols with a short biography of Styan Thirlby which he had first suggested (Apps. A and B).

CHAPTER II

"THE DIGNITY OF LITERATURE"

[1] *Life,* III, 310-311. Cf. II, 125; III, 182; IV, 113-114; V, 59; *Preface to the English Dictionary, Works,* V, 49; *English Poets,* II, 226; Ch. IV, below, esp. the discussion of the *Rambler.* See also *Letters of Walpole,* ed. Mrs. Toynbee, VIII, 268, *et passim;* Smollett, *Roderick Random* (Oxford, 1930), Vol. II, Ch. 26. A general account of eighteenth-century authorship conditions is to be found in A. S. Collins, *Authorship in the Days of Johnson* (N.Y., 1929).

[2] For political reasons and for want of other matters to write about, eighteenth-century journalists "lived by pointing out stains in each other's washing" (J. R. Sutherland, *Defoe* [Philadelphia and N.Y., 1938], p. 113).

[3] See *Craftsman* (March 21, 1740/1), letter by John Torbuck "From my lodgings in Newgate, March 9, 1740" (cf. issue for April 4, 1741) ; and *Treachery, Baseness, and Cruelty Displayed to the Full; in the Hardships and Sufferings of Mr. Henry Haines, Late Printer of the Country Journal, or Craftsman* (London, 1740).

[4] *The Letters of David Hume,* ed. J. Y. T. Greig (Oxford, 1932), I, 415, 417, 436; II, 209, 269; *passim.*

[5] *The Case of Authors by Profession or Trade* (London, 1758), pp. 20 ff., *et passim.*

[6] See John Forster, *The Life and Times of Oliver Goldsmith* (Boston and N.Y., 1900), I, 137; *Critical Review,* VII (1759), 37-38; *The Vicar of Wakefield,* Ch. XX; *Enquiry into the Present State of Polite Learning in Europe* (1759), Ch. IX; *Citizen of the World* (1762), No. 93. Cf. Charlotte Lennox, *The Female Quixote,* 2nd ed. (London, 1752), Bk. VI, Ch. XI, p. 119.

[7] *Enquiry into the Present State of Polite Learning,* Ch. IX.

[8] *Citizen of the World,* No. 75.

[9] Letter dated June 9, 1704, in *The Works of John Locke* (London, 1823), X, 291-292.

[10] Richardson was a force in quelling at least one attempted insurgence of the printers. Thomas Birch wrote to Philip Yorke on Oct. 1, 1748:

> The Business of Printing has of late met with great Interruption from a Rebellion of the Compositors against their Masters upon a Demand of a Shilling a Sheet to be added to their pay; which the latter have refus'd, and are resolv'd to stand still for the present, & starve the Seceders into Submission, who have no pretence for complaint, a compositor of common Skill and Industry being able to earn 30 s. a Week: & I am told, that Bettenham, while he was a Journeyman, us'd constantly to get near 50 s. Richardson has kept the Masters firm to their Interests, & drawn his Pen, (which, you know, is a very ready & copious one) upon the Subject, & wrote a circular Letter to his Brethren. (B.M. Add. MS. 35,398.)

[11] See *Life,* IV, 35; VI, 14-15, 215; Collins, p. 45. Cf. [Edmund Law, Bishop of Carlisle], *Observations Occasioned by the Contest About Literary Property* (Cambridge, Oxford, and London, 1770), pp. 6 ff.; *Anecdotes,* III, 462.

[12] C. J. Longman and J. E. Chandler, *The House of Longman 1724-1800* (London, 1936), pp. 6-9. But cf. E. C. Mossner and Harry Ransom, "Hume and the 'Conspiracy of the Booksellers,'" *University of Texas Studies in English,* XXIX (1950), 162-182. See also R. W. Chapman, "Authors and Booksellers," in *Johnson's England,* ed. A. S. Turberville (Oxford, 1933), II, 310-330.

[13] *Life,* II, 424-427, 426n.-427n. See Ransom, "The Rewards of Authorship in the Eighteenth Century," *University of Texas Studies in English* (July 8, 1938), 47-66. One of the few instances in which Johnson's high regard for booksellers was shaken resulted from his misunderstanding of the contract for the *Universal Visiter.* See Ch. III, below. On the whole, he had great respect for the responsibilities and judg-

ment of the Trade. For example, when Dr. John Calder was commissioned to edit Ephraim Chambers' *Cyclopaedia*, the booksellers in 1776 asked Johnson to read a specimen of Calder's work. Largely because of his adverse criticism they dissolved their contract, and Calder wrote Johnson a distressed letter. Johnson thereupon vainly interceded in a letter to one of the booksellers, Archibald Hamilton, commenting:

I have advised him, and he has promised, to be hereafter less tenacious of his own determination, and more pliable to the direction of the proprietors and the opinions of those whom they may consult.

See *Letters*, II, 103-104 [No. 453]; Nichols, *Illustrations of the Literary History of the Eighteenth Century* (London, 1822), IV, 800-814.

[14] *A Vindication of the Exclusive Right of Authors to Their Own Works* (London, 1762), p. 40.

[15] *A Modest Plea for the Property of Copyright* (Bath and London, 1774), p. 16.

[16] [Thomas Gordon?], *A Dedication to a Great Man, Concerning Dedications* (London, 1718), p. 32.

[17] *A Letter to the Society of Booksellers, on the Method of Forming a True Judgment of the Manuscript of Authors* (London, 1738), pp. 6 ff., 43-44.

[18] Anecdotes, V, 32n.-33n.

[19] *G.M.*, VI (1736), 353; Clayton Atto, "The Society for the Encouragement of Learning," *The Library*, 4th ser. XIX (1938), 263-288; *Anecdotes*, II, 97. The organization's name was obviously derived from the copyright law (8 Anne, c. 19), "An Act for the Encouragement of Learning." After having failed to sell *Irene* to the bookseller John Gray, Cave submitted the drama to the Society, which also declined to publish it. See *Letters*, I, 11 [No. 8]. Booksellers in the aggregate were known as the "Trade" (*Life*, III, 285n.).

[20] *General Index*, III, li.

[21] *Cave, Works*, VI, 428-435. Johnson revised this sketch for Nichols from *G.M.*, XXIV (1754), 55-58.

[22] *J.H.C.*, XXI (1727), *passim*; *J.H.L.*, XXVII (1747), 109.

[23] Carlson, pp. 25-27.

[24] Johnson's life of Cave; *Life*, III, 311.

[25] *Letters*, I, 85 [No. 87].

[26] Undated letter by Thomas Marryat (Bodleian Library, Add. MS. C. 89, f. 247-248).

[27] The B.M. copy was the property of Thomas Birch, who under date of "7 Sept. 1765" wrote: "The Author is now Vicar of Olney in Northamptonshire a chaplain of Morden College on Black Heath."

[28] *Poems on Various Subjects* (London, 1739), pp. 192-198.

[29] Hawkins, pp. 46n. ff.

[30] Boswell's *Letters*, II, 395n. *Sunday Thoughts* went to five editions by 1801.

[31] *Life*, II, 279n.-280n., 520.

[32] Bodleian Library, Add. MS. C. 89, f. 247-248.

[33] Hawkins, p. 48n.

[34] P. A. Scholes, *The Life and Activities of Sir John Hawkins* (London, 1953), pp. 5-7; *General Index*, III, l, lvi.

[35] The first of several eighteenth-century sketches of Boyse was by Robert Shiels, one of Johnson's *Dictionary* amanuenses, although the credit for this (and several other biographies) was taken by Theophilus Cibber, *Lives of the Poets of Great Britain and Ireland* (London, 1753), V, 160-176. Johnson probably supplied Shiels with information. See Sir Walter Raleigh, *Six Essays on Johnson* (Oxford, 1910), pp. 119-125; E. A. Bloom, "The Paradox of Samuel Boyse," *N&Q*, n.s. I (1954), 163-165.

[36] Cibber's *Lives*, V, 170-176; *Miscellanies*, I, 228.

[37] *Miscellanies*, II, 411.

[38] Cibber's *Lives*, V, 169.

[39] Hawkins, pp. 159n.-160n.

[40] *General Index, III,* liv.

[41] (London, 1767), pp. 3, 7.

[42] *European Magazine*, XXX (1796), 160. Boswell (*Life*, IV, 192-193) substituted the name of Smart for that of Boyse.

[43] *Life*, II, 52.

[44] *Life*, I, 116n.-117n.

[45] Disraeli, I, 15. Churchill satirized Guthrie in *The Author.*

[46] The epigram *Ad Ricardum Savage* (*G.M.*, VIII, 210), which Boswell attributed to Johnson, is possible evidence of an association between Savage and Johnson as early as April, 1738. But cf. Hawkins, p. 51; *Life*, I, *passim.*

[47] The mystery of Savage's birth is as far from resolution as ever. The most objective biography is by Clarence Tracy, *The Artificial Bastard* (Cambridge, Mass., 1953). See also the Rev. Montagu Pennington, *Memoirs of the Life of Mrs. Elizabeth Carter* (Boston, 1809), p. 49.

[48] Birch Correspondence (Oct. 19, 1736), B. M. Slo. 4318, f. 44; *Dunciad*, ed. Sutherland, pp. xxv-xxvi; *Life*, I, 61n.-62n.; *Gleanings*, V, 12.

[49] *Mrs. Carter's Memoirs*, pp. 48 ff. Thomas Birch was also attracted to Miss Carter (Clifford, p. 202).

[50] Carlson, p. 16. Allusions to unidentified poems which Savage contributed to *L.M.* are made in some of his communications to Birch (B. M. Slo. 4318, f. 41, 47-48, 53-54).

[51] F. A. Pottle, "The Dark Hints of Sir John Hawkins and Boswell," *MLN*, LVI (1941), 325-329; *English Poets*, II, 398 and *n.*

[52] *A Letter to Samuel Johnson, LL.D.* (London, 1770), p. 33.

[53] *English Poets*, II, 338, 398; Hawkins, pp. 52 ff.; *Miscellanies*, I, 371.

[54] Hawkins, p. 89.

[55] *English Poets*, II, 413-414.

[56] B. M. Slo. 4318, f. 41.

[57] *English Poets*, II, 380.

[58] Raleigh, pp. 18-20.

[59] *G.M.*, LIV^2 (1784), 901; Anecdotes, VIII, 415; V, 15.

[60] *English Poets*, II, 312; Raleigh, pp. 119-125.

[61] Cibber's *Lives*, V, 32.

[62] *Life*, I, 165. The date of the meeting has been hypothesized by Hilles, ed. *Portraits by Sir Joshua Reynolds*, p. 56.

[63] *English Poets*, III, 335; cf. *Adventurer*, No. 84, on projectors.

[64] Francis Fawkes and William Woty, *Some Account of the Life and Writings of Mr. William Collins, Poetical Calendar* (London, 1763), XII, 107-112; cf. J. Langhorne's *Memoirs of the Author, The Poetical Works of Mr. William Collins* (London, 1765). See *Life*, I, 382; *English Poets*, III, 338. Johnson's account of Collins was reprinted in periodicals several times (Hazen and McAdam, *A Catalogue of an Exhibition of First Editions*, p. 20).

[65] *English Poets*, III, 334 ff.; *Life*, I, 276-277, 382-383; *Letters*, *passim.*

[66] *Life*, II, 164; III, 32; *English Poets*, III, 411-420.

[67] B. M. Slo. 4318, f. 39-54; B. M. Add. MS. 4302, f. 94.

[68] *Poems*, pp. 107-108.

[69] Hawkins, p. 209.

[70] *Censura Literaria*, 2nd ed. (London, 1815), VII, 176.

[71] No. 283 in the *Catalogue* of Johnson's library.

[72] *G.M.,* VIII (1738), 279; *Life,* I, 139; *Mrs. Carter's Memoirs,* p. 12; *Censura Literaria,* VII, 188.

[73] *Mrs. Carter's Memoirs,* pp. 33-34.

[74] *A Series of Letters between Mrs. Elizabeth Carter and Miss Catherine Talbot,* ed. Pennington (London, 1808), II, 221.

[75] *Life,* IV, 275.

[76] See *Critical Review,* XVIII (1764), 366-371; *Life,* III, 443-449; P. W. Sergeant, *Liars and Fakers* (London, 1925); *DNB;* Jules le Febre-Deumier, *Célébrités Anglaises* (Paris, 1895); Smollett, *Humphry Clinker* (Melford's letter of June 10).

[77] *An Historical and Geographical Description of Formosa,* ed. N. M. Penzer, Vol. II, *The Library of Impostors* (London, 1926).

[78] Letter to Anthony Collins (May 29, 1704), Locke's *Works,* X, 291. He was ridiculed in an "advertisement" in *Spectator,* No. 14 (*Life,* III, 449).

[79] Hawkins, p. 547; *G.M.,* VII (1737), 256; X (1740), 360; XIX (1749), 144; LIV[2] (1784), 891-892; the Birch correspondence in the *B.M.,* cited; Edward Hart, "The Contributions of John Nichols to Boswell's Life of Johnson," *PMLA,* LXVII (1952), 391-410; L. M. Knapp, *Tobias Smollett* (Princeton, 1949), pp. 163, *et passim.* See Penzer, ed. *Description of Formosa,* pp. xvi-xvii.

[80] *Life,* III, 314; IV, 187, 274; *Works,* IX, 239; Hawkins, p. 547*n.*

[81] Emanuel Bowen, *A Complete System of Geography* (London, 1747), II, 251; Psalmanazar's *Memoirs,* 2nd ed. (London, 1765), p. 1.

[82] *Miscellanies,* II, 424.

[83] *G.M.,* XXXIII (1763), 257.

CHAPTER III

THE GRUB STREET HISTORIAN

[1] *Life,* III, 19; Hawkins, pp. 84, 363. After the *Gentleman's Magazine,* the *Literary Magazine* represents Johnson's most important connection with a miscellany. Requiring virtually an entire chapter for discussion, it is best considered out of chronological order. The history of the magazine and Johnson's political essays are taken up here, his book reviews in Ch. V, below.

[2] Faden apparently initiated the magazine, the first number bearing his imprint as publisher, i.e., "Printed for W. Faden." The remainder of Vol. I, however, was printed for Richardson. See *Prefaces,* pp. 126-128.

[3] H. R. Plomer, *A Dictionary of Printers and Booksellers in England from 1726 to 1775* (Oxford, 1932), pp. 87-88; *Life,* IV, 443. Faden acquired some notoriety in 1756, when he testified that Archibald Bower "was a Jesuit, and had been the instrument of converting Hoyle and his wife to the Romish religion." See *Literary Magazine,* No. 3, p. 132; *Critical Review,* I (1756), 543. The poetry section of No. 1 (p. 29) includes a prologue written by Murphy for a Drury Lane benefit, April 3, 1756.

[4] According to Murphy, *Miscellanies,* I, 413-414. Griffith Jones (see below) is suggested in *DNB* as a printer of the magazine.

[5] Hawkins, p. 352.

[6] *Life,* I, 283-285. Croker thought the *Literary Magazine* grew out of Johnson's scheme for a *Bibliothèque.*

[7] *Life,* I, 307. Boswell states he undertook "to superintend and contribute largely" to the magazine.

[8] *Miscellanies,* I, 414. Cf. *Idler,* No. 102.

[9] *Letters*, I, 25-26 [No. 19], 86 [No. 90], 89 [No. 94]; *et passim; Life*, I, 303*n.*-304*n.; Miscellanies*, I, 413.

[10] Murphy, like Hawkins, identified Johnson only as a reviewer.

[11] *Letters*, I, 92-93 [No. 98.1], 426. The reference to a "Life" is puzzling, because in neither the Aug. nor Sept. issues—following the letter—is there a formal biographical essay. It is possible but highly improbable that Chambers' piece was set up in type—as it obviously was—and then omitted from the magazine. In the book section for Aug. (No. 4, pp. 169-171), however, there appears an account of Ben Jonson's *Works* (1756), ed. Peter Whalley, which I suggest as the subject of Johnson's allusion. Ostensibly a review, it is in fact a brief biography extracted from Whalley and captioned by the editor *The Life of Ben Jonson*. Furthermore, it fills Johnson's request for "any performances from Oxford." Whalley was a fellow of St. John's College, Oxford, and space is given in the review to Jonson's residence in Christ Church College and his receiving a master's degree. For the Chambers-Johnson relationship, see E. L. McAdam, Jr., *Dr. Johnson and the English Law* (Syracuse, 1951), pp. 65-122.

[12] A comparable eulogy, which Johnson believed was written by Murphy, preceded a reprinting of the proposals in the *London Chronicle*, April 12-14, 1757, p. 358. See *Life*, I, 327-328.

[13] *Letters*, I, 105-106 [No. 113]. He is referring to a biography of Sir Thomas Browne, which he had prepared for the second ed. of the *Christian Morals* (1756).

[14] *A Defence of Mr. Kenrick's Review of Dr. Johnson's Shakespeare*, p. 16*n.* As editor of the *London Review of English and Foreign Literature*, Kenrick made Johnson the subject of several censorious reviews: I (1775), 32-42, 61-63, 228-231; XI (1780), 294-302.

[15] *Anecdotes*, III, 465-466; *DNB; Prefaces*, p. 126. Jones, a printer, was also editor of the *London Chronicle*, the *Daily Advertiser*, and the *Public Ledger*. With Smollett and Goldsmith, he was a contributor to the *British Magazine* (for which Johnson also wrote one essay). As a resident of Bolt Court, he was long a neighbor and friend of Johnson. The belief that Goldsmith contributed to the *Literary Magazine* has been discredited by R. W. Seitz, "Goldsmith and the *Literary Magazine*," *RES*, V (1929), 410-430, though he shows that three of the Chinese Letters were influenced by Johnson's political articles in the magazine. Recently, however, the argument that Goldsmith contributed to the *Literary Magazine* has been advanced by Morris Golden, "Goldsmith's Attributions in the 'Literary Magazine,'" *N&Q*, n.s. III (1956), 432-435, 489-493. There are striking similarities between this preliminary address and the *Preliminary Discourse* of the *London Chronicle*, which Johnson wrote in 1757 (see below). The two prefaces offer the very good possibility that Johnson organized the plan of the *London Chronicle* as well as of the *Literary Magazine*.

[16] Johnson ridiculed *Douglas* as a "foolish play" without ten good lines in it. *Life*, II, 320; V, 360.

[17] Essay in *Works*, VI, 123-142. In *Idler*, No. 8, he accused the British troops of cowardice, though in the *Debates, Works*, X, 448, and the *British Magazine*, I (1760), 37-39, he took an opposite position.

[18] *Works*, VI, 231-232. *Present State* in *Works*, VI, 113-123.

[19] *English Poets*, II, 393.

[20] Cf. his anti-American sentiments in the review of Evans' *Map of the Middle British Colonies in America*, Ch. V, below.

[21] *Life*, I, 310.

[22] This treatment of the *Observations* is an amplification of an article by D. J. Greene, "The Johnsonian Canon: A Neglected Attribution," *PMLA*, LXV (1950), 427-434.

[22] *Works,* VI, 236.

[24] See Ch. VII, below.

[25] In the *Memoirs of the King of Prussia* (below) Johnson praised the French for their "spirit and activity." *Works,* VI, 460. Since writing my analysis of the *Historical Memoirs,* I have seen another recent attribution to Johnson of this item. It is to be found in an article by D. J. Greene, "Johnson's Contributions to the *Literary Magazine,*" RES, n.s. VII (1956), 367-392. I do not, however, share Greene's opinion that two other essays and several reviews may now probably be charged to Johnson's pen. The essays are: *The History of Minorca, extracted from the history written in the form of letters by Mr. Armstrong in 1740,* No. 1, pp. 11-14; *Abstract of the Charge and Defence of Mr. A. Bower,* No. 3, pp. 126 (*sic*)-133. The available evidence to support acceptance of these pieces and the reviews (noted in Ch. V) does not seem to me to be adequate.

[26] *Life, passim; Works,* VI, 101, 199; X, 418. See also *English Poets,* III, 328; *Rambler,* No. 79; *Idler,* No. 31; *Miscellanies,* II, 16, 424. The romantic fiction that Johnson was an active warrior has been exploited by, among others, Charles Russell, "Johnson the Jacobite," *Fortnightly Review,* CXVII (1922), 229-240. See Clifford, pp. 288-290.

[27] Note the satirical letters on the Militia Bill in the *Literary Magazine:* No. 6, p. 314; No. 8, p. 394; related articles in No. 15, pp. 277-280, and No. 17, pp. 369-371.

[28] *Life,* I, 103n.-105n.; *et passim.*

[29] *Life,* II, 220, 321-322; V, 390-391; *English Poets,* II, 257.

[30] *Life,* II, 251.

[31] Basil Williams, *The Whig Supremacy, 1714-1760* (Oxford, 1949), pp. 210-211, 329-331. Johnson's essay in *Works,* VI, 142-152.

[32] *Parliamentary Debates,* in *Works,* X, 450. Several of the *Debates,* indeed, covering topics related to the British army and payments to foreign troops, probably gave Johnson a factual basis for his observations in the *Literary Magazine.*

[33] In the essay on the Militia Bill, Johnson had advocated restoration of the term "trained bands" in preference to "militia forces."

[34] Williams, *passim; Boswell on the Grand Tour, 1764,* ed. F. A. Pottle (London, 1953), pp. 4-5, *et passim.*

[35] *Literary Magazine,* No. 7, pp. 327-333; No. 8, pp. 383-390; No. 9, pp. 439-442; *Works,* VI, 435-474. See *Bibliography,* pp. 75-76; Chapman and Hazen, "Johnsonian Bibliography," pp. 139-140; *Life,* I, 308. As part of a 96-page treatise W. Salmon reproduced Johnson's essay (pp. 1-49) with some alterations: *Memoirs of the Life of the Heroic Frederick III, King of Prussia* (Nottingham, 1758). The conclusion of the third installment gives the impression that Johnson had intended to continue beyond 1745. Although the article is captioned in the *Literary Magazine Memoirs of the King of Prussia,* an error has been perpetuated—notably in Boswell's "Chronological Catalogue" (*Life,* I, 20) and the *Bibliography* (p. 75)—by identification of the piece as *Memoirs of Frederick III, King of Prussia.* Johnson's subject was Frederick II.

[36] *Works,* X, 434-455.

[37] Voltaire called Johnson "a superstitious dog." William Temple shared Johnson's low opinion of Frederick's morality, but Boswell—who in 1764 failed repeatedly to win an audience with Frederick—was struck with hero-worship. At the time Boswell was apparently unaware of Johnson's *Memoirs;* at least, he made no mention of them. *Boswell on the Grand Tour, 1764,* pp. 270, 292-293, *et passim; Life,* I, 435.

[38] But cf. *Life,* II, 180.

[39] The anti-Catholic attitude is pronounced, the *Literary Magazine* being proud

of adhering strictly "to the principles of sound religion and true patriotism." See No. 16, p. 330; No. 17, p. 390; and fn. 3 above. For analysis of possible political reasons leading to Johnson's separation, see Greene, "Johnson's Contributions to the *Literary Magazine."*

⁴⁰ *Anecdotes,* II, 551. The *Poetical Scale* was also attributed to Goldsmith, by James Prior, *The Life of Oliver Goldsmith* (Philadelphia, 1837), pp. 127-128. Cf. Golden, *loc. cit.*

⁴¹ G. J. Gray, "A Bibliography of the Writings of Christopher Smart," *Transactions of the Bibliographical Society,* VI (1903), 275; Chapman and Hazen, "Johnsonian Bibliography," pp. 135-136; Graham, pp. 169, 374. R. E. Brittain, "Christopher Smart in the Magazines," *The Library,* 4th ser., XXI (1941), 320-336.

⁴² *Life,* I, 228; *Anecdotes,* VI, 175; *Bibliography,* p. 38. Smart and Rolt were principals of the *Universal Visiter,* and Johnson wrote the preface for Rolt's *Dictionary of Trade and Commerce* (1756). Colman and perhaps Thornton wrote for the *Adventurer.* Thornton, author of a sophisticated parody of the *Rambler,* wrote *Idler,* No. 15, and Warton, Johnson's Oxford friend, wrote *Idler,* Nos. 33, 93, 96. See R. B. Botting, "Christopher Smart in London," *Studies of the State College of Washington,* VII (1939), 9-10; E. G. Ainsworth and C. E. Noyes, *Christopher Smart,* in *University of Missouri Studies,* XVIII, No. 4 (1943), 40-41.

⁴³ *Letters,* I, 36-38 [Nos. 32-34]; *Student,* II (1751), 260-269, 290-294, 331-334; *Works,* VI, 413,428.

⁴⁴ *Life,* I, 208n. One of the signatures under which Smart wrote poetry is "Zosimus Zephyrinus." *Rambler,* No. 12, is signed "Zosima"; the earlier *Essay on Epitaphs,* in *G.M.,* also contains this name.

⁴⁵ *Life,* I, 397.

⁴⁶ See *Life,* III, 58; *Miscellanies,* I, 100, 107; II, 19; *English Poets,* I, 377; Hawkins, p. 543.

⁴⁷ See Olive M. Griffiths, *Religion and Learning: A Study in English Presbyterian Thought* (Cambridge, 1935).

⁴⁸ *English Poets,* I, 210; *Life,* V, 61, 383; *et passim.*

⁴⁹ *Life,* II, 104. Cf. Parson Adams' distaste for Presbyterianism, in *Joseph Andrews,* Bk. III, Ch. V.

⁵⁰ *Life,* III, 138; IV, 75-76, 197-198; Hawkins, pp. 19, 162-164; *English Poets,* I, 257.

⁵¹ *Life,* II, 250-251; IV, 12. Cf. Ch. VII, below.

⁵² *Life,* II, 150.

⁵³ *Life,* II, 103-104; V, 121. He admired Methodist preaching; see *Life,* I, 458-460; II, 123.

⁵⁴ *Life,* V, 48.

⁵⁵ For contributors to the *Universal Visiter,* see: Claude Jones, "Christopher Smart, Richard Rolt, and *The Universal Visiter," The Library,* 4th ser., XVIII (1937-1938), 212-214; R. B. Botting, "Johnson, Smart, and the *Universal Visiter," MP,* XXXVI (1938-1939), 293-300; Brittain, "Christopher Smart in the Magazines," *loc. cit.;* Arthur Sherbo, "Christopher Smart and *The Universal Visiter," The Library,* 5th ser., X (1955), 203-205; Ainsworth and Noyes, p. 79.

⁵⁶ Stuart Piggott, "New Light on Christopher Smart," *TLS,* XXVIII (1929), 474.

⁵⁷ *Life,* II, 345.

⁵⁸ According to Sherbo, *loc. cit.,* Smart may have written for the *Visiter* as late as July or August.

⁵⁹ *Critical Review,* I (1756), 85-87.

⁶⁰ *Ibid.,* p. 287.

⁶¹ Hawkins, p. 352n.; *Life,* I, 306.

[62] *Poems*, p. 399.

[63] *Universal Visiter*, pp. 111-115; *Works*, V, 310-320. No. 553 in the *Catalogue* is *Essays in Agriculture*.

[64] Hawkins, p. 469.

[65] *A Journey to the Western Islands of Scotland*, in *Works*, IX, *passim*.

[66] *Life*, III, 353; IV, 164. See *Johnson's England*, I, 261-299,

[67] *Universal Visiter*, pp. 159-166. Identified in *Works*, V, 355-362, as *A Project for the Employment of Authors*. Cf. "Johnson on Authorship," Ch. IV, below.

[68] "I should like to know, Naevolus, why you so often look gloomy when I meet you, knitting your brow like a vanquished Marsyas." *Juvenal and Persius*, trans. G. G. Ramsay (Cambridge and London, 1950), p. 181.

[69] Gilbert Highet, *Juvenal the Satirist* (Oxford, 1954), p. 117.

[70] *Life*, I, 193.

[71] Cf. *Adventurer*, No. 115, and *Rambler*, No. 145.

[72] *G.M.*, X (1740), 593-596; *Works*, V, 259-266.

[73] And he so defines it in the *Dictionary*.

[74] *English Poets*, I, 36.

[75] *Life*, II, 407.

[76] Cf. *Life*, V, 154, 366. Kenrick accused Johnson of writing in the *Visiter* "severe and carping criticisms on the epitaphs of Pope," in *A Defence of Mr. Kenrick's Review of Dr. Johnson's Shakespeare*, p. 13.

[77] Cf. *Miscellanies*, II, 373.

[78] See *Works*, I, 150-154; *Miscellanies*, II, 416; Bloom, "Dr. Johnson's Landlord," *N&Q*, n.s. I (1954), 350-351.

[79] Botting, "Johnson, Smart, and the *Universal Visiter*," *loc. cit.*

[80] *The History of the English Language*, in the *Dictionary*.

[81] *Life*, IV, 35n., 381n.

[82] Portugal was an important market for British manufactures. See *Johnson's England*, I, 228-229.

[83] Similarly, indirect allusion is made to the £100,000 voted by Parliament for Portuguese relief after the Lisbon earthquake of 1755. One of the pieces attributed to Johnson, probably erroneously, is a review of *An Authentic Account of the Present State of Lisbon. . . Extracted from a pamphlet intitled A Satirical Review of the Manifold Falsehoods and Absurdities hitherto published concerning the Earthquake*, in *Literary Magazine*, I (1756), 20-22. See *Life*, I, 309n., 544.

[84] *Works*, V, 218-219; cf. VI, 233.

[85] For biographies of Gwynn and Chambers, see *DNB;* also, Thomas Hardwick, *A Memoir of the Life of Sir William Chambers*, I, xxxvii-li, in Chambers' *A Treatise on the Decorative Part of Civil Architecture*, ed. Joseph Gwilt (London, 1825). Further details of Johnson's relationship with Gwynn are in Sec. 5 of this chapter.

[86] Perhaps Reynolds, who apparently also met Johnson about this time, effected the meeting. Chambers became a part of the group among whom were Johnson, Reynolds, Goldsmith, Garrick, Burney. See Hilles, ed. *Portraits by Sir Joshua Reynolds*, pp. 56-57; *Life*, IV, 469.

[87] *Life*, IV, 188, 513.

[88] *A Treatise on Civil Architecture* (London, 1759), p. iii. The title as it appears in fn. 85 was altered in the third edition (1791). The second edition (1768) retained the original title. Among the subscribers to the first edition were Reynolds and Gwynn.

[89] Long a text-book for architectural students, the *Treatise* was extolled by Horace Walpole as "the most sensible book, and the most exempt from prejudices, that ever was written on that science" (*Life*, IV, 187n.).

[90] *Prefaces*, pp. 131-132; Ralph Straus, *Robert Dodsley* (London, 1910), pp. 96-

99; F. A. Pottle, "The Incredible Boswell," *Blackwood's Magazine*, CCXVIII (1925), 149-165; J. P. Emery, "Murphy's Criticisms in the London *Chronicle*," *PMLA*, LIV (1939), 1099-1104.

[91] *Life*, I, 318; *Boswell on the Grand Tour, 1765-1766*, ed. Pottle (London, 1955), pp. 258-259, 338-343.

[92] *Life*, II, 103.

[93] *Life*, IV, 150. Cf. *Letters, passim; Miscellanies*, I, 235; J. L. Clifford, *Hester Lynch Piozzi* (Oxford, 1941), p. 67.

[94] *Life*, I, 317*n*. See Hannah More, *Letters*, ed. R. B. Johnson (London, 1926), p. 91.

[95] *Miscellanies*, II, 397.

[96] For his review of Grainger's poem *Sugar Cane*, see Ch. V, below. Johnson reprinted the proposals for his Shakespeare edition in the *Chronicle* (April 12-14, 1757, pp. 358-359). *Life*, I, 327-329, 545. He probably wrote the concluding paragraph of a vindication of Dr. James which appeared in the *Chronicle*, Feb. 20-22, 1777, and thereafter. See Hazen, "Samuel Johnson and Dr. James," *loc. cit.*

[97] *London Chronicle*, April 29-May 2, 1769, p. 410; *Life*, I, 378; IV, 77. See also Wimsatt, *Prose Style*, p. 55*n*.

[98] *Life*, I, 378. Cf. C. G. Osgood, "Lady Phillipina Knight and Her Boswell," *Princeton University Library Chronicle*, IV (Feb.-April, 1943), 46-47.

[99] *Anecdotes*, IX, 675-677; *Life*, IV, 484; VI, 482. One of Johnson's godchildren was William Mudge, son of Dr. John Mudge.

[100] *Life*, IV, 76-77.

[101] Mudge published individual sermons and a volume, *Sermons on Different Subjects* (London, 1739).

[102] *Life*, II, 173; III, 247-248; IV, 105. See Aston's *Sermon Preached at the Cathedral Church of St. Paul* (1745), attributed to Johnson.

[103] *Life*, IV, 98.

[104] *Life*, III, 247; II, 123.

[105] *Daily Gazetteer*, Dec. 1, 8, 15, 1759; *Works*, V, 303-310; *Letters*, I, 446-452.

[106] *Life*, I, 352.

[107] Hawkins, p. 373; *Malahide Papers*, IX, 211; *Anecdotes*, II, 232*n*.-233*n*. Cf. Smollett's praise of Mylne in *Humphry Clinker* (*Life*, I, 352*n*.).

[108] *Life*, I, 361; II, 25, 438-440; V, 454; *Malahide Papers*, XI, 166-172; *Letters*, II, 189, 240 [Nos. 533, 570]; *Prefaces*, pp. 38-42.

[109] *Life*, I, 352-353.

[110] *London Gazette*, Tues., Jan. 6, to Sat., Jan. 10, 1761, p. 1. Whimsically, Johnson once alluded to the authoritative tone of the newspaper as "the formality of the Gazette" (*Life*, I, 428).

CHAPTER IV

"THE ANXIOUS EMPLOYMENT OF A PERIODICAL WRITER"

[1] Graham, *English Literary Periodicals*, pp. 119 ff.; *Bibliography*, pp. 25 ff.

[2] *English Poets*, II, 96, 150.

[3] Hawkins, pp. 219 ff., 259 ff.; *Life*, I, 215; *General Index, III*, xliv; *Miscellanies*, II, 350; I, 391.

[4] Birch correspondence, Oct. 30, 1750. B. M. Add. MS. 35,398.

[5] Hawkins, p. 326; G. B. Hill, ed. *Letters of Samuel Johnson* (N.Y., 1892), I, 29*n*. Johnson wrote the preface to Payne's *New Tables of Interest*, 1758 (*Prefaces*, pp. 142-146).

[6] *Anecdotes*, VIII, 415; *General Index, III*, xlivn.

[7] *The Correspondence of Samuel Richardson*, ed. Anna Laetitia Barbauld (London, 1804), I, 166-170.

[8] Birch correspondence, Oct. 30, 1750, and Sept. 7, 1751. B. M. Add. MS. 35, 398. Cf. Johnson's pessimistic outlook (*Miscellanies*, II, 350).

[9] *Rambler*, No. 208; *Life*, I, 203; *Bibliography*, p. 25; Hawkins, p. 271; D. N. Smith, "The Contributors to *The Rambler* and *The Idler*," *Bodleian Quarterly Record*, VII (1934), 508-509. See also J. L. Clifford, "Further Letters of the Johnson Circle," *Bulletin of the John Rylands Library*, XX (1936), 268-285. All subsequent references to the *Rambler*, *Adventurer*, and *Idler* are based upon the text of the *Works*, Vols. II-IV.

[10] *Miscellanies*, II, 414; Hawkins, p. 382. Cf. *Thraliana*, I, 163 and *n*.

[11] *Miscellanies*, II, 215-216.

[12] *English Poets*, III, 218.

[13] *Richardson's Correspondence*, I, 166-170.

[14] *Bibliography*, p. 33.

[15] The extensive nature of Johnson's changes has been examined by D. N. Smith, *Johnson and Boswell Revised* (Oxford, 1928), p. 12; C. B. Bradford, "Johnson's Revisions of the Rambler," *RES*, XV (1939), 302-314. Cf. Alexander Chalmers, ed. *British Essayists* (London, 1802), XVI, xx ff.

[16] *Carter-Talbot Letters*, II, 14-15.

[17] D. R. Lang, *Dr. Samuel Johnson in America* (Urbana, 1939; U. of Ill. diss.), p. 121. Selections from the *Rambler* were printed in the Colonies as early as 1750.

[18] Hawkins, p. 269; *Life*, I, 208; *Malahide Papers*, I, 71; Graham, p. 120.

[19] E. D. Leyburn, "The Translations of the Mottoes and Quotations in the Rambler," *RES*, XVI (1940), 169-177; *Poems*, pp. 127-142; *Letters*, I, 40 [No. 29]; see in *An Account of the Life of Dr. Samuel Johnson* (London, 1805) a letter to Johnson by Hill Boothby (July 1, 1754), p. 65.

[20] *Richardson Correspondence*, I, 164 ff.

[21] *Letters on the Improvement of the Mind* (London, 1773), Letter VIII.

[22] Reprinted in *G.M.*, XX (1750), 465.

[23] *Carter-Talbot Letters*, I, 371; *et passim*. None of the three *Rambler* essays contributed by these ladies is notable for cheerfulness.

[24] Birch correspondence noted above.

[25] *The Female Quixote*, Bk. VI, Ch. XI, pp. 119-120. Johnson perhaps assisted Mrs. Lennox with one chapter of the novel (*Prefaces*, p. 90). See *Rambler*, No. 23.

[26] (London, 1767). See *Life*, II, 44; Hawkins, p. 347.

[27] *The Sale of Authors* (London, 1767), pp. iii-iv.

[28] Graham, pp. 122-123.

[29] Birch to Yorke, Aug. 22, 1752. B. M. Add. MS. 35, 398. See B. C. Nangle, *The Monthly Review, First Series, 1749-1789* (Oxford, 1934), p. 21, for the sole number of the *Impertinent* (1752); and Botting, "Christopher Smart in London," *loc. cit.*, p. 29. The author was Dr. John Hill.

[30] *Miscellanies*, I, 408; *Life*, I, 356n. The *Rambler* was frequently reprinted without authority; e.g., between 1751 and 1753 the *Universal Magazine* reproduced fifteen essays. See Hazen, "Samuel Johnson and Dr. James," *loc. cit.* Cf. *G.M.*, XX (1750), 324, 370, 406-408.

[31] *Malahide Papers*, VII, 171. Among the numerous literary debts of Johnson's friend Joseph Baretti is his close imitation of the *Rambler* in his essay serial, *La Frusta Letteraria*. See C. J. M. Lubbers-Van der Brugge, *Johnson and Baretti* (Groningen, 1951), *passim*. Mrs. Piozzi made frequent borrowings from the *Rambler* for inclusion in her *British Synonymy*.

[32] William Roberts, *Memoirs of the Life and Correspondence of Mrs. Hannah*

More (London, 1834), I, 49. Cf. Mme. D'Arblay, *Diary and Letters,* I, 55. Another feminine votary was Anne Perry, author of *Anningait and Ajutt. . . . Inscribed to Mr. Samuel Johnson* (London, 1761), a rendering of *Rambler,* Nos. 186 and 187, in heroic couplets.

³³ *Life,* I, 280.

³⁴ Boswell's *Letters,* I, 22. Cf. *Boswell in Holland, 1763-1764,* ed. F. A. Pottle (London, 1952), *passim; Boswell on the Grand Tour, 1764,* p. 109.

³⁵ *Letters,* III, 28 [No. 843]. Cf. *Life,* IV, 90.

³⁶ *Life,* I, 208.

³⁷ E. A. Bloom, "Symbolic Names in Johnson's Periodical Essays," *MLQ,* XIII (1952), 333-352; Raleigh, *Six Essays on Johnson,* pp. 12-18. See also Hugh Walker, *English Satire and Satirists* (London, 1925), pp. 136, *passim;* W. B. C. Watkins, *Perilous Balance* (Princeton, 1939), pp. 29-30, 45 ff.

³⁸ *Thraliana,* I, 161-162; *Miscellanies,* I, 456; *Life,* I, 216.

³⁹ Hawkins, p. 453n.; *An Account of the Life of Johnson,* p. 38; Chalmers, XVI, xlv-xlviii.

⁴⁰ *Prayers and Meditations,* in *Works,* IX, 205.

⁴¹ J. W. Krutch, *Samuel Johnson* (N.Y., 1944), pp. 108 ff.

⁴² C. B. Bradford, *Samuel Johnson's 'Rambler'* (New Haven, 1937; Yale diss.). Cf. Murphy, *Miscellanies,* I, 465.

⁴³ *Letters of Hannah More,* p. 33. See *Life,* I, 252; Boswell's *Letters,* II, 425; *Bibliography,* p. 39; Hawkins, pp. 292 ff.

⁴⁴ *Adventurer,* No. 140; Chapman and Hazen, "Johnsonian Bibliography," pp. 136-137; *Hebrides,* p. 202; L. F. Powell, "Johnson's Part in the Adventurer," *RES,* III (1927), 420-429.

⁴⁵ *Monthly Review,* VII (1752), 373-376. The *Review* reprinted No. 4 and, later, No. 140 (X [1754], 189-192).

⁴⁶ *Carter-Talbot Letters,* II, 189. Cf. *Malahide Papers,* XVIII, 319; and Samuel Rogers, *Recollections of Table Talk* (N.Y., 1856), p. 96.

⁴⁷ Wimsatt, p. 135; *Life,* I, 223, 233, 252.

⁴⁸ *A Defence of Mr. Kenrick's Review of Johnson's Shakespeare,* p. 15n. Cf. Mme. D'Arblay, *Memoirs of Dr. Burney* (London, 1832), I, 268.

⁴⁹ Frances Reynolds, *Recollections,* in *Miscellanies,* II, 298; *Malahide Papers,* IX, 258. But cf. *Life,* I, 233; *English Poets,* III, 1.

⁵⁰ *Letters,* I, 47-48 [No. 46]; Arthur Sherbo, "The Translation for the Motto of 'The Adventurer,' No. 126," *N&Q,* CXCVI (1951), 497-498.

⁵¹ Powell, "Johnson's Part in the Adventurer," *loc. cit.,* p. 426.

⁵² *Letters,* I, 53 [No. 51].

⁵³ *An Account of the Life of Johnson,* pp. 42, 48; *Life,* I, 252.

⁵⁴ *Life,* I, 254, 540; *Thraliana,* I, 184.

⁵⁵ B. M. Add. MS. 4316, f. 168, undated letter.

⁵⁶ *Prefaces,* pp. 206-209; *Life,* I, 330n.; Boylston Green, "Possible Additions to the Johnson Canon," *Yale University Library Gazette,* XVI (1942), 70-79.

⁵⁷ Hawkins, pp. 363-364.

⁵⁸ *Life,* I, 331; Hawkins, pp. 381n.-382n.; *Prefaces,* p. 208.

⁵⁹ *Life,* I, 202; III, 411; *Memoirs of Dr. Burney,* II, 258; *Miscellanies,* I, 391; II, 215.

⁶⁰ *Works,* IV, 150; *Bibliography,* pp. 79 ff.; F. W. Hilles, *The Literary Career of Sir Joshua Reynolds* (Cambridge, 1936), pp. 21-22; Smith, "The Contributors to *The Rambler* and *The Idler," loc. cit.*

⁶¹ *Miscellanies,* II, 65.

⁶² *Memoirs of Dr. Burney,* I, 117-127.

⁶³ *Queeney Letters,* ed. the Marquis of Lansdowne (London, 1932), p. 223.

[64] *Hebrides*, p. 185.

[65] *Bibliography*, pp. 83-85; *Life*, I, 335n. Revisions of the *Idler*, after initial publication, were far less drastic and thorough than those of the *Rambler*, according to Boylston Green, *Samuel Johnson's 'Idler'* (New Haven, 1941; Yale diss.), pp. 10-20.

[66] Green, *ibid.*, p. 27.

[67] The *British Magazine* also reprinted *Idler*, Nos. 89, 97, 104. See D. N. Smith, *Johnson and Boswell Revised*, p. 17; Chapman and Hazen, "Johnsonian Bibliography," p. 142.

[68] *Thraliana*, I, 162, 766; *Life*, I, 332n.

[69] A. M. Broadley, *Doctor Johnson and Mrs. Thrale* (London, 1910), p. 121.

[70] Cf. *Prayers and Meditations, Works*, IX, 215-216; *Rasselas*, Ch. XLV.

[71] B. M. Add. MS. 35, 399.

[72] Especially in *Rambler*, Nos. 1, 3, 14, 16, 21, 23, 25, 26, 27, 49, 56, 91, 117, 136, 143, 145, 146, 163, 169, 184, 193, 208; *Adventurer*, Nos. 58, 85, 95, 115, 137, 138 (cf. [34], [41], 45, 50, 53, 62, 67, 69, 81, 84, 99, 102, 107, 108, 111, 119, 120, 126, 128); *Idler*, Nos. 1, 2, 3, 6, 7, 55, 59, 60, 61, 65, 85, 102; and cf. *Reflections on the Present State of Literature, Universal Visiter*, April, 1756, pp. 159-166.

[73] *English Poets*, II, 125.

[74] *Life*, I, 463; II, 362. Cf. II, 12n.; *Boswell's London Journal, 1762-1763*, ed. F. A. Pottle (N.Y., 1950), p. 331.

[75] Cf. *English Poets*, III, 43-44; *Essay on the Origin and Importance of Small Tracts and Fugitive Pieces, Works*, V, 191-192. See also *Life*, III, 377; but cf. IV, 305-306.

[76] Cf. *Life*, III, 423.

[77] Cf. *Life*, I, 538; Swift, *A Digression Concerning Critics*, in *A Tale of a Tub*, Sec. III.

[78] *Life*, I, 154 and n.

[79] *London Chronicle*, III (May 4-5, 1758), 431.

[80] See App. A.

[81] Cf. *Life*, I, 425; II, 40; IV, 34; V, 79.

[82] See Godfrey Davies, "Dr. Johnson on History," *Huntington Library Quarterly*, XII (1948), 1-21.

[83] *Hebrides*, p. 390. Cf. *Idler*, No. 29; *Vanity of Human Wishes*, ll. 135-138; biography of Morin, Ch. I, above; Pope's *Essay on Criticism*, ll. 474 ff.

[84] Cf. *London*, ll. 51-52, 178-181; *Vanity of Human Wishes*, ll. 73-84, 159-160, 229-232; Swift's dedication to Lord Somers, *A Tale of a Tub*; Steele's *Spectator*, No. 214. See *Prefaces, passim*; J. H. Sledd and G. J. Kolb, *Dr. Johnson's Dictionary* (Chicago, 1955), pp. 85-104.

CHAPTER V

JOHNSON AS BOOK REVIEWER

[1] Eighteenth-century reviewers customarily received two guineas a printed sheet (16 pages), but sometimes four, and—in one recorded instance—six guineas (*Life*, IV, 214 and n.). See Bloom, "Labors of the Learned," *SP*, LIV (1957).

[2] Michael Johnson stocked current periodicals, such as De la Roche's *Memoirs*, in his Lichfield book shop and Johnson had access to them (Clifford, *Young Sam Johnson*, p. 70).

[3] Among the contributors to the *Monthly* were: Gilbert Stuart, the historian; Charles Burney, the musician and father of Fanny Burney; George Colman, the

elder; David Garrick, Ralph and George Griffiths, John Hawkesworth, Arthur Murphy, Tobias Smollett, Bonnell Thornton, William Woodfall, and Oliver Goldsmith. Among the *Critical*'s reviewers were Smollett, Goldsmith, the Rev. Joseph Robertson, and Johnson. See Nangle, *The Monthly Review, First Series, passim;* R. S. Crane, *New Essays by Oliver Goldsmith* (Chicago, 1927); Arthur Friedman, "Goldsmith's Contributions to the Critical Review," *MP*, XLIV (1946), 23-52; C. F. Tupper, "Essays Erroneously Attributed to Goldsmith," *PMLA*, XXXIX (1924), 325-342.

⁴ Dr. John Shebbeare, *The Occasional Critic* (London, 1757), pp. 16 ff.

⁵ *Life*, IV, 214; I, 283-285.

⁶ *Life*, III, 44.

⁷ *Life*, IV, 150.

⁸ XII (1742), 128-131, 204-206, 256-258, 297-300; *Works*, VI, 4-9.

⁹ Cross, *The History of Henry Fielding*, I, 360-361.

¹⁰ *Rambler*, No. 13; *English Poets*, II, 89; III, 175, 272.

¹¹ *English Poets*, III, 207.

¹² *Life*, V, 175.

¹³ *Hebrides*, pp. 162-163.

¹⁴ *G.M.*, XXX (1760), 453-456; *Works*, VI, 80-89. Tytler and Johnson met socially in Edinburgh in 1773 (*Hebrides, passim*). Tytler returned Johnson's praise with a favorable commentary on the *Journey to the Western Islands* (*Life*, II, 305).

¹⁵ *Life*, V, 40

¹⁶ Arthur Sherbo attributes to Johnson a review of Keysler's *Travels Through Germany*, etc., in No. 5, pp. 240-247. See "A Possible Addition to the Johnson Canon," *RES*, n.s. VI (1955), 70-71. Greene, "Johnson's Contributions to the *Literary Magazine*," also accepts the review of Keysler and suggests the following reviews as Johnson's: Stephen White's *Collateral Bee-Boxes*, No. 1, pp. 27-28; *"On Ancient Characters"—A Letter from J. Ames to John Booth*, No. 2, pp. 77-78; Peter Whalley's *Works of Ben Jonson*, No. 4, pp. 169-171; John Free's *Sermon Preached at St. John's in Southwark*, No. 4, p. 186; Charles Parkins' *Impartial Account of the Invasion under William, Duke of Normandy*, No. 4, pp. 186-187; *A Scheme for preventing a further Increase of the National Debt*, No. 4, pp. 188-190; *An Account of the Conferences held, and Treaties made, between Major-General Sir William Johnson, and the Chief Sachems and Warriors of the Mohawks, Onondagas, Cayugas, Senekas. . . .*, No. 4, pp. 191-193; R. Lovett's *Subtil Medium Proved*, No. 5, pp. 231-234; Hoadly and Wilson's *Observations of a Series of Electrical Experiments*, No. 5, pp. 234-239. Several of these reviews (esp. of White, Ames, and Free) are much too slight to justify identification of authorship without concrete data. The review of Whalley may be argued more strongly for Chambers than for Johnson (See Ch. III, fn. 11). The others, while highly conjectural, invite further study.

¹⁷ No. 6, pp. 299-309; No. 7, pp. 336-351 (*sic*).

¹⁸ *J.H.L.*, XXIX (1756-1760), 60-64, 67. The *Monthly Review*, XVI (1757), lists numerous pamphlets on the affair. See *Malahide Papers*, VIII, 128; *English Poets*, III, 408; *Life*, I, 314-315. Suggestive of Johnson's attitude toward contemporary military writings is a review of "The Cadet," *Literary Magazine*, No. 7, p. 335 (*sic*). In the introduction he comments: "The book is of no great use but to military men, and the following quotation will show that it is written in a dialect which none but they can understand."

¹⁹ *Literary Magazine*, No. 13, pp. 171-175; No. 14, pp. 251-253; No. 15, pp. 301-306; *Life*, I, 315-316. The review of Jenyns' *Free Inquiry* and the extended notice of Hanway's *Journal* in Nos. 13-15 (May to July, 1757), were Johnson's final contributions to the magazine. The majority of his reviews were printed in the first

seven numbers (May to Nov., 1756). He wrote no reviews for publication between Nos. 7 and 13 (Nov., 1756-May, 1757), and then only two pieces—on Hanway and Jenyns. He contributed no political articles between Nos. 4 and 6, his last being the serialized article on the King of Prussia in Nos. 7 to 9 (Nov., 1756-Jan., 1757). Boswell attributes the decline of the *Literary Magazine* to Johnson's cessation of activities (*Life*, I, 320).

[20] Basil Willey, *The Eighteenth Century Background* (London, 1950), pp. 48-57.

[21] *Life*, IV, 149.

[22] B. H. Bronson, *Johnson Agonistes & Other Essays* (Cambridge, 1946), p. 34; Raleigh, *Six Essays on Johnson*, pp. 22-26. See also *Life*, I, 316*n.*; and in *Carter-Talbot Letters*, IV, 164, Miss Carter's belated defense of Jenyns' philosophy.

[23] *Literary Magazine*, No. 2, pp. 89-91.

[24] *Life*, II, 125.

[25] *Literary Magazine*, No. 3, pp. 141-143. Cf. *Works*, VI, 499-503.

[26] *Ibid.*, No. 6, pp. 282-288; *English Poets*, III, 306; *Life*, I, 312.

[27] No. 1, pp. 30-32. Cf. *Idler*, No. 88, and Ch. II, above.

[28] *Literary Magazine*, No. 4, pp. 193-197.

[29] *Ibid.*, No. 4, pp. 171-176. Cf. *Life*, III, 333, and "Symbolic Names in Johnson's Periodical Essays," *loc. cit.*

[30] *Literary Magazine*, No. 1, pp. 32-35. As a sample Johnson extracted No. 93 (July 27, 1754), an Eastern parable about a reformation which follows an excess of acquisitiveness. See *Life*, I, 355; III, 33.

[31] No. 1, pp. 35-38.

[32] P. F. Leedy, "Genres Criticism and the Significance of Warton's Essay on Pope," *JEGP*, XLV (1946), 140-146. Cf. *Life*, I, 448; II, 166-167.

[33] Cf. Johnson on pastorals in *English Poets*, III, 224-225; *Rambler*, Nos. 36, 37; *Adventurer*, No. 92. He is silent about Theocritus in the life of Pope, and virtually so in the life of Philips (III, 316). His review of Warton contains a good deal more opinion than is suggested by E. N. Hooker, "The Reviewers and the New Criticism, 1754-1770," *PQ*, XIII (1934), 189-202.

[34] No. 6, pp. 281-282; *Prefaces*, p. 90.

[35] No. 1, pp. 39-41. See *English Poets*, I, 87; *Catalogue*, No. 330.

[36] *Life*, II, 212, 259.

[37] *Life*, III, 256.

[38] *Life*, III, 36. Pope is his brilliant exception (*English Poets*, III, 236-239).

[39] No. 1, pp. 41-42; No. 5, pp. 239-240. Johnson apologized for the four-months interval between the two parts of the review. "The truth is that this work not being forced upon our attention by much public applause or censure, was sometimes neglected, and sometimes forgotten, nor would it, perhaps, have been now resumed, but that we might avoid to disappoint our readers by an abrupt desertion of any part."

[40] *English Poets*, III, 411; *Life*, IV, 56.

[41] *Life*, I, 311.

[42] No. 2, pp. 80-86.

[43] *Life*, III, 369; cf. IV, 22.

[44] *Literary Magazine*, No. 4, pp. 176-185. Aside from trade considerations there was an exotic appeal for European imaginations in distant regions, some of which is represented in works like Lobo's *Voyage to Abyssinia*, Du Halde's *Description de la Chine*, Guyon's *Dissertation on the Amazons*, Psalmanazar's *History of Formosa*, and even *Rasselas*.

[45] *Literary Magazine*, No. 2, pp. 91-97.

[46] *Ibid.*, No. 6, pp. 293-299.

[47] No. 3, pp. 136-141.

[48] *Literary Magazine,* No. 3, pp. 143-145. *Life,* V, 247.

[49] No. 4, pp. 167-168; No. 5, pp. 225-229; No. 6, pp. 288-293; *Life,* I, 311.

[50] *Works,* V, 7. Cf. Ch. VII, below, and Pope's *Essay on Criticism,* ll. 424-427.

[51] *Life,* II, 74-75.

[52] No. 7, pp. 335-342; No. 13, pp. 161-167; *Life,* I, 313-314.

[53] No. 14, pp. 253-256; *Works,* VI, 32-37; *Life,* I, 314; II, 61. Among attacks which he might have answered were Kenrick's *Review of Dr. Johnson's New Edition of Shakespeare* (London, 1765); *A Defence of Mr. Kenrick's Review;* Andrew Henderson's *Letter to Dr. Samuel Johnson on his Journey to the Western Isles* (London, 1775), and his *Second Letter to Dr. Samuel Johnson. In which his Wicked and Opprobrious Invectives are Shewn* (London, 1775); [Anon.], *A Letter to Dr. Samuel Johnson Occasioned by his Late Political Publications* (London, 1775). Johnson was annoyed at James Barclay's presumption in answering Kenrick's *Review* (*Life,* I, 498). He once "wished he had copies of all pamphlets written against him, as it is said Pope had" (*Malahide Papers,* XIV, 244).

[54] *Life,* III, 32. *Catalogue,* Nos. 631-634, 636, 649, is evidence of his interest in current reviews, magazines, and pamphlets.

[55] *Life,* IV, 214-215.

[56] *Life,* III, 170-171.

[57] *Life,* IV, 57-58 (Boswell disagrees). Cf. *English Poets,* III, 452.

[58] XV (1763), 314-318; *Bibliography,* pp. 102-103.

[59] *Life,* V, 97.

[60] *Life,* II, 380; III, 104.

[61] XVIII (1764), 458-462.

[62] *Portraits by Sir Joshua Reynolds,* p. 77.

[63] Forster, II, 154 ff.; III, 204; *Life,* II, 5-7, 236; III, 321. In 1770 Johnson contributed four lines to the *Deserted Village,* which he considered inferior to *The Traveller.*

[64] I (1757), 1.

[65] XVI (1764), 12, 20, 28. See *Prefaces,* pp. 168-171; Life, I, 481.

[66] XVIII (1764), 270-277. In a letter to Percy (Aug., 1765) Grainger wrote: "I am perfectly satisfied with the reception the Sugar Cane met with, and am greatly obliged to you and Mr. Johnson for the generous care you took of it in my absence." Earlier (April 6, 1764) Grainger had written to Percy: "Sam. Johnson says he will review it in the *Critical*" (*Life,* I, 481*n.*-482*n.*). Johnson had encouraged Grainger's translation of Tibullus (Grainger, *A Letter to Tobias Smollett. . . . Upon a Late Translation of Tibullus* [London, 1759]). The *Monthly Review,* XXXI (1764), 105-118, two months before Johnson's piece in the *Critical,* predicted *Sugar Cane* would succeed for its utility rather than for its entertainment.

[67] *Prefaces,* p. 168.

[68] *Miscellanies,* II, 265-266; *Malahide Papers,* XI, 179. The line was never printed. See G. S. Alleman, "Mice and the Muse," *TLS,* Aug. 13, 1938, p. 531. Many equally ridiculous lines, however, remain.

[69] *Life,* II, 454.

CHAPTER VI

PIRACY, COPYRIGHT, AND THE ENCOURAGEMENT OF LEARNING

[1] *A Vindication of the Exclusive Right of Authors* (London, 1762), pp. 37-39.

[2] *An Essay on the Regulation of the Press* (Jan. 7, 1703/4), ed. J. R. Moore (Oxford, 1948), pp. xiii, 25-28. Cf. *Defoe's Review,* ed. A. W. Secord (N.Y., 1938), *passim;* Laurence Hanson, *Government and the Press, 1695-1763* (Oxford, 1936), pp. 9-10.

[3] E.g., John How, *Some Thoughts on the Present State of Printing and Bookselling* (London, 1709), pp. 11-13.

[4] *The Case of the Booksellers Right to their Copies, or Sole Power of Printing their Respective Books* (n.d.). See also *More Reasons . . . for the Bill for Encouraging Learning, and for Securing Property of Copies of Books to the Rightful Owners Thereof* (n.d.).

[5] *J.H.C.,* XVI (1709), 281, 240.

[6] *Statutes at Large from the Eighth to the Twelfth Year of Queen Anne,* by Danby Pickering (Cambridge, 1764), XII, 82-87: 8 Anne, c. 19 (1709). See F. S. Siebert, *Freedom of the Press in England, 1476-1776* (Urbana, 1952), pp. 74-82, *et passim.*

[7] *A Short State of the Publick Encouragement Given to Printing and Book-selling in France, Holland, Germany, and at London* (n.d.). See also *A Letter from Mr. S. Buckley. . . Concerning a New Edition of Thuanus's History, Present State of the Republick of Letters,* I (1728), 158 ff.; *Life,* III, 162; IV, 410; *Works,* V, 181, 189; *Catalogue,* No. 10.

[8] Prior to the Act of 1709, there had been a regulation for the deposit of three books. Printers and booksellers had to be warned frequently by officials of the Stationers Company of the need for compliance. See Broadsides dated "Stationers-Hall," June 5, 1690, and April 26, 1694 (B.M. 1887. b. 58 [1,2]). Personal letters were ultimately recognized under copyright law like any other creative literary works. Harry Ransom, "The Personal Letter as Literary Property," *University of Texas Studies in English,* XXX (1951), 116-131.

[9] *Thoughts of a Tory Author Concerning the Press* (London, 1712), pp. 6-7.

[10] Collins, *Authorship in the Days of Johnson,* pp. 64 ff.

[11] *A Letter from an Author. . . Concerning Literary Property* (London, 1747); *An Enquiry into the Nature and Origin of Literary Property* (London, 1762). The *Enquiry* was refuted in *A Vindication of the Exclusive Right of Authors.*

[12] *Life,* I, 287-288. Cf. [Thomas Gordon?], *A Dedication to a Great Man,* pp. 25-26; [Law], *Observations Occasioned by the Contest about Literary Property,* pp. 6-7.

[13] *A Letter to the Society of Booksellers, on the Method of Forming a True Judgment of the Manuscript of Authors* (London, 1738). Bishop Law, *Observations,* pp. 6-7, denied the good intentions of the Society and discussed its failure. See Clayton Atto, "The Society for the Encouragement of Learning," *The Library,* 4th ser. XIX (1938), 263-288; *Anecdotes,* II, 97; *G.M.,* VI (1736), 353; *Letters,* I, 11 [No. 8]; Clifford, p. 235. Cf. Swift's interest in coöperative publishing, *Works,* ed. Sir Walter Scott (Edinburgh, 1814), I, 415-416.

[14] Collins, p. 77. *The Case of Authors and Proprietors of Books* (London, n.d.) argues on behalf of the booksellers for extension, but not perpetuity, of the 1709 copyright provisions.

[15] *J.H.L., passim;* Sir Frank MacKinnon, "Notes on the History of English Copy-

right," *The Oxford Companion to English Literature,* 2nd ed., Sir Paul Harvey (Oxford, 1937), pp. 880 ff.

[16] Collins, pp. 60 ff.; A. W. Pollard, "Some Notes on the History of Copyright in England, 1662-1774," *The Library,* 4th ser. III (1922), 97-114; Hellmut Lehman-Haupt, L. C. Wroth, and R. G. Silver, *The Book in America,* 2nd ed. (N.Y., 1951), pp. 108 ff., 203. Among the many authors affected by the Irish piracies were Richardson and Goldsmith: *The Case of Samuel Richardson. . . with Regard to the Invasion of his Property in the History of Sir Charles Grandison* (London, Sept. 14, 1753), p. 3; *An Address to the Public, on the Treatment which the Editor of Sir Charles Grandison has Met With* (London, 1754); A. D. McKillop, *Samuel Richardson, Printer and Novelist* (Chapel Hill, 1936), pp. 214-215; Forster, I, 130, 140-142. William Kenrick made comparable charges against Richardson in *An Address to the Artists and Manufacturers of Great Britain* (London, 1774), p. 47.

[17] Hawkins, p. 326.

[18] Ralph, *The Case of Authors,* pp. 61-62; *Life,* I, 345n.

[19] *G.M.,* IX (1739), 288-292.

[20] *Dunciad,* pp. 147n., 457; *The Works of Alexander Pope,* ed. Whitwell Elwin (London, 1871), VI, 111-112; Swift, *Journal to Stella,* Letters XIII, XXVIII; Johnson, *The Preface to the Preceptor, Works,* V, 240; Carlson, *The First Magazine,* pp. 118 ff.; Cibber's *Lives of the Poets,* V, 146-159.

[21] LVII² (1787), 555-557. See *Life,* IV, 549.

[22] McAdam, *Dr. Johnson and the English Law,* pp. 10-14. He probably abridged a parliamentary debate of 1657, as well as such works as Du Halde's *Description* and, undoubtedly, others which have not yet been verified. See Ch. I, above.

[23] *Life,* II, 237; but cf. III, 29, 227.

[24] Johnson's belief in this principle is substantiated by the introductory paragraph of his review of Hanway's *Journal, Literary Magazine,* No. 13, p. 161, where he maintained "an author is no longer the sole master of a book which he has given to the public."

[25] *Life,* I, 71; II, 226; IV, 308.

[26] *Hebrides,* p. 49. Nevertheless, Boswell had denied Zélide authority in her translation of the *Account of Corsica* either to alter or abridge the work (*Boswell in Holland,* p. 363n.).

[27] James Burrow, *The Question Concerning Literary Property* [in *Millar vs. Taylor*] (London, 1773), p. 10.

[28] Boswell, *The Decision of the Court of Session* [in *Hinton vs. Donaldson*] (London and Edinburgh, 1774), pp. 6-8.

[29] *Life,* IV, 383n. Cf. Defoe, *An Essay on the Regulation of the Press,* p. 26.

[30] W. A. Copinger and F. E. S. James, *On the Law of Copyright,* 8th ed. (London, 1948), p. 129. See *Grand Magazine of Magazines,* II (1759), 217-222, 301, 304; *London Chronicle,* V (1759), 378-380, 410-411, 423, 448; Straus, *Robert Dodsley;* Plomer, *A Dictionary of Printers and Booksellers,* pp. 76-77, 147.

[31] Copinger and James, p. 54.

[32] *Life,* III, 294.

[33] *Life,* I, 438-439. Cf. *Boswell's London Journal,* pp. 312-313; *English Poets,* I, 141-142; II, 435-436; *Poems,* p. 25.

[34] *Some Thoughts on the State of Literary Property* (London, 1764), p. 7; *Considerations on the Nature and Origin of Literary Property* (Edinburgh, 1767).

[35] Burrow, *The Question Concerning Literary Property; Letters of David Hume to William Strahan,* ed. G. B. Hill (Oxford, 1888), pp. 275-278 [No. 73].

[36] *Another Letter to Mr. Almon, in Matter of Libel* (London, 1770), p. 148.

[37] *J.H.L.,* XXXIV (Feb. 15, 1774), 24; *J.H.C.,* XXXV (1775), 299.

[38] *Hebrides*, p. 32.

[39] *Life*, I, 439; cf. II, 345.

[40] *Life*, II, 272-273; *Malahide Papers*, IX, 145. See also *Letters of Hume to Strahan*, pp. 274 ff.; Catherine Macaulay, *A Modest Plea for the Property of Copyright* (Bath and London, 1774); *Walpole Letters*, ed. Mrs. Toynbee, VIII, 423.

[41] Sir William Blackstone, *Commentaries on the Laws of England*, 9th ed. (London, 1783), II, 405-407; *Life*, II, 259. In an analogous instance (the review of the Duchess of Marlborough's memoirs), referring to the monarchs in power, Johnson clearly argued for the principle of occupancy.

[42] *Life*, V, 87; Blackstone, *Commentaries*, I, 125. See Ch. VII, below.

[43] *Letters of Hume to Strahan*, pp. 275-278.

[44] *Letters*, I, 398-399 [No. 349]. In *Miscellanies*, II, 442n., Hill identifies Strahan as the intended recipient of this letter. Cf. *Considerations on the Nature and Origin of Literary Property*, pp. 33-34. On annotations see *Life*, II, 212, 259; *Walpole's Correspondence*, ed. Lewis, XIV, 98.

[45] *Life*, III, 110-111, 370. See *English Poets*, I, 324-326.

[46] *The R. B. Adam Library Relating to Dr. Johnson and his Era* (Oxford, 1929), III, 152-153.

[47] M. R. Small, *Charlotte Ramsay Lennox* (New Haven, 1935), pp. 50-54; *Prefaces*, p. 115. See also *Prefaces*, p. 110; Chapman, "Johnsonian Bibliography," p. 140 (with reference to the possibility that Johnson wrote the dedication of the *Memoirs*).

[48] J. D. Wright, "Some Unpublished Letters to and from Dr. Johnson," *Bulletin of the John Rylands Library*, XVI (1932), 56-57. Cf. *Works*, VI, 477-478; *English Poets*, I, 360.

[49] Wright, "Some Unpublished Letters," *loc. cit.;* but cf. Small, pp. 50-54.

[50] *Life*, IV, 275. See also *Letters*, II, 431 [No. 736.1].

CHAPTER VII

JOHNSON ON A FREE PRESS

[1] W. E. Hocking, *Freedom of the Press* (Chicago, 1947), p. 69.

[2] *Life*, IV, 234.

[3] *Life*, II, 130. Ironically, Thomas Townshend in 1774 attacked both Johnson and Shebbeare for licentious writing (*Parliamentary History*, XVII [1771-1774], 1054-1058). Cf. Defoe's attitude toward liberty in *The Great Law of Subordination Consider'd* (London, 1724), Letter II, p. 18; and Pope's ("licensed blasphemies") in *An Essay on Criticism*, l. 553. However Johnson disagreed with Milton's politics, he certainly concurred with the distinction made in Sonnet XII between liberty and license.

[4] *Citizen of the World*, Letter 50. See also David Hume, *Essays Moral, Political, and Literary*, ed. T. H. Green and T. H. Grose (London, 1912), I, 94-98, 306 ff.; Adam Smith, *An Inquiry into the Nature and Causes of the Wealth of Nations*, ed. Edwin Cannan (N.Y., 1937), p. 141; Voltaire, *Letters on the English*, No. 7; *Walpole's Correspondence*, III, 192; Plato, *Laws*, III, 701.

[5] *Life*, III, 224.

[6] *Life*, II, 252n.

[7] *Laws*, III, 697; cf. *Republic*, VIII, 557B. See Z. S. Fink, *The Classical Republicans* (Evanston, Ill., 1945).

[8] *Politics*, III, 8; IV, 4, 8; V, 1, 8, 9; VI, 2, 4. Cf. John Locke, *The Second Treatise of Civil Government*, ed. J. W. Gough (Oxford, 1946), pp. 13, 42-43, 47.

[9] *The Discourses of Niccolò Machiavelli*, trans. L. J. Walker (New Haven, 1950), I, 238 [I. 10. 7] and I, 5. See *Life*, IV, 381n.

[10] *Life*, II, 249. Cf. II, 243; III, 59 ff.; *Works*, V, 476, 481-486. Prof. Clifford (*Young Sam Johnson*, pp. 285-287) has called attention to Johnson's views on subordination incorporated in the sermon written for the Rev. Henry Hervey Aston in 1745. See also Locke, *A Letter Concerning Toleration*, ed. Gough (Oxford, 1946), *passim;* Rousseau, *The Social Contract*, trans. H. J. Tozer (London, 1924), Ch. 4, sec. 8; Smith, *Wealth of Nations*, pp. 651, *et passim;* John Stuart Mill, *On Liberty*, ed. R. B. McCallum (Oxford, 1946), pp. 11 ff.

[11] *English Poets*, III, 446.

[12] *Ibid.*, 411-412; *Life*, IV, 56; Ch. V, above. Cf. *Boswell's London Journal*, p. 317; *Thraliana*, I, 207.

[13] *English Poets*, III, 289.

[14] *Ibid.*, I, 157; *Works*, VI, 262 [*Taxation no Tyranny*].

[15] *Life*, I, 394.

[16] *The False Alarm, Thoughts on the Late Transactions Respecting Falkland's Island, Taxation no Tyranny;* note also his *Literary Magazine* articles and reviews. See Wilkes' retort to *The False Alarm* in *A Letter to Samuel Johnson* (London, 1770); and H. J. Laski, *Political Thought in England from Locke to Bentham* (London, 1925), p. 178.

[17] *Life*, II, 348.

[18] Lewis Melville, *The Life and Letters of Tobias Smollett* (London, 1926), p. 193; *Walpole's Correspondence*, ed. Lewis, XI, *passim;* Walpole, *Memoirs of the Reign of George III* (London and N.Y., 1894), II, 48-49; III, 83; *The Letters of David Hume*, ed. Greig, II, 244-245.

[19] E.g., *A Letter to Dr. Samuel Johnson Occasioned by his Late Political Publications.* Cf. *Letters of Philip Dormer Stanhope*, ed. Bonamy Dobrée (London and N.Y., 1932), pp. 2563 ff.

[20] *The Militia Bill* and *Observations on his Britannick Majesty's Treaties.*

[21] *Taxation no Tyranny*, in *Works*, VI, 234, 257; cf. *Life*, II, 244. Bronson (*Johnson Agonistes*, pp. 44-45) justifies Johnson's conservatism in politics, which is in contrast to his radical interest in the individual.

[22] Locke, *The Second Treatise of Civil Government*, p. 13; Smith, *Wealth of Nations*, pp. 670 ff.; Hume, *Of Refinement in the Arts*, in *Essays*, I, 306 ff.; see also Plato, *Republic*, VIII, 557B and *Laws*, III, 698; Aristotle, *Politics*, V, 9.

[23] *Life*, II, 374; *Adventurer*, Nos. 67, 126, 128; Ch. VI, above.

[24] *Life*, II, 170. See also Fielding, *Champion* (Nov. 4, 1740; Dec. 17, 1741) and *The Historical Register for the Year 1736*, dedication *To the Public;* John, Lord Hervey, *Memoirs of the Reign of George the Second*, ed. J. W. Croker (London, 1848), I, 319.

[25] In his review of Lucas' *Essay on Waters*.

[26] Esp. in *Taxation no Tyranny*. See also *On School Chastisement*, *Works*, V, 467-470; *Letters*, II, 310 [No. 636]; *Thraliana*, I, 207; Hume, *Letters*, ed. Greig, II, 244-245.

[27] *Life*, III, 262. Smith, *Wealth of Nations*, pp. 670 ff.: Civil government is for the protection of property, for the defense of the rich against the poor; subordination is therefore essential.

[28] *Life*, II, 153; *False Alarm*.

[29] *Life*, II, 244.

[30] *English Poets*, I, 157.

[31] *Life*, I, 408; II, 219; III, 26; V, 106; *Boswell's London Journal*, pp. 314-316, 320.

[32] *Life*, IV, 81.

[33] *False Alarm*, in *Works*, VI, 159.

[34] As summarized in the first amendment to the Constitution, and by Alexander

Hamilton, who wrote in *Federalist*, No. 84, that liberty of the press must "depend on public opinion, and on the general spirit of the people and of the government."

[35] Laski, *Political Thought*, p. 15.

[36] Hocking, *Freedom of the Press*, p. 12. Cf. *Walpole's Correspondence*, ed. Lewis, II, 89; III, 232.

[37] Spokesmen in the second half of the century who believed in the importance and existence of an "unusual degree of liberty" in Britain, without necessarily approving of unbounded freedom, were Hume, *Of Liberty of the Press*, in *Essays*, I, 94-98; Thomas Erskine, *Celebrated Speech . . . in Support of the Liberty of the Press* (Edinburgh, 1793).

[38] E.g., at the time of Johnson's entry into London, *Craftsman, Common Sense,* William Guthrie's *Old England.* "Official" retorts were usually made by the *Daily Gazetteer.*

[39] *The Life of Father Paul Sarpi.*

[40] *An Essay on the Origin and Importance of Tracts and Fugitive Pieces*, in *Works*, V, 191; cf. G.M. preface of 1753. See also Fielding's *Covent Garden Journal*, Nos. 55, 60; *Walpole's Correspondence*, V, 92; Kingsley Martin, *French Liberal Thought in the Eighteenth Century* (Boston, 1929); Albert Bachman, *Censorship in France from 1715 to 1750* (N.Y., 1934).

[41] *A Complete Vindication of the Licensers of the Stage*, in *Works*, V, 329-344; political essays in the *Literary Magazine.*

[42] See parliamentary *Debate on a Seditious Paper*, in *Works*, X, 26-47; the case of the Scottish Society of Procurators, *Life*, IV, 128-131, 497, and *Malahide Papers*, XV, 41.

[43] *Life*, II, 60-61.

[44] *English Poets*, II, 361.

[45] *Covent Garden Journal*, Nos. 49, 51, 55, 60; *The Works of Henry Fielding*, ed. Leslie Stephen (London, 1882), VI, 319 ff., 407-437; Walpole, *Memoirs of George III*, III, 117; IV, 112; [Candor (John Almon?)], *A Letter to the Public Advertiser* (London, 1764); Forster, III, 23; etc.

[46] *The Expedition of Humphry Clinker* (Oxford, 1930), letter dated June 2, pp. 122-123. Cf. Smollett's difficulties with the libel laws: Knapp, *Tobias Smollett*, pp. 230-233, and *Critical Review*, V (1758), 438-439. Of libel in general there is no record of Johnson's opinions, although he was a forceful advocate of the truth at all costs. See *Life*, III, 16n. The literature of the period abounds with protests against libelous writings, but there were equally justified complaints against arbitrary, excessively severe prosecutions: e.g., Walpole, *Memoirs of George III*, I, 256; III, 117; IV, 112; Fielding, *Works*, VI, 319 ff., 407, 437; [T. Hayter?], *An Essay on the Liberty of the Press* (London, 1754); Hume, *History of England* (N.Y., 1879), VI, 342; *Letters on the Subject of the Proper Liberty of the Press* (London and Dublin, 1790); [Erskine], *The Whole Proceedings of the Trial. . . against John Stockdale* (Dublin, 1790).

[47] Hocking, pp. 69-70.

[48] *Commentaries*, IV, 151-153. Cf. Zechariah Chafee, Jr., *Free Speech in the United States* (Cambridge, Mass., 1941), pp. 9-10; G. J. Patterson, *Free Speech and a Free Press* (Boston, 1939), p. 67; Rousseau, *Social Contract*, p. 218.

[49] *Life*, IV, 216.

[50] *A Complete Vindication of the Licensers of the Stage*, in *Works*, V, 344. Defoe (*The Great Law of Subordination*, p. 20) wrote, "Liberty is a word of endearment, 'tis the hereditary favourite of the people."

[51] *English Poets*, I, 108. Francis Blackburne, *Remarks on Johnson's Life of Milton* (London, 1780), p. 59, finds the discussion of *Areopagitica* a contradictory "see-saw

of arguments pro and con." See Johnson's attitude toward Cheynel in the *Student,* Ch. III, above.

[52] Gabriel Peignot, *Essai Historique sur la Liberté D'Écrire* (Paris, 1832), pp. 108-109, parallels Johnson's fear of complete freedom for the masses. Of Johnson's statement he said, "Ces réflexions sont fort judicieuses."

[53] *The Works of John Milton* (N.Y., 1931), IV, 297-298.

APPENDIX A

SOME FUGITIVE PIECES

[1] *General Index, III,* xxvii-xxviii; Sherbo, "Two Additions to the Johnson Canon," *JEGP,* LII (1953), 543-545. Miss Talbot (*Carter-Talbot Letters,* II, 74) indicated that Johnson meant to write occasionally for the *Daily Advertiser,* but gave no further clues.

[2] *Proposals for Printing Every Fortnight, (Price Sixpence) The Publisher Containing Miscellanies in Prose and Verse Collected by J. Crokatt, Bookseller.* Printed in facsimile with note by R. W. Chapman (Oxford, 1930). See also by Chapman, "Johnson's Works: A Lost Piece and a Forgotten Piece," *London Mercury,* XXI (1930), 438-441.

[3] Plomer, *Dictionary of Printers and Booksellers,* p. 66. According to the "conditions" at the end of the *Proposals,* the *Publisher* was to appear first in Nov., 1744. The "conditions" also stipulate the manner by which the *Publisher* would be delivered, thus telling us something about eighteenth-century circulation techniques:

The numbers, as published, shall be sent by the editor to the gentlemen's abode, that will please to leave their directions at the following coffee houses [seventeen of them in various sections of London], where books are kept for that purpose. Parcels and letters directed to him (post paid) will be received, and letters duly answered, . . .

[4] D. J. Greene, "The Johnsonian Canon: A Neglected Attribution," *PMLA,* LXV (1950), 433.

[5] *Bibliography,* p. 36; *Prefaces,* 77-84.

[6] D. J. Greene, "Was Johnson Theatrical Critic of the Gentleman's Magazine?", *RES,* n.s. III (1952), 158-161.

[7] *Prefaces,* pp. 205 ff. Boylston Green's attempt ("Possible Additions to the Johnson Canon," *Yale University Library Gazette,* XVI [1942], 70-79) to prove Johnson's authorship of five *Observations* in the *Chronicle* between Aug. 19 and Sept. 30, 1758, is on circumstantial grounds and inconclusive.

[8] First attributed in the *European Magazine,* XIII (1788), 77.

[9] E. L. McAdam, Jr., "New Essays by Dr. Johnson," *RES,* XVIII (1942), 197-207.

[10] *Life,* V, 274 and *n.,* 550; *Hebrides,* p. 239 and *n.*; Forster, II, 62.

[11] Quoted by McAdam, "New Essays by Dr. Johnson," p. 199.

[12] Cf. *Fireworks,* in *G.M.,* XIX (1749), 8, also an attack on public wastefulness; and the eulogistic address to George III in the *London Gazette,* Jan. 6-10, 1761, p. 1.

[13] See *Letters,* III, 262 [No. 1133], to Griffith Jones.

[14] *Poems,* p. 55; *Life,* I, 227-228.

[15] *European Magazine,* XVI (1789), 4; *Prefaces,* pp. 19-20; *Life,* I, 464, 550-552; *English Poets,* I, 87.

[16] *Prefaces,* p. 217. Professor Sherbo has suggested to me that Smart was probably in confinement, and thus incapable of working. There is, indeed, a reasonable possibility that his family confined him to his home between 1756 and 1760, and then placed him in an asylum. See C. D. Abbott, "Christopher Smart's Madness," *PMLA,*

XLV (1930), 1014-1022. Goldsmith, among others, was helping to raise money on his behalf.

[17] *Prefaces,* p. 217; *Life,* I, 345, 546; IV, 382*n.* See Johnson's *G.M.* travel essays. Among his projects was a *Collection of Travels.*

[18] *European Magazine,* XVI (1789), 5; *Life,* II, 503.

[19] *Life,* V, 411-413 and *n.*

[20] *Letters,* II, 27-29 [No. 390]; cf. I, 361-364 [No. 327].

[21] The passage has been deleted from subsequent editions of the *Journey.*

[22] Clifford, *Hester Lynch Piozzi, passim; Life,* II, 286; III, 440, 442; IV, 344; *Thraliana,* I, 453-454.

[23] Croker, ed. Boswell's *Life of Johnson,* I, 252*n.*

[24] *Historical Chronicle,* in *G.M.,* XXXIX (1769), 162; see also 635, 637; *Thraliana,* I, 122*n.*-123*n.* Mawbey contributed prose and verse to *G.M.* for years *(DNB).*

[25] *English Poets,* II, 114.

[26] *Anecdotes,* II, 551; IV, 264-271; *Life,* IV, 161; *Letters,* II, 514 [No. 812]; *English Poets,* III, 116.

[27] One work continues to remain questionable in the Johnson canon. It is the dedication to a musical periodical, *Monthly Melody: or Polite Amusement for Gentlemen and Ladies: being a Collection of Vocal and Instrumental Music Composed by Dr. Arne* (London, 1760). There is no substantial reason for admitting it, but neither can it be dismissed finally. See *Life,* II, 2; *Bibliography,* p. 98; *Prefaces,* pp. 243-246; Hazen and McAdam, *A Catalogue of an Exhibition of First Editions,* p. 18.

INDEX

This is a selective index of names and titles. References to Johnson's biography, attitudes, and works are listed under his name. See Appendix B for complete journalistic canon.